6. Can a local account be used in a trust relationship? Explain.

7. In a complete trust domain model that uses 4 different domains, what is the total number of trust relationships required to use a complete trust domain model?

Exam Questions

The following questions are similar to those you will face on the Microsoft exam. Answers to these questions can be found in section Answers and Explanations, later in the chapter. At the end of each of those answers, you will be informed of where (that is, in what section of the chapter) to find more information..

1. ABC Corporation has locations in Toronto, New York, and San Francisco. It wants to install Windows NT Server 4 to encompass all its locations in a single WAN environment. The head office is located in New York. What is the best domain model for ABC's directory services implementation?

   A. Single-domain model

   B. Single-master domain model

   C. Multiple-master domain model

   D. Complete-trust domain model

2. JPS Printing has a single location with 1,000 users spread across the LAN. It has special printers and applications installed on the servers in its environment. It needs to be able to centrally manage the user accounts and the resources. Which domain model would best fit its needs?

   A. Single-domain model

   B. Single-master domain model

   C. Multiple-master domain model

   D. Complete-trust domain model

5. What must be created to allow a user account from one domain to access resources in a different domain?

   A. Complete Trust Domain Model

   B. One Way Trust Relationship

   C. Two Way Trust Relationship

   D. Master-Domain Model

Answers to Review Questions

1. Single domain, master domain, multiple-master domain, complete-trust domain. See section, Windows NT Server 4 Domain Models, in this chapter for more information. (This question deals with objective Planning 1.)

2. One user, one account, centralized administration, universal resource access, synchronization. See section, Windows NT Server 4 Directory Services, in this chapter for more information. (This question deals with objective Planning 1.)

6. Local accounts cannot be given permissions across trusts. See section, Accounts in Trust Relationships, in this chapter for more information. (This question deals with Planning 1.)

Answers and Explanations: For each of the Review and Exam questions, you will find thorough explanations located at the end of the section. They are easily identifiable because they are in blue type.

Exam Questions: These questions reflect the kinds of multiple-choice questions that appear on the Microsoft exams. Use them to become familiar with the exam question formats and to help you determine what you know and what you need to review or study more.

Suggested Readings and Resources

The following are some recommended readings on the subject of installing and configuring NT Workstation:

1. Microsoft Official Curriculum course 770: *Installing and Configuring Microsoft Windows NT Workstation 4.0*

   • Module 1: Overview of Windows NT Workstation 4.0

   • Module 2: Installing NT Workstation 4.0

2. Microsoft Official Curriculum course 922: *Supporting Microsoft Windows NT 4.0 Core Technologies*

   • Module 2: Installing Windows NT

   • Module 3: Configuring the Windows NT Environment

3. *Microsoft Windows NT Workstation Resource Kit Version 4.0* (Microsoft Press)

   • Chapter 2: Customizing Setup

   • Chapter 4: Planning for a Mixed Environment

4. Microsoft TechNet CD-ROM

   • *MS Windows NT Workstation Technical Notes*

      • MS Windows NT Workstation Deployment Guide – Automating Windows NT Setup

      • An Unattended Windows NT Workstation Deployment

5. Web Sites

   • www.microsoft.com/train_cert

Suggested Readings and Resources: The very last element in each chapter is a list of additional resources you can use if you wish to go above and beyond certification-level material or if you need to spend more time on a particular subject that you are having trouble understanding.

Exam 70-059 Internetworking with Microsoft TCP/IP on Microsoft Windows NT 4.0

Planning

OBJECTIVE	PAGE REFERENCE
Given a scenario, identify valid network configurations.	Chapter 1—objective covered throughout the chapter pg. 3

Installation and Configuration

OBJECTIVE	PAGE REFERENCE
Given a scenario, select the appropriate services to install when using Microsoft TCP/IP on a Microsoft Windows NT Server computer.	Chapter 2—Services pg. 59–60
On a Windows NT Server computer, configure Microsoft TCP/IP to support multiple network adapters.	Chapter 2—Installing TCP/IP pg. 49–59
Configure scopes by using DHCP Manager.	Chapter 4—Configuring the DHCP Server pg. 109–115
Install and configure a WINS server.	Chapter 5—objective covered throughout the chapter pg. 131
· Import LMHOSTS files to WINS.	Chapter 5—Importing Mappings pg. 142–143
· Run WINS on a multihomed computer.	Chapter 5—WINS on a Multihomed Computer pg. 139
· Configure WINS replication.	Chapter 5—Replication pg. 145–148
· Configure static mappings in the WINS database.	Chapter 5—Adding Static Mappings pg. 141–142
Configure subnet masks.	Chapter 3—Subnetting pg. 79–87
Configure a Windows NT Server computer to function as an IP router.	Chapter 2—pg. 47 and Chapter 6—pg. 167
· Install and configure the DHCP Relay Agent.	Chapter 2—DHCP Relay Installation and Configuration pg. 56–57
Install and configure the Microsoft DNS Server service on a Windows NT Server computer.	Chapter 7—Implementing Microsoft DNS servers pg. 219–229
· Integrate DNS with other name servers.	Chapter 7—Integration with WINS pg. 228
· Connect a DNS server to a DNS root server.	Chapter 7—objective covered throughout the chapter pg. 197
· Configure DNS server roles.	Chapter 7—Types of DNS Servers pg. 203–205
Configure HOSTS and LMHOSTS files.	Chapter 8—objective covered throughout the chapter pg. 243
Configure a Windows NT Server computer to support TCP/IP printing.	Chapter 9—objective covered throughout the chapter pg. 271
Configure SNMP.	Chapter 10—objective covered throughout the chapter pg. 289

MCSE

Second Edition

TCP/IP

Exam: 70-059

New
Riders

Rob Scrimger
Kelli Adam

MCSE Training Guide: TCP/IP, Second Edition
Copyright © 1999 by New Riders Publishing

International Standard Book Number: 1-56205-920-3

Library of Congress Catalog Card Number: 98-86323

Printed in the United States of America

First Printing: October, 1998

01 00 99   4 3 2 1

Trademarks

Warning and Disclaimer

EXECUTIVE EDITOR
Mary Foote

ACQUISITIONS EDITOR
Nancy Maragioglio

DEVELOPMENT EDITOR
Chris Zahn

MANAGING EDITOR
Sarah Kearns

PROJECT EDITOR
Christopher Morris

COPY EDITOR
Greg Pearson

INDEXER
Tina Trettin

TECHNICAL EDITORS
Dale Holmes
Tim Crothers

SOFTWARE DEVELOPMENT SPECIALIST
Jack Belbot

PROOFREADER
Jeanne Clark

PRODUCTION
Heather Stephenson

Contents at a Glance

PART V Troubleshooting

PART VI Final Review

PART VII Appendixes

Table of Contents

5 Windows Internet Name Service (WINS)   131

PART III: Connectivity

PART IV: Monitoring and Optimizing

PART V: Troubleshooting

15 Troubleshooting Microsoft TCP/IP   429

PART VI: **Final Review**

PART VII: Appendixes

About the Authors

Currently, **Robert Scrimger**, MCT, MCSE+Internet, is the Product Stream Leader, Microsoft, for Learnix, where he spends a great number of hours arguing the merits of Windows NT versus Solaris. After spending several years in the field with companies such as Bell Canada International, Canada Post, and Ricoh Canada, he moved into training, which he has been doing for over 10 years. This was fate more than design, since the reason for the change was that the small company he was working for went bankrupt—and the first ad he saw was for a computer trainer.

"Over the years, I have seen many different technologies evolve—some succeeding and some not. However, the one common thread I have observed is that the more things change, the more they stay the same. This perhaps is most appropriate as the front note to a book on TCP/IP, a technology that has its beginnings in the early days of the Cold War.

In this there is a great truth that I will pass on to help you in your studies—*understand the concepts*! If you know what something is supposed to do—figuring out how to work it is simple. For example, a word processor must be able to save files—this could be as simple as File, Save or as complex as Esc :wq {enter}—but the concept is the same in both cases."

Rob is also the author of *Sams Teach Yourself MCSE Internet Information Server 4 in 14 Days*.

During the last 10 years, **Kelli Adam** (MCT, MCSE+I) has earned an international reputation for technical training, support, and computer networking. Respected by Microsoft as an industry leader, she is regularly contracted to write exams and teach courses for Microsoft Certified Professionals (MCPs). In addition to providing technical consulting, managing Web hosting and media streaming servers, and speaking at computer conferences, Kelli also makes time to run ConnectOS Corporation, which she founded in 1995. At the end of her day, she goes home to her two house bunnies, husband, and new baby in Kirkland, Washington. Kelli can be reached at kadam@connectos.com.

Dedication

Rob Scrimger: *This is dedicated to my parents.*

Acknowledgments

Rob Scrimger: First and foremost I want to thank my family for putting up with me as I went through another book. Next I would like to acknowledge the aid and encouragement of the development editor, Chris Zahn, who helped to make this a fun book, and the technical editors, Dale Holmes and Tim Crothers: Dale made sure I made sense and Tim checked the binary and generally kept me honest. Finally, I'd like to thank Nancy Maragioglio for involving me in this project and Kelli Adam for the groundwork reorganizing the previous edition.

TELL US WHAT YOU THINK!

As the reader of this book, *you* are our most important critic and commentator. We value your opinion and want to know what we're doing right, what we could do better, what areas you'd like to see us publish in, and any other words of wisdom you're willing to pass our way.

As the Executive Editor for the Certification team at Macmillan Computer Publishing, I welcome your comments. You can fax, email, or write me directly to let me know what you did or didn't like about this book—as well as what we can do to make our books stronger.

Please note that I cannot help you with technical problems related to the topic of this book, and that due to the high volume of mail I receive, I might not be able to reply to every message.

When you write, please be sure to include this book's title and author, as well as your name and phone or fax number. I will carefully review your comments and share them with the author and editors who worked on the book.

Fax: 317-581-4663

Email: certification@mcp.com

Mail: Mary Foote
            Executive Editor
            Certification
            Macmillan Computer Publishing
            201 West 103rd Street
            Indianapolis, IN 46290 USA

How to Use This Book

New Riders Publishing has made an effort in the second editions of its Training Guide series to make the information as accessible as possible for the purposes of learning the certification material. Here, you have an opportunity to view the many instructional features that have been incorporated into the books to achieve that goal.

CHAPTER OPENER

Each chapter begins with a set of features designed to allow you to maximize study time for that material.

List of Objectives: Each chapter begins with a list of the objectives as stated by Microsoft.

Objective Explanations: Immediately following each objective is an explanation of it, providing context that defines it more meaningfully in relation to the exam. Because Microsoft can sometimes be vague in its objectives list, the objective explanations are designed to clarify any vagueness by relying on the authors' test-taking experience.

OBJECTIVES

Microsoft provides the following objectives for "Connectivity":

Add and configure the network components of Windows NT Workstation.

▶ This objective is necessary because someone certified in the use of Windows NT Workstation technology must understand how it fits into a networked environment and how to configure the components that enable it to do so.

Use various methods to access network resources.

▶ This objective is necessary because someone certified in the use of Windows NT Workstation technology must understand how resources available on a network can be accessed from NT Workstation.

Implement Windows NT Workstation as a client in a NetWare environment.

▶ This objective is necessary because someone certified in the use of Windows NT Workstation technology must understand how NT Workstation can be used as a client in a NetWare environment and how to configure the services and protocols that make this possible.

Use various configurations to install Windows NT Workstation as a TCP/IP client.

▶ This objective is necessary because someone certified in the use of Windows NT Workstation technology must understand how TCP/IP is important in a network environment and how Workstation can be configured to use it.

CHAPTER 4

Connectivity

OUTLINE

Chapter Outline: Learning always gets a boost when you can see both the forest and the trees. To give you a visual image of how the topics in a chapter fit together, you will find a chapter outline at the beginning of each chapter. You will also be able to use this for easy reference when looking for a particular topic.

STUDY STRATEGIES

▶ Disk configurations are a part of both the planning and the configuration of NT Server computers. To study for Planning Objective 1, you will need to look at both the following section and the material in Chapter 2, "Installation Part 1." As with many concepts, you should have a good handle on the terminology and know the best applications for different disk configurations. For the objectives of the NT Server exam, you will need to know only general disk configuration concepts—at a high level, not the nitty gritty. Make sure you memorize the concepts relating to partitioning and know the difference between the system and the boot partitions in an NT system (and the fact that the definitions of these are counter-intuitive). You should know that NT supports both FAT and NTFS partitions, as well as some of the advantages and disadvantages of each. You will also need to know about the fault-tolerance methods available in NT—stripe sets with parity and disk mirroring—including their definitions, hardware requirements, and advantages and disadvantages.

Of course, nothing substitutes for working with the concepts explained in this objective. If possible, get an NT system with some free disk space and play around with the Disk Administrator just to see how partitions are created and what they look like.

You might also want to look at some of the supplementary readings and scan TechNet for white papers on disk configuration.

▶ The best way to study for Planning Objective 2 is to read, memorize, and understand the use of each protocol. You should know what the protocols are, what they are used for, and what systems they are compatible with.

As with disk configuration, installing protocols on your NT Server is something that you plan for, not something you do just because it feels good to you at the time. Although it is much easier to add or remove a protocol than it is to reconfigure your hard drives, choosing a protocol is still an essential part of the planning process because specific protocols, like spoken languages, are designed to be used in certain circumstances. There is no point in learning to speak Mandarin Chinese if you are never around anyone who can understand you. Similarly, the NWLink protocol is used to interact with NetWare systems; therefore, if you do not have Novell servers on your network, you might want to rethink your plan to install it on your servers. We will discuss the uses of the major protocols in Chapter 7, "Connectivity." However, it is important that you have a good understanding of their uses here in the planning stage.

Study Strategies: Each topic presents its own learning challenge. To support you through this, New Riders has included strategies for how to best approach studying in order to retain the material in the chapter, particularly as it is addressed on the exam.

INSTRUCTIONAL FEATURES WITHIN THE CHAPTER

These books include a large amount and different kinds of information. The many different elements are designed to help you identify information by its purpose and importance to the exam and also to provide you with varied ways to learn the material. You will be able to determine how much attention to devote to certain elements, depending on what your goals are. By becoming familiar with the different presentations of information, you will know what information will be important to you as a test-taker and which information will be important to you as a practitioner.

Objective Coverage Text: In the text before an exam objective is specifically addressed, you will notice the objective is listed and printed in color to help call your attention to that particular material.

Warning: In using sophisticated information technology, there is always potential for mistakes or even catastrophes that can occur through improper application of the technology. Warnings appear in the margins to alert you to such potential problems.

EXAM TIP

Only One NTVDM Supports Multiple 16-bit Applications
Expect at least one question about running Win16 applications in separate memory spaces. The key concept is that you can load multiple Win16 applications into the same memory space only if it is the initial Win16 NTVDM. It is not possible, for example, to run Word for Windows 6.0 and Excel for Windows 5.0 in one shared memory space and also run PowerPoint 4.0 and Access 2.0 in another shared memory space.

Exam Tip: Exam Tips appear in the margins to provide specific exam-related advice. Such tips may address what material is covered (or not covered) on the exam, how it is covered, mnemonic devices, or particular quirks of that exam.

Note: Notes appear in the margins and contain various kinds of useful information, such as tips on the technology or administrative practices, historical background on terms and technologies, or side commentary on industry issues.

---

8   Chapter 1   PLANNING

INTRODUCTION

Microsoft grew up around the personal computer industry and established itself as the preeminent maker of software products for personal computers. Microsoft has a vast portfolio of software products, but it is best known for its operating systems.

Microsoft's current operating system products, listed here, are undoubtedly well-known to anyone studying for the MCSE exams:

◆ Windows 95

◆ Windows NT Workstation

◆ Windows NT Server

NOTE

Strange But True Although it sounds backward, it is true: Windows NT boots from the system partition and then loads the system from the boot partition.

Some older operating system products—namely MS-DOS, Windows 3.1, and Windows for Workgroups—are still important to the operability of Windows NT Server, so don't be surprised if you hear them mentioned from time to time in this book.

Windows NT is the most powerful, the most secure, and perhaps the most elegant operating system Microsoft has yet produced. It languished for a while after it first appeared (in part because no one was sure why they needed it or what to do with it), but Microsoft has persisted with improving interoperability and performance. With the release of Windows NT 4 which offers a new Windows 95-like user interface, Windows NT has assumed a prominent place in today's world of network-based computing.

WINDOWS NT SERVER AMONG MICROSOFT OPERATING SYSTEMS

WARNING

Don't Overextend Your Partitions and Wraps It is not necessary to create an extended partition on a disk; primary partitions might be all that you need. However, if you do create one, remember that you can never have more than one extended partition on a physical disk.

As we already mentioned, Microsoft has three operating system products now competing in the marketplace: Windows 95, Windows NT Workstation, and Windows NT Server. Each of these operating systems has its advantages and disadvantages.

Looking at the presentation of the desktop, the three look very much alike—so much so that you might have to click the Start button and read the banner on the left side of the menu to determine which operating system you are looking at. Each offers the familiar Windows 95 user interface featuring the Start button, the Recycling

STEP BY STEP

5.1 Configuring an Extension to Trigger an Application to Always Run in a Separate Memory Space

1. Start the Windows NT Explorer.

2. From the View menu, choose Options.

3. Click the File Types tab.

4. In the Registered File Types list box, select the desired file type.

5. Click the Edit button to display the Edit File Type dialog box. Then select Open from the Actions list and click the Edit button below it.

6. In the Editing Action for Type dialog box, adjust the application name by typing **cmd.exe /c start /separate** in front of the existing contents of the field (see Figure 5.15).

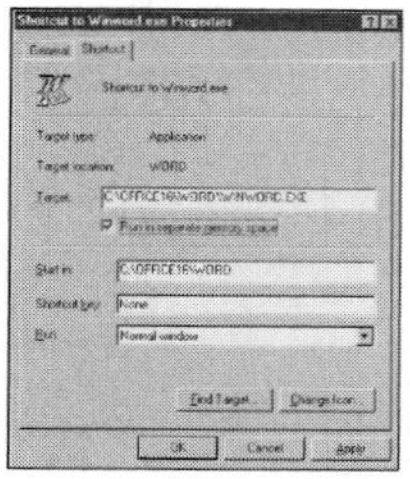

FIGURE 5.15
Configuring a shortcut to run a Win16 application in a separate memory space.

Step by Step: Step by Steps are hands-on tutorial instructions that walk you through a particular task or function relevant to the exam objectives.

Figure: To improve readability, the figures have been placed in the margins so they do not interrupt the main flow of text.

---

14   Chapter 1   PLANNING

You must use NTFS if you want to preserve existing permissions when you migrate files and directories from a NetWare server to a Windows NT Server system.

Windows 95 is Microsoft's everyday workhorse operating system. It provides a 32-bit platform and is designed to operate with a variety of peripherals. See Table 1.1 for the minimum hardware requirements for the installation and operation of Windows 95. Also, if you want to allow Macintosh computers to access files on the partition through Windows NT's Services for Macintosh, you must format the partition for NTFS.

MAKING REGISTRY CHANGES

To make Registry changes, run the REGEDT32.EXE program. The Registry in Windows NT is a complex database of configuration settings for your computer. If you want to configure the Workstation service, open the HKEY_LOCAL_MACHINE hive, as shown in Figure 3.22.

The exact location for configuring your Workstation service is

    HKEY_LOCAL_MACHINE\System\CurrentControlSet\Services\
    LanmanWorkstation\Parameters

To find additional information regarding this Registry item and others, refer to the Windows NT Server resource kit.

This summary table offers an overview of the differences between the FAT and NTFS file systems.

REVIEW BREAK

Choosing a File System

But if the system is designed to store data, mirroring might produce disk bottlenecks. You might only know whether these changes are significant by setting up two identical computers, implementing mirroring on one but not on the other, and then running Performance Monitor on both under a simulated load to see the performance differences.

This summary table offers an overview of the differences between the FAT and NTFS file systems.

In-Depth Sidebar: These more extensive discussions cover material that perhaps is not as directly relevant to the exam, but which is useful as reference material or in everyday practice. In-Depths may also provide useful background or contextual information necessary for understanding the larger topic under consideration.

Review Break: Crucial information is summarized at various points in the book in lists or tables. At the end of a particularly long section, you might come across a Review Break that is there just to wrap up one long objective and reinforce the key points before you shift your focus to the next section.

CASE STUDIES

Case Studies are presented throughout the book to provide you with another, more conceptual opportunity to apply the knowledge you are developing. They also reflect the "real-world" experiences of the authors in ways that prepare you not only for the exam but for actual network administration as well. In each Case Study, you will find similar elements: a description of a Scenario, the Essence of the Case, and an extended Analysis section.

CASE STUDY: REALLY GOOD GUITARS

ESSENCE OF THE CASE

Here are the essential elements in this case:

- need for centralized administration
- the need for WAN connectivity nation-wide
- a requirement for Internet access and e-mail
- the need for Security on network shares and local files
- an implementation of Fault-tolerant systems

SCENARIO

Really Good Guitars is a national company specializing in the design and manufacturer of custom acoustic guitars. Having grown up out of an informal network of artisans across Canada, the company has many locations but very few employees (300 at this time) and a Head Office in Churchill, Manitoba. Although they follow the best traditions of hand-making guitars, they are not without technological savvy and all the 25 locations have computers on-site which are used to do accounting, run MS Office applications, and run their custom made guitar design software. The leadership team has recently begun to realize that a networked solution is essential to maintain consistency and to provide security on what are becoming some very innovative designs and to provide their employees with e-mail and Internet access.

RGG desires a centralized administration of its

continues

Essence of the Case: A bulleted list of the key problems or issues that need to be addressed in the Scenario.

Scenario: A few paragraphs describing a situation that professional practitioners in the field might face. A Scenario will deal with an issue relating to the objectives covered in the chapter, and it includes the kinds of details that make a difference.

Analysis: This is a lengthy description of the best way to handle the problems listed in the Essence of the Case. In this section, you might find a table summarizing the solutions, a worded example, or both.

CASE STUDY: PRINT IT DRAFTING INC.

continued

too, which is unacceptable. You are to find a solution to this problem if one exists.

ANALYSIS

The fixes for both of these problems are relatively straightforward. In the first case, it is likely that all the programs on the draftspeople's workstations are being started at normal priority. This means that they have a priority of 8. But the default says that anything running in the foreground is getting a 2-point boost from the base priority, bringing it to 10. As a result, when sent to the background, AutoCAD is not getting as much attention from the processor as it did when it was the foreground application. Because multiple applications need to be run at once without significant degradation of the performance of AutoCAD, you implement the following solution:

1. On the Performance tab of the System Properties dialog box for each workstation, set the Application Performance slider to None to prevent a boost for foreground applications.

2. Recommend that users keep the additional programs running alongside AutoCAD at a minimum (because all programs will now get equal processor time).

The fix to the second problem is to run each 16-bit application in its own NTVDM. This ensures that the crashing of one application will not adversely affect the others, but it still enables interoperability between the applications because they use OLE (and not shared memory) to transfer data. To make the fix as transparent as possible to the users, you suggested that two things be done:

1. Make sure that for each shortcut a user has created to the office applications, the Run in Separate Memory Space option is selected on the Shortcut tab.

2. Change the properties for the extensions associated with the applications (for example, .XLS and .DOC) so that they start using the /separate switch. Then any file that is double-clicked invokes the associated program to run in its own NTVDM.

CHAPTER SUMMARY

KEY TERMS

Before you take the exam, make sure you are comfortable with the definitions and concepts for each of the following key terms:

• FAT

• NTFS

• workgroup

• domain

This chapter discussed the main planning topics you will encounter on the Windows NT Server exam. Distilled down, these topics revolve around two main goals: understanding the planning of disk configuration and understanding the planning of network protocols.

◆ Windows NT Server supports an unlimited number of inbound sessions; Windows NT Workstation supports no more than 10 active sessions at the same time.

◆ Windows NT Server accommodates an unlimited number of remote access connections (although Microsoft only supports up to 256); Windows NT Workstation supports only a single remote access connection.

Key Terms: A list of key terms appears at the end of each chapter. These are terms that you should be sure you know and are comfortable defining and understanding when you go in to take the exam.

Chapter Summary: Before the Apply Your Learning section, you will find a chapter summary that wraps up the chapter and reviews what you should have learned.

EXTENSIVE REVIEW AND SELF-TEST OPTIONS

At the end of each chapter, along with some summary elements, you will find a section called "Apply Your Knowledge" that gives you several different methods with which to test your understanding of the material and review what you have learned.

Chapter 1   PLANNING   **23**

APPLY YOUR KNOWLEDGE

This section allows you to assess how well you understood the material in the chapter. Review and Exam questions test your knowledge of the tasks and concepts specified in the objectives. The Exercises provide you with opportunities to engage in the sorts of tasks that comprise the skill sets the objectives reflect.

Exercises

1.1   Synchronizing the Domain Controllerys

The following steps show you how to manually synchronize a backup domain controller within your domain. (This objective deals with Objective Planning 1.)

Estimated Time: Less than 10 minutes.

1. Click Start, Programs, Administrative Tools, and select the Server Manager icon.

2. Highlight the BDC (Backup Domain Controller) in your computer list.

3. Select the Computer menu, then select Synchronize with Primary Domain Controller.

12.2   Establishing a Trust Relationship between Domains

The following steps show you how to establish a trust relationship between multiple domains. To complete this exercise, you must have two Windows NT Server computers, each installed in their own domain. (This objective deals with objective Planning 1.)

Estimated Time: 10 minutes

1. From the trusted domain select Start, Programs, Administrative Tools, and click User Manager for Domains. The User Manager.

FIGURE 1.2
The login process on a local machine.

2. Select the Policies menu and click Trust Relationships. The Trust Relationships dialog box appears.

4. When the trusting domain information has been entered, click OK and close the Trust Relationships dialog box.

Review Questions

1. List the four domain models that can be used for directory services in Windows NT Server 4.

2. List the goals of a directory services architecture.

3. What is the maximum size of the SAM database in Windows NT Server 4.0?

4. What are the two different types of domains in a trust relationship?

5. In a trust relationship which domain would contain the user accounts?

Exercises: These activities provide an opportunity for you to master specific hands-on tasks. Our goal is to increase your proficiency with the product or technology. You must be able to conduct these tasks in order to pass the exam.

Review Questions: These open-ended, short-answer questions allow you to quickly assess your comprehension of what you just read in the chapter. Instead of asking you to choose from a list of options, these questions require you to state the correct answers in your own words. Although you will not experience these kinds of questions on the exam, these questions will indeed test your level of comprehension of key concepts.

6. Can a local account be used in a trust relationship? Explain.

7. In a complete trust domain model that uses 4 different domains, what is the total number of trust relationships required to use a complete trust domain model?

Exam Questions

The following questions are similar to those you will face on the Microsoft exam. Answers to these questions can be found in section Answers and Explanations, later in the chapter. At the end of each of those answers, you will be informed of where (that is, in what section of the chapter) to find more information..

1. ABC Corporation has locations in Toronto, New York, and San Francisco. It wants to install Windows NT Server 4 to encompass all its locations in a single WAN environment. The head office is located in New York. What is the best domain model for ABC's directory services implementation?

A. Single-domain model

B. Single-master domain model

C. Multiple-master domain model

D. Complete-trust domain model

2. JPS Printing has a single location with 1,000 users spread across the LAN. It has special printers and applications installed on the servers in its environment. It needs to be able to centrally manage the user accounts and the resources. Which domain model would best fit its needs?

A. Single-domain model

B. Single-master domain model

C. Multiple-master domain model

D. Complete-trust domain model

5. What must be created to allow a user account from one domain to access resources in a different domain?

A. Complete Trust Domain Model

B. One Way Trust Relationship

C. Two Way Trust Relationship

D. Master-Domain Model

Answers to Review Questions

1. Single domain, master domain, multiple-master domain, complete-trust domain. See section, Windows NT Server 4 Domain Models, in this chapter for more information. (This question deals with objective Planning 1.)

2. One user, one account, centralized administration, universal resource access, synchronization. See section, Windows NT Server 4 Directory Services, in this chapter for more information. (This question deals with objective Planning 1.)

6. Local accounts cannot be given permissions across trusts. See section, Accounts in Trust Relationships, in this chapter for more information. (This question deals with Planning 1.)

Exam Questions: These questions reflect the kinds of multiple-choice questions that appear on the Microsoft exams. Use them to become familiar with the exam question formats and to help you determine what you know and what you need to review or study more.

Answers and Explanations: For each of the Review and Exam questions, you will find thorough explanations located at the end of the section. They are easily identifiable because they are in blue type.

Suggested Readings and Resources

The following are some recommended readings on the subject of installing and configuring NT Workstation:

1. Microsoft Official Curriculum course 770: *Installing and Configuring Microsoft Windows NT Workstation 4.0*

   • Module 1: Overview of Windows NT Workstation 4.0

   • Module 2: Installing Windows NT Workstation 4.0

2. Microsoft Official Curriculum course 922: *Supporting Microsoft Windows NT 4.0 Core Technologies*

   • Module 2: Installing Windows NT

   • Module 3: Configuring the Windows NT Environment

3. *Microsoft Windows NT Workstation Resource Kit Version 4.0* (Microsoft Press)

   • Chapter 2: Customizing Setup

   • Chapter 4: Planning for a Mixed Environment

4. Microsoft TechNet CD-ROM

   • *MS Windows NT Workstation Technical Notes*

      • MS Windows NT Workstation Deployment Guide – Automating Windows NT Setup

      • An Unattended Windows NT Workstation Deployment

5. Web Sites

   • www.microsoft.com/train_cert

   • www.prometric.com/testingcandidates/ assessment/chosetest.html (take online

Suggested Readings and Resources: The very last element in every chapter is a list of additional resources you can use if you want to go above and beyond certification-level material or if you need to spend more time on a particular subject that you are having trouble understanding.

Introduction

MCSE Training Guide: TCP/IP, Second Edition is designed for advanced end-users, service technicians, and network administrators with the goal of certification as a Microsoft Certified Systems Engineer (MCSE). The Internetworking with Microsoft TCP/IP on Microsoft Windows NT 4.0 exam (70-059) measures your ability to implement, administer, and troubleshoot information systems that incorporate Microsoft TCP/IP.

This book is your one-stop shop. Everything you need to know to pass the exam is in here, and Microsoft has approved it as study material. You do not have to take a class in addition to buying this book to pass the exam. However, depending on your personal study habits or learning style, you may benefit from buying this book *and* taking a class.

This book also can help advanced users and administrators who are not studying for the exam but are looking for a single-volume reference on Microsoft's TCP/IP implementation.

HOW THIS BOOK HELPS YOU

This book conducts you on a self-guided tour of all the areas covered by the Internetworking with Microsoft TCP/IP on Microsoft Windows NT 4.0 exam and teaches you the specific skills you need to achieve your MCSE certification. You'll also find helpful hints, tips, real-world examples, exercises, and references to additional study materials. Specifically, this book is set up to help you in the following ways:

- ◆ **Organization**. This book is organized by major exam topics and individual exam objectives.

Every objective you need to know for the Internetworking with Microsoft TCP/IP on Microsoft Windows NT 4.0 exam is covered in this book. The objectives are not covered in exactly the same order as they are listed by Microsoft, but we have attempted to organize the topics in the most logical and accessible fashion to make it as easy as possible for you to learn the information. We have also attempted to make the information accessible in the following ways:

- The full list of exam topics and objectives is included in this introduction.

- Each chapter begins with a list of the objectives to be covered.

- Each chapter also begins with an outline that provides you an overview of the material and the page numbers where particular topics can be found.

- We also repeat objectives in the margin where the material most directly relevant to it is covered (unless the whole chapter addresses a single objective).

- Information on where the objectives are covered is also conveniently condensed in the tearcard at the front of this book.

- ◆ **Instructional Features**. This book has been designed to provide you with multiple ways to learn and reinforce the exam material. Following are some of the helpful methods:

  - *Objective Explanations*. As mentioned previously, each chapter begins with a list of the objectives covered in the chapter. In addition, immediately following each objective is an explanation of it in a context that defines it more meaningfully.

- *Study Strategies*. The beginning of the chapter also includes strategies for how to approach studying and retaining the material in the chapter, particularly as it is addressed on the exam.

- *Exam Tips*. Exam tips appear in the margin to provide specific exam-related advice. Such tips may address what material is covered (or not covered) on the exam, how it is covered, mnemonic devices, or particular quirks of that exam.

- *Review Questions and Summaries*. Crucial information is summarized at various points in the book in lists or tables. Each chapter ends with a summary as well.

- *Key Terms*. A list of key terms appears at the end of each chapter.

- *Notes*. These appear in the margin and contain various kinds of useful information, such as tips on technology or administrative practices, historical background on terms and technologies, or side commentary on industry issues.

- *Warnings*. When using sophisticated information technology, there is always the potential for mistakes or even catastrophes that can occur because of improper application of the technology. Warnings appear in the margin to alert you to such potential problems.

- *In-Depths*. These more-extensive discussions cover material that may not be directly relevant to the exam, but which is useful as reference material or in everyday practice. In-depths may also provide useful background or contextual information necessary for understanding the larger topic under consideration.

- *Step By Steps*. These are hands-on, tutorial instructions that lead you through a particular task or function relevant to the exam objectives.

- *Exercises*. Found at the end of the chapters in the "Apply Your Knowledge" section, exercises may include additional tutorial material as well as other types of problems and questions.

- *Case Studies*. Presented throughout the book, case studies provide you with a more-conceptual opportunity to apply and reinforce the knowledge you are developing. They include a description of a scenario, the essence of the case, and an extended analysis section. They also reflect the real-world experiences of the authors in ways that prepare you not only for the exam but for actual network administration as well.

◆ **Extensive practice test options**. The book provides numerous opportunities for you to assess your knowledge and practice for the exam. The practice options include the following:

- *Review Questions*. These open-ended questions appear in the "Apply Your Knowledge" section at the end of each chapter. They allow you to quickly assess your comprehension of what you just read in the chapter. Answers to the questions are provided later in the section.

- *Exam Questions*. These questions also appear in the "Apply your Knowledge" section. They reflect the kinds of multiple-choice questions that appear on the Microsoft exams. Use them to practice for the exam and to help you determine what you know and what you need to review or study further. Answers and explanations for them are provided.

- *Practice Exam.* A practice exam is included in the "Final Review" section. The "Final Review" section and the practice exam are discussed below.

- *Top Score.* The Top Score software included on the CD-ROM provides further practice questions.

> NOTE
>
> For a complete description of the New Riders Top Score test engine, please see Appendix D, "Using the Top Score Software."

◆ **Final Review.** This part of the book provides you with three valuable tools for preparing for the exam.

- *Fast Facts.* This condensed version of the information contained in the book will prove extremely useful for last-minute review.

- *Study and Exam Tips.* Read this section early on to help you develop study strategies. It also provides you with valuable exam-day tips and information on new exam/question formats, such as adaptive tests and simulation-based questions.

- *Practice Exam.* A full practice exam is included. Questions are written in the styles used on the actual exam. Use it to assess your readiness for the real thing.

The book includes other features, such as sections titled "Suggested Reading and Resources," which direct you toward further information that could aid you in your exam preparation or your actual work. There are several valuable appendixes as well, including a glossary (Appendix A), an overview of the Microsoft certification program (Appendix B), and a description of what

is on the CD-ROM (Appendix C). These and all the other book features mentioned previously will provide you with thorough preparation for the exam.

For more information about the exam or the certification process, contact Microsoft:

Microsoft Education: (800) 636-7544

Internet: ftp://ftp.microsoft.com/Services/MSEdCert

World Wide Web:
http://www.microsoft.com/train_cert

CompuServe Forum: GO MSEDCERT

What the Internetworking with Microsoft TCP/IP on Microsoft Windows NT 4.0 Exam (#70-059) Covers

The Internetworking with Microsoft TCP/IP on Microsoft Windows NT 4.0 exam (70-059) covers the five main topic areas represented by the conceptual groupings of the test objectives: Planning, Installation and Configuration, Connectivity, Monitoring and Optimization, and Troubleshooting. Each chapter represents one or more of these main topic areas. The exam objectives are listed by topic area in the following sections.

Planning

- Given a scenario, identify valid network configurations.

Installation and Configuration

- Given a scenario, select the appropriate services to install when using Microsoft TCP/IP on a Microsoft Windows NT Server computer.

- On a Windows NT Server computer, configure Microsoft TCP/IP to support multiple network adapters.

- Configure scopes by using DHCP Manager.

- Install and configure a WINS server.

  - Import LMHOSTS files to WINS.

  - Run WINS on a multihomed computer.

  - Configure WINS replication.

  - Configure static mappings in the WINS database.

- Configure subnet masks.

- Configure a Windows NT Server computer to function as an IP router.

  - Install and configure the DHCP Relay Agent.

- Install and configure the Microsoft DNS Server service on a Windows NT Server computer.

  - Integrate DNS with other name servers.

  - Connect a DNS server to a DNS root server.

  - Configure DNS server roles.

- Configure HOSTS and LMHOSTS files.

- Configure a Windows NT Server computer to support TCP/IP printing.

- Configure SNMP.

Connectivity

- Given a scenario, identify which utility to use to connect to a TCP/IP-based UNIX host.

- Configure an RAS server and dial-up networking for use on a TCP/IP network.

- Configure and support browsing in a multiple-domain routed network.

Monitoring and Optimization

- Given a scenario, identify which tool to use to monitor TCP/IP traffic.

Troubleshooting

- Diagnose and resolve IP addressing problems.

- Use Microsoft TCP/IP utilities to diagnose IP configuration problems.

  - Identify which Microsoft TCP/IP utility to use to diagnose IP configuration problems.

- Diagnose and resolve name-resolution problems.

HARDWARE AND SOFTWARE YOU'LL NEED

A self-paced study guide, this book was designed with the expectation that you will use Windows NT 4.0 as you follow along through the exercises while you learn. However, the theory covered in *MCSE Training Guide: TCP/IP, Second Edition* is applicable to a wide range of network systems in a wide range of actual situations, and the exercises in this book encompass that range.

Your computer should meet the following criteria:

- On the Microsoft Hardware Compatibility List

- 486DX2 66Mhz (or better) processor for Windows NT Server

- 340MB (or larger) hard disk for Windows NT Server, 100MB free and formatted as NTFS

- 3.5-inch 1.44MB floppy drive

- VGA (or Super VGA) video adapter

- VGA (or Super VGA) monitor

- Mouse or equivalent pointing device

- Double-speed (or faster) CD-ROM drive (optional)

- Network Interface Card (NIC)

- Presence on an existing network, or use of a 2-port (or more) miniport hub to create a test network

- Microsoft Windows NT Server version 4.0 (CD-ROM version)

It is easier to obtain access to the necessary computer hardware and software in a corporate business environment. It can be difficult, however, to allocate enough time within the busy workday to complete a self-study program. Most of your study time will occur after normal working hours, away from the everyday interruptions and pressures of your regular job.

ADVICE ON TAKING THE EXAM

More extensive tips are found in the "Final Review" section titled "Study and Exam Tips," but keep this advice in mind as you study:

- **Read all the material.** Microsoft has been known to include material not expressly specified in the objectives. This book has included additional information not reflected in the objectives in an effort to give you the best possible preparation for the examination—and for the real-world network experiences to come.

- **Do the Step by Steps and complete the Exercises in each chapter.** They will help you gain experience using the Microsoft product. All Microsoft exams are task- and experienced-based and require you to have experience using the Microsoft product in a real networking environment.

- **Use the questions to assess your knowledge.** Don't just read the chapter content; use the questions to find out what you know and what you don't. Study some more, review, then assess you knowledge again.

- **Review the exam objectives.** Develop your own questions and examples for each topic listed. If you can make and answer several questions for each topic, you should not find it difficult to pass the exam.

> **NOTE**
>
> **Exam-Taking Advice** Although this book is designed to prepare you to take and pass the Internetworking with Microsoft TCP/IP on Microsoft Windows NT 4.0 certification exam, there are no guarantees. Read this book, work through the questions and exercises, and when you feel confident, take the Practice Exam and additional exams using the Top Score test engine. This should tell you whether or not you are ready for the real thing.
>
> When taking the actual certification exam, make sure you answer all the questions before your time limit expires. Do not spend too much time on any one question. If you are unsure about a question, answer it as best you can; then mark it and review it when you have finished the rest of the questions.

Remember, the primary object is not to pass the exam—it is to understand the material. After you understand the material, passing the exam should be simple. Knowledge is a pyramid; to build upward, you need a solid foundation. This book and the Microsoft Certified Professional programs are designed to ensure that you have that solid foundation.

Good luck!

NEW RIDERS PUBLISHING

The staff of New Riders Publishing is committed to bringing you the very best in computer reference material. Each New Riders book is the result of months of work by authors and staff who research and refine the information contained within its covers.

As part of this commitment to you, the NRP reader, New Riders invites your input. Please let us know if you enjoy this book, if you have trouble with the information or examples presented, or if you have a suggestion for the next edition.

Please note, however, that New Riders staff cannot serve as a technical resource during your preparation for the Microsoft certification exams or for questions about software- or hardware-related problems. Please refer instead to the documentation that accompanies the Microsoft products or to the applications' Help systems.

If you have a question or comment about any New Riders book, there are several ways to contact New Riders Publishing. We will respond to as many readers as we can. Your name, address, or phone number will never become part of a mailing list or be used for any purpose other than to help us continue to bring you the best books possible. You can write to us at the following address:

New Riders Publishing
Attn: Publisher
201 W. 103rd Street
Indianapolis, IN 46290

If you prefer, you can fax New Riders Publishing at 317-817-7448.

You also can send email to New Riders at the following Internet address:

certification@mcp.com

NRP is an imprint of Macmillan Computer Publishing. To obtain a catalog or information, or to purchase any Macmillan Computer Publishing book, call 800-428-5331.

Thank you for selecting *MCSE Training Guide: TCP/IP, Second Edition!*

PLANNING

This chapter helps you prepare for the exam by covering the following Planning objective:

Given a scenario, identify valid network configurations.

▶ This is a very general objective as there are many aspects of a valid network configuration. Essentially, this objective indicates that you will need to have the background provided by the Networking Essentials exam and understand what configurations of TCP/IP are valid.

▶ This chapter does not cover this objective entirely, and you will need to understand IP Addressing, subnetting, and routing to fully prepare yourself for the exam. These topics are covered in subsequent chapters. This chapter covers some of the technologies that are used to connect networks, the basics of the TCP/IP Network Architecture, and more.

CHAPTER 1

Introduction to Networking with TCP/IP

As you read through this chapter, you should concentrate on the following key items:

► You should understand the four layers in the TCP/IP network architecture and what function each performs.

► You should know which technologies are available to connect network segments together and what the key differences are among them.

► You should understand the need for segmenting a network.

As technology evolves at an ever-increasing pace, time and distance seem to take on new meanings for all of us. Nowhere is this truer than in the computer industry, where the computers of today are often made obsolete by the systems that will arrive next week. In the midst of this constant change, it is good sometimes to reflect on some of the technologies that have been around seemingly forever. Transmission Control Protocol/Internet Protocol (TCP/IP), whose development began in 1957, is one of these technologies.

When you sit at a computer today and "surf the Web," you are connecting to servers all over the world—traveling almost instantly to remote continents. Or perhaps you can visit a chat room and discover that the person you have been "talking" with is halfway around the world. Most people never take the time to consider the miracle of clicking on a link and connecting to servers all over the world, or about the steps that are involved in making this possible.

In this text you will discover the components that make the journey possible. As we look at TCP/IP and its implementation in Microsoft Windows NT, you will learn basic concepts that apply to all forms of TCP/IP no matter who implements them.

Before you can understand TCP/IP and where it fits into the networking model, you need to understand the basics. This chapter will start with a review of the introductory concepts of networking.

From there the chapter moves into the main components of the TCP/IP stack and what they do. Finally, various methods of connecting network segments will be reviewed.

INTRODUCTORY CONCEPTS

The TCP/IP suite of protocols provides a "language" that can be used for computers to talk to each other. For a language to be used to communicate, there must be some way for the words to be transferred from one person to another (such as using a telephone to communicate with a distant relative) and some common, conventional reference for the ideas behind the conversation. This section will discuss the methods that can be used to move the conversation from one system to another.

The Components of a Network

Put simply, a *network* is a collection of machines that have been linked together physically and on which software components have been added to facilitate communication and sharing of information. By this definition, a network might be as simple as the computers shown in Figure 1.1. In fact, Figure 1.1 shows the simplest kind of network that can be created: two machines connected by a piece of coaxial cable. This example is deceptively simple and hides a fairly complex arrangement of pieces that must work together to enable these two machines to communicate.

Figure 1.2 shows the main hardware and software components required to enable communication between these two machines.

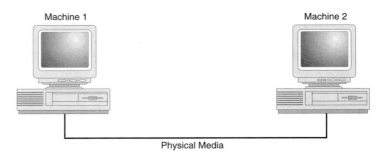

FIGURE 1.1
An example of a simple network.

The components shown in Figure 1.2 are defined here:

FIGURE 1.2
The various components involved in a network.

◆ **OS.** This is the operating system; more specifically, this is the user interface that you use to connect to other computers on the network.

◆ **RDR.** The RDR, or redirector, intercepts requests for resource access and, if required, passes the request to the network. The redirector (or client, if you will) can talk only to a server that understands what it is talking about, or that has a common frame of reference.

◆ **SVR.** The server component receives and services the requests from a redirector.

◆ **Protocol.** The requests from the redirector and the responses from the server are encapsulated in a transport protocol. The protocol (such as TCP/IP) then finds the other computer and moves the data to the target machine.

◆ **Network Card.** The protocol works with the Network Card to physically move the data to the other computer.

The Physical Layer

One of the key components of the network is the wire that sticks out of the back of your computer. This wire connects you to your network and probably, with TCP/IP enabled, to the rest of the world. The type of wiring used is determined by the network topology that is employed.

A number of topologies can be used to establish a physical connection: 10Base-T Ethernet, 10Base-2 Ethernet, Token Ring, FDDI, and others. Each of these topologies requires the appropriate hardware, such as a network card in the machine that acts as the interface to the network. This card has a unique address that identifies each computer on the network.

The Physical Address

A physical address is used to distinguish machine A from machine B in a way the network cards can understand. This physical address, a unique identifier assigned to a network card, is often referred to as the Media Access Control (MAC) address, the hardware address, or the ethernet address. All these terms represent the same thing; but to keep things simple, this text will refer to this identifier as the MAC address.

A MAC address is a 48-bit address represented by six pairs of hexadecimal values (for example, 00-C0-DF-48-6F-13). The MAC address, which is assigned by the manufacturer of the network card before it is shipped to be sold, is designed to be unique and is used to help identify a single machine on a network. At this level of the networking model, the Physical layer, data being passed over the network appears to be nothing more than the transmission and error-checking of negative and positive voltages—represented as 1s and 0s—on the wire. These 1s and 0s are transmitted in a group (the size of which is based on the type of network used) called a frame. Within the frame, various pieces of information can be deciphered.

The network card is responsible for determining whether the data is intended for it or another network card. Each network card is given a set of rules that it obeys. First, there is a preamble used to synchronize the card so it can determine where the data within the frame begins.

After the network card determines where the data begins, it discards the preamble before continuing to the next process. Next, the network card deciphers the data to determine the physical address for which the frame is destined. If the destination address matches the physical address of the network card, or if it is a broadcast, it continues to process the information and pass the remaining data to the protocol. If the destination address specifies some other machine's physical address, the network card silently discards the data within the frame and starts listening for other messages.

It is relatively easy to determine the MAC address of a machine running Windows NT 4.0. To do so, follow these steps:

> **NOTE**
>
> **Broadcasts and Addresses**
> Broadcasts are transmissions sent to a broadcast address so that all machines on the network will receive the information.

STEP BY STEP

1.1 Checking the MAC Address

1. From the Start menu, select Programs, Command Prompt.

2. Type **IPCONFIG /all** in the command prompt window.

3. Read the information provided by the IPCONFIG utility until you see a section called "Ethernet Address" (or "Physical Address" in some topologies). The value represented in this section is the physical address of the machine.

Network Topologies

There are three main types of networks that are in use today. These networks differ in the distances that they can cover and in speed. The next few sections look at the three common types of networks, followed by a discussion of hybrid networks.

The Bus Configuration

The bus configuration has its roots in coaxial cable (similar to what the cable company uses with a single conductor within a shielded cover). This configuration makes possible simple networks in which desktop machines are connected so that they can share information with each other. Network traffic (the data) is carried by the wire, or bus, to all connected machines.

Any time a machine needs to talk with another, it addresses a frame for that computer (which means it needs to know the MAC address for the computer) and sends it on the wire. The address is normally resolved using a broadcast that queries every system on the network, asking the system you are trying to communicate with to send back

> **NOTE**
>
> **Coaxial Cable Versus Twisted-Pair Cable** Coaxial cable was initially the most popular form of transmission media; however, most new installations use twisted-pair cable. This medium is facilitated by the use of hubs that connect several stations to a single bus.

its MAC address (this address resolution is handled in TCP/IP by Address Resolution Protocol).

Using this method, clients (RDR) and servers (SRV) can be randomly placed on the network because they are all able to listen to frames sent by a machine. The main selling point behind this type of network is that it is simple to set up and can scale fairly well with the addition of relatively inexpensive hardware, such as repeaters or bridges. However, adding more machines to a bus-type network also adds more traffic that will compete for the wire during transmission—creating a traffic jam.

To illustrate this, imagine two machines try to communicate and send their frames on the wire at the same time. This is the electrical equivalent of a car wreck for 1s and 0s—or what is commonly referred to as a collision on the network.

Any machine listening on the network for frames has no idea what to make of the chaotic confusion that results from a collision. Imagine trying to listen to 15 or 20 people trying to talk at the same time to different people, and even possibly in different languages. Thankfully, network cards are designed with rules to alleviate some of the chaos surrounding collisions and for avoiding them in the future.

One common design—Carrier-Sense Multiple Access with Collision Detection (CSMA/CD)—implements a standard set of rules for the transmission of frames on a network. CSMA/CD defines the relative politeness of machines on the network. When a network card wants to use the wire to transmit data, it listens first to determine whether another machine is already in the process of transmitting. If the network is idle (silent), the machine may transmit its own frames. If, in the course of transmitting, another network card also begins to transmit, a collision occurs. Each network card stops transmitting and waits a random amount of time; when this time expires, each card again listens. If all is clear, the card retransmits the data.

At the blazing speeds that data is transferred, it might seem that collisions are not a problem, and on small networks this is true; however, as networks grow in size, and as the amount of data being transferred between machines grows, the number of collisions increases. It is possible to put so many machines on a network segment that the capability of machines to communicate is slowed down greatly, if not stopped altogether. If too many machines try to communicate at the same time, it is nearly impossible for network cards to transmit data without collisions. This problem is referred to as saturating your bandwidth (the amount of sustainable data transfer rate) and should be avoided.

The Ring Configuration

The ring configuration provides an alternative method for the transmission of data from one computer to another over a network segment. This configuration relies on the passing of a token from computer to computer.

In this type of network, one of the machines is designated the creator of a token. The token, which is the vehicle that carries all network communication, is sent from one machine to another in a circular loop until it travels all the way around. A token can either be flagged "In Use" or "Free." If a network card receives a free token, the system places data in it and addresses it for another computer (again, the MAC address must be resolved first by using a broadcast). The system then flags the token as "In Use."

The token is then passed from network card to network card, and each checks the MAC address. If a network card determines that the token is addressed to a different destination, it silently ignores it. When the destination address receives the frame, it formulates a reply, addresses the token for the original computer, and sends it back. Again, the token is passed from one network card to another until it reaches its origin. Assuming that communication between the two machines is done, the originator of the communication releases the token by setting its flag to "Free" and passing it to the next network card.

In a ring-based network, the only communication occurring on the network is by the machine that currently has control of the token. The risk of collisions is completely eliminated. Not only that, but the lack of collisions means that network cards don't have to be quite so polite and can send much-larger frames. By using larger frame sizes, ring-based networks can transfer much-larger amounts of data at any one time than can be transferred in the bus configuration.

There is a downside to ring-based networks, however. If any system is frozen, it cannot send or receive the token. The ring essentially breaks if a machine crashes, and the communications network is down.

As with bus-based networks, software and hardware implementations have been developed to eliminate such problems; but ring networks are typically more expensive and more difficult to maintain and service than a bus configuration. The main selling point behind this type of configuration is the amount of data that can be transferred at one time through the significantly larger frame sizes.

The Star Configuration

In the ring configuration, traffic problems are eliminated by only allowing one system to talk on the network at a time. Obviously, there are limitations when only one system can talk on the network at one time. The star configuration was designed to get around this limitation. The star configuration reduces the traffic that any one machine has to compete with to communicate on the network. This is accomplished through the implementation of smart hardware known as fast switches.

In a bus configuration, a circuit is created between two systems and data is transferred from system to system. However, all these circuits are on the same wire, leading to collisions. The switch in a star configuration isolates the network segments (or even individual computers) so that collisions do not occur between network cards. All data is designed to flow through the switch. A virtual circuit is then created between two machines to allow them to communicate with each other. The virtual circuit lasts only as long as is necessary to transfer data. After the machines finish communicating, the virtual circuit is destroyed, and the segments are isolated from each other once again.

To visualize this, you might think of the switch in the middle acting as telephone operators did back in the days when connections were made between a caller and receiver by plugging cables into their respective sockets. Switches perform essentially the same task—but significantly quicker than a person can do it. Again, the connection lasts only as long as the two machines are communicating.

After the machines stop, the connection is broken, and the path between the two machines no longer exists. In a very small environment, each machine is assigned a port on the switch; in most situations, however, this is not practical. Switches of this kind are typically very expensive and would not be used for a small number of machines. Most switches are used in hybrid configurations, in which additional hubs are used to provide additional bandwidth to hundreds of machines.

The key characteristic of the star configuration is that each machine with its own port receives the maximum bandwidth that the medium can carry. Each machine sees only the traffic for the connections it has established because of the physical configuration of the network—*whereas a virtual circuit connects sections together logically though this configuration appears the same as a bus configuration.* This is one of the more expensive solutions to minimizing bandwidth bottlenecks, but it works very well when implemented.

Although the discussions of topology is important, you should bear in mind that this is the physical connection between systems and acts as the lowest layer in the network architecture. For a network to function, there must be a common language spoken on the network and some common functions available. In the next section you will learn about the TCP/IP architectural model, which provides those commonalties.

INTRODUCTION TO **TCP/IP**

The Transmission Control Protocol/Internet Protocol (TCP/IP) is an industry-standard suite of protocols designed to be routable, robust, and functionally efficient. TCP/IP was originally designed as a set of wide area network (WAN) protocols for the express purpose of maintaining communication links and data transfer between sites in the event of an atomic or nuclear war. Since those early days, development of the protocols has passed from the hands of the military and has been the responsibility of the Internet community.

The evolution of these protocols from a small, four-site project into the foundation of the worldwide Internet has been extraordinary. And, despite more than 25 years of work and numerous modifications to the protocol suite, the ideas inherent to the original specifications are still intact. Following are some of the advantages of TCP/IP:

◆ **An industry-standard protocol.** Because TCP/IP was developed by the Department of Defense, it is not in the public domain. This means the Internet community as a whole decides whether a particular change or implementation is worthwhile. Although this slows down the implementation of new features, it guarantees that changes are thought out and compatible with other implementations of TCP/IP. The definitions of new features, which are publicly available over the Internet, detail how the protocol suite should be used and implemented.

◆ **Utilities for connecting dissimilar operating systems.** Many connectivity utilities have been written for the TCP/IP suite, including the File Transfer Protocol (FTP) and Terminal Emulation Protocol (Telnet). Because these utilities use the standard Windows Sockets API, connectivity from one machine to another is not dependent on the network operating system used on either machine. For example, a Windows NT server running an FTP server could be accessed by a UNIX FTP client to transfer files without either party having to worry about compatibility issues. Just as easily, a Windows NT computer running a Telnet client can access and run commands on an IBM mainframe running a Telnet server.

◆ **The Sockets interface.** The Windows Sockets API provides developers a standard interface (based on the Berkeley standard) for the development of client/server applications. All implementations of TCP/IP use the Sockets interface between applications (many of which are called, confusingly, protocols) and the network protocols; therefore, applications such as FTP and Telnet can be developed and used on different computers.

◆ **Access to the Internet.** TCP/IP is the protocol of the Internet and allows access to a wealth of information that can be found at thousands of locations around the world.

The rest of this section will look at the TCP/IP protocol stack and provide you with an overview of the main protocols that are used in the TCP/IP model.

The TCP/IP Architectural Model

TCP/IP maps to a four-layer architectural model. This model, called the TCP/IP Architectural Model, is broken into the Network Interface, Internet, Transport, and Application layers.

The Network Interface layer is responsible for communicating directly with the network. It must understand the network architecture being used, such as token-ring or ethernet, and provide an interface allowing the Internet layer to communicate with it. The Internet layer is responsible for communicating directly with the Network Interface layer.

The Internet layer is primarily concerned with the routing and delivery of packets through the Internet Protocol (IP). The protocols in the Transport layer must use IP to send data. The Internet Protocol includes rules for how to address and direct packets, fragment and reassemble packets, provide security information, and identify the type of service being used. However, because IP is not a connection-based protocol, it does not guarantee that packets transmitted onto the wire will not be lost, damaged, duplicated, or out of order. This is the responsibility of higher layers of the networking model.

Other protocols that exist in the Internet layer are the Internet Control Messaging Protocol (ICMP), Internet Group Management Protocol (IGMP), and Address Resolution Protocol (ARP). Each of these is described in more detail later in this chapter.

The Transport layer is responsible for providing communication between machines for applications. This communication can be connection-based or connectionless. Transmission Control Protocol (TCP) is the protocol used for connection-based communication between two machines, providing reliable data transfer. User Datagram Protocol (UDP) is used for connectionless communication, such as broadcasts, in which reliability is not required.

The Application layer of the Internet Protocol suite is where the client and server applications are located. These applications use the socket interface to work with either TCP or UDP to move data from system to system. Numerous protocols have been written for use in this layer, including Simple Network Management Protocol (SNMP), File Transfer Protocol (FTP), Simple Mail Transfer Protocol (SMTP), and many others.

The interface between the Network Interface layer and the Internet layer does not pass a great deal of information, but it must follow certain rules. It must listen to all broadcasts and send the rest of the data in the frame to the Internet layer for processing; if it receives any frames that do not have an IP frame type, they must be silently discarded (or passed to a different transport protocol). In Windows NT this interface—called the Network Driver Interface Specification (NDIS)—allows the network card to work with TCP/IP and other protocols at the same time.

The interface between the Internet layer and the Transport layer must be able to provide each layer full access to such information as the source and destination addresses, whether TCP or UDP should be used in the transport of data, and all other available mechanisms for IP. Rules and specifications for the Transport layer give it the capability to change these parameters or to pass parameters it receives from the Application layer to the Internet layer. The most important thing to remember about these boundary layers is that they must use the agreed-upon rules for passing information from one layer to the other.

The interface between the Transport layer and the Application layer is written to provide an interface to applications whether they are using the TCP or UDP protocol for transferring data. The interface uses the Windows Sockets to transfer parameters and data between the two layers. The Application layer must have full access to the Transport layer to change and alter parameters as necessary.

The layers provide only guidelines, however; the real work is done by the protocols that are contained within the layers. This chapter describes the TCP/IP protocol as a suite of protocols, not just two (TCP and IP). The six protocols that provide the basic functionality of TCP/IP are

- ◆ Transmission Control Protocol (TCP)
- ◆ User Datagram Protocol (UDP)
- ◆ Internet Protocol (IP)
- ◆ Internet Control Message Protocol (ICMP)
- ◆ Address Resolution Protocol (ARP)
- ◆ Internet Group Management Protocol (IGMP)

Figure 1.3 shows where each of these protocols resides in the architectural model.

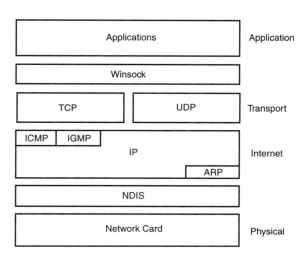

FIGURE 1.3
The core protocols that make up TCP/IP.

Transmission Control Protocol

The Transmission Control Protocol is a connection-based protocol; this means that it requires the establishment of a session before data is transmitted between two machines. Because TCP sets up a connection between two machines, it is designed to verify that all packets sent by a machine are received on the other end. If, for some reason, packets are lost, the sending machine will resend the data. Therefore, it is because a session is established that delivery of packets can be considered reliable. However, there is additional overhead involved with using TCP to transmit packets to support connection-oriented communications.

Connection-Oriented Communication

TCP achieves reliable delivery of packets by using an assigned sequence number to track the transmission and receipt of individual packets during communication. A session is able to track the progress of individual packets by monitoring when a packet is sent, determining in what order it was sent, and notifying the sender when it is received so it can send more. Figure 1.4 illustrates how TCP sets up a connection-oriented session between two machines.

FIGURE 1.4
A TCP session is established using a three-way handshake.

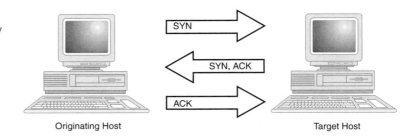

The first step in the communication process is for the initiating machine to send a message indicating a desire to synchronize the systems. This is handled by setting a flag in the TCP header (information that describes what to do with the data); this indicates that the system wants to synchronize sequence numbers.

Next, the target system formulates a reply by acknowledging the sequence number that was sent (in fact, the acknowledgment number is the next sequence number that the system expects to receive). Just as the initiating system did, the target will set a flag indicating that the initiating system should set its acknowledgment numbers.

The initiating system then acknowledges the sequence number that was sent to it, and there is now a session between the two systems. Whenever data is sent, a sequence number is sent and acknowledged.

After a session is created between the two computers, data can be transferred continuously until the session is either disrupted or shut down. Data is sent in pieces, each of which forms a TCP Segment— a combination of the data and a TCP Header (known as encapsulation). The system takes the data stream from the application layer and makes as many TCP Segments as are required. Shutting down the session is also done with a three-way handshake, with the exception that the systems use the finish (FIN) flag.

Figure 1.5 illustrates the format of a TCP header. The header includes all the parameters that are used to guarantee delivery of packets and to provide error-checking and control. Notice that the header specifies a source and destination port for the communication. This tells TCP where it is supposed to send the data and where the data came from (a discussion of ports and sockets follows).

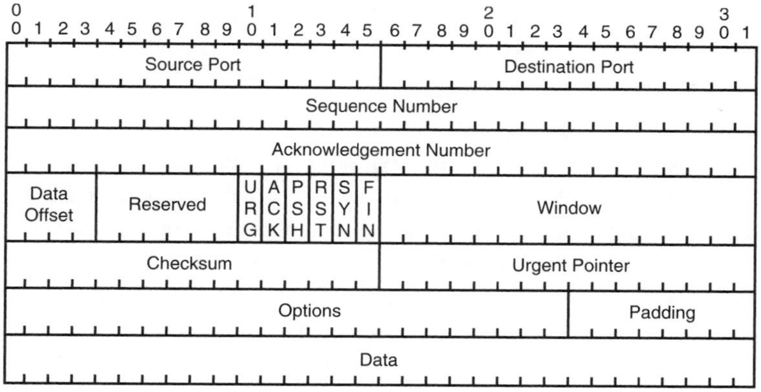

FIGURE 1.5
The breakdown of the TCP header.

Notice that the header includes sections defining the sequence numbers and acknowledgment numbers that were discussed previously. The data from the application is treated as a stream of information with no defined starting or ending points. This data has to be broken up into smaller pieces, because the underlying network can transmit only so much data at one time. Other parameters include the SYN and FIN options for starting and ending communication sessions between two machines; and the current size of the receive window, which tells the other system how big the pieces of data can be.

The header also includes a checksum for verifying the header information and other options that can be specific to particular implementations of TCP/IP. The last part of the frame is the actual data being transmitted. A full discussion of each of these parameters is beyond the scope of this book or the TCP/IP test. Other academic texts and RFCs on the Internet describe in fuller detail the specifications for each parameter.

In addition to synchronizing the acknowledgment numbers, the three-way handshake sets the initial size for the receive window on each host. To provide reliable delivery, TCP breaks the data stream into packets in sequence. The packets are sent and are acknowledged before new data can be sent.

To do this, the send window on each host is set to the size of the receive window on the other host. The packets from the data stream are placed in the send window and transmitted. As the other system acknowledges the receipt of the packets, the send window is moved past (slides by) the acknowledged data, and more packets can be sent.

Sliding Windows

TCP uses the concept of sliding windows for transferring data between machines. Each machine has both a send window and a receive window that it uses to buffer data and make the communication process more efficient. TCP guarantees the delivery of data; however, packets can be lost on the network or dropped during routing. Therefore, TCP must keep track of the packets on both machines (which is why there is a sequence number and an acknowledgment number). By using a window, TCP needs to keep track of only part of the data; data that the window has passed has been delivered, and the data the window will pass over is not on the wire yet.

The receive window allows a machine to receive packets out of order and reorganize them while it waits for more packets. This reorganization may be necessary because TCP uses IP to transmit data, and IP does not guarantee the orderly delivery of packets.

Figure 1.6 shows the send and receive windows that exist on machines that have TCP/IP installed. By default, window sizes in Windows NT are a little more than 8KB in size, representing the data eight standard ethernet frames will carry.

The TCP send window will hold the packet until it is acknowledged. However, if no acknowledgment is forthcoming, TCP will resend the packet. When data is sent, a retransmit timer is set. If this expires, the packet is re-sent and the timer reset to two times its original value. This will continue until the retransmit reaches the maximum retransmit time period (around 16 seconds).

FIGURE 1.6

The data that is active on the network is in the send window.

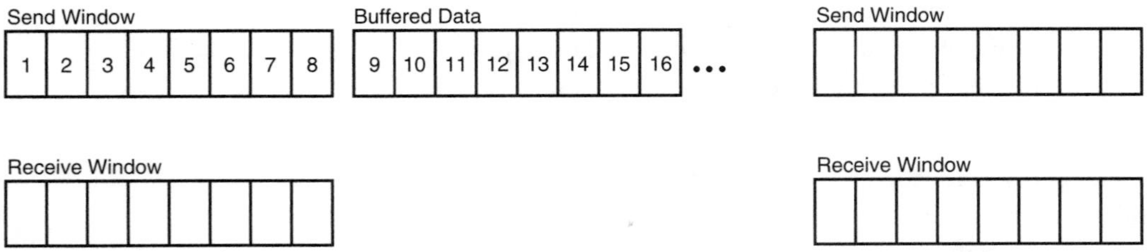

Acknowledgments

As the receiving window receives packets, it sends acknowledgments to the send window that the packets arrived intact. When the send window receives acknowledgments for data it has sent, it slides the window to the right so that it can send any additional data stored in memory. However, it can slide over only as many spaces as acknowledgments it has received.

By default, a receive window sends an acknowledgment for every two sequenced packets it receives. Therefore, assuming no network problems, if the send window in Figure 1.7 sends eight packets to the receive window on the other machine, four acknowledgment packets come back. An acknowledgment is sent for packets 1 & 2, 3 & 4, 5 & 6, and 7 & 8. The sending window slides over to the next eight packets waiting to be sent and sends those to the receiving window. In this manner, the number of acknowledgments sent over the network is reduced, and the flow of traffic is increased.

As long as the acknowledgments are flowing back regularly from the receiving machine, data is streamed smoothly and efficiently. However, on busy networks, packets can get lost. Because TCP provides reliable delivery, the window cannot slide past any data that has not been acknowledged. If the window cannot slide, no more data beyond the window is transmitted; TCP eventually will then have to shut down the session, and the communication will fail.

FIGURE 1.7
The send window will slide after acknowledgments are received.

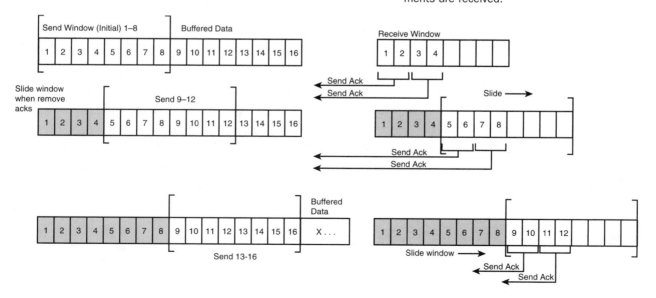

TCP, therefore, will wait a certain amount of time before either retransmitting data or sending acknowledgments for packets that arrive out of sequence. Each window is given a timer: the send window has the Retransmit Timer and the receive window has the Delayed Acknowledgment Timer. These timers help define what to do when communication isn't flowing smoothly. In the sending window, a Retransmit Timer is set for each packet, specifying how long to wait for an acknowledgment before making the assumption that the packet did not get to its destination. After this timer has expired, the packet is re-sent and the retransmit timer is set to two times its initial value.

This doubling of the retransmit timer will continue until the maximum number of retries is hit. If this value—which is set in the Registry—is exceeded, the TCP session is closed and errors are reported to the application.

Window NT Registry Retransmission Subkey

You can find the Registry location for changing the number of times to retry a transmission in the following subkey:

```
HKEY_LOCAL_MACHINE\SYSTEM\CurrentControlSet\Services\Tcpip\
Parameters
```

The Registry parameter and value is

```
TcpMaxDataRetransmissions (REG_DWORD).
```

The default value is 5.

In the receiving window, a Delayed Acknowledgment Timer is set for those packets that arrive out of order. Remember, by default an acknowledgment is sent for every two sequenced packets. If packets arrive out of order (if, for instance, 1 and 3 arrive, but 2 is missing), an acknowledgment for two sequenced packets is not possible.

When packets arrive out of order, the Delayed Acknowledgment Timer is set on the received packet from the pair. In the parenthetical example, a Timer is set on packet number 1. The Delayed

Acknowledgment Timer is hard-coded for 200 milliseconds. As data is acknowledged and passed to the Application layer, the receive window slides to the right, enabling more data to be received. Again, if a packet doesn't show up, the window is not able to slide past it.

User Datagram Protocol

The second protocol that lives in the Transport layer is the User Datagram Protocol (UDP). This protocol does not create a session between the two communicating machines before data is transmitted. Because of this, UDP cannot guarantee that packets are delivered, that they are delivered in order, or that they will be retransmitted if they are lost.

Given the apparent unreliability of this protocol, some may wonder why a protocol such as UDP was developed. But observe the relative simplicity of the header format of UDP (see Figure 1.8) as compared to TCP (refer to Figure 1.5).

Notice that sending a UDP datagram has very little overhead involved. A UDP datagram has no synchronization parameters or priority options. All that exist are the source port, destination port, the length of the data, a checksum for verifying the header, and then the data.

There are actually a number of good reasons to have a transport protocol that does not require a session to be established. For one, very little overhead is associated with UDP—there is no need to keep track of sequence numbers, Retransmit Timers, Delayed Acknowledgment Timers, and retransmission of packets. UDP is quick and streamlined functionally; it's just not guaranteed. This makes UDP perfect for communications that involve broadcasts, general announcements to the network, or real-time data because a session is not created with each receiving station.

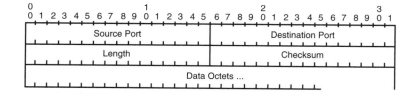

FIGURE 1.8

The UDP header is much simpler than the TCP header.

Internet Protocol

A number of protocols are found in the Internet layer, including the most important protocol in the entire suite, the Internet Protocol (IP). The reason this is the most important protocol is that the Transport layer cannot communicate at all without communicating through IP in the Internet layer. IP is responsible for the handling, addressing, and routing of packets on a network. It is a connectionless delivery system, but delivery of packets is not guaranteed. (Reliability is provided by the higher layers, either through TCP or by higher-layer applications, in the case of UDP.)

IP also has a number of parameters that can be set. Figure 1.9 illustrates a sample datagram for IP and the various characteristics that can be configured.

Of the parameters that can be controlled and set in the IP packet in Figure 1.9, pay close attention to the Time to Live, Protocol, Source Address, and Destination Address. These parameters are what specify where a datagram is supposed to be sent, where it came from, how long a packet has to get to its destination before it is discarded by the network, and what protocol (such as TCP or UDP) the data should be passed to.

Addressing

The most fundamental element of the Internet Protocol is the address space that IP uses. Each machine on a network is given a unique 32-bit address called an Internet address, or IP address, in addition to the MAC address of the network card. Although IP addresses are 32-bit addresses, they are expressed in a dotted, decimal notation (such as 209.204.204.64) to make them simpler to use and understand.

IP addresses are divided into five categories called classes; there are currently A, B, C, D, and E classes of addresses. The unique address given to a machine is derived from the class A, B, or C addresses. A class D address is used for combining machines into one functional group (multicasting). Class E addresses are considered experimental and are not currently available.

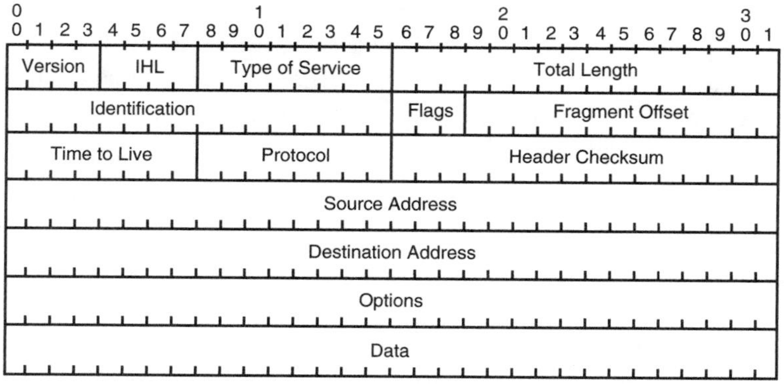

```
 0                   1                   2                   3
 0 1 2 3 4 5 6 7 8 9 0 1 2 3 4 5 6 7 8 9 0 1 2 3 4 5 6 7 8 9 0 1
+-------+-------+---------------+-------------------------------+
|Version|  IHL  | Type of Service|          Total Length        |
+-------+-------+---------------+-----+-------------------------+
|      Identification            |Flags|      Fragment Offset   |
+---------------+----------------+-----+-------------------------+
|  Time to Live |    Protocol    |        Header Checksum        |
+---------------+----------------+-------------------------------+
|                        Source Address                          |
+----------------------------------------------------------------+
|                     Destination Address                        |
+----------------------------------------------------------------+
|                           Options                              |
+----------------------------------------------------------------+
|                            Data                                |
+----------------------------------------------------------------+
```

FIGURE 1.9
The header for an IP datagram.

It is important to understand that the IP protocol cannot be used to directly communicate with another machine. At the Physical layer, all communication is done using the MAC address. The IP address is used to find which network a machine is on so the physical address can be used to talk to it. In other words, the IP address is used for routing (moving packets between networks), and the MAC address is used for direct communications (host-to-host or from the router to the host.)

IP receives information in the form of packets from the Transport layer, from either TCP or UDP, and sends out data in IP datagrams. The size of a datagram depends on the type of network that is being used, such as token-ring or ethernet. If a packet has too much data to be transmitted in one datagram, it is broken into pieces and transmitted through several datagrams (this is called fragmentation). Each of these datagrams has to then be reassembled by TCP or UDP.

Fragmentation and Reassembly

Fragmentation and reassembly occur when data is too large to be transmitted on the underlying network. Combining a token-ring and ethernet network is the most common example. Token-ring networks support much-larger frame sizes and, therefore, support larger datagram sizes.

When moving data from a token-ring to an ethernet network, IP must break down the data into manageable chunks through a process called fragmentation. After data is fragmented, each datagram gets a fragment ID, identifying all the fragments that belong together. The datagrams also receive a fragment offset so that each fragment can be reassembled at the destination machine. This whole process is transparent to the user.

After the fragments have been received and reassembled at the destination machine, the data can be sent up to the higher layers for processing.

Routability

As noted previously, the primary job of IP is the routing of IP datagrams from one network to another. This is possible because the 32-bit IP address is made up of two parts: the network ID (which identifies your network) and the host ID (which identifies your system on the network).

The system uses the subnet mask (a special number that tells your system which part of the address is the network address) to determine which part is which. In simplest terms, the IP layer compares the local IP address and subnet mask to extract the network ID. Then the target machine's IP address is compared to the local subnet mask to extract a network ID (later you will discover this is not necessarily the target machine's network ID). If the two network IDs match, the system is local; otherwise, the packet needs to be routed. Normally, IP will forward the packet to a default gateway (which is the router to use when you don't have other instructions).

Time-to-Live

The default Time-to-Live (TTL) specification is set to 128 in Windows NT. This number represents either 128 router hops or 128 seconds, or a combination of the two. Each time a router handles a datagram, it decrements the TTL by one. If a datagram is held up at a router, the router decrements the TTL by one for each second the packet sits waiting.

If the datagram gets routed through congested routers, traffic jams, narrow-bandwidth communication avenues, and so on, the TTL may expire. If the TTL expires before the datagram reaches its destination, it is discarded from the network. This prevents datagrams from running around a network indefinitely, which could wreak havoc with bandwidth and the synchronization of data. Without a specific TTL, a packet could, in theory, start circling the globe, endlessly looping through the networks and using up bandwidth. If more and more packets did this, the entire network would eventually crash.

As you can see, the TTL plays a vital role in making a TCP/IP network function. ICMP works with IP to allow the network to function by reporting events, such as the discarding of a packet.

Internet Control Message Protocol

Internet Control Message Protocol (ICMP), a part of the Internet layer, is responsible for reporting errors and messages regarding the delivery of IP datagrams. It can also send "source quench"—which tells a system to slow its transmission rate—and other tuning signals during the transfer of data between two machines, without the intervention of the user.

The tuning signals sent by ICMP are designed to fine-tune and optimize the transfer of data automatically. ICMP is the protocol that warns you when a destination host is unreachable, or informs you of how long it took to get to a destination host.

ICMP messages can be broken down into two basic categories: the reporting of errors and the sending of queries. Error messages include the following:

◆ **Destination unreachable.** The `Destination unreachable` error message is generated by ICMP when an IP datagram is sent out and the destination machine either cannot be located or does not support the designated protocol. For instance, a sending machine may receive a `Destination host unreachable` message when trying to communicate through a router that does not know which network to send a datagram to.

◆ **Redirect.** The important thing to realize about `Redirect` messages is that only routers in a TCP/IP environment, not individual machines, send them. Networks may have more than one router (for redundancy); if a router detects a better route to a particular destination, it forwards the first packet it receives, but it sends a redirect message to the machine telling it to use the other route.

◆ **Source quench.** Sometimes a machine has to drop incoming datagrams because it has received so many that it can't process them all. In this case, a machine can send a Source quench message to the source, indicating that it needs to slow up transmission. The Source quench message can also be sent by a router if it is between the source and destination machines and is encountering trouble routing all the packets in time. Upon receiving a Source quench message, the source machine immediately reduces its transmissions. However, it continues to try to increase the amount of data, as time progresses, to the original amount of data it was sending before.

◆ **Time exceeded.** The Time exceeded error message is sent by a router whenever it drops a packet due to the expiration of the TTL. This error message is sent to the source address to notify the machine of a possible infinite routing loop or that the TTL is set too low to get to the destination.

ICMP also includes general message queries. The two most commonly used are the following:

◆ **Echo request.** The echo request is a simple, directed datagram that asks for acknowledgment that a particular IP address exists on the network. If a machine with this IP address exists and receives the request, it is designed to send an ICMP echo reply.

◆ **Echo reply.** This reply is sent back to the destination address to notify the source machine of its existence. The Packet Internet Groper (PING) utility reports the existence of the IP address and how long it took to get there.

The PING utility is the most familiar tool for verifying that an IP address on a network actually exists. This utility uses the ICMP echo request and reply mechanisms.

Internet Group Management Protocol

Internet Group Management Protocol (IGMP) is a protocol and set of specifications that allows machines to be added and removed from IP group addresses, using the class D range of addresses mentioned previously. IP allows the assignment of class D addresses to groups of machines so that they may receive broadcast data as one functional unit; this is referred to as multicasting. Machines can be added and removed from these units or groups, or they can be members of multiple groups.

Most implementations of the TCP/IP protocol stack support IGMP on the local machine; however, routers designed to broadcast IGMP messages from one network to another are still in the experimental stage. Routers are designed to initiate queries for multicast groups on local network segments to determine whether they should be broadcasting on that segment. If at least one member of an IGMP group exists or answers with an IGMP response, the router processes IGMP datagrams and broadcasts them on the segment.

Address Resolution Protocol

Unless IP is planning to initiate a full broadcast on the network, it has to know the physical address of the machine to which it is going to send datagrams (broadcasts are sent to FF-FF-FF-FF-FF-FF). To gather this information, it relies on Address Resolution Protocol (ARP). Remember that IP is used to determine routes and move packets from network to network. The MAC address is always used for direct communications (that is, sending information on the wire).

ARP is responsible for finding a map to any local physical address that IP may request. If ARP does not have a map in memory, it has to find one on the network. ARP uses a local broadcast, asking all the systems on the network if they have the IP that is being resolved. This is done using an ARP broadcast packet that contains the IP address and MAC of the originating host; these can then be stored at the target machine. The target stores the address and responds with a packet that contains its MAC address. The originating machine then stores this in the local ARP cache. The two systems now have each other's IP and MAC addresses and can communicate.

ARP can resolve only the address of a local machine. When an IP address is determined to be on a remote subnet, IP sends the packet to the default gateway; in this case, ARP is used to find the MAC address of the gateway.

> **NOTE**
>
> **The ARP Cache** The ARP cache is short-lived. Addresses that are used are kept for ten minutes; addresses that are not used are kept for two minutes.

Sockets and Application Protocols

In our previous discussion, we looked at the various protocols that are involved in the TCP/IP stack. There was also a discussion of the boundary layers. The two key boundaries were the Sockets interface and NDIS. Although a discussion of the NDIS interface might be interesting, it is beyond the scope of this book.

The Sockets interface, however, is critical to TCP/IP and is fundamental in making the protocol suite as flexible and useful as it is. Sockets are the interface between the Application layer protocols, such as FTP and NetBIOS, and the Transport layer protocols.

In the Windows NT environment the Winsock API (Windows Sockets) handles the sockets. A socket (which is a number) provides an endpoint for communications. If you think about the number of different services that might be running on a computer, it makes sense that something is required to identify which service a packet is for.

To communicate, you actually require three pieces of information: an IP address, the transport protocol (TCP or UDP), and the socket number. For example, to open a session with an FTP server running on a computer at 194.23.49.23, the system opens this socket: 194.23.49.23:TCP:21. This could be expanded as IP address 194.23.49.23, protocol TCP, port address 21.

The FTP server responds to the port on your machine that you used to initiate the communications. For example, you might be known as 201.52.14.2:TCP:1523. The server will use this port to identify a request from you, and it will respond to this port number. This lets FTP support hundreds or thousands of users simultaneously without sending data to the wrong client.

The first 1,024 port numbers are defined as well-known ports. These reserved ports are assigned by the Internet Assigned Numbers Authority (IANA). Ports in this range are nearly always server ports; that is, the FTP server will open port 21 and listen for incoming traffic on it (hence, the term "listening" or "server" port.)

When a client application starts, it will grab the next available port above 1,023 and actively open the port to send data. This means that the client application does not always have the same port number (which also means that you can FTP to more than one server at a time or open multiple connections to the same server at the same time).

Most of the server-side ports are listed in a file called "services." For a default Windows NT installation, this file is in the C:\WINNT\SYSTEM32\DRIVERS\ETC directory.

All requests from a client (RDR) to a server (SVR) use sockets in the TCP/IP world. Unfortunately, not all protocols that we use work directly with sockets.

NetBIOS over TCP/IP

No discussion of the implementation of TPC/IP on Windows NT is complete without discussing how NetBIOS (the application protocol used by Windows NT) is implemented. NetBIOS supports three main networking functions that are then used by NetBIOS services (such as the Windows NT redirector and server) to communicate over the network.

The functions that must be supported for NetBIOS to communicate are:

◆ **Data Transfer.** Any transport protocol that will work with NetBIOS must be able to transfer data from one station to another. Because this is a primary function of all transport protocols, there are few that cannot be used. TCP/IP connection-oriented transfers use TCP, and connectionless transfers use UDP.

◆ **Session Management.** NetBIOS uses sessions to transfer data and implement security across the network. Because TCP can create a session, this is easily implemented over TCP/IP.

◆ **Name Management.** NetBIOS uses computer names rather than IP addresses to communicate. There is no translation for this in the TCP/IP world; as you will see in future chapters, many ways to get around this have been developed.

Although the basic functions for NetBIOS to work are available in TCP/IP, NetBIOS does not know how to use sockets. Therefore, some other service is required to handle the interface between the NetBIOS application protocol and the TCP/IP transport protocol. This is accomplished by the NetBIOS Helper (which you can see in the services list). The NetBIOS helper lives on ports 137, 138, and 139; it uses these ports to service the NetBIOS requests.

RFCs

Anyone interested in learning more about TCP/IP should read the series of published standards called Requests For Comments (RFCs). These standards, which can be thought of as the living documents of the Internet, are constantly under various stages of completion, acceptance, or planned obsolescence.

A particular RFC number describes a single enhancement or feature to the TCP/IP protocol. Whenever a significant change to a feature is recommended or suggested, and enough of the Internet community agrees on the change, a new RFC is created to discuss the new implementation and place it under further study.

RFCs are referred to as the living documents of the Internet because they are never updated or deleted—much like the Constitution of the United States. Every addition or change is an amendment to the original. Therefore, a change requires the creation of a new RFC number, which always references the original RFC it is intended to replace or enhance.

To keep track of whether RFCs are current, under progress, or no longer used, a classification system was created indicating the status of any individual RFC. These classifications are Required, Recommended, Elective, Limited Use, and Not Recommended.

When you read an RFC, you may notice that different terminology is used. For instance, in the case of a particular implementation detail that is Required, the terminology used in the RFC says that this implementation "must" be used. In the case of a Recommended implementation, the RFC uses the word "should" throughout. The Elective portions are discussed in terms of how a protocol "may" handle a particular feature. And, of course, for those implementations that are Not Recommended, the use of "should not" is often seen. To view Internet RFCs, check out the following URL:

```
http://www.internic.net
```

CONNECTING NETWORK SEGMENTS

Now that you have seen the topologies and the protocols that will tie the systems together, you should understand that TCP/IP is used to connect networks. This ability to join networks is important because a finite number of systems can be placed on a single network.

This section will discuss some of the technologies that are used to join networks. This is provided more as background information than as required knowledge in the TCP/IP world. The discussion will look at how repeaters, bridges, and routers factor into the networking equation.

Repeaters

One of the first challenges that network engineers needed to overcome was the distance a signal can travel. The technologies that are used to create networks are limited by the distance that they can carry a signal without a loss in strength.

Signal weakness is a problem if you need to connect systems in a large building where the signal may have to travel more than a few hundred feet. To overcome this, designers came up with a simple device—a repeater—that can sit on the wire and listen for traffic.

Essentially, a repeater is a simple device that works at the Physical layer. When traffic is received, the repeater does exactly what its name suggests—repeats the traffic on the other network. This means that all the traffic from each of the networks is repeated on the other. As you saw previously, a network card (in ethernet) will listen for quiet before attempting to transmit. With all the traffic of two networks floating around waiting for a moment to transmit, data sharing becomes more difficult and retransmission becomes more common.

Bridges

Obviously, the repeater was able to extend the distance a network could traverse; however, the price paid in increased traffic means that repeaters are not practical in larger networks.

Engineers, then, needed to develop a device that passes only the traffic that is required—which is not every piece of traffic. This is where a bridge comes in. A bridge acts much like a repeater in that it passes traffic from one network to another. The difference is that the bridge listens to all traffic on all interfaces and builds a list of the MAC addresses that reside on each interface.

As this list builds, the amount of traffic that a bridge must pass diminishes quickly. When traffic is received, a bridge will do one of three things with it:

◆ If the destination MAC and the originating MAC are on the same interface (network adapter), the bridge does nothing. If the originating address is unknown, it will be added to the address table for the interface.

◆ If the destination MAC and the originating MAC are on different interfaces, the bridge retransmits the traffic on the correct interface. Again, if the originating address is unknown, it will be added to the address table for the interface.

◆ If the destination address is unknown or is the broadcast address, the traffic will be retransmitted on all interfaces.

Routers

Repeaters and bridges are active devices—that is, they listen to and act on nearly all the traffic that passes by them. These technologies can effectively link systems that are connected to their physical interfaces. However, they are restricted in the size to which they can grow.

The ability to connect to a computer halfway around the world requires a router. Routers contain two or more network interfaces (like bridges and repeaters); however, they sit passively on the network waiting for traffic that is directed to them. When a router receives a packet, it is passed to the IP layer, which determines a route for the packet to the destination machine or to the next router. The ability to move data from one router to the next is what allows IP to move your data so far.

Observe the following output; this is a path through a series of routers going halfway around the world:

```
Tracing route to world.comat.com.sg [203.127.148.8] over a
maximum of 30 hops:


  1     80 ms     70 ms     70 ms   tnt01.magma.ca [204.191.36.88]
  2     60 ms     80 ms     60 ms   core1-vlan5.magma.ca [206.191.0.129]
  3     60 ms     81 ms     90 ms   border2-e3.magma.ca [206.191.0.9]
  4     80 ms     80 ms    101 ms   205.150.227.1
  5    100 ms    181 ms     90 ms   a10-0-0.102.bb1.ott1.a10-0-0.102.bb1.tor2.uunet.ca [205.150.242.89]
  6    100 ms    101 ms    110 ms   ATM11-0-0.BR2.TCO1.ALTER.NET [137.39.250.69]
  7    120 ms    110 ms     91 ms   332.atm3-0-0.cr2.tco1.alter.net [137.39.13.18]
  8    200 ms    211 ms    210 ms   189.ATM6-0-0.BR2.LND1.Alter.Net [137.39.30.177]
  9    211 ms    260 ms    230 ms   332.ATM6-0-0.CR2.LND1.Alter.Net [146.188.5.29]
 10    260 ms    250 ms    241 ms   167.Hssi9-0.GW1.MCM1.Alter.Net [146.188.3.46]
 11    391 ms    410 ms    421 ms   Hssi1-0.CR1.SGP1.Alter.Net [146.188.2.6]
 12    401 ms    450 ms    501 ms   Fddi2-0.AR2.SGP1.Alter.Net [210.80.7.226]
 13    430 ms    441 ms    421 ms   SingNET-gw.customer.Alter.Net [210.80.8.2]
 14    491 ms    530 ms    511 ms   eunos.singnet.com.sg [165.21.102.3]
 15    541 ms    391 ms    380 ms   atm-qt-tp.singnet.com.sg [165.21.49.201]
 16    471 ms    410 ms    421 ms   clementi.singnet.com.sg [165.21.80.4]
 17    630 ms    731 ms    481 ms   165.21.18.226
 18    431 ms    440 ms    461 ms   world.comat.com.sg [203.127.148.8]

Trace complete.
```

CASE STUDY: THE SUNSHINE BREWING COMPANY

ESSENCE OF THE CASE

You have been hired to design and implement a networking solution that will unite all the offices into a secure network. Here are some of the key issues that you need to look at:

- There are about 61 locations that need to be connected.

- There are several existing networks.

- The locations are primarily of three types: headquarters, production, and sales.

- There are currently no standards in place.

- All the offices have some form of Internet connectivity.

At the end of every chapter of this book you will find a case study. As you read through the chapters, you should think about how the technology can be applied.

The same company will be used in the case studies throughout the book to allow you to see its progression through the different topics that are covered. Presented here is an overview of Sunshine Brewing Company (SBC) as it is now. This is a fictional company based on various companies that the author has worked with.

SCENARIO

The Sunshine Brewing Company started out as many companies do—as a local enterprise. Initially, two computers were used: one handled payroll and other administrative functions, the other dealt with the accounts payable and receivable and inventory.

The first office opened in Kamloops in 1983. Since then, the company has expanded several times and now has offices across North America and in Pacific Rim countries. There are five production facilities in North America and one in Australia. In addition, there are 52 sales offices, a regional headquarters in Australia, and one in the United States. The headquarters are still located in Kamloops.

CASE STUDY: THE SUNSHINE BREWING COMPANY

As the company expanded, so too did the number of computers that were used. The company has generally allowed the local offices to deal with the automation and, as such, there are a fair number of different computers involved, as well as several types of networks. The only guideline to date is that all the offices must be able to send and receive mail through the Internet.

ANALYSIS

Obviously, there are several different aspects of this case that will need to be looked at as you travel through this book. Hopefully, the information from this chapter leads you to the conclusion that this organization will need to use

TCP/IP because of the distribution of the centers. (Also, you should recognize that the company will need to spend a lot of money.) When relating this to the exam or to the real world, the decision to use TCP/IP is primarily based on the need to communicate over a long distance.

In this scenario we also see that there are several different types of networks involved, so TCP/IP's capability to connect different types of computers (and topologies) will also be required as a unifying force.

There is not enough information here to really even begin the network design; however, as you get into future chapters, more details will be added.

CHAPTER SUMMARY

KEY TERMS

Before you take the exam, make sure you are comfortable with the definitions and concepts for each of the following key terms:

• ARP

• bridge

• byte-stream communications

• ethernet

• ICMP

• IGMP

• IP

• MAC

• NDIS

• repeater

• router

• sliding window

• sockets

• TCP

• token ring

• UDP

• Winsock

The point of this chapter was to introduce TCP/IP as a transport protocol and to help you understand its role in networking. Here are several key points that you should now be aware of:

◆ You should understand the need to have both a server and a client component, and that the same system can act in both roles at the same time.

◆ You should understand that every network card has a unique address and that all network traffic will be sent to the MAC address of a network card—not an IP address.

◆ You should be aware of different network topologies and that each has advantages and disadvantages. Further, you need to understand that there are different amounts of information that can be transmitted over each topology.

◆ You need to know the four layers of the TCP/IP model: Application, Transport, Internet, and Network Access; and the two key boundary layers: Sockets and NDIS.

◆ You need to understand that the basic difference between TCP and UDP is that TCP is used for reliable delivery (such as file transfer) and UDP is used for unreliable delivery (such as broadcasts).

◆ You need to understand the concept of byte-stream communications as it pertains to TCP—that is, how TCP treats the data to be sent as a series of bytes without any boundaries (rather than a series of messages).

◆ You need to understand the concepts of sliding windows and the use of sequence numbers and acknowledgment numbers and their effect on byte-stream communications.

◆ You need to understand that IP is used to determine if a packet is local or remote, and that IP is responsible for finding a route if the packet is remote.

◆ You need to be familiar with ICMP, IGMP, and ARP. Specifically, you need to know in which cases each is used: ICMP for error messages and controlling flow, IGMP for multicasting, and ARP for address resolution.

CHAPTER SUMMARY

◆ You need to understand that sockets provide a connection point for different services or clients on a computer, and that there are certain well-known port numbers.

◆ You need to understand that NetBIOS acts as a Socket application when using TCP/IP as a transport protocol; it does this by using the NetBIOS Helper service to handle the socket communications.

◆ You need to understand the basic differences among repeaters, bridges, and routers.

Now that you have seen the theory behind TCP/IP, you are ready to learn about the installation of the TCP/IP protocol. In Chapter 2, you will see how to assign IP addresses and other parameters. In Chapter 3, IP addressing will be discussed in detail.

APPLY YOUR KNOWLEDGE

Just like the Case Studies, Apply Your Knowledge sections can be found at the end of each chapter. These will normally contain three sections: Exercises, Review Questions, and Exam Questions. In this chapter there are no exercises due to the introductory, general nature of the material.

Review Questions

1. The president of your company calls you into a meeting and asks you about the transition to the TCP/IP protocol that you're planning for the corporate-wide network. The president expresses some concern about getting locked into a proprietary protocol that will put the company at the mercy of a software company. How do you respond?

2. Your network administrator has told you to integrate your IBM mainframes, NetWare servers, Macintosh clients, and Windows 95 and Windows NT machines with a common protocol. Is TCP/IP able to connect all these different systems together?

3. One of your users has been reading up on the UNIX environment because the company is planning to migrate to the TCP/IP protocol. This user is worried that the Windows network is using the NetBIOS API, and that NetBIOS doesn't work over TCP/IP. Is this a valid concern?

Exam Questions

1. What interface is used between TCP/IP applications and the transport protocols?

A. Winsock

B. Sockets

C. NDIS

D. NetBIOS

2. How many layers are in the TCP/IP model?

A. 3

B. 4

C. 7

D. 9

3. Which protocol is responsible for routing packets between networks?

A. ICMP

B. IGMP

C. ARP

D. IP

4. Which of the following are used to determine if a computer is on the same network or a different network?

A. IP address

B. Default gateway

C. MAC address

D. Subnet mask

5. Which statement describes the main difference between a bridge and a router?

A. A bridge is used to extend the distance a network can span.

B. A bridge is an active device, and a router is a passive device.

C. Bridges and routers both use tables to determine what action to take.

D. There is no difference between a bridge and a router.

6. When you send a packet on the network, you will always be sending it to which of the following addresses?

A. The TCP/IP address

B. The network ID

C. The host ID

D. The MAC address

7. What is the name of the service that is required to enable NetBIOS servers to run over TCP/IP?

A. TCP

B. Windows Internet Naming Service

C. NetBIOS Helper

D. NetBIOS over TCP/IP Service

8. You are designing a small network that will handle 50 clients and 10 servers. There is no connection to the Internet and the company does not plan to change this. All the systems are on a single floor, and you will also be installing the wiring.

You decide to use TCP/IP as the protocol and create two subnets. You will use a router to connect the two segments so that broadcast traffic is kept to a minimum. How good is the solution that you have chosen?

A. This is the best possible solution.

B. This is a good solution.

C. This solution works, but it is far from optimal.

D. This solution does not work.

9. The company that you are working for is currently in the process of taking over another organization. You are currently using NetBIOS Frame as your network protocol, with switched ethernet (star configuration) as your backbone. All your systems run Windows NT or Windows 95.

The other organization uses a combination of UNIX workstations and Macintosh systems. It also uses an IBM mainframe to handle financial and engineering tasks. All of these use TCP/IP.

You have been asked to look at what will be required to connect your office with theirs, and you have decided to do the following: convert your network so that it uses TCP/IP, continue to run switched ethernet, and assign a different network ID to each segment connected by the switch. You will then use routers to connect to the other office. How well does this solution work?

A. This is the best possible solution.

B. This is a good solution.

C. This solution works but is far from optimal.

D. This solution does not work.

10. Your organization will be connecting to the Internet in the near future, and you will need to provide access to all the desktops on your network. At the same time, you want to ensure that people outside your network are not able to connect to your servers (except the Web server).

APPLY YOUR KNOWLEDGE

You decide you will run TCP/IP only on the systems that will need to connect to the Internet and on the Web server. In addition, you will run a second common protocol on all internal systems to allow them to connect to the local servers. You will disable file- and print-sharing on all systems except the internal servers. How well does this solution work?

A. This is the best possible solution.

B. This is a good solution.

C. This solution works but is far from optimal.

D. This solution does not work.

Answers to Review Questions

1. Tell the president that TCP/IP is an industry-standard suite of protocols that is not owned or developed by one company. The Internet community works on the establishment of these standards and the evolution of the protocols, and no implementation is considered mandatory until the whole community agrees upon a good implementation. See the "RFCs" section of this chapter.

2. TCP/IP has been developed as a cross-platform, client/server suite of protocols and enables IBM mainframes, NetWare servers, Macintosh clients, Windows 95 and Windows NT machines, and, of course, UNIX systems to be integrated. See the "Introduction to TCP/IP" section of this chapter.

3. This is an unnecessary concern because Microsoft's TCP/IP protocol stack includes NetBT (NetBIOS over TCP/IP), which enables all NetBIOS API calls to use TCP/IP as a protocol. See the "NetBIOS over TCP/IP" section of this chapter.

Answers to Exam Questions

1. **A.** The Winsock interface is used in Windows NT to provide Sockets functionality. This allows application protocols such as NetBIOS to use port numbers to communicate. NDIS is the interface between the transport protocols and the network card. See the "Sockets and Application Protocols" section of this chapter.

2. **B.** The TCP/IP Network model is a four-layer model: Application, Transport, Internet, Physical. See the "Introduction to TCP/IP" section of this chapter.

3. **D.** The Internet Protocol is used to route packets between networks. The other three choices all work with IP: ARP is used to resolve IP addresses to MAC addresses on the local segment, ICMP is used to provide error and status reporting, and IGMP is used to enable multicasting. See the "Internet Protocol" section of this chapter.

4. **A** and **D.** The IP address and the subnet mask are used to determine the network ID. This will be compared with the network ID of the target machine to see if IP should use ARP to find the MAC address of local machine or the default gateway. See the "Internet Protocol" section of this chapter.

5. **B.** Both devices use a table to determine where to send the packet next; however, the bridge actively grabs all traffic physically off the network (at the Network Access layer) to see if it needs to be

APPLY YOUR KNOWLEDGE

moved to another network, whereas the router sits passively until packets are sent to it (which is done at the Transport layer). See the "Connecting Network Segments" section of this chapter.

6. **D.** Because the only address that can be recognized by the network card is the MAC address, data must always be sent to this address. See the "Address Resolution Protocol" section of this chapter.

7. **C.** Although the NetBIOS over TCP/IP Service would make sense, NetBIOS over TCP/IP or NBT is the name given to the entire process of running NetBIOS networking over the TCP/IP protocol. The service that handles socket communications for NetBIOS is the NetBIOS Helper service. See the "NetBIOS over TCP/IP" section of this chapter.

8. **B.** In this case, you could place all of the systems on a single segment running 100 Mbps ethernet. This would remove all the issues that will appear

with routing and keep the network simple. Also, in this case you would probably run NetBIOS Frame because it is faster on a small network than TCP/IP. See the "Network Topologies" section of this chapter.

9. **D.** This is almost a perfect solution. However, if you start assigning different network IDs to the segments when they are connected to a switch, they will not be able to communicate. This is because the switch makes all the systems look like they are on the same physical network. However, the IP addresses would place them on different physical networks. See the "Bridges" section of this chapter.

10. **A.** Within the current context, this is the best solution because it provides security by using the separate protocol and disabling the server service on any system that will connect to the Internet. In the real world, this would be better accomplished through the use of a proxy server. See the "Bridges" section of this chapter.

Suggested Readings and Resources

1. Berg, Glenn. *MCSE Training Guide: Networking Essentials, Second Edition.* New Riders, 1998.

2. Derfler, Frank Jr. *Using Networks.* Que, 1998.

INSTALLATION AND CONFIGURATION

This chapter helps you prepare for the exam by covering the following Installation and Configuration objectives:

On a Windows NT Server computer, configure Microsoft TCP/IP to support multiple network adapters.

▶ This straightforward objective is included to ensure that you understand how to configure TCP/IP and, in a case where there is more than one network card, how to configure each card with a separate address.

Given a scenario, select the appropriate services to install when using Microsoft TCP/IP on Microsoft Windows NT computers.

▶ This objective is included to ensure that you know about the different services available for TCP/IP on Windows NT. This is covered in this chapter with an overview of the services, which are then described in detail in later chapters.

Install and configure the DHCP Relay Agent.

▶ This objective is actually a subobjective of "Configure a Windows NT Server computer to function as an IP router." It is included here as part of the installation of TCP/IP to ensure that you know how to install the DHCP Relay service on a Windows NT computer. DHCP is covered in detail in Chapter 4, "Dynamic Host Configuration Protocol (DHCP)"; and IP routing is covered in Chapter 6, "IP Routing."

CHAPTER 2

Installing Microsoft TCP/IP

STUDY STRATEGIES

As you read through this chapter, you should concentrate on the following key items:

▶ You should understand the configuration options that are available for TCP/IP under Windows NT and know where the options are set.

▶ You should know what services are available and understand what each of the services does.

▶ You should understand how to install the DHCP Relay service on Windows NT.

▶ You should know how to enable IP forwarding.

▶ You should know how to install multiple network cards and configure different cards with different addresses.

Before you can explore the various aspects of TCP/IP, you obviously have to install the protocol. This chapter is given over to that particular task. In addition, the various services that you can install will also be covered.

INSTALLING **TCP/IP**

Installing TCP/IP in Windows NT is very simple: all that is required is either an installed modem or a network card. (Although you could install the protocol without either, it would be pointless.)

Objective: On a Windows NT Server computer, configure Microsoft TCP/IP to support multiple network adapters.

One of the issues that Microsoft has identified as an exam topic is installing TCP/IP when your Windows NT computer has multiple network adapters. The next section will look at the Network dialog box that is used to configure network settings.

You can access the Network dialog box in one of two ways: right-click the Network Neighborhood and choose Properties; or choose Start, Settings, Control Panel and double-click the Network icon.

Either of these methods will bring up the Network dialog box (see Figure 2.1).

There are five tabs on the Network dialog box:

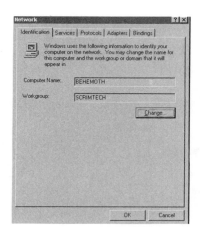

FIGURE 2.1
The Network dialog box with the Identification tab showing. This dialog box is used to control network settings.

◆ **Identification.** The Identification tab is used to change the NetBIOS name of the computer or to change the workgroup or domain to which the computer belongs.

◆ **Services.** From the Services tab you can add or remove network services. You can also change the properties for an installed service or update the driver.

◆ **Protocols.** This is where you install or remove TCP/IP or any other protocol. You can also change a protocol's properties and update the driver.

◆ **Adapters.** From this tab you can add or remove adapters. You can also change the properties for an adapter or update its driver.

◆ **Bindings.** This tab is used to control the bindings—the logical connections between an application protocol and a transport protocol, or between a transport protocol and a network adapter.

Installing a Network Adapter

As stated previously, before you install the protocol you should install the network adapter. To do this, follow these steps.

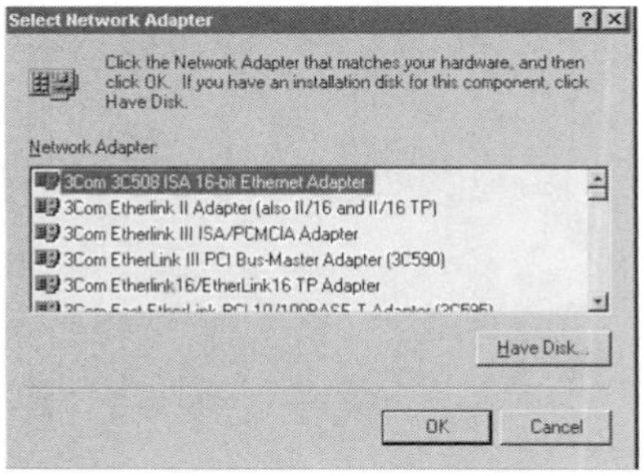

FIGURE 2.2
The Select Network Adapter dialog box lets you choose the adapter installed in your system.

FIGURE 2.3
The Setup dialog box for the MS Loopback Adapter.

FIGURE 2.4
A warning is given when you attempt to install the same driver a second time.

FIGURE 2.5
The system will need to restart to initialize the drivers for the network adapters.

STEP BY STEP

2.1 Installing a Network Card

1. Access the Network dialog box and select the Adapters tab.

2. Click the Add button; this will bring up the Select Network Adapter dialog box.

3. From the list (see Figure 2.2), choose your network adapter (if you don't have one, choose the MS Loopback Adapter). If your card is not listed and you have a disk from the manufacturer, you can click the Have Disk button, which brings up a dialog box asking you for the location of the files. Enter the location (normally the A: drive) and click OK; you will be presented with a list of options from the disk. When you are done, click OK.

4. Any required settings will be requested. This varies from card to card, so you need to follow the dialog box on the screen (see Figure 2.3). Beware that just accepting the defaults works only about half the time. Click OK when the dialog box is complete.

5. Windows NT will now prompt you for the location of the source files; enter this information (if it's not there) and click Continue.

6. If required, repeat steps 2 through 5 for the other network cards in your system. If the cards are of the same type, you may get a warning (see Figure 2.4); choose OK to continue.

7. Click Close when the adapters are installed. You may be asked for the information for the new cards for one or more protocols. TCP/IP settings are covered in the next section, "Installing the TCP/IP Protocol." (For NWLink you can choose defaults.)

8. Finally, you are asked to restart your computer (see Figure 2.5). Choose Yes.

Installing the TCP/IP Protocol

After you have your network cards installed, you may have to install the TPC/IP protocol (which can be done at the same time). Installing the TCP/IP protocol is as simple as installing the network cards. The steps are as follows.

STEP BY STEP

2.2 Installing the TCP/IP Protocol

1. Open the Network dialog box and choose the Protocols tab.

2. Click the Add button, which will bring up the Select Network Protocol dialog box.

3. Choose TCP/IP Protocol (see Figure 2.6) from the list and click OK.

4. You will be asked if you wish to use DHCP to configure TCP/IP. If you are using DHCP, choose Yes; otherwise choose No.

5. When prompted, enter the path to your Windows NT source files.

6. Click Close when the protocol is installed. If you choose No for the DHCP prompt, you will now be asked for the configuration information for the network cards.

7. Finally, you will be asked to restart your computer. Choose Yes.

Whether you are installing a new card or just adding the TCP/IP protocol, you need to configure TCP/IP for the network card.

Configuring TCP/IP

TCP/IP configuration is performed in the Microsoft TCP/IP Properties dialog box (see Figure 2.7). This dialog box is used when you install the protocol or network card, or after the installation to

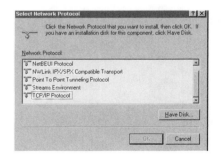

FIGURE 2.6
The Select Network Protocol dialog box is used to add protocols to Windows NT.

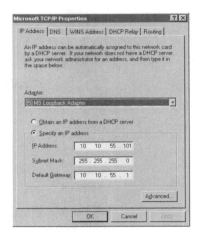

FIGURE 2.7
TCP/IP configuration is performed in the Microsoft TCP/IP Properties dialog box.

reconfigure TCP/IP for a network card. To access the Microsoft TCP/IP Properties dialog box, follow these steps.

STEP BY STEP

2.3 Accessing the TCP/IP Properties

1. Open the Network dialog box and choose the Protocols tab.

2. Double-click on TCP/IP Protocol (or click once to select it, and then click the Properties button).

There are five tabs in the Microsoft TCP/IP dialog box:

◆ **IP Address.** This tab is used for basic TCP/IP configuration, such as the IP address and subnet mask (these two fields are required; all others are optional).

◆ **DNS.** The DNS (Domain Name System) tab allows you to configure host information for your computer and to enter information about DNS servers, which are used to resolve hostnames.

◆ **WINS Address.** The WINS (Windows Internet Name Service) tab is used to configure how the system resolves NetBIOS names. The difference between hostnames and NetBIOS names is explained in Chapter 5, "Windows Internet Name Service (WINS)."

◆ **DHCP Relay.** This lets you configure a station to act as a DHCP Relay Agent, which is discussed in Chapter 4. (This tab does not, by default, appear in Windows NT Workstation; the service must first be installed.)

◆ **Routing.** This tab lets you determine whether your system will act as a router, forwarding packets that are received from one network to another network.

Basic TCP/IP Configuration

The basic configuration of TCP/IP is all done on the IP Address tab. The first choice you need to make is whether to configure TCP/IP manually or using DHCP, which will be discussed in more detail shortly.

If you are configuring your system manually, you need to set an IP address and subnet mask for each of the network cards and configure your default gateway. The following steps cover this configuration.

STEP BY STEP

2.4 Basic TCP/IP Configuration

1. Open the Network dialog box, and on the Protocols tab double-click TPC/IP Protocol.

2. Choose the network adapter to configure from the Adapter drop-down list box.

3. Choose Obtain an IP address from a DHCP Server if you will receive your configuration automatically.

   OR

   Enter the assigned IP address for the adapter and the subnet mask for the segment that the adapter is attached to.

4. Repeat steps 2 and 3 for each card that is installed.

5. If you are manually configuring TCP/IP, enter the Default Gateway address (this is the address of your router).

6. Click OK to set the properties, and then close the Network dialog box. You will need to restart your computer.

This configuration will allow your system to communicate with the network; however, you will be able to communicate with remote systems only by IP address—not by name.

Configuring Name Resolution

There are two types of names that you can use in the TCP/IP world: hostnames (used by Winsock applications as aliases to the hosts on a network) and NetBIOS names. Hostnames can be just about anything, and a single host might have several names. You can even add your own names for different hosts using the HOSTS file located (for a default install) in C:\WINNT\SYSTEM32\DRIVERS\ETC. (For details, see Chapter 8, "Name Resolution.")

> **NOTE**
>
> **DNS**   The naming convention on the Internet is called the domain name System. This system runs using DNS servers (which run a DNS Service) and resolvers that query the DNS servers.

The NetBIOS name is used by NetBIOS applications (such as the Windows NT Workstation service) when connecting to another computer. When you use this name for connecting to other systems, the real name of the system must be used.

Configuring your system for name resolution follows the same steps as outlined previously for the basic TCP/IP configuration. The difference is that the entries are made on the DNS and WINS Address tabs. The next two sections cover the options on these tabs.

The DNS Tab

DNS, or domain name System, is a system that allows computer names to be resolved using a worldwide distributed database (for details, see Chapter 7, "Microsoft Domain Name System"). Configuring your system to use a DNS server (a computer that resolves names) is done on the DNS tab (see Figure 2.8).

Following are the options available on the DNS tab:

◆ **Host Name.** The hostname is the TCP/IP name of the computer. This can be different than the NetBIOS name. However, if the NetBIOS name is ever changed, the hostname will be reset. In Figure 2.8 the hostname is "behemoth."

◆ **Domain.** Here you enter the name of the domain that the computer belongs to. This is not a Windows NT domain but an Internet domain, normally. The hostname and domain name are combined to form the Fully Qualified Domain Name (FQDN) of the system. In Figure 2.8 the computer is called "behemoth.scrimtech.com."

◆ **DNS Service Search Order.** This area is used to add a list of computers on your network that run a DNS service. You should configure at least one DNS server in this area, but adding an extra server will provide redundancy if one is down. (If you add several servers and lose connectivity, however, your system will freeze for a long time as each server is tried, and you must wait for it to time out.)

◆ **Domain Suffix Search Order.** When a name is sent to the DNS server to be resolved, it is first sent with the local domain name attached. For example, if you enter "irobot," the system would try irobot.scrimtech.com. If the DNS server does not

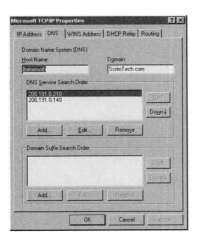

FIGURE 2.8
The DNS tab lets you set the computer's domain and the addresses of DNS servers that it should use.

have an entry for this name, the system will try adding each of the entries that are listed in this text box as a suffix. Finally, the name will be tried without any extensions.

Normally, you should configure at least one DNS service entry for a computer. Remember that this will resolve only hostnames, whereas NetBIOS name configuration is done on the WINS Service tab.

The WINS Service Tab

NetBIOS name resolution is configured in a couple of places, but the basic information is kept on the WINS Address tab. NetBIOS name resolution, which can be complicated, is discussed in detail in Chapters 5 and 8. Here only the options on the WINS Address tab (see Figure 2.9) will be discussed.

These are the options that can be configured on the WINS Address tab:

◆ **Adapter.** Each of the adapters can be configured to use a different WINS server; this will let you select which adapter you are configuring.

◆ **Primary WINS Server.** This is the first WINS server that should be tried when you are resolving NetBIOS names.

◆ **Secondary WINS Server.** If the first server cannot resolve the address after about 30 seconds (that is, 3 attempts at 15 second intervals), this WINS server will be tried.

◆ **Enable DNS for Windows Resolution.** If this is selected, the system will try the DNS server if the WINS server is unable to resolve the name to an IP address.

◆ **Enable LMHOSTS Lookup.** If this option is selected, the LMHOSTS files found by default in the C:\WINNT\ SYSTEM32\DRIVERS\ETC directory can be used to locate servers on other networks when the WINS server is down.

◆ **Import LMHOSTS.** If you are installing a system (notably a backup domain controller) the system might need to contact the primary domain controller. Because the WINS client would require you to reboot (which is difficult during installation), Microsoft included this button to allow you to import an LMHOSTS file from a disk during installation.

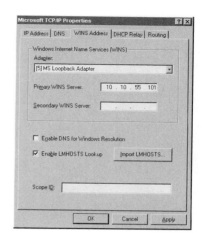

FIGURE 2.9
The WINS Address tab is used to configure NetBIOS name resolution.

◆ **Scope ID.** If this is entered, it is added to the NetBIOS name during communications. If the system you wish to communicate with does not have the same scope, you will not be able to see it. This can cause problems if you are not careful.

At this point, you should have configured the basic address and the name resolution for your computer. This is all that is required in most cases. The other options in the Microsoft TCP/IP Properties dialog box are options used for advanced configuration, which is explained in the next section.

Advanced Configuration

TCP/IP advanced configuration options allow you to add extra IP addresses, default gateways and security; the DHCP Relay Agent; and routing capabilities. The next few sections will cover these topics.

DHCP Relay Installation and Configuration

As you will learn in Chapter 4, DHCP requires the use of broadcasts. Normally, routers do not forward broadcasts to other networks (unless they support BOOTP relay as described in RFC1542); therefore, DHCP would be limited to a single network. To get around this problem without having to reconfigure (or replace) your routers, Microsoft includes the DHCP Relay Agent.

Objective: Install and configure the DHCP Relay Agent.

There are actually two stages to setting up a relay agent: first you need to install the service, and then you can configure it. To do this, follow these steps.

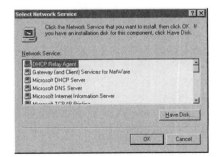

FIGURE 2.10
The DHCP Relay Agent service should be installed before you configure it.

STEP BY STEP

2.5 Installing the DHCP Relay Agent Service

1. Open the Network dialog box and choose the Services tab.

2. Click Add and select the DHCP Relay Agent (see Figure 2.10). Click OK.

3. When prompted, enter the path to your Windows NT source files.

4. Click Close to close the Network dialog box and choose Yes when prompted to restart your computer.

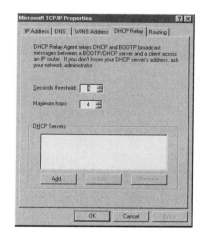

FIGURE 2.11
Configuring the DHCP Relay Agent.

After the DHCP Relay Agent is installed, you can configure it on the Microsoft TCP/IP Properties page (see Figure 2.11). Following are the available options:

◆ **Seconds threshold.** This is the number of seconds the service waits before forwarding the broadcast. This allows a DHCP server to respond, if there is one on this subnet.

◆ **Maximum hops.** This is the greatest number of networks that can be traversed as requests are forwarded to the DCHP server. Setting a large number may cause the client to time out.

◆ **DHCP Servers.** This is where you can enter the IP address of a known DHCP server. The agent will send the client's request to each of the servers listed.

Routing

Any machine that has an IP address from more than one valid subnet and an IP layer can perform routing. The Routing tab is easy to configure (see Figure 2.12). If you want routing enabled, check the Enable IP Forwarding check box; otherwise, leave it cleared.

Before you enable routing, your system will need to have two IP addresses (normally on different network cards). Chapter 6 covers routing in greater detail.

Advanced IP Address Configuration

Back in Figure 2.7, you may have noticed an Advanced button. Selecting this button will bring up the Advanced IP Addressing dialog box (see Figure 2.13).The first few options in this dialog box are similar to those we looked at earlier. These are reviewed here along with other options.

◆ **Adapter.** Here you can change the configuration of an adapter.

◆ **IP Addresses.** This area will allow you to add, edit, or remove addresses for the selected network adapter (see the dialog box

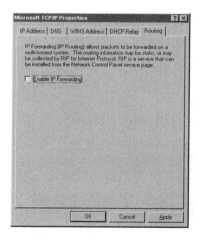

FIGURE 2.12
The Routing tab is the simplest one to configure.

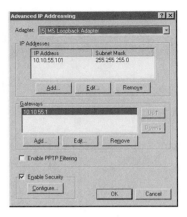

FIGURE 2.13
You can add extra IP addresses and gateways and perform other configurations in the Advanced IP Addressing dialog box.

FIGURE 2.14
Adding or editing IP addresses.

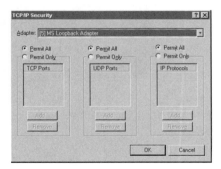

FIGURE 2.15
The TCP/IP Security dialog box can be used to lock out protocols that you don't want people to be able to use.

in Figure 2.14). To remove an address, select it in the list and click Remove. To edit addresses, select the address and click Edit. To add an adapter, Click Add.

◆ **Gateways.** This area will allow you to add extra gateway addresses. This will provide your system with alternate addresses if the primary is not available.

◆ **Enable PPTP Filtering.** The Point to Point Tunneling Protocol (PPTP) can be used to create a secure channel for communications across the network (for details, see Chapter 12, "Remote Access Service and TCP/IP"). Setting this option will disable all protocols on the select card except for PPTP. This should be selected on the exposed interface of your RAS server if you are running PPTP Virtual Private Networks (VPN).

◆ **Enable Security.** This option allows you to specify which protocols can be used on the computer. If you enable security, you will be able to shut down any sockets that you are not using, leaving fewer places for hackers to attack.

When you enable security, a Configure button lets you configure which ports are available for each of the protocols (see Figure 2.15).

Using the TCP/IP dialog box requires the following simple steps.

STEP BY STEP

2.6 Security Settings

1. Choose the Adapter to configure (normally, the adapter that connects to the Internet).

2. For each protocol that you want to restrict, select Permit Only.

3. Using the Add and Remove buttons, create a list of the ports that users are allowed to connect to for each protocol.

4. Click OK when you have finished.

5. Close the other dialog boxes and restart your computer.

Service Packs

Now that you have read about the installation and configuration of network adapters and the TCP/IP protocol, there is a final bit of information that must be noted: Microsoft Windows NT is not perfect!

Occasionally, errors are found and need to be corrected. This is the role of a service pack. At the time of this writing, Service Pack 3 and several patches are available.

Whenever you install files from the original media—by adding a protocol, adapter, or service—you are putting files on your system that might have been updated in a service pack. The real problem is that other components that have been updated may not work correctly with the new files you have added.

To avoid this, you must reapply the latest service pack and any ensuing patches every time you add anything that takes files from the original CD.

SERVICES

Objective: Given a scenario, select the appropriate services to install when using Microsoft TCP/IP on Microsoft Windows NT computers.

Along with TCP/IP, several other related services are available in Windows NT. As a wrap-up to the installation and a look forward to other chapters, the following list describes some of these services:

- ◆ **Internet Information Server (IIS) 2.0.** IIS provides you the ability to share information with any type of computer that can use the TCP/IP protocol. IIS includes FTP, Gopher, and WWW servers. The current release of IIS—version 4.0—is included in the NT Option Pack available from the Microsoft Web site (www.microsoft.com). This is not covered in this book because the focus is on the TCP/IP exam; however, several books cover configuring IIS, such as *MCSE Training*

Guide: IIS 4 from New Riders and *Teach Yourself Internet Information Server in 14 Days* from Sams.

◆ **Line Printer Daemon.** This server allows you to share printers with many different types of hosts, including mainframes and UNIX-based hosts. See Chapter 9, "TCP/IP Printing Services," for details.

◆ **Dynamic Host Configuration Protocol (DHCP).** DHCP provides automatic configuration of remote hosts, making management of a TCP/IP environment easy. See Chapter 4 for details.

◆ **DHCP Relay Agent.** This extends the capabilities of the DHCP service by allowing it to work across various subnets. Although this was discussed earlier, you should see Chapter 4 for more details.

◆ **Windows Internet Name Service (WINS).** Without the ability to find another computer on the network, you would never be able to communicate. The WINS server provides a centralized method of name management that is both flexible and dynamic. See Chapter 5 for details.

◆ **WINS Proxy Agent.** Some clients are not or cannot be configured for WINS. The WINS Proxy Agent, part of the WINS client, will allow a WINS client to provide name resolution to a non-WINS client. See Chapter 5 for details.

◆ **Simple Network Management Protocol Agent (SNMP Agent).** If you want to track the performance of your TCP/IP protocols or use SNMP managers, you will want to install the SNMP agent. See Chapter 10, "Implementing the Microsoft SNMP Service," for details.

◆ **DNS Server Service.** Whereas the WINS server provides the ability to find NetBIOS names, the DNS server works with hostnames to allow you to integrate your systems into or resolve hosts on the Internet. See Chapter 7 for details.

CASE STUDY: ROLLING OUT MICROSOFT WINDOWS NT AND TCP/IP

ESSENCE OF THE CASE

Several important facts arise out of the preceding discussion:

- There will be a requirement to reconfigure laptops frequently due to travel.

- Consideration will need to be given to communications from the branches to the regional headquarters.

- Remote access will need to be configured to allow the laptops to connect to the different offices.

- An IIS server will be required to bring the Web site in-house. The system will need to be configured to reduce the risk of invasion. (This will also require name servers.)

- You will need to provide connections to the Microsoft Exchange network.

- You will need to set up the Windows NT systems in the production centers to connect to the Solaris systems.

- Systems in any location will need to be able to connect to all the systems within the Sunshine network.

Now that you have an understanding of installing TCP/IP and an overview of the main services that are available in TCP/IP, it is time to revisit Sunshine Brewing Company. In this chapter, you will start to look at the issues involved in the roll-out of Microsoft Windows NT and TCP/IP.

SCENARIO

After some initial discussions, you have started to build up a picture of the requirements that Sunshine Brewing Company has and the various networks that are in place already.

The three headquarters all use NetWare for file and print services, as well as basic email. The current email package is cc:Mail, but it will be replaced with Microsoft Exchange; and an SMTP gateway is running in each of the headquarters locations.

The main headquarters in Kamloops currently has a 256Kb digital line to the Internet. The Web site, www.ScrimTech.com/SunshineBrewing.htm, is maintained at the ISP; Sunshine brewing would like to bring this in-house along with email services and register the domain www.sunshine.ca. There are 150 employees: 25 in the executive level, 50 in sales, and the rest support staff covering administration, personnel, and logistics.

The U.S. head office is located in New Orleans. This office has 80 employees: 20 in the executive level, 40 in sales, and 20 support staff. The Australia head office is located in Toowoomba, Queensland. This office has 50 employees: 10 in the executive level, 30 in sales, and 10 in

continues

continued

support. Both offices have a 56k connection to the Internet.

The 52 sales offices average 20 employees, usually consisting of a manager, 10–15 salespeople, and about 5 support staff. Mail is handled by individual accounts through a local ISP in each city. The sales offices need to be able to connect to the regional headquarters to upload and download sensitive information such as pricing. These offices currently don't have networks.

Sunshine Brewing would like to upgrade all the executive- and sales-level personnel to Pentium laptops running Windows NT Workstation. They need to be able to dial into the different offices or connect to the local network for access to mail, the intranet, and the Internet. The support staff will use desktops with Windows 95. Existing equipment will be used where possible.

The production centers currently use Solaris to control bottling and production systems. Email is currently executed using Telnet and ELM (a character-based email package). The Solaris system is required to run the bottling and production systems. There are typically 60 employees at each of the centers, most of whom have little need for email. About five employees working at the supervisor level need to be able to connect to the regional offices.

ANALYSIS

What you are starting to get are the requirements that the client is imposing. In this case there is a need for security, even though the Internet may be used as a backbone for this network. This will require configuring advanced options for TCP/IP and creating VPNs using PPTP.

Also, a significant number of employees will be traveling with laptops, and you will need to be able to automatically configure and reconfigure them on-the-fly. This sounds like a good reason for using DHCP.

If DHCP is used, then it is possible that addresses will change. This means that some dynamic method is required for name resolution—in other words, WINS. This can, as you will see, be tied to the DNS server to create a Dynamic DNS server.

In the next few chapters, you will start to see the specific implementation details being added; as you read through the next chapter and the scenario, stop and think about how you would handle the allocation of IP networks.

CHAPTER SUMMARY

This chapter covered the installation and configuration of Microsoft TCP/IP on Windows NT Server. As you saw, the installation can be relatively simple depending on the options that you choose.

The first option that you will need to decide on is whether to use DHCP. In most cases you will want to use DHCP to avoid the administrative overhead of manually assigning IP addresses.

Remember that, although all the options were discussed here, you will not normally implement them together. The basic configuration should include a single adapter configured with an IP address and subnet mask, a default gateway, and the IP addresses of a WINS server and a DNS server.

The chapter finished with an overview of the services and the role they play. When implementing services, the key word is planning; many organizations have problems with their Windows NT network because the rollout was not planned properly.

These are key elements to keep in mind from this chapter:

◆ You need to know how to install one or more network adapters and configure them to work with Windows NT.

◆ You need to be able to install the TCP/IP protocol and configure it for each adapter in the system.

◆ You need to understand the options that are presented for configuring TCP/IP.

◆ You need to know about the Routing tab and that you need more than one address to use it. The installation of IP Routing is covered in this chapter, but further details are provided in Chapter 6.

◆ You need to understand what a DHCP Relay Agent does and how to install and configure it.

◆ You need to understand that configuration can be done manually or through DHCP, and that DHCP normally leads to fewer configuration errors.

KEY TERMS

• default gateway

• DHCP

• DNS

• IP address

• routing

• subnet mask

• WINS

CHAPTER SUMMARY

◆ You need to know the services that are available for TCP/IP on Windows NT and their purpose.

Now that you have an understanding of the theory and know how to install the protocols (and adapters and services), the next chapter will look at assigning addresses and creating logical networks.

Exercises

In this set of exercises, you will install and configure the MS Loopback Adapter. This will provide you with networking capabilities whether or not you have a network card. The exercises in the rest of this text will assume you are using this configuration; if you are not, you will need to substitute your own IP address, hostname, and NetBIOS names.

2.1   Adding a Network Adapter

This exercise will take you through the addition of TCP/IP and a network adapter. Furthermore, you get a chance to enter TCP/IP configuration parameters for the adapter you are adding.

Estimated Time: About five minutes.

1. Choose Start, Settings, Control Panel from the taskbar.

2. Double-click the Network icon.

3. Click the Add button, which brings up the Select Network Adapter dialog box.

4. From the list choose the MS Loopback Adapter and click OK.

5. Select a frame type of 802.3.

6. When prompted, enter the location of the NT source files and click Continue.

7. Choose the Protocols tab.

8. Click the Add button, which brings up the Select Network Protocol dialog box.

9. Choose TCP/IP Protocol from the list and click OK.

10. A dialog box appears asking if you want to use DHCP; click No.

11. When prompted, enter the location of the NT source files and click Continue.

12. Click the Close button to close the Network Dialog box.

13. When the Microsoft TCP/IP Properties dialog box appears, enter the IP address as **10.1.0.1** and the subnet mask as **255.255.0.0.** Click OK.

14. Finally, you are asked to restart your computer. Choose Yes.

This exercise provides you with an opportunity to install a Network adapter and the TCP/IP protocol. See the sections on "Installing a Network Adapter" and "Installing TCP/IP" to review the information.

2.2   Configuring Name Resolution

In this exercise you will add the name resolution configuration for your computer. This will give you a chance to reconfigure TCP/IP and explore the options available.

Estimated Time: About five minutes.

1. Right-click on the Network Neighborhood and choose Properties.

2. From the Network dialog box, choose the protocol tab and double-click the TCP/IP Protocol.

3. Click on the DNS tab. You should notice that the hostname is the same as the NetBIOS name (computer name). Enter **mcp.com** as the Domain name.

4. In the DNS Service search order area, click the Add button and enter **10.1.0.1** as the IP address.

5. Click the WINS Address tab. Enter the same address as the primary WINS server.

APPLY YOUR KNOWLEDGE

6. Click OK to close the Microsoft TCP/IP Properties dialog box. Then click Close to close the Network dialog box.

7. When prompted, restart your computer.

This exercise gives you an opportunity to reconfigure the TCP/IP protocol. If you would like to review all the options, see the section titled "Configuring TCP/IP."

Review Questions

1. What minimum configuration parameters are required to install TCP/IP?

2. In addition to configuring the DHCP Relay tab, what else must you do to run the DHCP Relay Agent?

3. You have installed the TCP/IP protocol, but after restarting your system you receive errors. What could the problem be?

4. If you already have TCP/IP configured and you install an additional network adapter, what parameters are required?

5. You have installed TCP/IP and it seems to be running correctly. However, you cannot connect to a server in your warehouse. What could the problem be?

Exam Questions

1. Which of the following are the two methods of configuring the TCP/IP protocol on a client station?

   A. WINS

   B. DHCP Boot Relay

   C. Manually

   D. A DHCP server

2. Which of the following is true of hostnames?

   A. Hostnames are an alias for a computer name.

   B. Hostnames are an alias for an IP address.

   C. The hostname and NetBIOS name must be the same.

   D. The hostname is an FQDN.

3. Where is the NetBIOS name for a computer changed?

   A. On the DNS tab of the TCP/IP configuration.

   B. On the Identification tab of the Network dialog box.

   C. In the Registry.

   D. It is set during installation and cannot be changed.

4. You have enabled DNS resolution for NetBIOS names, and the DNS server is functioning correctly. In most cases everything seems to be working; however, there is a server that you cannot connect to using Microsoft Networking. Which of the following could be the error?

   A. You are trying to connect to the hostname instead of the NetBIOS name.

   B. A local hosts files is providing the wrong IP address.

   C. The DNS server cannot resolve the name to an IP address.

   D. The system is configured on a different DNS domain than your own.

APPLY YOUR KNOWLEDGE

5. Which services can be implemented on Windows NT to assist in the use and deployment of TCP/IP across your NetBIOS network?

    A. DNS server

    B. WINS server

    C. DHCP server

    D. SNMP agent

6. Which of the following will allow DHCP requests to be forwarded to a DHCP server on a remote subnet?

    A. RFC1542-compliant routers

    B. WINS Proxy agent

    C. The BOOTP Relay service

    D. The DHCP Relay service

7. Your company has offices in the United States and Canada. Your Internet domain has been registered in both countries and, as a result, the full name of some of your servers ends in ".com" and some in ".ca". Your system is part of the ".ca" domain, but you often have to use systems from the ".com" domain. When using systems in the United States, you have to enter the full name or else you cannot connect. What can you do to fix this problem?

    A. Use a WINS server.

    B. Enter a second DNS server address for a server in the United States.

    C. Add the U.S. domain name to the domain suffix search order.

    D. You cannot avoid this problem.

8. Your organization is using PPTP to create secure connections across the Internet. However, the

system that is used as a connection point is being attacked by hackers who have hung the system several times.

If an effort to stop this from happening, you go to the Advanced TCP/IP Configuration and select PPTP filtering for all the network adapters in the system. How well does this solution work?

    A. The solution will work and is the correct implementation.

    B. The solution works but is not the correct implementation.

    C. The solution appears to work but in fact doesn't.

    D. The solution does not work.

9. Your company wants to use DHCP to configure all the hosts that use its intranet. Furthermore, the company wishes to keep the number of DHCP servers to a minimum to reduce the possibility of configuration errors.

The routers that your company uses do not forward any broadcasts, so you intend to install a DHCP Relay Agent on each subnet where there is a DHCP server and configure all clients using DHCP Relay tab. How well will this solution work?

    A. The solution will work and is the correct implementation.

    B. The solution works but is not the correct implementation.

    C. The solution appears to work but in fact doesn't.

    D. The solution does not work.

APPLY YOUR KNOWLEDGE

10. Your organization uses a combination of Sun stations running Common Desktop Environment (CDE) and Windows 95 stations. The Sun stations use TCP/IP already, but the Windows 95 stations use NetBIOS Frame. Your company is in the process of implementing Oracle Server on NT and wants to use TCP/IP so that all stations will be able to use it.

You intend to configure the Windows 95 stations with TCP/IP as you install the Oracle client. You will assign the addresses manually and add the hostnames to the DNS server so the Windows 95 stations will be able to find each other. How well does this solution work?

A. This is the best possible solution.

B. This is a good solution.

C. This solution works but is far from optimal.

D. This solution does not work.

Answers to Review Questions

1. At a minimum, TCP/IP requires that you configure an IP address and a subnet mask. However, if you want to communicate with servers outside your segment, you need to add the default gateway along with a WINS server address and/or a DNS server address. See "Configuring TCP/IP."

2. The configuration tab for the DHCP Relay is used to configure the DHCP Relay Agent. You will need to install and configure this service. See "DHCP Relay Installation and Configuration."

3. Whenever you install files from the original disk, you need to reapply the service pack. In this case, the system probably had a service pack installed before you added TCP/IP. See "Service Packs."

4. All that is ever required is the IP address and subnet mask. In a case where you are configuring a second adapter, any other configuration that you require should already be in place, so these two parameters should be sufficient. See "Configuring TCP/IP."

5. There are many potential problems that you can run across in this case, but the most likely is a name resolution problem. Other problems that you might encounter: an invalid subnet mask, incorrect default gateway, invalid local router, invalid route at the router, incorrect name resolution, or general network errors. See "Configuring Name Resolution."

Answers to Exam Questions

1. **C** and **D.** There are two ways to configure a Microsoft client: you can manually enter the TCP/IP configuration or you can obtain your IP address from a DHCP server. The DHCP Boot Relay will forward your request to the DHCP server; however, it does not fulfill your request itself. WINS is used for NetBIOS name resolution and does not provide any configuration information. See "Configuring TCP/IP."

2. **B.** The hostname is used as a reference to an IP address. Most Winsock applications will communicate with the IP address rather than a name. Initially, the hostname and the computer name (NetBIOS name) are the same; however, the hostname can be changed. The hostname is then combined with the domain name to form the Fully Qualified Domain Name. See "The DNS Tab."

3. **B.** The computer name is used for all the protocols and, therefore, would not be set in the TCP/IP configuration. Although the name is stored and can be changed in the Registry, this is not the recommended place to do it. See "The DNS Tab."

4. **A, B, C,** and **D.** All these could be the problem. Because hostnames are aliases to the IP address and not the computer name, the name you would use for FTP is different than the one used for NetBIOS. However, when you try to connect using NetBIOS, you must use the correct name. Having a local hosts file that is out of date could resolve a correct name to the wrong address.

   Furthermore, if the DNS server has the wrong address, you will not be able to connect at all. If the wrong DNS domain is used, you will first try your DNS domain (which will be incorrect), and then just the name you entered (which the DNS server may not resolve). See "Configuring Name Resolution."

5. **B** and **C.** Implementing WINS will provide the ability to resolve NetBIOS names across different subnets; DHCP will help in assigning IP addresses and configuration information. The DNS is used for host-name resolution and would not aid in NetBIOS networking. SNMP is a management system for non-Microsoft systems and again doesn't aid in NetBIOS networking. See "Basic TCP/IP Configuration" and "The WINS Service Tab."

6. **A** and **D.** In the case of an RFC1542-compliant router, the BOOTP forwarding is enabled and the requests are forwarded automatically; this can add to the traffic carried by routers. The DHCP Relay service is a better choice because it will send the request to the DHCP server directly. See "DHCP Relay Installation and Configuration."

7. **C.** Although adding the address of a server in the United States domain might help, the best course of action is to add the United States domain suffix to the domain suffix search order area of the DNS tab in the TCP/IP configuration. Using a WINS server might also help, but because the type of connections is not mentioned, you cannot assume that only NetBIOS connections are being made. See "The DNS Tab."

8. **C.** Although this should slow down the hackers (the only way to stop them would be to take the system off the Internet), the users will be able to connect but will not be able to get anywhere. You should enable PPTP filtering only on the adapter that connects to the Internet, or else the system will not be able to communicate internally on the other adapters. See "Advanced Configuration."

9. **D.** This solution does not work. In this case you need to install the DHCP Relay service on a machine on each subnet that does not have a DHCP server, and then configure the agent with the IP address of a DHCP server. The agent will then be able to forward the requests to the DHCP server on behalf of the local clients. See "DHCP Relay Installation and Configuration."

10. **C.** This is not an optimal solution because there is still a lot of manual configuration required. This can lead to errors in the assignment of TCP/IP addresses and options and make updating the information more difficult. Furthermore, the Windows 95 stations should be using a WINS server to find each other. This provides more than simple name resolution; there will still be a DNS server that should be integrated with

APPLY YOUR KNOWLEDGE

the WINS server to provide full name resolution. Finally, you should always attempt to reduce the number of protocols that are used on a station, so

the NetBIOS Frame should be removed from the desktop computers. See "Installing the TCP/IP Protocol."

Suggested Readings and Resources

1. Siyan, Karanjit S. *Windows NT Server 4 Professional Reference.* New Riders, 1996.

2. Heywood, Drew. *Inside Windows NT Server 4.* New Riders, 1997.

3. Casad, Joe. *MCSE Training Guide: Windows NT Server 4.* New Riders, 1997.

4. Sirockman, Jason. *MCSE Training Guide: Windows NT Server 4 Enterprise.* New Riders, 1997.

This chapter helps you prepare for the exam by covering the following objectives:

Diagnose and resolve IP addressing problems.

▶ This objective is intended to stress the importance of the TCP/IP configuration and the purpose of the parameters.

Configure subnet masks.

▶ You will need to be able to create subnets and know which hosts are on which subnet throughout the exam. This is covered time and time again not only by itself, but also in conjunction with other questions. Essentially, you will need to be able to create subnets on-the-fly and, from a subnet mask, figure out the range of valid host IDs.

CHAPTER 3

IP Addressing and Subnetting

STUDY STRATEGIES

As you read through this chapter, you should concentrate on the following key items:

▶ Three classes of addresses—A, B, and C—can be used for host IDs.

▶ The starting octet can be used to determine the class of address.

▶ The IP address is made up of the network ID, possibly the subnet ID, and the host ID.

▶ The host ID on a network with all 0s refers to that network.

▶ The host ID with all 1s is the broadcast address.

▶ Addresses starting with 224 through 239 are class D, or multicasting, addresses.

▶ Subnetting is a very important part of the exam; each subnet is a physical segment on your network.

▶ Subnetting is simply a matter of turning on more bits in the subnet mask—the hard part is dealing with binary.

▶ The network ID, subnet ID, and host ID cannot be all 1s or all 0s for a host.

▶ Subnetting is the opposite of supernetting: subnetting takes a large network and breaks it into pieces, whereas supernetting combines smaller networks into a single, larger entity.

Now that you have installed the TCP/IP protocol, your system is ready to communicate on the network. This chapter returns to theory and introduces the key concepts of routing.

Routing is one of the key reasons for using TCP/IP; recall from the discussion in Chapter 1, "Introduction to Networking with TCP/IP," that the IP protocol is responsible for this. The use of the subnet mask was also introduced in Chapter 1 as the means of determining the portion of the address that represents a network versus the portion that represents the host on the network.

Here you will expand these concepts. First, this chapter will review the IP address and how it is used with the subnet mask to determine whether a machine is local or remote. Then you will be introduced to routing (which is covered fully in Chapter 6, "IP Routing"). Finally, the processes of subnetting and supernetting will be looked at as a means of dealing with large networks.

IP Addresses

Diagnose and resolve IP addressing problems.

In order for a network to function, all its devices require a unique address: the MAC address. For an intranet (or even the Internet) to work, a unique IP address is required. As you saw in Chapter 1, the IP address is made up of two parts: the network ID and the host ID. Each of these must be unique within its realm—that is, the host ID must be unique on the local network and the network ID must be unique throughout the entire intranet.

IP addresses are similar to street addresses. The address 110 Main Street identifies what street you are on and in which house on that street you live. TCP/IP addresses simply switch this around, identifying the more general information first (network ID), followed by the more specific (host ID). Thus, the street address expressed like a TCP/IP address would be Main Street 110.

The system views an IP address as a 32-bit binary number. Obviously, this would be difficult for most people to work with. Therefore, the address is entered in dotted decimal notation, such as 209.206.202.64. Each of the four numbers represents eight bits of the address, which means that each of the four can be between 0 and 255 (8 bits provide 256 possible combinations.)

UNDERSTANDING BINARY

As you start to work with subnet masking and some other functions of TCP/IP, you will occasionally need to work in binary. Therefore, this short refresher has been added to this chapter.

In the number 238, we see the 2 as two groups of one hundred, the 3 as three groups of ten, and the 8 as eight groups of one. Each of the numbers represents a number of groups; the groups are always based on 10 of the next-smaller groups (10 1s in 10, 10 10s in 100, and so on). The reason for this is simple: we have only 10 symbols that represent numbers (0–9). You take the digits, multiply by the group value, and add the results together to make the total ($2 \times 100 + 3 \times 10 + 8 \times 1 = 238$).

In binary there are only two symbols (0 and 1); therefore, each of the groups is two of the smaller group (for example, the 1 in 10 is two groups of 1, which equals 2; and the 1 in 100 is two groups of 2, which equals 4). Thankfully, when working with IP addresses you only use binary numbers eight digits at a time. The following chart shows the decimal values for the first eight positions in a primary number.

128	64	32	16	8	4	2	1

Using the chart you can convert the binary number 110110 to $1 \times 32 + 1 \times 16 + 0 \times 8 + 1 \times 4 + 1 \times 2 + 0 \times 1$, which equals 54. You should notice that, unlike with decimal numbers there will never be anything but a 1 to multiply the group (or positional) value by; therefore, we could simply say that 110110 stands for 32 + 16 + 4 + 2, or 54.

Therefore, converting from binary to decimal is simple addition. If this is true (it is), converting the other way (decimal to binary) should be a matter of simple subtraction. This is, in fact, the case.

If you wish to convert 83 to binary, start by figuring out the binary group value that is nearest but less than 83. Because 83 is larger than 64 but smaller than 128, the first bit to turn on (set to 1) is the 64 bit.

Now subtract 64 from 83 to get 19. Because 19 is smaller than 32 (the next-lowest binary group value), the 32 bit is left as 0. And because 19 is larger than 16, the 16 bit is turned on. Then subtract 16 from 19. This leaves 3, which is smaller than 8 and 4; thus, those two bits are turned off. Three, however, is bigger than 2, which is, therefore, turned on. This leaves a remainder of 1; thus, the last bit is also turned on. This means 83 in decimal is 1010011 in binary.

To complete the eight bits, known also as a *byte* or *octet*, you would add 0s to the front (left) side. In this case you would add a single 0 to complete the octet, yielding 01010011.

Address Classes

You may be wondering how much of an IP address represents the network and how much represents the host. The answer depends on the type of address you have. (Recall that there are three main classes of addresses: class A, B, and C.)

The most obvious difference among the three main types of addresses is the number of octets used to identify the network. Class A uses only the first octet to identify the network; this leaves 24 bits (or three octets) to identify the host. Class B uses the first two octets to identify the network, leaving 16 bits (two octets) for the host. Class C uses three octets for the network ID, leaving 8 bits (one octet) for the host.

The other difference among the classes of networks is how the address starts in binary: class A addresses start with 0, B with 10, and C with 110. Therefore, you can tell the class of a host's address by the first octet of its TCP/IP address. Knowing that the first octet represents the first eight bits of the IP address, and knowing the starting bits for the classes of addresses, you can determine the host address, or the last part of the IP address (see Table 3.1).

TABLE 3.1

TCP/IP ADDRESS CLASSES—FIRST OCTET

Class	Start (Binary)	Finish (Binary)	Start (Decimal)	Finish (Decimal)
A	00000001	01111111	1	127
B	10000000	10111111	128	191
C	11000000	11011111	192	223

A couple of rules determine what you can and cannot use for addresses. Neither the network ID nor the host ID can be signified by all 0s or by all 1s because each of these conditions has a special meaning. Also, the network with the first octet 127 is used solely for loop-back tests, in which your information loops back to your own IP protocol internally.

Because class A addresses use only the first octet to identify the network, there are a limited number of them—126, to be exact (as just mentioned, 127 is reserved.) However, each of these 126 networks can have many hosts on it because there are 24 bits (three octets) available for the host ID. Because each bit can be either on or off, the number of hosts can be articulated as 2^{24}, or 16,777,216. However, because the host ID cannot be all 0s or all 1s, you actually need to subtract 2, leaving 16,777,214 possible hosts on each class A network.

Class B addresses use the first two octets to identify the network; however, the first two bits are set to binary 10. This leaves 14 bits that can be used to identify the network—or 2^{14} possible combinations (six bits in the first octet and eight from the second) or 16,384 possible network IDs (because the first two digits are 10, you don't have to worry about addresses with all 0s or all 1s). Each of those network IDs has 16 bits left to identify the host; this allows 65,534 possible hosts ($2^{16}-2$).

Finally, there are class C networks, which use three octets, or 24 bits, to identify the network. Because the first three bits are always 110, there are 21 bits left to uniquely identify different network IDs. This yields 2^{21}, or 2,097,152, possible networks. With eight bits left for hosts, there can be 254 hosts on each network.

Table 3.2 summarizes all the possible TCP/IP addresses.

> **NOTE**
>
> **Determining the number of hosts**
> This is the basic formula for determining the number of hosts:
> $2^{number\ of\ host\ bits} - 2$.

TABLE 3.2

ADDRESS CLASS SUMMARY

Address Class	First Octet Start	Finish	Number of Networks	Hosts
A	1	126	126	16,777,214
B	128	191	16,384	65,534
C	192	223	2,097,152	254

Using the Standard Subnet Mask

Internet Protocol (IP) is responsible for determining whether a packet is for the local network; and, if it is not, for finding a route for the packet to the destination network and, eventually, the destination host. To understand how IP determines whether a host is on the local network, we must look at the subnet mask and its function.

As was just discussed, the IP address is a combination of the network ID and the host ID. The address itself is 32 bits long, and there are a varying number of bits that are used to identify the network and the host.

The subnet mask is a representation of the number of bits that represent the network ID. The portion that holds the network ID is set to all 1s, and the remainder (the host ID) is set to 0s. This means that you can use the logical AND (see the following In-Depth, "The AND'ing Process," for details) to extract the network ID from the IP address.

THE AND'ING PROCESS

A well-known (yet readily overlooked) example of the AND'ing process is found in file attributes. All attributes for a file on a standard FAT partition are stored in one byte in the directory entry. Because one byte is eight bits, you can see that there are eight different ons and offs that can be stored.

On a FAT partition, attributes include Read Only, Archive, System, Hidden, Directory, and Volume Label. The following chart shows an example of what this might look like.

R	A	S	H	D	V
0	1	0	1	0	0

Here the binary value is 010100 (decimal 20); however, this means nothing because it is the value of each individual bit that is of interest. This is where the logical AND and the concept of masking come in.

The logical AND is used to compare two bits and determine if they are both turned on or not. The following chart shows the result of bitwise (operations on bits) AND'ing.

First Bit	Second Bit	Result
1	1	1
1	0	0
0	1	0
0	0	0

This is useful when you need to extract the value of a single bit. To do this you can create a mask (which is a binary number) where all

continues

continued

the bits are 0s except for the bit you are looking for. Using the previous example, if you wanted to find out if a file is hidden, you could construct the mask 000100. As you can see in the next chart, this will extract the value of hidden bit.

	R	*A*	*S*	*H*	*D*	*V*
Attributes	0	1	0	1	0	0
Mask	0	0	0	1	0	0
Result	0	0	0	1	0	0

If the resulting value is 0, the bit was 0 (off); if the resulting value is anything else, then the bit was 1 (on).

A problem arises, though, in that your system cannot know the subnet mask of the system you want to communicate with. This means that you can extract your network ID, but you will not be able to extract the network ID of the target machine. However, if the target machine were on your local subnet, it would have the same subnet mask. This means that you can use your subnet mask and extract a possible network ID. If the ID you extract matches your own, the host should be local.

For example, if your IP address is 198.53.147.45 (subnet mask 255.255.255.0) and you are trying to connect to 198.53.147.98, your system will perform the comparisons shown in Table 3.3.

TABLE 3.3

AND'ING IP ADDRESSES AND SUBNET MASKS— LOCAL HOST

198.53.147.45	11000110	00110101	10010011	00101101
255.255.255.0	11111111	11111111	11111111	00000000
Local Network ID	**11000110**	**00110101**	**10010011**	**00000000**
198.53.147.98	11000110	00110101	10010011	01100010
255.255.255.0	11111111	11111111	11111111	00000000
Possible Network ID	**11000110**	**00110101**	**10010011**	**00000000**

As you can see, the results match exactly; therefore, the network ID in both cases is the same, and the systems are on the same network. Table 3.4 shows the same calculations with a target ID of 131.107.2.200.

TABLE 3.4

AND'ING IP ADDRESSES AND SUBNET MASKS—REMOTE HOST

198.53.147.45	11000110	00110101	10010011	00101101
255.255.255.0	11111111	11111111	11111111	00000000
Local Network ID	**11000110**	**00110101**	**10010011**	**00000000**
131.107.2.200	10000011	01101101	00000010	11001000
255.255.255.0	11111111	11111111	11111111	00000000
Possible Network ID	**10000011**	**01101101**	**00000010**	**00000000**

After the network IDs are known, they can be compared. The only case in which they should match is if the two hosts are on the same network. If the host that you are trying to reach is on the same network, the IP layer will now find that host and transmit the data to it. If not, you need to look for a route to the host. This can be done using the local routing table (see Chapter 6 for a full discussion).

SUBNETTING

Objective: Configure subnet masks.

As you reviewed the address classes in the previous sections, you may have noticed that in the case of class A or B networks there are a large number of hosts per network. Even a class C network with 254 hosts is too large to be handled effectively on a single segment. Therefore, you will need some way to break these larger networks into small pieces that your topology can handle.

The solution is very simple: just like cutting a cake so that members of a large group can each have a piece, you can cut your IP network into slices. This is accomplished using subnetting. *Subnetting* allows you to make a group of networks out of a single network address from your ISP. You will then be able to route between these networks internally, and through a main router externally.

To the outside world your entire network appears as a single entity; that is, it appears as if all of the systems are on a single network. However, trying to keep thousands of hosts on a single network is impossible because of the limitations in the topologies. This means you need to break down the network from what the Internet sees to a group of smaller, yet related, networks. This is done by subnetting.

To subnet a network, all you do is set two or more extra bits to 1 in the subnet mask. Remembering how IP uses the subnet mask, you can see this will force IP to recognize more of the hosts you are communicating with as being on a remote network. Table 3.5 shows the AND'ing process using a standard and a custom subnet mask.

TABLE 3.5

EXTRACTING THE TARGET NETWORK ID USING A STANDARD AND A CUSTOM SUBNET MASK

IP Address	10100000	00010000	10011010	00010111	160.16.154.23
Subnet Mask	11111111	11111111	00000000	00000000	255.255.0.0
Network ID	**10100000**	**00010000**	**00000000**	**00000000**	**160.16.0.0**
Subnet Mask	11111111	11111111	11110000	00000000	255.255.240.0
Network ID	**10100000**	**00010000**	**10010000**	**00000000**	**160.16.144.0**

Remember that the IP address is a 32-bit binary address with the first part as the network ID and the remainder as the host ID on that network. Obviously, if you use more bits for the network ID (to subnet it), you will have fewer bits for the hosts; essentially, you will reduce the number of hosts per network.

Creating Subnets

Subnetting is usually done only once and falls into the Planning stages of the network. Changing the subnetting scheme after a network is in place is a large job that involves the reprogramming of routers and, possibly, the reconfiguration of the hosts on your network.

Determining Your Addressing Needs

There are two critical factors that you must determine when choosing how to subnet your network. First, you need to know how many different subnets are needed, and then you need to know the maximum number of hosts required on any one subnet. Remembering that your network will probably grow at some time in the future, you should always design your network so that the growth you expect (and more) can be accommodated.

Defining Your Subnet Mask

For an IP address to be a remote address, the network portion of the address has to be different (in binary) from your own. In the case of subnetting, that means the bits in the portion you are using for subnetting have to change. The easiest way to figure out how many bits you will need is to write the number in binary. For example, it takes four bits to write the number 12 in binary (1100). This means you need to use four bits for a subnet mask to allow for at least 12 unique binary combinations.

The bits are added to the standard subnet mask to generate a custom subnet mask. To do this, you simply set the number of bits you require to 1. Table 3.6 uses a class B example to illustrate this.

TABLE 3.6			
THE NUMBER OF BITS NEEDED FOR SUBNETTING			
Standard Mask	11111111 11111111	00000000	00000000
Additional bits		**11110000**	
Custom Subnet Mask	11111111 11111111	11110000	00000000

You should notice that the extra bits are added in the position immediately after the bits from the standard subnet mask. Remember, the system sees this as a 32-bit number, not as four octets; thus, you turn on the next four bits regardless of where they are.

The last step in determining the subnet mask is simple: convert the custom subnet mask from binary to decimal one octet at a time—255.255.240.0. Now you can determine the number of networks and hosts that you will have available.

Determining the Number of Networks and Hosts

Because you now know the custom subnet mask, you can determine the number of networks that you will have. This is normally larger than the number you started with. When you convert 12 to binary (1100), not all of the bits are 1 (on). You have 12 combinations; however, more combinations are possible.

In this case you have used four bits, so you can have any combination of 0s and 1s in those four bits. That means there are 2^4 combinations, or 16. Like the host IDs and the network IDs, however, the subnet ID cannot be all 0s or all 1s; this means again subtracting two, resulting in 14 possible subnets.

You can also figure out how many hosts each subnet will have by using the standard formula. Start with the 16 bits that you can use for hosts on class B network, and then subtract the four used for the subnet mask. This means there are 12 bits available for host IDs. Take 2^{12} minus two, and you can have 4,094 hosts per network.

Because you will always include the bits that you want to subnet with immediately after the standard subnet mask, only certain numbers can be used for the subnet mask. Obviously, 255 and 0 are available: they make up the standard subnet mask. In a previous example, we took the four bits and put them on the left side of the octet, and the rest was padded with 0s. This is the same thing that will be done for all custom subnetting. Table 3.7 shows all the valid numbers for subnet masks.

TABLE 3.7

VALID SUBNET MASK NUMBERS

Bits Used	Octet in Binary	Decimal Value
1	Not Valid	Not Valid
2	11000000	192
3	11100000	224
4	11110000	240
5	11111000	248
6	11111100	252
7	11111110	254
8	11111111	255

You will notice that subnetting on one bit is not valid. This makes sense if you remember that the subnet ID cannot be all 1s or all 0s. Because the only possible subnet IDs with one bit would be either a 1 or a 0, the subnet ID would be all 1s or all 0s, which is not allowed.

Subnet IDs

Now that the hard work is done, you can figure out the subnet IDs that will in turn allow us to calculate the valid host IDs for each subnet. Looking at the preceding example, you can see that there are 16 possible combinations that exist in the subnetted octet. Looking at them as an entire octet, they can be converted to decimal. This will give us the subnet IDs as presented in Table 3.8.

TABLE 3.8

CALCULATING THE SUBNET IDs USING BINARY

Octet in Binary	Decimal Equivalent	Full Network ID
0000 0000	0	Not Valid
0001 0000	16	160.16.16.0
0010 0000	32	160.16.32.0
0011 0000	48	160.16.48.0
0100 0000	64	160.16.64.0
0101 0000	80	160.16.80.0
0110 0000	96	160.16.96.0
0111 0000	112	160.16.112.0
1000 0000	128	160.16.128.0
1001 0000	144	160.16.144.0
1010 0000	160	160.16.160.0
1011 0000	176	160.16.176.0
1100 0000	192	160.16.192.0
1101 0000	208	160.16.208.0
1110 0000	224	160.16.224.0
1111 0000	240	Not Valid

Again, there are the two values that are not valid because they consist of all 0s and all 1s. Looking at Table 3.8 you might notice that the subnet ID always increases by 16. The first half of the octet (the part being subnetted) is being increased by 1 each time, and the four other bits are ignored; therefore, we are counting by 16.

This, in fact, works for all possible subnetting scenarios. You will always end up counting by the position value of the last bit in the subnet mask. Table 3.9 shows this with a 3-bit subnet.

TABLE 3.9

SUBNET IDS FOR A 3-BIT SUBNET MASK

Octet in Binary	Decimal Equivalent	Full Network ID
000 00000	0	Not Valid
001 00000	32	160.16.32.0
010 00000	64	160.16.64.0
011 00000	96	160.16.96.0
100 00000	128	160.16.128.0
101 00000	160	160.16.160.0
110 00000	192	160.16.192.0
111 00000	224	Not Valid

In this case the last bit in the subnet mask has a position value of 32. Therefore, to calculate the subnet IDs, all you need to do is look at the position value for the last bit in the subnet mask. This will be the first valid subnet ID, and the value to increment by.

Table 3.10 summarizes all the information that we have looked at so far.

TABLE 3.10

SUMMARY TABLE FOR CALCULATING SUBNET MASK, SUBNET IDS, AND NUMBER OF SUBNETS

Position Value	64	32	16	8	4	2	1
Subnet bits	2	3	4	5	6	7	8

Subnets Available	2^2-2	2^3-2	2^4-2	2^5-2	2^6-2	2^7-2	2^8-2
	2	6	14	30	62	126	254
Subnet Mask	128+64	192+32	224+16	240+8	248+4	252+2	254+1
	192	224	240	248	252	254	255
Host bits	6	5	4	3	2	1	0

Using Table 3.10, look at a network with the class B address of 152.42.0.0. Suppose we need at least 28 subnets with a maximum of 300 hosts per subnet. In this case, there is more than one right solution.

Knowing that we need 28 subnets, the obvious answer is to use 5 bits for subnetting, which, as you can see, gives you up to 30 subnets. Therefore, you might use the 255.255.248.0 as the subnet mask. However, this will leave three bits for hosts in the third octet, plus the eight in the last octet, for a total of 11 bits. That would be 2,046 hosts per segment (2^{11}–2).

This is perfectly valid because it will allow you to have the correct number of subnets and meet (actually exceed) the minimum number of hosts per network desired. However, because you don't want to end up with subnets that have 2,046 hosts each, you might look at this problem in another way.

If we need to have 300 unique host IDs, we can write that number in binary (just like we did for the subnet bits in the beginning) and see how many bits we will need. The number 300 in binary is 100101100, which is nine bits. There are eight in the last octet, so we only really need one from the third octet to make nine.

We can, therefore, use seven bits for the subnet mask, giving us 2^7–2 (126) subnets, leaving us a lot of room for growth while still maintaining the minimum number of hosts per subnet required for acceptable performance. Both answers are correct, but remember to allow for growth.

Host IDs

The last step in subnetting is to figure out the actual host IDs and IP addresses for each of the subnets that you are creating. This is now very simple: The IDs available for each network are all the possible bit combinations between the subnet ID and the broadcast address for the

NOTE

Subnetting on more than eight bits
It is possible to subnet on more than eight bits. This would take the subnetting to the next octet, however. The numbers shown in the table can still be used depending on the number of bits you use. The exception is a 9-bit subnet, in which the subnet mask would include 128.

subnet. For example, if the subnet ID is 160.16.32.0 and the subnet mask is 255.255.240.0, the range is 160.16.32.1 to 160.16.47.254.

The first step is to figure out the next subnet ID. In the preceding case, the subnet mask is 255.255.240.0, which should tell you that there are four bits in the subnet mask. Therefore, the last bit in the subnet mask is in the 16 position; thus, the increment is 16. We can see now that the next valid subnet ID is 160.16.48.0.

Now that you know the current subnet ID and the next subnet ID, you can calculate the range of host IDs. Remembering that the IP address is really just a 32-bit number, you can add 1 to make the host portion something other than all 0s, as shown in Table 3.11; this gives you the first host's ID.

TABLE 3.11

FINDING THE FIRST HOST ID BY ADDITION

Subnet ID					
160.16.32.0	10100000	00010000	00100000	00000000	
Plus 1	00000000	00000000	00000000	00000001	
First Host ID	**10100000**	**00010000**	**00100000**	**00000001**	**160.16.32.1**

Finding the end of the valid host IDs is also simple. Take the next subnet ID (in the case of the last subnet, use the subnet mask—the subnet with all 1s) and subtract one. This will give you the address where all the hosts' bits are set to 1. This is the broadcast address; now you subtract one more to get the last host ID. This is shown in Table 3.12.

TABLE 3.12

FINDING THE LAST HOST ID BY SUBTRACTION

Next Subnet ID	10100000	00010000	00110000	00000000	160.16.48.0
Minus 1	00000000	00000000	00000000	00000001	
Broadcast address	10100000	00010000	00101111	11111111	160.16.47.255
Minus 1	00000000	00000000	00000000	00000001	
Last Host ID	**10100000**	**00010000**	**00101111**	**11111110**	**160.16.47.254**

Although the numbers will look different, the same math can be applied when subnetting class C addresses. For example, take 198.53.202.0 as a network address, and say we want two subnets. You end up with 198.53.202.64 and 198.53.202.128 as the two subnet IDs (with a subnet mask of 255.255.255.192). In Table 3.13 the example system is used to determine the valid hosts.

TABLE 3.13

HOST IDS FOR A SUBNETTED CLASS C ADDRESS

Subnet ID	Starting Host ID	Last Host ID
198.53.202.64	198.53.202.65	198.53.202.126
198.53.202.128	198.53.202.129	198.53.202.190

> **NOTE**
>
> **Proxy Servers**   Normally, this will be handled using a proxy server. Internally, the network will use a private network address; the proxy would accept requests from the internal network on the "fake" address and forward the request over the Internet using a real address. This allows many users to connect to the Internet using a single IP address.

SUPERNETTING (CLASSLESS INTERDOMAIN ROUTING)

As the world runs out of TCP/IP addresses, larger companies face a problem: there are no more class A or class B addresses available. If a company has 620 hosts on its network, it must have multiple class C addresses because it would not be able to obtain a class B address. This requires multiple routers to connect to the Internet—meaning even more addresses that the Internet has to handle for a single company.

Supernetting, or combining smaller networks into a single, larger entity, is a way to relieve the problem posed by the lack of class A and B addresses. A company with 620 hosts would require at least three class C addresses, leaving little room for growth. Also, if the distribution of the systems didn't match the distribution of addresses (say, 300 hosts in each of two locations, and 20 at head office), connecting the office could be problematic.

If you look at the subnetting you have just done, you see that because of the way binary works, you can break large networks into a group of smaller ones. Therefore, it makes sense that you should be able to join smaller networks into one large one. If we treat class C addresses as a subnetted class B address, using eight bits for the subnet mask, the problem just about resolves itself.

Looking at the previous example, the company mentioned could be a single subnet on a class B network. If you wanted to subnet a class B network, you would look at the 620 hosts as a maximum number of hosts per subnet. Writing 620 in binary lets you determine that 10 bits are needed for host IDs. Therefore, we could subnet a class B network on six bits, leaving two bits in the third octet and eight in the last octet for the host ID.

This sounds simple, but a class C address is not really a class B address—so you can't really do this. What your ISP can do however, is fake it. There are two bits in the third octet being used for the host ID in this example; two bits means there are four possible combinations. Your ISP will take four class C addresses, in which the only difference is the last two bits of the third octet; then they will actually be combined.

It is not important which addresses are used, only that they are sequential and all possible combinations of the last two bits of the third octet are included. Table 3.14 presents an example of four addresses that would work in this case.

TABLE 3.14

BINARY VIEW OF A SUPERNET

198.53.212.0	11000110	00110101	11010100	00000000
198.53.213.0	11000110	00110101	11010101	00000000
198.53.214.0	11000110	00110101	11010110	00000000
198.53.215.0	11000110	00110101	11010111	00000000

As you can see, all that changes is the last two bits in the third octet (you might also notice that, in supernetting, addresses with all 0s and all 1s are valid). In this case you can treat these four addresses as a subnetted class B address: 198.53.212.0. Using the standard class B subnet mask of 255.255.0.0, and adding the 6-bit subnet mask of 252, gives you 255.255.252.0.

CASE STUDY: IP ADDRESSES AND SUBNETTING

ESSENCE OF THE CASE

At this point we know that there are 61 locations that we will need to deal with in this network design. They break down into three types of offices with varying numbers of staff. The breakdown is as follows:

- Head office with about 150 employees

- Two regional offices with up to 80 employees each

- Six production centers with about 60 employees each

- Fifty-two sales offices with an average of 20 employees each

All the offices will need to be able to connect to the regional offices, and the sales- and executive-level users will be on roaming laptops.

Now that you have an understanding of the how IP addresses work and the concept of subnetting, it is time to go back to the Sunshine Brewing Company and see how you can apply what you have learned.

SCENARIO

Now that we are starting to look at how to split the network apart, we need to look at the different offices with a view toward the network requirements. With that in mind, a short recap of the information we have so far seems in order.

ANALYSIS

The key points thus far have not changed. However, we can now begin to build the basis for the network that will provide this company with the connectivity it requires and also some cost savings.

Given the size of the company, we can assume that the number of computers in any location is probably around 110 percent of the number of staff. In the small offices there might be one or two extra computers as servers, and in the larger offices there would be extra servers for the network. The production offices would certainly have a larger number of computers to run the production equipment; however, most of the employees use little more than email and would not require full-time access.

Given the number of full-time systems in the sales offices, there is really little need to segment those networks. Because there will be only a single segment, there will also be no need to subnet. The number of hosts can easily be

continues

CASE STUDY: IP ADDRESSES AND SUBNETTING

continued

handled by a partial class C network. This can be arranged through a local ISP. (To conserve IP addresses, ISPs will now assign a partial class C address—in other words, they perform the subnetting.)

Although the equipment in the production centers runs on Solaris, it does not need to be connected to the Internet. This will provide better security for the equipment. (In reality, very little in this organization would connect to the Internet—just the proxy servers, PPTP-enabled RAS servers, and Web servers.) The production centers, therefore, can also get by with a partial class C network.

The regional headquarters and the head office could get to a point where they will need a full class C address, so you want to provide that now. Because a class C network can handle 254 hosts, you need to look at how you will reduce traffic in these offices. Although you could do this with subnetting, you should use switched ethernet to avoid losing addresses and keep all 254 host IDs available in each office because they will logically all be on a single segment (this was discussed in Chapter 1.)

CHAPTER SUMMARY

KEY TERMS

- class A network
- class B network
- class C network
- custom subnet mask
- host ID
- multicasting
- network ID
- standard subnet mask
- subnet
- subnet ID
- subnet mask
- supernet

This chapter has covered how the IP address and subnet mask work together to define a network ID. Following up concepts from the first chapter, you were shown how the system will determine whether the host you are communicating with is local or remote.

You also were introduced to the process of subnetting, which is an extension of network IDs. Based on a given set of requirements, you should now be able to figure out a subnet mask for various situations, even those in which you are combining a group of class C networks.

The key pieces of information that you will need to know from this chapter are summarized in the following list:

◆ IP addresses start with the network ID (which is the actual network ID and the subnet ID) and a host ID.

◆ No part of the IP address can be either all 1s or all 0s.

◆ The network address that starts with 127 is used for diagnostics.

CHAPTER SUMMARY

◆ Three classes of addresses that can be used as a host ID:

Class	Start	Finish	Networks	Hosts
A	1	126	126	16,777,214
B	128	191	16,384	65,534
C	192	223	2,097,152	254

◆ The subnet mask is used with the IP address to extract the network ID.

◆ Subnetting is the process of turning more bits on (to 1) in the subnet mask.

◆ The numbers that can appear in a subnet mask are 0, 192, 224, 240, 248, 252, 254, 255, and 128. The 128 is used only when subnetting with more than one octet.

◆ You should have a single subnet mask for your entire organization.

◆ You will lose addresses when you need to subnet because those subnets with all 0s and all 1s will not be available.

◆ When you subnet, you will have $2^{number\ of\ subnet\ bits} - 2$ networks and $2^{number\ of\ remaining\ bits} - 2$ hosts per subnet.

◆ The bit position value for the last 1 in your subnet mask is the increment that you use when calculating the subnet IDs.

◆ Custom subnet masks are always appended to the normal subnet mask.

◆ Supernetting joins groups' addresses (normally class C addresses); you will always join 2^x networks together.

◆ Supernetting is performed to give you a single address on the Internet and normally happens at your ISP.

APPLY YOUR KNOWLEDGE

This section will give you a chance to test the knowledge you have gained in this chapter. The exercises in this section are paper-based because you would need several computers and a couple of routers to practice them in real life—and not everyone has that available.

Exercises

The following series of exercises will give you a chance to practice with the binary numbers that are used in subnetting.

3.1 Determining Bits Used

In this exercise you simply need to determine the number of bits needed to accommodate the number of networks given.

Estimated Time: About five minutes.

1. 84
2. 145
3. 7
4. 1
5. 15

In this case all you needed to do was either use the chart provided earlier in this chapter or write the number in binary and count the bits. Your answers should have been as follows:

1. 7 bits
2. 8 bits
3. 4 bits (using 3 bits would make the last subnet all 1s)

4. 2 bits (see note for number 3)
5. 5 bits (see note for number 3)

3.2 Calculating the Subnet Mask by Number of Subnets

Given a network ID and the required number of subnets, determine the subnet mask and the number of hosts per subnet.

Estimated Time: About 15 minutes.

1. Network ID 148.25.0.0 with 37 subnets
2. Network ID 198.63.24.0 with 2 subnets
3. Network ID 110.0.0.0 with 1,000 subnets
4. Network ID 175.23.0.0 with 550 subnets
5. Network ID 209.206.202.0 with 60 subnets

In this case you first needed to figure out the number of bits to use for the subnet and create the subnet mask. When that is done, simply calculate the number of bits remaining and figure out the number of hosts. The only trick here is that in two cases (4 and 5) the subnet mask goes beyond one octet (which is valid). Your answers should be as follows:

1. 255.255.252.0 with 1,022 hosts per subnet
2. 255.255.255.192 with 62 hosts per subnet
3. 255.255.192.0 with 16,382 hosts per subnet
4. 255.255.255.192 with 62 hosts per subnet
5. 255.255.255.252 with 2 hosts per subnet

APPLY YOUR KNOWLEDGE

3.3 Calculating the Subnet Mask by Number of Hosts

In this exercise you will calculate the subnet mask; however, the number of hosts is given, so you need to determine the number of subnets that will be available.

Estimated Time: About 15 minutes.

1. Network 63.0.0.0 with a maximum of 100 hosts per subnet

2. Network 198.53.25.0 with a maximum of 100 hosts per subnet

3. Network 154.25.0.0 with a maximum of 1,500 hosts per subnet

4. Network 121.0.0.0 with a maximum of 2,000 hosts per subnet

5. Network 223.21.25.0 with a maximum of 14 hosts per subnet

The answers are as follows:

1. 255.255.255.128 with 131,070 subnets available

2. 255.255.255.0 with no subnets available (in the previous example, the number 128 is valid because, in reality, 17 bits are used for the subnet ID; here you would need to use 1 bit, which is not valid)

3. 255.255.248.0 with 30 subnets available

4. 255.255.248.0 with 8,190 subnets available (the previous was a class B address, whereas this is a class A address—therefore making eight extra bits available for the subnet ID)

5. 255.255.255.240 with 14 subnets available

3.4 Determining Host IDs

For each of the following subnet IDs and subnet masks, determine the valid host IDs.

Estimated Time: About 10 minutes.

1. Subnet ID 148.56.64.0 with the subnet mask 255.255.252.0

2. Subnet ID 52.36.0.0 with the subnet mask 255.255.0.0

3. Subnet ID 198.53.24.64 with the subnet mask 255.255.255.192

4. Subnet ID 132.56.16.0 with the subnet mask 255.255.248.0

5. Subnet ID 152.56.144.0 with the subnet mask 255.255.254.0

The answers are as follows:

1. 148.56.64.1 to 148.56.67.254

2. 52.36.0.1 to 52.36.255.254

3. 198.53.24.65 to 198.53.24.126

4. 132.56.16.1 to 132.56.23.254

5. 152.56.144.1 to 152.56.145.254

3.5 Determining a Range of Host IDs from a Host ID

For the following hosts, determine the range of host IDs into which it falls.

Estimated Time: About 10 minutes.

1. IP address of 23.25.68.2 with subnet mask 255.255.224.0

APPLY YOUR KNOWLEDGE

2. IP address of 198.53.64.7 with subnet mask 255.255.255.0

3. IP address of 131.107.56.25 with subnet mask 255.255.248.0

4. IP address of 148.53.66.7 with subnet mask 255.255.240.0

5. IP address of 1.1.0.1 with subnet mask 255.255.0.0

The answers are as follows:

1. 23.25.64.1 to 23.25.95.254

2. 198.53.64.1 to 198.53.64.254

3. 131.107.56.1 to 131.107.63.254

4. 148.53.64.1 to 148.53.79.254

5. 1.1.0.1 to 1.1.255.254

Review Questions

1. Why is subnetting required?

2. What does subnetting do from a binary perspective?

3. How many different subnet masks are required for an organization with 17,938 hosts?

4. What is the function of a subnet mask?

5. What is the least number of bits that you can subnet on?

6. What is the first function that IP must perform? How does it do it?

7. What are the two pieces of a TCP/IP address?

8. How does the computer see a TCP/IP address?

Exam Questions

1. What class of IP address does 192.25.36.1 belong to?

   A. Class A

   B. Class B

   C. Class C

   D. Reserved

2. What class of IP address does 127.24.15.2 belong to?

   A. Class A

   B. Class B

   C. Class C

   D. Reserved

3. What class of IP address does 92.125.4.1 belong to?

   A. Class A

   B. Class B

   C. Class C

   D. Reserved

4. What class of IP address does 150.12.4.5 belong to?

   A. Class A

   B. Class B

APPLY YOUR KNOWLEDGE

C. Class C

D. Reserved

5. What is the default subnet mask for a class B network?

   A. 0.0.0.0

   B. 255.255.255.0

   C. 255.0.0.0

   D. 255.255.0.0

6. You have an assigned IP address of 200.25.12.0 and you currently have 10 subnets. You want to maximize the number of hosts you can have at each. What subnet mask should you use to maximize the number of available hosts?

   A. 255.255.255.192

   B. 255.255.255.224

   C. 255.255.255.240

   D. 255.255.255.248

   E. 255.255.255.252

7. What is the default subnet mask for a class A network?

   A. 0.0.0.0

   B. 255.255.255.0

   C. 255.0.0.0

   D. 255.255.0.0

8. You have an assigned IP address of 100.0.0.0 and 60 subnets, and you want to maximize the number of hosts you can have at each. What subnet mask should you use to maximize the number of available hosts per subnet?

   A. 255.192.0.0

   B. 255.224.0.0

   C. 255.240.0.0

   D. 255.248.0.0

   E. 255.252.0.0

9. What is the default subnet mask for a class C network?

   A. 0.0.0.0

   B. 255.255.255.0

   C. 255.0.0.0

   D. 255.255.0.0

10. You have an assigned IP address of 100.0.0.0 and only eight subnets, but you anticipate adding two more subnets next year. You want to maximize the number of hosts you can have on each subnet. What subnet mask should you use to maximize the number of available hosts?

    A. 255.192.0.0

    B. 255.224.0.0

    C. 255.240.0.0

    D. 255.248.0.0

    E. 255.252.0.0

APPLY YOUR KNOWLEDGE

Answers to Review Questions

1. Subnetting is required to allow organizations that have large numbers of hosts to break an assigned network ID down into small pieces. This is done for performance reasons or to accommodate different physical locations or topologies. See "Subnetting."

2. When you create a subnet, you are setting more of the bits in the subnet mask to 1. This will cause more of the IP address to be used as the network ID and, therefore, create more networks. See "Creating Subnets."

3. One. When you plan the network, all the hosts on the network should use the same subnet mask—regardless of the number of hosts. See "Defining Your Subnet Mask."

4. The subnet mask allows IP to strip the host ID from the IP address, leaving the network ID. See "Using the Standard Subnet Mask."

5. The subnetting RFC requires the subnet ID not be all 0s or all 1s. This means you cannot use one bit to subnet and that the least number of bits you can subnet on is 2. See "Creating Subnets."

6. IP must first determine if the address is a local or remote address. IP performs this function by AND'ing the local IP address with a subnet mask to determine the local network ID. Then IP will AND the subnet mask with the remote host to determine a possible network address. If the two network addresses are the same, the other host is local; otherwise, it is remote. See "Using the Standard Subnet Mask."

7. A TCP/IP address is made up of a network ID and a host ID. See "IP Addresses."

8. The computer views an address as a string of 32 bits; you work with addresses as a series of four octets in dotted decimal notation. See "IP Addresses."

Answers to Exam Questions

1. **C.** An IP address starting with 192 identifies a class C network. See "Address Classes."

2. **D.** An IP address starting with 127 signifies a reserved address. See "Address Classes."

3. **A.** An IP address starting with 92 identifies a class A network. See "Address Classes."

4. **B.** An IP address starting with 150 identifies a class B network. See "Address Classes."

5. **D.** The default subnet mask for a class B network is 255.255.0.0. See "Using the Standard Subnet Mask."

6. **C.** A subnet mask of 240 will make 14 hosts available on each subnet of a class C network. See "Determining the Number of Networks and Hosts."

7. **C.** The default subnet mask for a class A network is 255.0.0.0. See "Using the Standard Subnet Mask."

8. **E.** A subnet mask of 252 will make 262,142 hosts available on each subnet of a class A network. See "Determining the Number of Networks and Hosts."

APPLY YOUR KNOWLEDGE

9. **B.** The default subnet mask for a class C network is 255.255.255.0. See "Using the Standard Subnet Mask."

10. **C.** A subnet mask of 240 will make over a million hosts available on each subnet of a class A network. See "Determining the Number of Networks and Hosts."

Suggested Readings and Resources

1. Siyan, Karanjit. *Inside TCP/IP, Third Edition.* New Riders, 1997.

2. Heywood, Drew. *Networking with Microsoft TCP/IP, Certified Administrator's Resource Edition.* New Riders, 1997.

3. Komar, Brian. *Sams Teach Yourself TCP/IP Network Administration in 21 Days.* Sams, 1998.

4. Siyan, Karanjit. *Windows NT TCP/IP.* New Riders, 1998.

This chapter will help you prepare for the exam by covering the following objectives:

Configure scopes by using DHCP Manager.

▶ This objective ensures that you understand what DHCP is and how to use it. You also need to know about subnetting, IP addressing, and the options that can be set.

Install and configure the DHCP relay agent.

▶ This objective was actually covered in Chapter 2 as a subobjective of "Configure a Windows NT Server computer to function as an IP router." However, more pertinent material is included in this chapter, such as using DHCP across a router.

CHAPTER 4

Dynamic Host Configuration Protocol (DHCP)

STUDY STRATEGIES

As you read through this chapter, you should concentrate on the following key issues:

▶ You need to understand the four steps of the DHCP process, who initiates them, and when they are used.

▶ You need to understand the problem of running DHCP in a routed network and the solutions for it.

▶ You need to know about DHCP lease periods and when leases are renewed. You should also know what happens if the lease is not renewed.

▶ You should understand the options that work with Microsoft systems and how they can be set.

One of the biggest problems with using TCP/IP is the configuration of the client workstations. This can be very time-consuming, and several problems will arise due to incorrect configuration.

In this chapter, you will learn about the DHCP server that is included with TCP/IP on Windows NT. This server can reduce configuration problems and make it possible to address issues such as roaming users with laptops.

First, the theory of DHCP will be discussed. Then the actual implementation will be looked at from both the server and client perspectives.

UNDERSTANDING DHCP

DHCP is an open industry standard that enables the automatic TCP/IP configuration of DHCP client computers.

To configure Microsoft TCP/IP, you must know the correct values for several fields for each TCP/IP host (see Chapter 2, "Installing Microsoft TCP/IP," for a review of these), and you must know how to enter them manually. At a minimum, the host IP address and subnet mask need to be configured. However, in most cases, other parameters—such as WINS and DNS server addresses—also need to be configured on each host. DHCP relieves the need for manual configuration and provides a method of configuring and reconfiguring all TCP/IP-related parameters.

It is critical that the correct TCP/IP address is configured on each host; otherwise, hosts on the intranet might

- ◆ Fail to communicate
- ◆ Fail to initialize
- ◆ Cause other hosts on the intranet to hang

What DHCP Servers Can Do

The use of Microsoft's DHCP server greatly reduces the administrative overhead of managing TCP/IP client computers because it eliminates the need to manually configure clients. The DHCP server also allows for greater flexibility and mobility of clients on a TCP/IP network, without administrator intervention.

If used correctly, DHCP can eliminate almost all problems associated with TCP/IP. The administrator has only to enter the valid IP addresses, or ranges of IP addresses (called scopes), in the DHCP server database, which then assigns (or leases) the IP addresses to the DHCP client host.

Having all the TCP/IP configuration parameters stored on the DHCP server provides the following benefits:

◆ The administrator can quickly verify the IP address and other configuration parameters without having to go to each host. Also, reconfiguration of the DHCP database is accomplished at one central location, thereby eliminating the need to manually configure each host.

◆ DHCP does not lease the same IP address from a scope to two hosts at the same time; this prevents duplicate IP addresses, if done properly.

◆ The DHCP administrator can control which IP addresses are used by which hosts. This means that servers (other than DHCP servers) can also be DHCP clients; they still have a fixed IP address, but the other configuration will be dynamically updated.

◆ The chance of clerical and typing errors is reduced because the TCP/IP configuration parameters are entered in one place in the DHCP server database.

◆ Several options can be set for each DHCP scope (or globally for all scopes). These options, such as the default gateway and WINS server addresses, are configured on the client along with the IP address. They can also be set for individual machines that have a reserved address.

◆ If a host is physically moved to a different subnet, the DHCP server on that subnet automatically reconfigures the host with the proper TCP/IP configuration information.

NOTE

Updates to DHCP Server Originally, DHCP could not detect which IP addresses were already in use by non-DHCP clients. If a host had a manually configured IP address, and a DHCP scope configured with that same address, the DHCP server may have leased the address to a DHCP client, creating a duplicate IP address on the network. This problem was addressed in Service Pack 2, in which the DHCP server was updated to "ping" the IP address before leasing it.

Using DHCP

To enable automatic TCP/IP configuration by using DHCP, the administrator first enters the valid IP addresses as a scope in the DHCP server database, and then he activates the scope. The DHCP administrator then enters other TCP/IP configuration information that will be given to the clients. The administrator or user then selects Obtain IP Address Automatically from a DHCP server option on the client (found in the Microsoft TCP/IP Properties dialog box).

When a DHCP client host starts up for the first time, TCP/IP initializes and the client requests an IP address from a DHCP server by issuing a DHCPDISCOVER packet. The DHCPDISCOVER packet represents the client's IP lease request.

After a DHCP server receives the DHCPDISCOVER packet, the DHCP server offers (DHCPOFFER) one of the unassigned IP addresses from the scope of addresses that are valid for that host. This ensures that no two DHCP clients on that subnet have the same IP address. This DHCPOFFER information is then sent back to the host. If your network contains more than one DHCP server, however, the host may receive several DHCPOFFERs. In most cases, the host or client computer accepts the first DHCPOFFER that it receives. The client then sends a DHCPREQUEST packet containing the IP address offered by the DHCP server.

The DHCP server then sends the client an acknowledgment (DHCPACK) that contains the IP address originally sent and a lease for that address for a specified period. After 50 percent of the lease time expires, the client attempts to renew its lease with the DHCP server that assigned its TCP/IP configuration. (The renewal request is sent automatically, assuming the host still has TCP/IP initialized, can communicate with the DHCP server, and is still on the same subnet or network.)

After 87.5 percent of the active lease period, the client, if still unable to contact and renew the lease with the original DHCP server, attempts to communicate with any DHCP server to renew its configuration information. If the client cannot make contact with a DHCP server and consequently fails to maintain its lease, the client must discontinue use of the IP address and begin the entire process again by issuing a DHCPDISCOVER packet.

Limitations of DHCP

Although DHCP can substantially reduce the headaches and time required for administering IP addresses, you should note a few limiting characteristics of DHCP:

◆ DHCP does not detect IP addresses already in use by non-DHCP clients on a network. These addresses should be excluded from any scopes configured on the DHCP server. As previously noted, this problem was fixed in Service Pack 2 for Windows NT 4.0.

◆ A DHCP server does not communicate with other DHCP servers and cannot detect IP addresses leased by them. Therefore, two DHCP servers should not use the same IP address in their respective scopes.

◆ DHCP servers cannot communicate with clients across routers unless BOOTP forwarding is enabled on the router or the DHCP relay agent is enabled on the subnet.

◆ As with manually configured TCP/IP, incorrect values configured for a DHCP scope can cause unexpected and potentially disastrous results on the intranet.

Other than the IP address and subnet mask, any values configured manually through the Network dialog box of a DHCP client override the DHCP server scope settings. If you intend to use the server-configured values, be sure to clear the values from the host TCP/IP configuration dialog boxes. Enabling DHCP on the client host does not automatically clear any existing values other than the IP address and subnet mask.

Planning a DHCP Implementation

As with all network services that you will use, you should plan the implementation of DHCP in advance. A few conditions that must be met will be covered in the next few sections.

Network Requirements

The following requirements must be met to implement Microsoft TCP/IP using DHCP:

◆ The DHCP server service must be running on a Windows NT server.

◆ The DHCP server must have a manually configured IP address.

◆ A DHCP server must be located on the same subnet as the DHCP clients; or, the clients' subnet must have a DHCP relay agent running; or, the routers connecting the two subnets involved must be able to forward DHCP (BOOTP) datagrams.

◆ Pools, or scopes, of IP addresses must be configured on the DHCP server.

It is easiest to implement DHCP with only one DHCP server on a subnet (local network segment). If more than one DHCP server is configured to provide addresses for a subnet, either could provide the address; there is no way to specify which server to use as you can in WINS. Because DHCP servers do not communicate with each other, a DHCP server has no way of knowing if an IP address is leased to a client from another DHCP server.

To prevent two DHCP servers from assigning the same IP address to two clients, you must ensure that each IP address is made available in a scope on only one DHCP server on the intranet. In other words, the IP address scopes cannot overlap or contain the same IP addresses.

If no DHCP server is available to lease an IP address to a DHCP client—due to hardware problems, for example—the client cannot initialize. For this reason, you may want to have a second DHCP server, with unique IP address scopes, on the network. This scenario works best when the second DHCP server is on a different subnet connected by a router that forwards DHCP datagrams.

A DHCP client accepts the first IP address offer it receives from a DHCP server. This address would normally be from the DHCP server on the local network because its IP address-request broadcast would reach the local DHCP server first. However, if the local DHCP server is not responding, and if the DHCP broadcasts were forwarded by the router, the DHCP client could accept a lease offer from a DHCP server on a remote network.

Finally, the DHCP server must have one or more scopes created by using the DHCP Server Manager application (found in Start, Programs, Administrative Tools, DHCP Manager). A scope, as you learned, is a range of IP addresses available for lease by DHCP clients; for example, 200.20.5.1 through 200.20.5.20 may be a scope for a given subnet, and 200.20.6.1 through 200.20.6.50 may be a scope for another subnet.

Client Requirements

A Microsoft TCP/IP DHCP client can be any of the following Microsoft TCP/IP clients:

◆ Windows NT server 3.5 or later that is not a DHCP server

◆ Windows NT Workstation 3.5 or later

◆ Windows 95

◆ Windows for Workgroups 3.11 running the Microsoft TCP/IP-32 software from the Windows NT Server CD-ROM

◆ Microsoft Network Client for MS-DOS 3.0 from the Windows NT Server CD-ROM

◆ LAN Manager server for MS-DOS 2.2c from the Windows NT server CD-ROM

If some clients on the network do not use DHCP for IP address configuration, their IP addresses must not be made available for lease to the DHCP clients. Non-DHCP clients can include clients that do not support Microsoft DHCP (ones not on the preceding list) and clients that must always use the same IP address, such as WINS servers, DNS servers, and other DHCP servers.

Although you can use DHCP Manager to reserve an IP address for use by only a specific WINS or DNS server, this technique is not recommended. If a DHCP server with the proper address for these servers is not available on the network for some reason, the client is not assigned an IP address and cannot initialize TCP/IP.

Using Multiple DHCP Servers

It is not recommended that you have more than one DHCP server on a subnet because there is no way to control which DHCP server a client receives an IP address lease from. Any DHCP server that receives a client's DHCP request broadcast can send a DHCP offer to that client. The client accepts the first lease offer it receives from a DHCP server.

If more than one subnet exists on a network, it is generally recommended that a DHCP server be on each subnet. However, if the DHCP relay agent or routers that support the forwarding of BOOTP broadcasts are used, a single DHCP server can handle requests for DHCP addresses.

A DHCP server has an IP address scope configured for each subnet to which it sends DHCP offers. If the DHCP server receives a relayed DHCP request from a remote subnet, it offers an IP address lease from the scope for that subnet. To ensure that a DHCP client can receive an IP address lease even if a DHCP server is not functioning, you should configure an IP address scope for a given subnet on more than one DHCP server. Thus, if a DHCP client cannot obtain a lease from the local DHCP server, the DHCP relay agent or router passes the request to a DHCP server on a remote network that can offer a DHCP lease to the client.

For example, consider a network with two subnets, each with a DHCP server, joined by a RFC 1542–compliant router. For this scenario, Microsoft recommends that each DHCP server contain approximately 75 percent of the available IP addresses for the subnet the DHCP server is on, and 25 percent of the available IP addresses for the remote subnet. Most of the IP addresses available for a subnet can be obtained from the local DHCP server. If the local DHCP server is unavailable, the remote DHCP server can offer a lease from the smaller range of IP addresses available from the scope on the remote DHCP server.

If the range of IP addresses available is 120.50.7.10 through 120.50.7.110 for Subnet A and 120.50.8.10 through 120.50.8.110 for Subnet B, you could configure the scopes on each DHCP server as follows:

Subnet	DHCP Server A	DHCP Server B
A	120.50.7.10 - 120.50.7.84	120.50.7.85 - 120.50.7.110
B	120.50.8.10 - 120.50.8.34	120.50.8.35 - 120.50.8.110

Using Scope Options

Each time a DHCP client initializes, it requests an IP address and subnet mask from the DHCP server. The server is configured with one or more scopes—each containing a range of valid IP addresses—

along with the subnet mask for the scopes and additional optional DHCP client configuration information (known as scope options).

For example, the default gateway for a subnet is often configured as a scope option for a given subnet. If any scope options are configured on the DHCP server, they are given to the DHCP client along with the IP address and subnet mask to be used by the client. The common scope options supported by Microsoft DHCP clients are shown in Table 4.1.

TABLE 4.1

SCOPE OPTIONS SUPPORTED BY MICROSOFT DHCP CLIENTS

Scope Option	Option Number
Router	3
DNS server	6
DNS Domain Name	15
NetBIOS Name server (such as WINS)	44
NetBIOS Node Type	46
NetBIOS Scope ID	47

NOTE

Leasing Addresses to Non-Microsoft Clients   It is possible to lease addresses to non-Microsoft clients including BOOTP clients; in this case, you may have to add a client reservation. Then you will be able to configure options for that single client.

The Scope Options Configuration dialog box in the DHCP Manager application contains many other scope options (such as Time Server) that can be sent to the clients along with the other TCP/IP configuration information. The Microsoft DHCP clients, however, ignore and discard all the scope option information except for the options listed in Table 4.1.

INSTALLING THE DHCP SERVER SERVICE

The DHCP server service can be installed on a computer running Microsoft TCP/IP and Windows NT Server 3.5 or later version. The following steps describe how to install the DHCP server service on a Windows NT Server 4.0 computer.

1. Open the Network dialog box and choose the Services tab.

2. Click the Add button and choose the Microsoft DHCP Service from the list that appears (see Figure 4.1) and click OK.

3. When prompted, enter the directory for the NT source files.

4. Click Close on the Network dialog box and, when prompted, restart your computer.

The DHCP server must have a manually configured IP address, subnet mask, and default gateway. It cannot be assigned an address from another DHCP server, even if an address is reserved for the DHCP server.

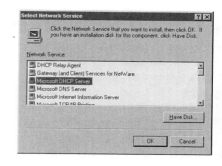

FIGURE 4.1
The DHCP server is added in the Select Network Service dialog box.

CONFIGURING THE **DHCP** SERVER

Objective: Configure scopes by using DHCP Manager.

After a DHCP server has been installed on your intranet, you need the following configuration:

◆ One or more IP address scopes (ranges of IP addresses to be leased) must be defined on the DHCP server.

◆ Non-DHCP client IP addresses must be excluded from the defined scopes.

◆ The options for the scope, such as the default gateway for a subnet, must be configured.

◆ IP address reservations for DHCP clients requiring a specific IP address must be created.

◆ The DHCP clients must have automatic DHCP configuration enabled and should have unwanted, manually configured TCP/IP parameters deleted.

Each of these is discussed in the following sections.

Creating Scopes

For a DHCP server to lease IP addresses to the DHCP clients, a range of valid IP addresses for those clients must be configured on the DHCP server. Each range of IP addresses is called a scope. One scope must be configured on the server for each subnet that the

WARNING

Excluding IP addresses from the scope If any hosts are not using DHCP but have an IP address that falls within the IP address pool, the IP addresses of these hosts must be excluded from the scope. If these IP address are not excluded, DHCP does not know that they already are in use and might assign the IP address to a DHCP client, causing a duplicate IP address on the network.

If you want certain DHCP clients to use a specific IP address out of the scope, you can assign it from the Add Reserved Clients dialog box, as described later in this section.

DHCP server provides IP address leases for. The DHCP server is normally configured with a scope for the local subnet (the subnet the DHCP server is on) and, optionally, with a scope for each remote subnet that it will provide addresses for, as discussed earlier. This will provide backup in case one server goes down.

The following steps are used to configure a scope on the DHCP server.

STEP BY STEP

4.1 Configuring a Scope on the DHCP Server

1. Start the DHCP Manager (Start, Programs, Administrative Tools, DHCP Manager).

2. Select the local DHCP server "Local Machine" by clicking the entry, and then choose Create from the Scope menu item. The Create Scope dialog box is displayed (see Figure 4.2).

3. Type the starting and ending IP addresses for the first subnet in the Start Address and End Address fields of the IP Address Pool.

4. Type the subnet mask for this scope in the Subnet Mask field.

5. If required, type a single IP address or a range of IP addresses to be excluded from the scope. Repeat if required.

6. If you do not want the IP address leases to expire, select the Unlimited option under Lease Duration (if you do this, the configuration of the client will never be updated).

   If you want to force the DHCP clients to renew their leases periodically, choose the Limited To option and type the lease duration in days, hours, and minutes. By default, the Lease Duration is three days.

7. In the Name field, type the name to be used for referring to the scope in the DHCP Manager (for example, **52 Subnet Scope**).

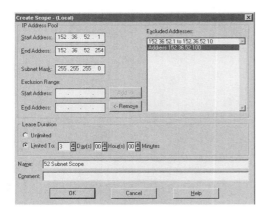

FIGURE 4.2
This dialog box is used to create scopes for the DHCP server.

8. In the Comment field, type an optional descriptive comment for the scope.

9. Click OK to create the scope. The server will now ask if you want to activate the scope (see Figure 4.3). Choose Yes to activate it.

FIGURE 4.3
After the scope is created, you are asked if you wish to activate it.

Scope Options

As discussed earlier, configuration options can be sent to the client along with the IP address and subnet mask. There are two types of options: those set on the scope and those set for all scopes on the server (global). The value set in a scope option overrides a value set for the same DHCP option in a global option. Any values manually configured on the DHCP client—through the Network Control Panel applet or the Microsoft TCP/IP Configuration dialog box, for example—override any DHCP-configured options.

The following steps outline how to view and define options for a DHCP server.

STEP BY STEP

4.2 Viewing and Defining Options for a DHCP Server

1. Start the DHCP Manager tool.

2. Choose either Scope or Global from the DHCP Options menu. This will bring up DHCP Options dialog box (see Figure 4.4).

3. Configure the required DHCP options. First, from the unused Options list, select an option and click Add. The option is added to the Active Options list. Then choose Value, and the value for the option will be displayed (see Figure 4.5).

You can now edit any of three types of values. First, there are strings (such as Domain name), which you can simply enter (see Figure 4.6).

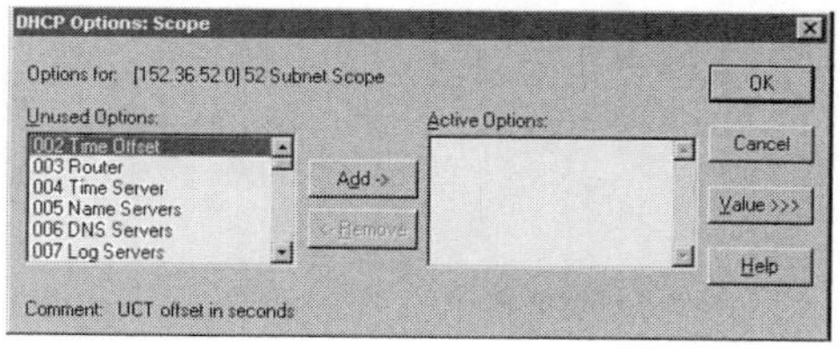

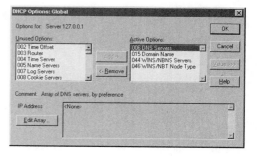

FIGURE 4.4
The DHCP Options dialog is used to add configuration options. Shown are the scope options.

FIGURE 4.5
The DHCP Options dialog box, with the value section showing that no DNS server address (<None>) is entered.

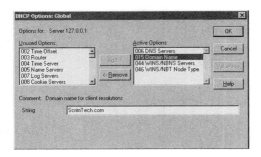

FIGURE 4.6
Entering a string uses a standard text box.

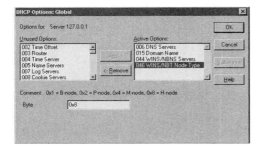

FIGURE 4.7
Entering a hexadecimal value is as easy as a string.

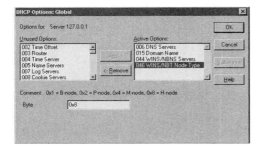

FIGURE 4.8
To enter IP addresses, use the IP Address Array Editor.

Second, there are hexadecimal values (such as NetBIOS node type), which you can enter (see Figure 4.7).

And, finally, there are IP address ranges. For these, you click Edit Array (refer to Figure 4.5), and another dialog box appears (see Figure 4.8) allowing you to enter one or more IP addresses.

4. When all the required options are entered, click OK. The options you have entered will appear in the right-hand pane (see Figure 4.9). Verify the options, and then exit the DHCP manager.

Address Reservations

Some DHCP clients require a specific IP address to be assigned to them each time they renew their IP address lease. Those IP addresses can be reserved for DHCP clients by using the DHCP Manager tool.

Following are examples of clients that should have an IP address reservation:

◆ Servers on a network with non–WINS-enabled clients. If a server on such a network does not always lease the same IP address, the non-WINS clients might not be able to connect to the servers using NetBIOS over TCP/IP (NetBT).

◆ Any other host that is expected to have a specific IP address that other hosts use to connect to it.

The following steps outline how to reserve an IP address from a scope for a specific DHCP client.

STEP BY STEP

4.3 Reserving an IP Address from a Scope for a Specific DHCP Client

1. Determine the hardware address for the DHCP client with the IP address to be reserved from the scope. This can be done by typing **ipconfig /all** at a client's command

prompt. Here is an example of output that would be returned:

```
Ethernet adapter NDISLoop1:
    Description . . . . . . . . : MS LoopBack Driver
    Physical Address. . . . . . : 20-4C-4F-4F-50-20
    DHCP Enabled. . . . . . . . : No
    IP Address. . . . . . . . . : 200.20.1.30
    Subnet Mask . . . . . . . . : 255.255.255.0
    Default Gateway . . . . . . : 200.20.1.1
```

2. Start the DHCP Manager and select the DHCP server to be configured.

3. Select the scope containing the IP address to be reserved.

4. Choose Add Reservations from the Scope menu. The Add Reserved Clients dialog box is displayed (see Figure 4.10).

5. In the IP Address field, type the IP address to be reserved for the DHCP client.

6. In the Unique Identifier field, type the hardware address of the network card for the IP address used. The hardware address should be typed without hyphens.

7. In the Client Name field, type a name for the client to be used only in DHCP Manager. This value is purely descriptive and does not affect the client in any way.

8. In the Client Comment field, type any comments for the client reservation (optional).

9. Choose Add. The reservation is enabled.

10. Choose Active Leases from the Scope menu of DHCP Manager. The Active Leases dialog box is displayed, and the reservations are shown (see Figure 4.11).

DHCP Clients

Automatic DHCP configuration must be enabled for a client to use DHCP to obtain IP address information. The procedure is slightly different for Windows NT and Windows for Workgroups clients.

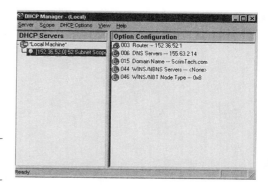

FIGURE 4.9
The DHCP Manager with options set. Options with an icon of a group of computers are scope options; the icon globes refer to global options.

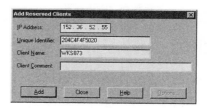

FIGURE 4.10
Client reservations are added using the Add Reserved Clients dialog box.

FIGURE 4.11
You can see the reservation in the Active Leases dialog box.

Windows NT and Windows 95 as DHCP Clients

You can enable Automatic DHCP configuration either before or after Microsoft TCP/IP is installed. To ensure that the DHCP TCP/IP parameters are used instead of any configured manually on the host, you should, preferably, enable automatic DHCP configuration as Microsoft TCP/IP is installed. To do this, follow these steps.

STEP BY STEP

4.4 Enabling Automatic DHCP Configuration

1. Open the Network dialog box, and then choose the Protocols tab and double-click the TCP/IP protocol.

2. Select the Obtain an IP address from a DHCP server check box (see Figure 4.12). The previous IP address and subnet mask values disappear. Ensure that all other configuration parameters you want DHCP to supply are cleared.

3. Close the TCP/IP configuration dialog box and the Network Setting dialog box. Restart the system when prompted.

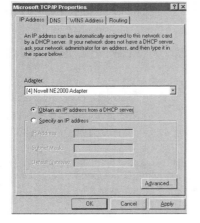

FIGURE 4.12
Select Obtain an IP Address from a DHCP Server to tell your client to use DHCP.

Windows for Workgroups as a DHCP Client

Configuring Windows for Workgroups as a DHCP client is simple.

STEP BY STEP

4.5 Configuring Windows for Workgroups as a DHCP Client

1. Double-click the Network Setup icon in the Network program group of the Windows for Workgroups client (if this is not available, run **winsetup /z**). The Network Setup dialog box will appear (see Figure 4.13).

FIGURE 4.13
The Network Setup dialog from Windows for Workgroups.

2. Choose the Drivers button, select Microsoft TCP/IP, and
choose the Setup button (see Figure 4.14). The TCP/IP
Configuration dialog box is displayed.

3. Select the Enable Automatic DHCP Configuration check
box, and then choose OK (see Figure 4.15). The dialog
box closes, and you are prompted to restart the computer.

4. Do not configure any other parameters unless you want to
override the options set in the DHCP scope, which is not
recommended.

5. Click OK on each dialog box to close it, and then restart
your computer.

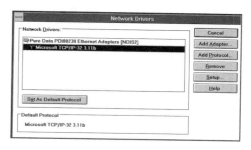

FIGURE 4.14
Select the TCP/IP protocol and click Setup.

USING THE IPCONFIG UTILITY

The IPCONFIG command-line utility is installed with Microsoft
TCP/IP for Windows NT and Windows for Workgroups clients. (In
Windows 95, a graphical interface called WINIPCFG is used.) This
command-line utility and diagnostic tool can be used to

◆ Display detailed information about a computer

◆ Renew a DHCP IP address lease

◆ Release a DHCP IP address lease

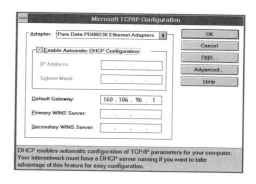

FIGURE 4.15
Checking the Enable Automatic DHCP
Configuration box enables the DHCP client.

Displaying Information

To display the complete TCP/IP information about the local host,
run the IPCONFIG /all command from a command prompt. This
command lists several pieces of information; however, only certain
parts of the information relate to DHCP. For each network interface
card bound to TCP/IP on the host, IPCONFIG /all displays the following:

◆ Whether DHCP is enabled for automatic IP address configuration for the network card

◆ The IP address of the network card

◆ The subnet mask for the network card

◆ The default gateway for the network card

◆ The address of the DHCP server that leases the IP address

◆ The IP lease expiration date and time

Following is an example of output after you type **ipconfig/all** at a command prompt:

```
C:\>ipconfig/all

Windows NT IP Configuration
Host Name . . . . . . . . . : binky.gopherit.com
DNS servers . . . . . . . . : 200.20.16.122
Node Type . . . . . . . . . : Hybrid
NetBIOS Scope ID. . . . . . :
IP Routing Enabled. . . . . : No
WINS Proxy Enabled. . . . . : No
NetBIOS Resolution Uses DNS : Yes
Ethernet adapter NDISLoop1:
Description . . . . . . . . : MS LoopBack Driver
Physical Address. . . . . . : 20-4C-4F-4F-50-20
DHCP Enabled. . . . . . . . : No
IP Address. . . . . . . . . : 200.20.1.30
Subnet Mask . . . . . . . . : 255.255.255.0
Default Gateway . . . . . . : 200.20.1.1
Primary WINS server . . . . : 16.255.1.50
```

Renewing a Lease

The IPCONFIG /renew command typed at a command prompt causes the DHCP client immediately to attempt to renew its IP address lease with a DHCP server. The DHCP client sends a DHCPREQUEST message to the DHCP server to receive a new lease duration and any options that have been updated or added to the scope. If a DHCP server does not respond, the DHCP client continues to use the current lease information.

The IPCONFIG /renew command is usually performed after scope options or scope address information has been changed on the DHCP server and when you want the DHCP client to have these changes immediately.

By default, the IPCONFIG /renew command renews all leases for each network adapter on a multihomed computer. To renew the lease for only a specific network adapter, type **ipconfig /renew <adapter>**, where <adapter> is the specific adapter name.

Releasing a Lease

You can type the IPCONFIG /release command at a command prompt to have the DHCP client advise the DHCP server that it no longer needs the IP address lease. The DHCP client sends a DHCPRELEASE message to the DHCP server to have the lease marked as released in the DHCP database.

The IPCONFIG /release command is usually performed when the administrator wants the DHCP client to give up its lease and possibly use a different lease. For example, the DHCP client's IP address can be reserved for another host or deleted from the DHCP database scope; then you can run the IPCONFIG /release command to have the DHCP client give up that IP address lease and be forced to receive a different lease. This is also useful when equipment moves from subnet to subnet: if you release the address and shut down the computer when you bring it up on another subnet, it will obtain a new lease automatically.

By default, the IPCONFIG /release command releases all leases for each network adapter on a multihomed computer. To release the lease for only a specific network adapter, type the **ipconfig /release <adapter>** command, where <adapter> is the specific adapter name.

COMPACTING THE DHCP DATABASE

Entries in the DHCP database are continually being added, modified, and deleted throughout the IP address leasing process. When entries are deleted, the space is not always completely filled with a new entry because of the different sizes of each entry. After some time, the database contains unused space that can be recovered by compacting the database. This process is analogous to defragmenting a disk drive.

Microsoft recommends compacting the DHCP database once every month or once every week, depending on the size of the intranet. This compaction increases transaction speed and reduces the disk space used by the database.

The jetpack utility compacts the DHCP database (DHCP.mdb) into a temporary database, which is then automatically copied to DHCP.mdb and deleted. The command used is JETPACK DHCP.mdb temp_name.mdb, where "temp_name.mdb" is any file-name specified by the user, with extension .mdb.

The following shows how to compact the DHCP database:

STEP BY STEP

4.6 Compacting the DHCP Database

1. Stop the DHCP server service by using the Control Panel, Server Manager, or a command prompt. (To stop the service from a command prompt, type **net stop dhcpserver**.)

2. Type **cd \systemroot\system32\dhcp**, where "systemroot" is C:\WINNT by default. This changes to the DHCP directory.

3. Type **jetpack dhcp.mdb dhcptemp.mdb**. This compacts dhcp.mdb into dhcptemp.mdb; copies it back to dhcp.mdb; and automatically deletes dhcptemp.mdb.

4. Type **net start dhcpserver**. This restarts the DHCP server service (or starts the service from the control panel or the Server Manager).

BACKING UP THE DHCP DATABASE

By default, the DHCP database is automatically backed up at a specific interval. You can change the default interval by editing the

DHCP server BackupInterval parameter value contained in the Registry, as such:

```
SYSTEM\current\currentcontrolset\services\DHCPServer\
Parameters
```

Backing up the DHCP database enables recovery from a system crash or DHCP database corruption.

RESTORING A CORRUPT DHCP DATABASE

If the DHCP database becomes corrupt, it can be restored from a backup in one of the following ways:

◆ It can be restored automatically.

◆ You can use the RestoreFlag key in the Registry.

◆ You can manually replace the corrupt database file.

Automatic Restoration

The DHCP server service automatically restores the backed-up copy of the database if it detects that it is corrupt. If the database has become corrupt, stop and restart the DHCP server service.

Registry RestoreFlag

If a corrupt DHCP database is not automatically restored from a backup when the DHCP server service is started, you can force a restoration by setting the RestoreFlag key in the Registry. To do this, perform the following steps:

STEP BY STEP

4.7 Setting the RestoreFlag Key in the Registry

1. Stop the DHCP server service from a command prompt by typing **net stop dhcpserver**.

2. Start the Registry Editor (REGEDT32.EXE).

3. Open the HKEY_LOCAL_MACHINE\SYSTEM\ CurrentControlSet\Services\DHCPserver\Parameters key, and then select RestoreFlag.

4. Change the value to **1** in the data field, and choose OK. Close the Registry Editor.

5. Restart the DHCP server service from a command prompt by typing **net start dhcpserver**. The database is restored from the backup, and the RestoreFlag entry in the Registry automatically resets to 0.

Copying from the Backup Directory

You can manually replace a corrupt database file with a backed-up version by performing the following steps:

STEP BY STEP

4.8 Manually Replacing a Corrupt DHCP Database File

1. Stop the DHCP server service from a command prompt by typing **net stop dhcpserver**.

2. Change to the DHCP directory by typing **cd \system-root\system32\dhcp\backup\jet**, where "systemroot" is WINNT, for example.

3. Copy the contents of the directory to the \systemroot\ system32\DHCP directory.

4. Type **net start dhcpserver** from a command prompt to restart the DHCP server service.

CASE STUDY: IMPLEMENTING DHCP

ESSENCE OF THE CASE

As you consider this part of the Sunshine Brewing Company's network, the need for DHCP is very obvious. The need to provide addressing for an army of laptop users demands it. However, because only a small number of addresses are in each location, and because you need to handle redundancy and dial-in connections, there will be some extra drains on the IP address pool. Some of the items that you need to consider include the following:

- The locations with partial class C addresses will not have many adressed to spare, so you will need to be careful how many are used for backup.

- Given the size of the local offices, the back-up of the DHCP server could be a problem: this requires a second machine, which some offices may not have.

- A laptop will occasionally still have a lease from the last location that it was connected to; this could cause a problem as its user logs on to a different network.

- The backbone of the network is the Internet; therefore, you cannot control the types of routers that connect the offices together.

Now that you have learned about DHCP, it is time to take this knowledge back to the Sunshine Brewing Company.

SCENARIO

At this point, you know there are 61 different locations that you need to deal with. Each of these will use a class C or partial class C network.

You need to deal with a few servers in this case. However, a large number of laptops will constantly need to be configured to work on the network. There should also be some consideration of making the DHCP servers redundant.

Recall that the production environments have several Sun boxes; however, these will be on a separate network and don't require real addresses.

The following section offers solutions that could be used to fulfill the DHCP requirements of the network.

ANALYSIS

In this case the analysis, and therefore your recommendations, are fairly straightforward: You need to implement DHCP in each local office. Because this is a Windows NT network, you also need in each office a BDC that will be able to act as a DHCP server. Because there will be some offices with other servers, implement a policy that all servers must be configured with static IP addresses and options.

This leaves the client computers and the laptops for you to deal with. One of the first issues is the number of addresses that you will need per network. Because you want to provide backup for the DHCP server, you will need extra addresses—the exact number will fluctuate depending on the

continues

CASE STUDY: IMPLEMENTING DHCP

continued

number of people visiting an office at any one time. This solution also requires a policy that determines the number of required addresses for a location. Given the size of the organization and the number of people who might travel, each location needs to have 1.5 times the number of actual systems for IP address space, as a minimum.

The backup for the DHCP server will be handled using the DHCP Relay Agent, which will be able to cross the Internet (because it is a directed transmission). This will be installed either on a Windows NT Server or a Windows NT Workstation

in the local office, and it will be given the address of another office's DHCP server.

The laptop issue (retaining an old address) can be solved by including a script that will issue these commands:

```
IPCONFIG /RELEASE
IPCONFIG /RENEW
```

This, combined with a lease duration of eight hours, should allow the laptops to work without error. The dial-in issue is already addressed by using PPTP over a dial-in connection to a local ISP.

CHAPTER SUMMARY

KEY TERMS

- address reservation
- DHCPACK
- DHCPDISCOVER
- DHCPNACK
- DHCPOFFER
- DHCPREQUEST
- global options
- jet
- lease duration
- scope
- scope options

This chapter has covered the installation and configuration of the DHCP server. The use of DHCP makes implementing TCP/IP much easier in a large organization because all addressing configuration is performed on the DHCP server.

The key issues to remember are these:

◆ DHCP is a four-step process: DHCPDISCOVER, DHCPOFFER, DHCPREQUEST, and DHCPACK.

◆ The DHCP server must be a Windows NT server that requires manual TCP/IP configuration.

◆ All DHCP traffic is broadcast and will not pass routers; therefore, you need to configure your router to pass this traffic or configure a DHCP Relay Agent for each subnet.

◆ For the purposes of the exam, know that DHCP does not check the address it is leasing, and that it does communicate with other servers.

◆ DHCP can configure TCP/IP options for clients; however, options configured locally will not be overwritten.

◆ For a BOOTP client (such as a network printer) to use DHCP, a client reservation is required.

APPLY YOUR KNOWLEDGE

Exercises

Through the following set of exercises you will have a chance to install and configure a DHCP server. You need to have a Windows NT server and network card installed to do these exercises (the MS Loopback adapter will work).

4.1   Installing the DHCP Server

This exercise will take you through the installation of the DHCP server.

Estimated Time: About five minutes.

1. Open the Network dialog box and choose Add from the Services tab.

2. Select Microsoft DHCP Server and click OK.

3. Enter the path for your Windows NT source files. Close the Network Setting dialog box and restart your computer.

4. From the Start menu, choose Programs, Administrative Tools. Verify that the DHCP Manager is installed.

For a review of installing a DHCP server, please see the "Installing the DHCP Server Service" section of this chapter.

4.2   Configuring a DHCP Scope

In this exercise, you will configure and activate a DHCP scope.

Estimated Time: About five minutes.

1. Start the DHCP Manager. Double-click the Local Machine to ensure you are connected to it.

2. Choose Scope, Create from the menu. The Create Scope dialog box appears.

3. Enter the following information for the IP Address Pool:

   Start Address   **148.53.66.1**

   End Address   **148.53.127.254**

   Subnet Mask   **255.255.192.0**

4. To add an exclusion, enter **148.53.90.0** into the Start Address and **148.53.90.255** into the End Address. Click the Add button.

5. Leave the duration at default, and enter **Test Subnet 1** as the Name. Click OK.

6. You will be prompted to activate the scope; choose Yes.

For a review of this material please see the "Creating Scopes" section of this chapter.

4.3   Adding Options to the DHCP Server

Now that the server is installed and you have created a scope, choose the scope options that will be added when a lease is acquired.

Estimated Time: About 10 minutes.

1. Click the scope that was created in the previous exercise. (If you get an error, click OK to continue. This is an undocumented feature—a bug. Close the DHCP Manager and reopen it to stop this.)

2. From the menu, choose DHCP Options, Scope.

3. From the list of Unused Options, choose 003 Router and click Add.

4. Click on the Values button to see the rest of the dialog box. Currently, there is no router listed.

APPLY YOUR KNOWLEDGE

5. Choose Edit Array. In the dialog box that appears, enter **148.53.64.1** in the IP Address field. Click Add to add the address to the list.

6. Choose OK to close the IP Address Array Editor, and then choose OK to close the DHCP Options: Scope dialog box. The router option should appear in the Options Configuration panel.

7. Choose DHCP Options, Global from the menu, and add the following options:

   006 DNS Servers

   015 Domain Name

   044 WINS/NBNS Servers (you will get a message when you add this one)

   046 WINS/NBT Node Type

8. Add the configuration for these options, using the following values:

DNS Server	**148.53.64.8**
Domain Name	**ScrimTech.com**
WINS/NBNS Servers	**198.53.64.8**
WINS/NBT Node Type	**0x8**

9. Click OK.

For a review of this material please see the "Scope Options" section of this chapter.

4.4   Creating an Additional Scope

For practice, you will now add another scope to the DHCP server. Notice as you create the scope that the global options apply to the new scope.

Estimated Time: About five minutes.

1. Add another DHCP scope using the following values:

   IP Address Pool

Start Address	**148.53.140.0**
End Address	**148.53.191.255**
Subnet Mask	**255.255.192.0**

2. Set the lease duration for **14** days, and the name of the scope to **Test Subnet 2**.

   There should be a number listed for each scope in the DHCP Manager. The number given is the subnet ID for the scope. This scenario used a Class B address, which is split into two subnets: 148.53.64.0 and 148.53.128.0.

3. Set the default gateway for this scope to **148.53.128.1**.

4. This scope will not be used immediately; therefore, deactivate it by choosing Scope, Deactivate.

For a review of this material, please see the "Creating Scopes" section of this chapter.

4.5   Creating a Client Reservation

In this last exercise, you will create a client reservation.

Estimated Time: About five minutes.

1. Highlight the first subnet (148.53.64.0).

2. Choose Scope, Add Reservations from the menu.

3. In the Add Reserved Clients dialog box, change the IP address to **148.53.66.7**.

4. Enter the unique identifier **0000DE7342FA**, and then enter the client name as **Rob**.

APPLY YOUR KNOWLEDGE

5. Click Add.

6. Enter the IP address **148.53.66.9**, with the unique identifier **00D4C9C57D34**. The client name is **Judy**. Click Add, and then choose Done.

7. Choose Scope, Active Leases to verify the reservations have been added.

For a review of this material, please see the "Address Reservations" section of this chapter.

Review Questions

1. Which fields in the TCP/IP configuration will DHCP overwrite on a DHCP client that previously had TCP/IP manually configured?

2. Name three benefits of using DHCP to automatically configure a client for TCP/IP.

3. What extra steps should you take after installing two DHCP servers on a subnet?

4. What are the router requirements on an internetwork for enabling a DHCP client to communicate with a DHCP server on a remote subnet?

5. What steps should you take to ensure that DHCP does not assign an IP address that is already in use by a non-DHCP client?

6. Is it possible for two DHCP clients on an internetwork to lease the same IP address at a given time? Why or why not?

7. A DHCP client is having difficulty communicating with hosts on an adjacent subnet. You do some troubleshooting and determine that the DHCP client is not using the default gateway that is set in the scope option for that subnet. What could be causing this problem?

8. How many DHCP servers are required on an internetwork of 10 subnets, each with 200 hosts and with BOOTP forwarding routers connecting the subnets? How many would you recommend and why?

9. Through which two methods can a DHCP client be configured to use DHCP for automatic TCP/IP configuration?

Exam Questions

1. Before a client can receive a DHCP address, what must be configured on the DHCP server?

   A. The DHCP Relay Agent

   B. A scope for the client's subnet

   C. A scope for the server's subnet

   D. A hostname

2. What is the recommended method of providing backup to the DHCP server?

   A. Configure two DHCP servers with the same scope.

   B. Configure a BOOTP server.

   C. Replicate the database using directory replication.

   D. Configure two DHCP servers with different sections of the scope.

APPLY YOUR KNOWLEDGE

3. What is the effect of setting the lease duration to Unlimited?

   A. DHCP configuration options will never be updated.

   B. There is no effect.

   C. There will be an increase in network traffic.

   D. Addresses cannot be shared dynamically.

4. In what environment is it advisable to have a short lease duration?

   A. In static environments where addresses don't change often

   B. When you have fewer hosts than IP addresses

   C. In environments where you have hosts moving and many changes to IP addresses

   D. When you have more hosts than IP addresses

5. What portions of the DHCP process does the server initiate?

   A. Lease acquisition.

   B. Lease renewal.

   C. Lease release.

   D. No processes are initiated by the server.

6. How must a Windows NT Server be configured before you install a DHCP server?

   A. The WINS server must be installed.

   B. The server requires a static IP configuration.

   C. TCP/IP must not be installed.

   D. The server must be a BDC.

7. What information is required to define a scope?

   A. Starting and ending address and the subnet mask

   B. Subnet ID and the number of addresses to lease

   C. Number of hosts to be leased

   D. The name of the scope

8. Which clients cannot use a DHCP server?

   A. MS LAN Manager for DOS 2.2c

   B. Windows NT Workstation

   C. MS LAN Manager for OS/2 2.2c

   D. Windows 95

9. How do you configure a client to use DHCP?

   A. Install the DHCP client service.

   B. Select the automatic configuration icon from the control panel.

   C. DHCP will automatically configure all clients.

   D. Select Obtain IP Address Automatically in the TCP/IP configuration.

10. What is the difference between a global option and a scope option?

    A. Global options affect all systems on the network, whether DHCP clients or not.

    B. Scope options are set in the DHCP manager for individual scopes.

    C. Global options affect the clients on scopes where no scope options are configured.

    D. There is no difference in the options, just in how they are entered.

11. Why would you use a client reservation?

    A. To provide dynamic configuration of TCP/IP options with a static IP address.

    B. To be able to control all the IP addresses.

C. This is required for any host that cannot be a DHCP client but that uses an address in the scopes range.

D. You cannot reserve addresses.

12. What is required for a client reservation?

A. The NetBIOS name of the client

B. The HOST name of the client

C. The MAC address of the client

D. The WINS address of the client

13. What happens to the client if you delete its lease?

A. It immediately stops using the address.

B. It will not be able to initialize at next startup.

C. Nothing until it attempts to renew the address.

D. The host will stop working.

14. The administrator of DesCal Corp. is in the process of implementing DHCP on the company's network. The DesCal network currently has 400 computers that are located on 5 separate subnets. Because of the potential problem of duplicate IP addresses when there is more than one DHCP server, the administrator decides to use only one DHCP server.

The administrator configures a DHCP Relay Agent on each subnet and creates a scope for each subnet on the DHCP server. Then the administrator configures the following global options: router, domain name, DNS server, NBNS/WINS server, and NBNS Node Type. How does this solution work?

A. This is the best possible solution.

B. This is a good solution.

C. This solution works, but is far from optimal.

D. This solution does not work.

15. The network administrator of Suds 'n Stuff is attempting to install and configure Windows NT on the company's local area network. Suds 'n Stuff has two offices, each of which is connected by a router to the Internet. Each office has about 80 machines and a class C address.

The administrator decides to use a WINS server in each location and place the PDC and a BDC in the corporate office and two BDCs in the production office. The administrator decides to make the BDC in the corporate office and one of the BDCs in the production office the DHCP server. Each is configured to handle addresses on the local token-ring network rather than using a single DHCP server in the corporate office. How does this solution work?

A. This is the best possible solution.

B. This is a good solution.

C. This solution works, but is far from optimal.

D. This solution does not work.

Answers to Review Questions

1. The IP address and subnet mask are no longer used when the Obtain an IP address from a DHCP server check box is selected. See "DHCP Clients."

2. The following are benefits of using DHCP (see "What DHCP Servers Can Do"):

   • The administrator can quickly verify the IP address and other configuration

APPLY YOUR KNOWLEDGE

parameters without having to check each host individually.

- DHCP does not lease the same IP address from a scope to two different hosts at the same time.
- The DHCP administrator controls which IP addresses are used by which hosts.
- Clerical and typing errors can be reduced.
- Multiple scope options can be set, reducing the amount of manual configuration.
- An IP address may be leased for a limited time.
- A host can be automatically reconfigured when it moves to a different subnet.

3. These are the extra steps that should be taken after two DHCP servers have been installed on a subnet (see "Using Multiple DHCP Servers"):

- You must ensure that the IP address ranges on each DHCP do not overlap. A given IP address must not be in a scope on more than one DHCP server in an intranet.
- You should consider having the DHCP servers on separate subnets connected by a router configured as a DHCP relay agent.

4. To use a router on an intranet that will enable a DHCP client to communicate with a DHCP server on a remote subnet, the router must possess the following characteristics (see "Planning a DHCP Implementation"):

- It must support RFC 1542.
- It must be configured to forward BOOTP packets between the subnets.

5. To ensure that DHCP does not assign an IP address that is already in use by a non-DHCP client, the non-DHCP client IP address should be excluded from that subnet's scope. See "Creating Scopes."

6. Yes, it is possible for two DHCP clients on an intranet to lease the same IP address—if each received its lease from a different DHCP server and the DHCP server scopes contained overlapping IP addresses. See "Using Multiple DHCP Servers."

7. The DHCP client might still have a manually configured default gateway that is no longer correct. See "Using Scope Options."

8. Only one DHCP server is required, although it is usually recommended that each subnet have a DHCP server. Having one DHCP server on each subnet reduces DHCP lease broadcasts on a remote subnet. The DHCP servers can also be configured with ranges of unallocated IP addresses for each other's subnets; this allows another DHCP server to lease a DHCP client an IP address if the DHCP server on that client's subnet is unavailable. You must, however, ensure that the IP address scopes do not overlap so that any given IP address is found in only one scope on the intranet. See "Planning a DHCP Implementation."

9. You can select the Enable Automatic DHCP Configuration check box before or after Microsoft TCP/IP is installed and configured. See "DHCP Clients."

APPLY YOUR KNOWLEDGE

Answers to Exam Questions

1. **B.** A scope for each client subnet must be configured on the DHCP server. See "Configuring the DHCP Server."

2. **D.** Configuring two DHCP servers with different sections of the scope is the recommended method of providing backup to a DHCP server. See "Using Multiple DHCP Servers."

3. **A.** DHCP configuration options will never be updated if the lease is set to Unlimited. See "Creating Scopes."

4. **C.** A short lease duration is ideal for environments where you are moving hosts often. See "Creating Scopes."

5. **D.** In DHCP all processes are initiated by the client and not by the server. See "Using DHCP."

6. **B.** A DHCP server cannot be a DHCP client and must have a static address. See "Installing the DHCP Server Service."

7. **A.** Starting and ending addresses and the subnet mask are required to define a scope. See "Creating Scopes."

8. **C.** MS LAN Manager for OS/2 2.2c clients cannot use DHCP. See "DHCP Clients."

9. **D.** Selecting Obtain IP Address Automatically in the TCP/IP configuration will configure a client to use DHCP. See "DHCP Clients."

10. **B.** Scope options are set in the DHCP Manager for individual scopes. See "Scope Options."

11. **A.** A client reservation is used to provide a static IP address. See "Address Reservations."

12. **C.** The MAC address of a client must be given to configure a client reservation. See "Address Reservations."

13. **C.** If you delete a client's lease, nothing will happen until it attempts to renew the address. When this occurs, the server will send a NACK (Negative Acknowledgment), and the system will start the DHCP process over, starting with the DHCPDISCOVER. See "DHCP Clients."

14. **D.** This is a nearly workable solution and will provide a TCP/IP address to each host and all the configuration information. The only problem here is that the router address is configured as a global option. This means that none of the computers will be able to communicate outside the local network except for the subnet where the router is valid. See "Using Scope Options."

15. **B.** There is no redundancy in this case. The link speed to the Internet and, therefore, the other office is slow. However, because the number of requests should be incredibly low, the administrator should configure redundancy notable, given the number of extra addresses. In this case the only way the redundant address would be available is using a DHCP Relay agent. See "Planning a DHCP Implementation."

Suggested Readings and Resources

1. Komar, Brian. *Teach Yourself TCP/IP Network Administration in 21 Days*. Sams, 1998.

2. TechNet:
   - Windows NT Resource Kit Networking Guide—Configuring DHCP.
   - Windows NT Resource Kit Networking Guide—Planning for DHCP Implementation.

This chapter will help you prepare for the exam by covering the following objective and its subobjectives:

Install and configure a Windows Internet Name Service (WINS) server.

> **Import LMHOSTS files to WINS.**
>
> **Run WINS on a multihomed computer.**
>
> **Configure WINS replication.**
>
> **Configure static mappings in the WINS database.**

▶ One of the key services that is required to effectively run NetBIOS networking over TCP/IP is the capability to resolve NetBIOS names to TCP/IP addresses. This objective is included to ensure that you understand how to install and configure the WINS server.

CHAPTER 5

Windows Internet Name Service (WINS)

OUTLINE

STUDY STRATEGIES

As you read through this chapter you should concentrate on the following key items:

▶ You need to know how to install WINS.

▶ You need to know which operating systems can be clients and how to configure them as such.

▶ You need to know the effect of a multihomed WINS server.

▶ You need to know how to create a static address and the different types of addresses.

▶ You need to know how to set up replication with other WINS servers and how automatic replication takes place.

WINS provides name registration, renewal, release, and resolution services for NetBIOS names. This allows a WINS server to maintain a dynamic database linking NetBIOS names to IP addresses. The database is dynamic because each system can register its own name without the intervention of an administrator.

The WINS server receives registration, renewal, and release requests from WINS clients and uses them to update its database. Name resolution queries from WINS clients can then be resolved by the WINS server database.

Using the WINS server provides a marked improvement over using broadcast messages or static mappings for name registration, renewal, release, and resolution services. Instead of each computer sending a broadcast to all clients on its subnet for every name registration, each computer can send a directed message to the WINS server.

The same applies for name queries: Instead of sending a broadcast message to all clients on its subnet, a WINS client sends a directed message to the WINS server. For networks using static mappings, such as an LMHOSTS file, each computer has a fixed list of NetBIOS names and IP addresses (see Chapter 8, "Name Resolution," for details about LMHOSTS). This can become difficult to manage—or impossible when using dynamic IP address assignments, such as in environments using DHCP.

The following section looks at how WINS works and details the services that a WINS server provides to WINS clients.

> **NOTE**
>
> **WINS and Directed Communications**
> Because the communications are directed rather than broadcast, client computers can be configured to use WINS servers on the local subnet or on a different subnet because the directed traffic can cross the router.

How WINS Works

A WINS server provides name registration, renewal, release, and resolution services to client computers configured to use it. Just how these services are provided is an interesting combination of client and server processes. The four fundamental services provided by WINS are detailed in the following sections.

Name Registration

Name registration is the process by which the WINS server obtains information from WINS clients. Name registration, which occurs when a WINS client computer starts, allows the WINS database to be maintained dynamically, rather than statically.

When a WINS client starts up, it sends a name registration to its configured WINS server. This registration provides the computer name and IP address of the WINS client to the WINS server. If the WINS server is running and no other client has the same name registered, the server returns a successful registration message to the client. This message contains the name registration's time-to-live (TTL).

Just like the IP address, a unique name within the network is required for each computer; otherwise, network communication would be impossible. After WINS clients send name registration requests to the WINS server, the server ensures that the name registration is unique; no other computer may have the same name.

If the name is already registered, the WINS server will attempt to verify that the name is really in use. This is important because there are cases, such as with laptops, in which systems will move around. The WINS server will verify the name using the following guidelines:

◆ The server challenges the computer already holding the name registration to ensure that it is still active. If the computer does not answer the challenge, the registration proceeds.

◆ If the host that currently holds the name is a multihomed system (if it has multiple IP addresses and/or multiple network cards), a challenge is sent to each interface.

◆ If the original host answers the challenge, the registration request receives a negative acknowledgment, and an error is registered in the System Event Log of the client. The computer attempting to claim an existing name cannot communicate using NetBIOS on that adapter.

Name Renewal

After a WINS client's name is registered, it is assigned a time-to-live, and the name is removed from the WINS server's database. If there were no mechanism to renew leases, this would be an inefficient system: at the end of each registration's time-to-live, the client computer would have to go through the entire registration process again. To avoid this, WINS clients request a renewal to their name registration record before the time-to-live expires.

This process is straightforward and similar to the initial name registration process. After one eighth of the time-to-live value has passed, the client attempts to renew its name registration. If no response is received, the WINS client retries its renewal every two minutes, until half its time-to-live has passed.

At half the time-to-live, the WINS client tries to renew its lease with the secondary WINS server. The time-to-live is reset to zero; then, as with the primary WINS server, after one eighth of its time-to-live value has passed, the client begins trying to renew its name registration until it succeeds or half its time-to-live has passed. If it is still unsuccessful after half its time-to-live has passed, it reverts to its primary WINS server.

After a name renewal succeeds at any point in the process—with either the primary or secondary WINS server—the WINS client is provided with a new TTL value for its name registration.

Name Release

WINS clients send a name release request to the WINS server during an orderly shutdown. This release message is a request to deactivate the IP address and NetBIOS name mapping in the WINS server database. Computers that also use broadcast name resolution send a broadcast message indicating the name release to all computers on its subnet.

Upon receipt of the release request, the WINS server verifies that it has the IP address and NetBIOS name in its database. If an error occurs, the server sends a negative response to the WINS client. The following circumstances are possible errors that can cause the WINS server to send a negative response:

◆ If another client has a different IP address mapped to the same NetBIOS name.

◆ If the WINS database is corrupted.

◆ If the IP address or NetBIOS name specified does not exist within the WINS server's database.

If a computer is not shut down correctly, the WINS server does not know that the name has been released, and the name is not deactivated until the WINS name registration record expires.

Name Resolution

WINS clients typically send name resolution requests to the WINS server when the client computer tries to map a network drive. To connect to a network drive, the user needs to specify two things: a system name and a share name. The system name needs to be resolved to an IP address.

The basic flow of a name resolution request is as follows :

1. When a WINS client computer wants to resolve a name, it first checks its local NetBIOS name cache. You can view the cache using the NBTSTAT -c command, which is covered in detail in Chapter 8.

2. If the name is not in the local cache, a name query is sent to the primary WINS server. Three attempts are made at 15-second intervals; if the primary WINS server is unavailable, the request is sent three times to the secondary WINS server at the same interval. If either WINS server resolves the name, a verification message is sent to the client containing the requested NetBIOS name and IP address.

3. If neither the primary nor secondary WINS server is available, or if neither server can resolve the query, no response is sent to the client. The WINS client then attempts to resolve the name using (depending on the clients configuration) a local broadcast, the LMHOSTS or HOSTS file, or DNS.

See Chapter 8 for more details on name resolution.

IMPLEMENTATION CONSIDERATIONS

Because of the scaleable nature of Windows NT networks, your environment could range from one server and three workstations to a worldwide WAN with hundreds of servers and thousands of clients. Prior to implementing WINS, you need to examine a number of issues that will largely determine the best implementation for your particular environment. The following sections examine these issues in more detail.

WINS Server Considerations

WINS servers are the most critical element of a WINS deployment and critical for a successful deployment of Windows NT using TCP/IP. Determining how many WINS servers you need, where to place them, and how to configure them are important aspects of predeployment planning.

At an absolute minimum, you need one WINS server. Two WINS servers provide some degree of fault tolerance if the primary WINS server fails, because WINS servers are able to share database information.

WINS servers don't have a built-in limit on the number of clients that can be served. A basic rule of thumb is that one WINS server can handle up to 1,500 name registrations and about 4,500 name queries per minute. Microsoft recommends that you use one primary and one secondary WINS server per 10,000 clients.

One interesting component of the WINS server is that it supports database logging. *Database logging* is a fault-tolerance feature that maintains a log file, in addition to the database, that contains recent transaction information. If this feature is enabled, the database can be "rolled back" to a known state. However, this increases the required resources because all name registrations are processed twice. The benefit is fault tolerance: If logging is enabled, the most recent updates to the WINS database won't be lost if the WINS server software crashes.

If your network spans multiple subnets, client computers can be configured to use WINS servers on the local subnet or on a different subnet. Of course, this slows performance and increases traffic through routers. Also, if WINS servers are located on a different subnet than the WINS client computers, the availability of the routers becomes paramount—and if they are no longer available, neither are the WINS services.

WINS Client Considerations

Each WINS client must be configured to communicate with at least a primary WINS server, but it can be configured with both a primary and a secondary WINS server. This provides a certain degree of fault tolerance: if the primary WINS server is unavailable, the secondary WINS server can provide the same services. This can be configured manually or through the use of DHCP.

IMPLEMENTING WINS

Now that you have an understanding of the theory and benefits of WINS, this chapter will look at the installation and configuration of a WINS server. Remember that this service is available only on Windows NT Server.

Installing a WINS Server

Installing a WINS server is very simple and, in many cases, requires no further configuration. The WINS server is installed on a Windows NT Server in the same way as other services. The server should, however, have a static IP configuration (that is, it should not be a DHCP client). To install WINS, perform the following steps.

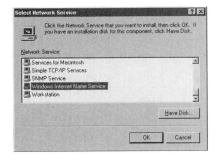

FIGURE 5.1
Adding the WINS service to a Windows NT Server.

STEP BY STEP

5.1 Installing WINS

1. Open the Network dialog box and choose the Services tab.

2. Click the Add button and choose the Windows Internet Name Service from the Select Network Service dialog box (see Figure 5.1).

3. When prompted, enter the path to your Windows NT source files.

4. Close the Network dialog box and restart the system.

After the WINS service is installed, you will need to configure your clients to see the WINS server. The next section deals with the configuration of the client computers both manually and using a DHCP server.

WINS on a Multihomed Computer

Normally, the WINS service should not be run on a computer that is multihomed (has two or more network cards) because the WINS server always registers its names in the local database. This is a problem if you are using DOS clients because they will always try the first IP address that they receive from the WINS server. Because the WINS server will register all of its IP addresses in order, the DOS client might not be able to reach resources on the WINS server from networks other than the one on which the first card is located.

WINS Clients

Nearly all Microsoft clients capable of networking can be a WINS client; the exception is the MS LAN Manager 2.2c for OS/2 client. The following list includes the clients that can work with WINS:

◆ Windows NT Server 3.5x, 4.0

◆ Windows NT Workstation 3.5x, 4.0

◆ Windows 95/98

◆ Windows for Workgroups with TCP/IP-32

◆ Microsoft Network Client 3.0 for MS-DOS

◆ LAN Manager 2.2c for MS-DOS

However, only the Windows-based clients can register their names with the WINS server. The DOS-based clients can use the WINS server for name resolution, but you must add static entries for them to the WINS server so their names can be resolved.

To configure these clients for WINS, the address of the primary WINS server must be specified on the client. The client can also configure the address of a secondary WINS server. You can either enter this information manually at the client, or it can receive the configuration information with its IP address from a DHCP server.

Manually Configuring a Client for WINS

To manually configure a WINS client, specify the WINS server address as part of the TCP/IP configuration. The following steps work for Windows NT.

STEP BY STEP

5.2 Manually Configuring a WINS Client

1. Open the Network dialog box and choose the Protocol tab.

2. Double-click the TCP/IP protocol and click the WINS Address tab.

3. Enter the address of a primary WINS server and secondary WINS server (see Figure 5.2).

   If multiple cards are installed, select each card from the drop-down list box and configure the WINS server addresses for each.

4. Click OK and close the Network dialog box.

5. Restart your computer when prompted.

Although this is simple, it does require that you visit each of the clients to update the TCP/IP configuration. If you are using DHCP, however, you can send the information to the client with the IP address lease.

Configuring a Client for WINS Using DHCP

Configuring WINS clients by using a DHCP server can reduce the time it takes to implement WINS. You need to add two properties to the DHCP global (or scope) options created on the DHCP server. Under the DHCP global options, add the following parameters:

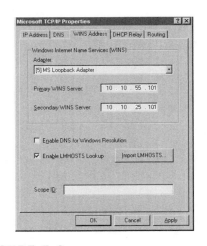

FIGURE 5.2
Entering the WINS server information can be done on the WINS Address tab.

◆ **044 WINS/NBNS Servers.** Configure this with the address of the primary WINS server and a secondary WINS server, if desired.

◆ **046 WINS/NBT Node.** By default, this is set to 0x0, a b-node broadcast. WINS clients should use h-node, so you should change the value of this parameter to 0x8. (To completely remove name resolution broadcasts, configure the clients as a 0x2 p-node.)

Configuring WINS to Work with Non-WINS Clients

A WINS server interacts in two ways with WINS clients. First, it registers the names of those clients. Second, it answers requests for name resolutions (name queries). You can enable both functions for non-WINS clients through additional configuration.

Registering Non-WINS Clients with Static Entries

You can register a non-WINS client with a WINS server by adding a static entry to the WINS database. With entries added for non-WINS clients, WINS clients can resolve more names without resorting to broadcasts or looking up the entries in an LMHOSTS file.

Adding Static Mappings

Static entries are added through the WINS Manager in the following way.

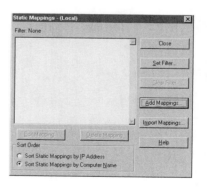

FIGURE 5.3
From the Static Mappings dialog box you can add, edit, or delete mappings.

STEP BY STEP

5.3 Adding Static Mappings

1. Start the WINS Manager (Start, Programs, Administrative Tools, WINS Manager).

2. From the menu, choose Mappings, Static Mappings. The Static Mappings dialog box appears (see Figure 5.3).

FIGURE 5.4
Adding static mapping is simple using the Add Static Mappings dialog box.

3. Click Add Mappings to add a mapping. The Add Static Mapping dialog box appears (see Figure 5.4).

4. Enter the name and IP address for the static host. Choose the type of mappings to create (these are explained in Table 5.1). Click the Add button.

5. Repeat step 4 until all mappings are entered. When you have finished, click Close.

6. The entries you added will now appear in the Static Mappings dialog box. After verifying the entries, close the Static Mappings dialog box.

Table 5.1 explains the different types of static mappings.

TABLE 5.1

TYPES OF STATIC MAPPINGS

Type of Mapping	Explanation
Unique	This registers a single computer name to a single IP address.
Group	Group names don't have an address assigned to them; instead, the WINS server returns 255.255.255.255 (the broadcast address). This causes the client to use a broadcast on the local subnet to resolve the name.
Domain Name	The domain-name mapping contains up to 25 IP addresses consisting of the PDC and as many as 24 BDCs in a domain. This enables computers to locate a domain controller for logon validation or pass through authentication.
Internet Group	This is a user-defined mapping used to store addresses for members of a group other than a domain (such as a work-group). This can contain up to 25 IP addresses.
Multihomed	A multihomed name is used to register a computer with more than one network adapter (or at least with more than one IP address). A multihomed entry can have up to 25 IP addresses.

Importing Mappings

You may have noticed an option to Import Mappings in the Static Mappings dialog box. This will allow you to import the contents of an LMHOSTS file, which was used in the days of LAN Manager (the "LM" in LMHOSTS) to resolve the addresses of TCP/IP-based servers in a LAN Manager network.

The Import Mappings option is included to allow you to easily create all the entries required during an upgrade process from LAN Manager to NT. If you are upgrading from a LAN Manager environment and planning to use this function, you will want to enable Migration in the WINS server configuration; this will allow the static mappings to be overwritten by the dynamic mappings as the systems are upgraded.

Resolving Names for Non-WINS Clients

You can also allow non-WINS clients to use a WINS server to resolve NetBIOS names by installing a *WINS proxy agent*. By definition, a non-WINS client cannot directly communicate with a WINS server to resolve a name. Instead, the non-WINS client resolves names by resorting to a name query broadcast. The proxy agent forwards any broadcasts for name resolution to the WINS server. The proxy agent must be located on the same subnet as the non-WINS clients to receive the broadcast for name resolution. The proxy agent must also be a WINS client.

When a non-WINS client broadcasts a name resolution request, a proxy agent that hears the broadcast checks its own NetBIOS name cache to see whether an entry exists for the requested name. If the entry doesn't exist, the proxy agent adds to the cache an entry for that name with the status of "pending." The proxy agent then sends a name resolution request for the same name to the WINS server. After the WINS server responds with the name resolution, the proxy agent adds the entry to its cache and removes the pending status from the entry.

The proxy agent does not forward the response to the non-WINS client making the request. When the non-WINS client broadcasts another request for the name resolution, the proxy agent finds an entry for the name in its cache, and the proxy agent can respond to the non-WINS client with a positive name resolution response.

The WINS proxy agent also forwards registration requests to the WINS server. However, registration requests for non-WINS clients are not added to the WINS server's database. The WINS server uses these forwarded registration requests to see whether there are any potential conflicts in its database with the requested name registration. You must still add static entries to the WINS database so that names of non-WINS clients can be resolved.

You must place a WINS proxy agent on each subnet where non-WINS clients are located so that those clients have access to the WINS server. A client resolves names only by using broadcasts, which are not routed; thus, those broadcasts never go beyond the subnet.

With a proxy agent on each subnet, broadcasts can then be forwarded to the WINS server. You can have two proxy agents on a subnet, but you shouldn't exceed this limit. Even having more than one proxy agent on a subnet can generate excessive work for the WINS server because each proxy agent forwards name resolution and name registration requests to the WINS server. The WINS server has to respond to duplicate messages from proxy agents if more than one proxy agent is on a subnet.

Any Windows-based WINS client can be a WINS proxy agent. To configure a Windows NT server or workstation to be a proxy agent, you must activate a parameter in the Registry. This proxy agent cannot be a WINS server, and it must be a WINS client. Following are the steps for enabling the proxy agent on a Windows NT computer. (For Windows 95 and Windows for Workgroups the configuration is simpler: you need only activate a switch in the TCP/IP configuration.)

STEP BY STEP

5.4 Enabling the WINS Proxy Agent

1. Start the Registry Editor (Start, Run type REGEDT32 and click OK).

2. Choose Window and select HKEY_Local_Machine on Local Machine from the menu.

3. Double-click the SYSTEM key to expand it. Then double-click CurrentControlSet. Expand the Services key next and locate NetBT. Expand the NetBT key and click on

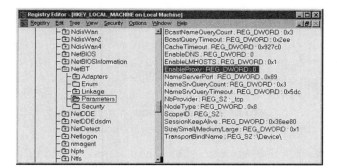

FIGURE 5.5
The Registry Editor with NetBT parameters.

the Parameters subkey (see Figure 5.5).

4. In the list of values, double-click on EnableProxy. Change this value from 0 to 1 (see Figure 5.6).

5. Click OK and close the Registry Editor.

6. Restart your computer.

FIGURE 5.6
Changing the value of EnableProxy from 0 to 1 in the DWORD Editor activates the proxy agent.

REPLICATION

Because WINS clients are configured to communicate only with specified WINS servers, the database on each WINS server may not have entries for all the WINS clients in the network. In fact, many TCP/IP implementations divide WINS clients among different WINS servers to balance the load. Unfortunately, WINS clients cannot resolve addresses registered with another WINS server unless the registrations from that server are copied to the client's WINS server.

WINS replication is the process used to copy one WINS server's database to another WINS server. You can configure a WINS server so that it automatically replicates its database with another WINS server. This way, clients registered with one WINS server can be added to the database of another server. Static mappings entered on one server are also replicated to replication partners. In fact, you can enter static entries on only one WINS server and have them propagated to any number of WINS servers through replication. After you enable replication, clients seeking name resolution can see not only entries from their server but also the entries of the replication partner.

Configuring Replication

To set up replication, you must configure a WINS server as a push partner or a pull partner (or, normally, as both). A *push partner* notifies another server of changed entries based on the number of changes, whereas a *pull partner* requests and receives entries from another server based on a scheduled time. You must always configure WINS servers in pairs; otherwise, replication won't work.

One of the WINS servers must be a push partner to send its entries out, while the other WINS server must be a pull partner to receive the entries. Replication does not occur unless both WINS servers are properly configured. If both WINS servers are configured as push and pull partners, then each server ends up with entries from the other server. In theory, the combined database on each WINS server should be the same. However, due to the lag time in replication, this doesn't always happen.

The following steps show how to configure a WINS server as a replication partner.

FIGURE 5.7
Adding another WINS server allows you to control the server as well as set up replication.

FIGURE 5.8
Configuring replication is done in the Replication Partners dialog box.

STEP BY STEP

4.5 Configuring a WINS Server as a Replication Partner

1. Start the WINS Manager.

2. From the Server menu, choose Add Server (see Figure 5.7). Type the TCP/IP address of the other WINS server; then choose OK.

3. Select your WINS server in the WINS Manager window.

4. From the Server menu, choose Replication Partners.

5. From the Replication Partners dialog box (see Figure 5.8), select the other WINS server.

6. In the Replication Options box, select either Push Partner or Pull Partner for this server.

7. Click OK.

Replication Considerations

Deciding which WINS server will be a push partner and which will be a pull partner is often driven by performance considerations. You often use a pull partner across slow WAN links because you can configure a pull partner to replicate only at certain times (such as at night, when the WAN link is not as heavily used). In that case, you could make the WINS server on each side of the WAN link a pull partner with the other WINS server. This is known as pull-pull replication.

On faster links, you can use push partners. Push partners replicate when a specified number of changes are made to the database. These updates can happen fairly frequently, but they are not too large because you are not waiting to replicate a whole day's worth of changes. If you want two WINS servers to have identical databases, you must configure each WINS server to be a push and a pull partner for the other server.

You can configure a replication partner to start replication in several ways:

◆ You can configure a startup replication for either a push or a pull partner.

◆ Replication can be completed at a specified interval, such as every 24 hours. This applies to pull replication.

◆ Replication can be completed when a push partner reaches a specified number of changes to the database. These changes include name registrations and name releases. When this threshold is reached, the push partner notifies all its pull partners that it has changes for replications.

◆ You can manually force replication from the WINS Manager.

Automatic Replication

WINS can automatically replicate with other WINS servers if your network supports multicasting. By default, every 40 minutes, each WINS server sends a multicast to the address 224.0.1.24. Any servers found through this multicast are automatically configured as push and pull partners, with replication set to occur every two hours. If the routers on your network do not support multicasting, the WINS servers see other servers only on the same subnet.

You can control this multicasting feature by editing the Registry in the following location:

```
HKEY_LOCAL_MACHINE\System\CurrentControlSet\Services\NetBT\
➥Parameters
```

Change the value of UseSelfFndPnrs to 0 to turn it off, and change the value of McastIntvl to a set the interval.

A WINS server replicates only its active and extinct entries; released entries are not replicated. A replication partner can have entries that are marked active even though its partner has released them. Released entries are not replicated; this reduces the traffic caused by computers booting and shutting down each day. However, if the registration changes for a system, it is considered a new entry, and it is replicated.

WINS SERVER CONFIGURATION

As you have seen, the WINS Manager tool is added to the Administrative Tools group. Use this tool to manage the local WINS server as well as remote WINS servers. You can use WINS Manager to view the WINS database, add static entries to the database, configure push and pull partners for replication, and back up and restore the WINS database.

You can use the WINS Server Configuration dialog box to configure how long entries stay in the WINS database (see Figure 5.9).

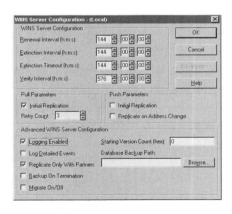

FIGURE 5.9
WINS server configuration options.

WINS Registration Intervals

Four options affect the length of time a registration will remain in the WINS server:

◆ **Renewal Interval.** This is the interval (time-to-live) given to a WINS client after it successfully registers its name. The client begins renewing the name registration when half this time has expired. The default is six days.

◆ **Extinction Interval.** This is the amount of time that must pass before the WINS server marks a released entry as extinct. The default is six days. An extinct entry is not immediately deleted; the time until removal is controlled by the following parameter.

◆ **Extinction Timeout.** This is the amount of time WINS waits before removing (scavenging) entries that have been marked extinct. The default is six days.

◆ **Verify Interval.** This applies if WINS servers are set up for replication. This is the interval at which the WINS server verifies that names in its database that came from other servers are still valid. The default—24 days—is also the minimum.

Initial Replication Configuration

You can configure the WINS server to replicate with its partners when it starts. Choose the Initial Replication option under Pull Parameters on the WINS Server Configuration dialog to have a pull replication partner replicate on startup. You can also specify the number of times the pull partner tries to contact the other WINS server as the pull partner performs the startup replication.

To configure a push partner to replicate upon startup, choose the Initial Replication option under Push Parameters. You can also configure the push partner to replicate when it has an address change.

Advanced Configuration Options

There are several options that appear only if you click the Advanced button. These options control how the WINS server functions, and you should configure them when you initially install the WINS server:

◆ **Logging Enabled.** You can activate the logging of entries to the WINS database. This log file will record changes that are made to the WINS database before they are made. By default, logging is already enabled, which gives the WINS server a backup via the log file. If you deactivate logging, the WINS server registers names more quickly—but you lose the backup support of the log file.

◆ **Log Detailed Events.** If you turn this on, the logging of WINS events in Event Viewer is more verbose. This means that you get more useful troubleshooting information from the log file. However, some performance degradation occurs when verbose logging is turned on.

◆ **Replicate Only With Partners.** By default, WINS replicates only with other WINS servers that are specifically configured as push or pull partners. If you want the WINS server to replicate automatically with other WINS servers, you must turn off this setting. This will allow your WINS server to pick up entries from a server that it learns about through a replication partner.

◆ **Backup On Termination.** If you set this option, the WINS database is automatically backed up when the WINS service is stopped. However, the database is not backed up when the Windows NT server is shut down.

◆ **Migrate On/Off.** If this switch is on, static entries that have the same address as a WINS client requesting registration are overwritten. This option is helpful if you are converting a computer from a non-Microsoft operating system to a Microsoft operating system with the same TCP/IP address. To have addresses resolved for this non-Microsoft machine in the past, you may have added a static entry to the WINS database. With the option on, the new dynamic entry can overwrite the old static entry.

◆ **Starting Version Count.** This specifies the largest version ID number for the database. Each entry in the database is assigned a version ID on which replication is based. A replication partner checks its last replicated entries against the version IDs of the records in the WINS database. The replication partner replicates only records with a version ID assigned later than the last records it replicated from this partner. Usually, you don't need to change this parameter. However, if the database becomes corrupted, you may need to adjust this number so that a replication partner replicates the proper entries.

◆ **Database Backup Path.** When the WINS database is backed up, it is copied to a local hard drive. This option specifies the path to a directory on a local drive where the WINS backups are stored. This directory can also be used to automatically restore the WINS database. You must specify a local drive path here before the system performs automatic backups.

BACKING UP THE WINS DATABASE

A database can be backed up automatically when WINS shuts down. You also can schedule or manually start a backup. All backups are copied to the backup directory specified in the Advanced Configuration options.

You can manually start a WINS backup from the Mappings menu in the WINS Manager. To schedule backups to occur automatically, configure the path for a backup directory. After you set this path, the WINS server automatically runs the backup every 24 hours.

Restoring the WINS Database

You can restore the WINS database from the backups you made previously. To restore the database, choose Restore database from the Mappings menu in WINS Manager.

WINS will automatically restore the database from the specified backup directory if it starts and detects a corrupted database. If you suspect the database is corrupt, you can stop and start the WINS service from Control Panel, Services to force this automatic restoration.

Files Used for WINS

The WINS database is stored in the directory \WINNT\ SYSTEM32\WINS. Several files make up the WINS database:

◆ **WINS.MDB.** This is the WINS database itself.

◆ **WINSTMP.MDB.** This is a temporary working file used by WINS. This file is normally deleted when the WINS server is shut down, but a copy could remain in the directory after a crash.

◆ **J50.LOG.** This is the transaction log of the WINS database.

◆ **J50.CHK.** This is a checkpoint file used by the WINS database. It is equivalent to a cache for a disk drive.

COMPACTING THE WINS DATABASE

You can compact the WINS database to reduce its size. However, WINS under Windows NT 4.0 is designed to automatically compact the database, so you shouldn't have to do it yourself.

To force manual compacting of the database, use the JETPACK utility in the \WINNT\SYSTEM32\WINS directory. (The WINS database is a JET database, so this utility packs that database.) To pack the database, you must first stop the WINS service; you cannot pack an open database.

Type the following command to compact the database:

```
jetpack WINS.mdb winstemp.mdb
```

This command compacts the database into the file winstemp.mdb, and then it copies the compacted database to WINS.mdb. The temporary file is deleted. After the database is compacted, you can restart the WINS service from Control Panel, Services.

CASE STUDY: ADDING NAME RESOLUTION TO THE SUNSHINE BREWING COMPANY NETWORK

ESSENCE OF THE CASE

There are other concerns that will need to be addressed as you configure the name resolution issue. Here are a few of these concerns:

• The company operates as a single-domain model; therefore, you will need to be able to perform name resolution between domain controllers to facilitate the synchronization of the domain-accounts database. This also means that every system will need to be able to find the primary domain controller so that they will be able to change passwords.

• There is a considerable number of laptop users who need to be able to find the resources from their local network regardless of where they travel.

• All users will need to be able to connect to the Microsoft Exchange network to collect and send email.

As you return to the Sunshine Brewing Company, you need to look at the issue of name resolution. Name resolution is used to connect to a system with an available server service (or other network service).

There are two keys issues that you will need to look at here. First, how many servers are there, and who has to connect to them? Second, where are the systems physically located?

SCENARIO

As you look at this network, you see four basic types of offices to address:

• **Head Office.** The largest of the offices, there are resources here that all users will require access to. This includes an SQL server (configured for TCP/IP on port 1433) and a series of newsgroups on an IIS 4.0 server.

• **Regional Offices.** These offices use the resources of the Head Office servers, including the SQL Server. They also have file and print servers for the local users.

• **Production Centers.** These offices need to connect to the Head Office SQL server to receive the orders for production. There is also the normal need to provide local file and print services.

• **Sales Offices.** These centers will need to be able to connect to the Head Office SQL server to post orders. They, too, need local file and print services.

continues

continued

ANALYSIS

Because you will need to be able to find several of the servers that are located at Head Office, and because you will need to deal with laptop users, you should use WINS to some degree.

There are basically four areas in which name resolution becomes a problem that cannot be handled on the local network:

- Connecting to Head Office
- Synchronizing the domain
- Connecting to Exchange
- Connecting to the home office for laptop users

These need to be considered carefully because you could, in theory, saturate the backbone Internet connections with WINS replication. You must also know the number of times that users will connect to local systems versus remote systems.

Before you can come to a full conclusion, you need to learn more about name resolution (see Chapter 8) so that you know what the LMHOSTS file can do. However, in the current situation the following solution might be workable.

To facilitate the local connections, establish a WINS server in each of the local offices. Then set up all the hosts to use the WINS server. Next, create a static entry for the servers that users connect to in the Head Office (these will need to be updated if the IP addresses change). This will allow for the connection to the Head Office without replication.

The Exchange server problem can be eliminated using the same strategy. The domain activity simply requires that you create a domain group on each of the WINS servers that lists all the domain controllers that are likely to become the PDC.

A problem still remains, though, with the laptop users having to connect to their home server. This could force you to use replication (which is not bad, but can use up the bandwidth to the Internet). An alternative solution is the LMHOSTS file; this lists the IP address and name of NetBIOS servers. You could configure each laptop with an LMHOSTS file that lists the user's home server and its IP address.

This is not necessarily the best solution. However, you will refine this scenario after you gain a better understanding of the entire name resolution issue.

CHAPTER SUMMARY

This chapter covered the installation and configuration of a WINS server. Additionally, the configuration of WINS clients and WINS proxies were discussed. You need to be familiar with all aspects of installation and configuration.

Following are the key items that you need to understand:

◆ You need to understand that the WINS server resolves NetBIOS names to IP addresses. Furthermore, it reduces over-all network traffic by using directed transmissions.

◆ You should be able to install the WINS server and configure WINS clients both manually and using DHCP.

◆ You need to understand the purpose of a WINS proxy agent and how to configure Windows NT as a proxy agent.

◆ You need to know what the configuration parameters for the WINS server are and how to set them.

◆ You need to know the types of static entries and how to add them.

◆ You must understand how and why to import the LMHOSTS files and the reason for the Migrate On/Off option in the con-figuration.

◆ You must understand that replication is set up in pairs—one push and one pull. Furthermore, you need to know the effect of the Replicate Only With Partners button.

◆ You should know about the Replicate with Self Finding Partners feature, and how to turn it off.

◆ You also need to know how to back up and compact the WINS database.

KEY TERMS
• extinction
• name registration
• name release
• name renewal
• name resolution
• NetBIOS name
• scavenging
• Verify Interval
• WINS
• WINS proxy
• WINS replication

APPLY YOUR KNOWLEDGE

Exercises

In this series of exercise you will have a chance to work with a WINS server.

5.1   Installing a WINS Server

In this exercise, you will install and configure your WINS server to use itself as the primary WINS server. Assume that you have installed Windows NT 4.0 Server with the TCP/IP protocol.

Estimated Time: About five minutes.

1. Right-click on Network Neighborhood and choose Properties from the menu. (Network Properties can also be accessed from the Network icon in Control Panel.)

2. Select the Services tab, and then choose Add. From the Network Service box, select Windows Internet Name Service, and then choose OK.

3. Select the Protocols tab, select TCP/IP Protocol, and then choose Properties.

4. Select the WINS Address tab. Enter the TCP/IP address of your Windows NT server as the primary WINS server.

5. Choose OK, and then close the Network Properties dialog box.

6. When prompted, choose Yes to restart your server.

For a review of the material in this exercise, see "Installing a WINS Server."

5.2   Adding Static Entries to a WINS Database

In this exercise, you will manually add static entries to the WINS database through WINS Manager.

Estimated Time: About 10 minutes.

1. Choose Start, Programs, Administrative Tools.

2. From the Administrative Tools menu, choose WINS Manager.

3. From the Mappings menu in WINS Manager, choose Static Mappings.

4. Choose Add Mappings.

5. In the computer box, type **ABDCE**.

6. In the IP Address box, type **131.107.2.25**.

7. In the Type box, select Unique.

8. Choose Add to save the entry.

9. Add an entry for a computer named "FGHIJ" with an IP address of 133.107.4.53 of a Group type.

10. Add an entry for a computer named "KLMNO" with an IP address of 136.107.3.34 of a Domain Name type. Note that with the Domain Name mappings you must also move the IP address down with the arrow before you can save it. This is because you can have multiple addresses (for multiple domain controllers) associated with a domain name.

11. Close the Add Static Mappings dialog. Note the mappings you have added.

12. Try editing each of the entries. Note that the type of each entry differs. Note also that the Edit Static Mapping dialog for the domain mapping differs from the dialogs for the unique and group types.

13. Explore the Edit Static Mapping dialogs; then close the Static Mappings dialog box.

14. In the WINS Manager window, choose Show Database from the Mappings menu.

APPLY YOUR KNOWLEDGE

15. Scroll down the mappings database and note the static entries you added. The static mappings are marked with a check in the S column.

16. Sort the database by expiration date. Scroll to the bottom of the database and note that the static mappings are there with a time stamp that won't let these entries expire.

17. Close the Show Database window.

For a review of this, see "Adding Static Mappings."

5.3   Importing an LMHOSTS File into the WINS Database

In this exercise, you will create and import an LMHOSTS file (explained fully in Chapter 8).

Estimated Time: About five minutes.

1. In Explorer, locate LMHOSTS.SAM. This file is located in the System32\Drivers\Etc subdirectory of your Windows NT root directory.

2. Edit LMHOSTS.SAM with Notepad.

3. Remove the # comment characters in front of the lines registering IP addresses for rhino, appname, popular, and localsrv.

4. Save this file as LMHOSTS. Now the file is ready for importing.

5. Choose Start, Programs, Administrative Tools.

6. From the Administrative Tools menu, choose WINS Manager.

7. From the Mappings menu in WINS Manager, choose Static Mappings.

8. Choose the Import Mappings button.

9. Browse to find the LMHOSTS file you modified, and then choose that file.

10. Choose Open.

11. Note that the names from the LMHOSTS file have been added to the static mappings.

12. Close the Static Mappings dialog.

13. From the Mappings menu, choose Show Database.

14. Note that the mappings you added from the LMHOSTS file are now in the WINS database.

For a review of this topic, see "Importing Mappings."

5.4   Configuring the WINS Server

This exercise will give you a chance to view and change the configuration of the WINS server.

Estimated Time: About 10 minutes.

1. Choose Start, Programs, Administrative Tools.

2. From the Administrative Tools menu, choose WINS Manager.

3. From the Server menu, choose Configuration.

4. Note the default times (six days, or 144 hours) for the Renewal Interval, Extinction Interval, and Extinction Timeout. These times dictate how quickly a WINS database entry moves from active to released, from released to extinct, and from extinct to being removed from the database, respectively. Note that Microsoft recommends you do not modify these values.

5. Note the default time for the verify interval—24 days (576 hours). This specifies when a WINS server verifies that entries it does not own (entries added to the database upon replication) are still active. The minimum value you can set for this parameter is 24 days.

APPLY YOUR KNOWLEDGE

6. Note the check box that allows you to perform push or pull replication when the WINS server initializes.

7. Choose the Advanced button.

8. Note two of the settings here that can affect WINS performance: Logging Enabled and Log Detailed Events. With Logging Enabled, WINS must first write any changes to the WINS database to the JET.LOG file. Then the changes are made to the database. This log file serves as an ongoing backup to the database should it crash during the write process. However, if a number of changes are made to the database simultaneously, logging can slow WINS performance. This is a problem when, for example, everyone powers up their computers in the morning and the clients try to register at the same time. With Log Detailed Events turned on, more-detailed messages are written to the Event Log. Note that both settings are turned on by default.

9. Note the default setting for Replicate Only With Partners. WINS replicates only with specified partners unless you turn this setting off. When it is deactivated, WINS tries to replicate with all the WINS servers it can locate through broadcasts.

10. Choose OK to close the Configuration dialog.

For a review of this material, see "WINS Server Configuration."

5.5 Configuring a DHCP Client to be a WINS Client

The purpose of this exercise is to configure DHCP clients to automatically receive WINS client configuration through the DHCP scope.

Estimated Time: About five minutes.

1. Choose Start, Programs, Administrative Tools.

2. From the Administrative Tools menu, choose DHCP Manager.

3. In the DHCP Manager window, choose the local machine.

4. Select the scope created under the local machine.

5. From the DHCP Options menu, select Scope.

6. In the Unused Options box, select 044 WINS/NBNS Servers and choose Add.

7. In the Unused Options box, select 046 WINS/NBNS Node Type and choose Add.

8. From the Active Options box, select 044 WINS/NBNS Servers and choose Value.

9. Choose Edit Array, type the address of your WINS server, and then choose Add.

10. Choose OK to close the IP Address Array Editor.

11. From the Active Options box, select 046 WINS/NBNS Node Type.

12. In the Byte box, change the value 0x1 (b-node broadcast) to 0x8 (h-node broadcast).

13. Choose OK. The scope options are now set for DHCP clients from this scope to automatically become clients of your WINS server.

For a review of this material, see "Configuring a Client for WINS Using DHCP."

Review Questions

1. How often must WINS clients renew their name registrations with the WINS server?

2. How are entries removed from the WINS database?

APPLY YOUR KNOWLEDGE

3. How can a WINS client resolve addresses that are located in another WINS server's database?

4. How do you configure a WINS server to receive entries from another WINS server's database?

5. How do you configure two WINS servers so they have identical databases?

6. How can you back up a WINS server database?

7. How can you restore a WINS server database? Does this ever happen automatically?

8. On what platform can you install WINS, and how do you install it?

9. When does push replication occur and when does pull replication occur?

10. How is a WINS client configured to use a WINS server?

Exam Questions

1. How does a WINS server gather entries to add to its database?

    A. It examines each packet sent on the network.

    B. It receives a copy of the browse list from the master browser on each network segment.

    C. WINS clients send a name registration to the WINS server.

    D. It retrieves a copy of the computer accounts in each domain.

2. Where does a client first look to resolve a NetBIOS name?

    A. In the NetBIOS name cache on the WINS server

    B. In the NetBIOS name cache on the WINS proxy agent

    C. In the NetBIOS name cache on the primary domain controller

    D. In the NetBIOS name cache on the client

3. How do you configure an automatic backup of the WINS database?

    A. Use the AT command to schedule the backup.

    B. Specify the name of the backup directory in WINS Manager.

    C. Specify the backup interval in WINS Manager.

    D. Install a tape device through Control Panel, SCSI Adapters.

4. When does a WINS client try to renew its registration?

    A. After three days

    B. One day before the registration expires

    C. Every 24 hours

    D. When one-eighth of the registration life has expired

5. By default, where does the WINS server first write changes to the database?

    A. To the log file

    B. To the database

    C. To the Registry

    D. To the temporary database

6. How do you configure replication to occur at specified intervals?

    A. Configure a WINS server to be a pull partner.

B. Use the AT command to schedule replication.

C. Configure a WINS server to be a push partner.

D. Edit the ReplIntrvl parameter in the Registry.

7. How can you add entries for non-WINS clients to a WINS server's database?

A. Configure the WINS server to be a pull partner for a DNS server.

B. Import an LMHOSTS file.

C. Install the WINS proxy agent on the segment with non-WINS clients.

D. Add the entries with WINS Manager.

8. When is an entry scavenged from the WINS database?

A. When a WINS client requests a name release.

B. When a name registration expires without renewal.

C. When an entry has been marked extinct.

D. When the extinction interval has elapsed.

9. What does a WINS server do if it receives a name registration request for a hostname already in its database?

A. It replaces the old entry with the newer one.

B. It queries the host of the existing registration to see whether the registration is still valid.

C. It denies the registration request.

D. It adds the registration as an alternative address for the existing name.

10. How do you install a WINS proxy agent on Windows NT?

A. From Control Panel, Network, Services

B. From Control Panel, Add Programs

C. By changing a Registry entry

D. By running the Network Client Administration tool from the WINS program group

11. How can you configure a WINS server to automatically replicate its database with any other WINS servers?

A. Specify All Servers as push partners for replication.

B. Turn on the Migrate On/Off switch in WINS Manager.

C. Change the UseSelfFndPnrs parameter in the Registry to 0.

D. Do nothing; this is the default configuration.

12. Which WINS server will a client decide to use?

A. The first WINS server that responds to a broadcast

B. The WINS server that WINS an election

C. The initial WINS server configured in TCP/IP

D. The primary WINS server specified in the DHCP scope options

13. What happens to a name registration when the host crashes?

A. The WINS server marks the record as released after it queries the client at half of TTL.

B. The name is marked as released after three renewal periods are missed.

C. The name is scavenged after the registration expires.

D. The name is released after the TTL is over.

APPLY YOUR KNOWLEDGE

14. On which platforms can you install a WINS server?

    A. On a Windows NT 3.51 member server

    B. On a Windows NT 4.0 workstation running the WINS proxy agent

    C. On a Windows NT 4.0 backup domain controller

    D. On a Windows NT 4.0 primary domain controller

15. How many WINS servers should be installed?

    A. One primary for each subnet and one secondary for every two subnets

    B. One primary for every 2,000 clients and one secondary for each additional 2,000 clients

    C. One primary and one secondary for every 10,000 clients

    D. One primary and secondary for each domain

16. How do you configure automatic address resolution for DHCP clients?

    A. Specify the NBNS/WINS Server option in the DHCP scope.

    B. Install a WINS server with an address specified by the DHCP scope.

    C. Schedule the active leases to be copied from DCHP Manager to an LMHOSTS file.

    D. Locate a DHCP relay agent on the same subnet as the WINS server.

17. Where should a WINS proxy agent be located?

    A. On the same subnet as non-WINS clients

    B. On the same subnet as the DHCP server

    C. On the same subnet as the DNS server

    D. On the same subnet as the DHCP Relay Agent

18. To configure a DHCP scope to use WINS, what should the WINS/NBT Node type be set to?

    A. 0x1

    B. 0x2

    C. 0x4

    D. 0x8

19. How can the WINS clients of one WINS server resolve the addresses of clients registered with another WINS server?

    A. The WINS server can be configured for recursive lookup to the other WINS server.

    B. The WINS server can be a replication partner of the other server.

    C. The client can be configured with the address of the other WINS server as its secondary WINS server.

    D. The WINS servers automatically synchronize their databases.

20. Where is WINS configuration information stored?

    A. In the \WINNT\SYSTEM32\WINS directory

    B. In the Registry

    C. In the WINS.CFG file in the WINNT directory

    D. In the J50.CHK file in the WINS directory

APPLY YOUR KNOWLEDGE

21. Which replication option is best for WINS servers separated by a slow WAN link?

    A. Pull replication configured to replicate after 100 changes

    B. Push replication configured to replicate after 100 changes

    C. Pull replication configured to replicate at 6 a.m. and 6 p.m.

    D. Push replication configured to replicate at 6 a.m. and 6 p.m.

22. The administrator of the local area network is trying to set up WINS. The local area network has a mix of clients, including DOS/Windows 3.1, Windows 95, and Windows NT Workstation. There are two segments on the network, and the types of systems are spread across the different networks.

    A Windows NT Server handles routing and file and print services between the two segments. The Administrator is planning to set up the WINS server on the router and use DHCP to distribute the WINS address and the IP addresses. How does this solution work?

    A. This is the best possible solution.

    B. This is a good solution.

    C. This solution works but is far from optimal.

    D. This solution does not work.

23. Your company has two offices connected by a T1 leased line. One office has three segments, connected using a fast Ethernet switch, that support 180 systems in total. The other office has a single segment that supports 50 users. You are converting to Windows NT from NetWare 3.12 and are planning the WINS implementation.

You decide that you will install WINS on a computer in the larger network and point all the systems to that WINS server. How good is this design?

A. This is the best possible solution.

B. This is a good solution.

C. This solution works but is far from optimal.

D. This solution does not work.

Answers to Review Questions

1. Clients first register their names with the WINS server when they start up. Upon successful registration, they receive a time-to-live for their registration from the WINS server. Clients try to renew the registration when half this time has elapsed. The default time-to-live is six days, so the WINS client tries to renew its registration after three days. After the client renews its registration, the new time to live is, again, six days; so in another three days the client renews its registration. See "How WINS Works."

2. Entries can be removed either when a client requests a release or when the registration expires. A client normally sends a registration release request when it shuts down. The WINS server marks released entries as inactive. If the client has not renewed its registration when its time-to-live expires (assuming the client has not released the registration), the WINS server marks the entry as released. After the specified extinction interval (the default is six days), the entry is marked extinct. The entry is not removed from the data-

APPLY YOUR KNOWLEDGE

base until the extinction timeout interval is reached (also six days, by default). In total, then, a client's address can remain in the WINS server database for 18 days (six days for the time-to-live, six days for the extinction interval, and six days for the extinction timeout) after the initial registration, even if the client never renews its registration. See "How WINS Works."

3. A WINS client queries only those WINS servers specified as its primary and secondary WINS servers. However, you can have a number of WINS servers on the network, with each server servicing a different set of clients. You can configure the WINS servers to copy their entries to another server through replication. See "How WINS Works."

4. Configure the target WINS server as a replication partner of the source WINS server. To receive entries from another server, the WINS server must be a pull partner. You must also configure the source WINS server as a replication partner. To send entries to another WINS server, the local WINS server must be a push partner. You must configure both servers as replication partners of the other WINS server, or else replication will not happen. See "Replication."

5. You must configure each server as both a push and a pull replication partner for the other WINS server. Being a push partner sends a WINS server's entries to its partner. Being a pull partner lets a WINS server receive entries from its partner. See "Replication."

6. You must specify a backup directory path in WINS Manager. When the WINS server starts, and every 24 hours thereafter, it automatically backs up this directory. You can also manually

back up a WINS server through WINS Manager. See "Backing Up the WINS Database."

7. You can restore a WINS database backup manually through WINS Manager. A WINS server attempts to automatically restore a backup when it detects a corrupt database upon startup. You can force this automatic restoration when you suspect a corrupt database by stopping and starting the WINS service. See "Backing Up the WINS Database."

8. You can install a WINS server on an NT server version 3.5x or 4.0. It can be on any variety of server: a member server, a backup domain controller, or a primary domain controller. You can install the WINS service during installation, but you normally install it later by configuring the network properties of the server through Control Panel, Network. See "Installing a WINS Server."

9. Push replication is configured to occur after a certain number of changes are made to the WINS database. This is usually used for replication partners on the same subnet, so replication can occur fairly often with only a small amount of traffic transmitted with each replication attempt.

Pull replication is configured to take place at certain time intervals. Pull replication first occurs at a specified starting time and then at specified intervals thereafter. Using the time setting for pull replication, you can schedule replication during hours when network traffic is at its lowest. This type of replication is typically used when a slow WAN link separates replication partners. During heavy traffic times on a WAN link, it is not usually desirable to have constant traffic between servers, such as the traffic generated by push replication. See "Replication."

APPLY YOUR KNOWLEDGE

10. If the client is manually configured with a TCP/IP address, the address of a primary WINS server must also be configured. Although not required, you can also configure the address of a secondary WINS server.

    If the client receives its TCP/IP address from the WINS server, you must configure the options of the DHCP scope to include the address of a primary WINS server. You can also specify the address of a secondary WINS server. One additional parameter you must configure in the DHCP scope is the type of broadcasts (h-node) used for WINS. See "WINS Clients."

Answers to Exam Questions

1. **C.** The WINS server builds its database based on the registration requests sent from the clients. Neither the browse list nor the computer's accounts list contains the IP address. WINS is intended to reduce traffic; reading the information on the network would rely on this and force all systems to use broadcasts. See "How WINS Works."

2. **D.** The client will always check the local NetBIOS name cache. This is kept in memory and, therefore, is the only cache it can check. See "How WINS Works."

3. **B.** All you need to do is specify the directory in the WINS configuration, and WINS will automatically backup every 24 hours. See "Backing Up the WINS Database."

4. **D.** A WINS client will start trying to renew its name registration at one-eighth of the time-to-live. If the server is not available, the client will try again every two minutes. See "Name Renewal."

5. **A.** The WINS server will use a log file to provide fault tolerance. This is the same system used by SQL servers to ensure that a database can be returned to a known consistent state. See "WINS Server Configuration."

6. **A.** If you configure the WINS servers to use pull replication, the servers will pull the changes at a given interval. This is useful when replication takes place over a slow WAN link. See "Replication."

7. **B** and **D.** If you have been using an LMHOSTS file, you can import the mappings in the Static Mappings dialog box. You can also add other entries there. See "Importing Mappings."

8. **D.** Scavenging is the removal of extinct intervals from the database; this is when entries will be removed. See "WINS Server Configuration."

9. **B.** The WINS server will verify the name is still in use. This allows systems to move from IP address to IP address (such as laptops might) and still be able to register their names. See "Name Registration."

10. **C.** Although configuring a proxy agent on Windows 95 or Windows for Workgroups is a simple configuration option, in Windows NT you need to modify the Registry to enable this function. See "Resolving Names for Non-WINS Clients."

APPLY YOUR KNOWLEDGE

11. **D.** When WINS is installed, the Use Self Finding Partners option is enabled. This uses a multicast address to allow WINS server to find each other and configure replication between themselves. See "Replication."

12. **D.** In this case the client would use the WINS server that was sent to it from the DHCP server. There is no Initial WINS Server entry in the configuration, only a Primary and a Secondary. See "WINS Clients."

13. **D.** The only time a WINS server will attempt to verify that a client exists is if there is another registration of the same name. Therefore, the WINS server will remove the registration only for a system that crashes after the time-to-live has expired. See "Name Release" and "WINS Server Configuration."

14. **A, C,** and **D.** The WINS server must be installed on Windows NT Server version 3.5 or above. See "Installing a WINS Server."

15. **C.** The Microsoft recommendation for WINS servers is one primary WINS server and one backup WINS server for every 10,000 computers. See "Implementing WINS."

16. **A.** You can add the WINS server address to the DHCP scope or global options. This will configure the DHCP clients to use the WINS servers automatically. See "Configuring a Client for WINS Using DHCP."

17. **A.** The purpose of a proxy agent is to receive NetBIOS name queries and respond to them for non-WINS clients. These queries are restricted

to the local subnet and, therefore, the WINS proxy needs to be on the same subnet as the non-WINS clients. See "Resolving Names for Non-WINS Clients."

18. **D.** The NBT Node Type should set to 0x8 to tell the system to use the WINS server and that it doesn't work to use a local broadcast. See "Configuring a Client for WINS Using DHCP."

19. **B** and **D.** The WINS server would need to have replication set up. This allows the clients to synchronize their databases. This could happen automatically with replication using "self finding partners." See "Replication."

20. **B.** As with all other NT services, the configuration of the WINS server is in the Registry. See "Automatic Replication."

21. **C.** Pull replication can be set for time-based replication. This is preferred for a slow link because the traffic from updates would normally slow the line during busy periods. See "Replication."

22. **D.** This solution does not work. The DOS clients will not be able to see the WINS Server for file and print services on one side of the router because the DOS client will always try to get the first IP address returned by the WINS server. See "WINS on a Multihomed Computer."

23. **B.** This is a good solution unless the leased line between the two offices goes down. If this happens, the systems on the smaller network must try to time out on the WINS server before they broadcast. See "Implementation Considerations."

Suggested Readings and Resources

1. Siyan, Karanjit S. *Windows NT Server 4 Professional Reference.* New Riders, 1996.

2. Heywood, Drew. *Inside Windows NT Server 4.* New Riders, 1997.

3. Maione, Dennis. *MCSE Training Guide: Windows NT Server 4, Second Edition.* New Riders, 1998.

4. Sirockman, Jason. *MCSE Training Guide: Windows NT Server 4 Enterprise, Second Edition.* New Riders, 1998.

5. *TechNet.* MS Windows NT Server 4.0— WINS Architecture and Capacity Planning.

This chapter helps you prepare for the exam by covering the following objective:

Configure a Windows NT Server computer to function as an IP router.

▶ This particular objective was actually covered in Chapter 2, "Installing Microsoft TCP/IP." However, this chapter is included to provide you with further information that will help you understand the purpose of IP. Even though this information is not specifically in the objectives list, knowing this material is critical to passing the exam.

CHAPTER 6

IP Routing

STUDY STRATEGIES

As you read through this chapter, you should concentrate on the following key items:

▶ You should understand the difference between dynamic and static routing.

▶ You need to know how to use the ROUTE command.

▶ You should understand how to add a static route.

▶ You should know how to integrate static and dynamic routers.

The first two chapters, which really began the discussion of routing, provided you with the building blocks that are required to understand routing. Remember from those chapters that the IP layer is responsible for finding a route to the target host if it determines (using the subnet mask) that the host is remote instead of local.

The process of AND'ing was introduced in Chapter 2. You were shown how the IP address of the sending host and the subnet mask undergo this process, which provides the system with the network ID of the local host. Then IP ANDs the IP address of the target host and the subnet mask of the sending host.

The result of the second AND'ing process matches the result of the first in only one case: if the target is on the local network. In this case IP has very little to do; it simply lets ARP find the MAC address of the remote host and sends the data to NDIS for transmission.

INTRODUCTION TO ROUTING

The routing process is only slightly different if the target host is remote. In this case IP checks the local routing table to see if there is a path to the remote network. All IP-enabled systems do this—not just routers.

Looking at a normal computer using TCP/IP, you will find a routing table. In Windows NT you can view this using either ROUTE PRINT or, for the UNIX folks, NETSTAT -r. The output from this command looks something like this:

```
Active Routes:

      Network Address          Netmask  Gateway Address        Interface   Metric
            0.0.0.0          0.0.0.0       10.10.3.1      10.10.3.200        1
           10.10.3.0  255.255.255.0     10.10.3.200      10.10.3.200        1
         10.10.3.200  255.255.255.255      127.0.0.1        127.0.0.1        1
      10.255.255.255  255.255.255.255    10.10.3.200      10.10.3.200        1
           127.0.0.0        255.0.0.0      127.0.0.1        127.0.0.1        1
           224.0.0.0        224.0.0.0    10.10.3.200      10.10.3.200        1
     255.255.255.255  255.255.255.255    10.10.3.200      10.10.3.200        1
```

The system performs the AND'ing process with each netmask of the target IP address. The result is then compared with the entry under Network Address. If the Network Addresses match, the route has been found and the packet is sent to the listed gateway address through the interface (network card).

The only strange part is that the system starts at the bottom of the list and works its way up. If you look closely at the routing table, you will notice that the most restrictive subnet masks are at the bottom and the least restrictive subnet masks are at the top (from 255.255.255.255 to 0.0.0.0).

By listing the subnet masks in this way, the system is essentially looking for routes to individual hosts, and then to whole networks. The top (or last) entry is the catch-all entry or, as you know it, the default gateway. (Try AND'ing anything you like with 0.0.0.0 and see if it doesn't come out as 0.0.0.0.)

If your system had two network cards, each on a separate network, there would be a route to each of these networks. If a system knows about two networks, it can pass traffic between them. This requires that you enable IP routing, which will tell your system to look at the destination IP address and, if a packet is not intended for your own system, to send the packet to its next destination (using the routing table). The routing table for a basic router might look like the following:

```
Active Routes:

Network Address          Netmask  Gateway Address      Interface    Metric
        0.0.0.0          0.0.0.0      10.10.3.254       10.10.3.1        1
       10.10.4.0    255.255.255.0       10.10.4.1       10.10.4.1        1
       10.10.4.1  255.255.255.255       127.0.0.1       127.0.0.1        1
       10.10.3.0    255.255.255.0       10.10.3.1       10.10.3.1        1
       10.10.3.1  255.255.255.255       127.0.0.1       127.0.0.1        1
  10.255.255.255  255.255.255.255       10.10.3.1       10.10.3.1        1
      127.0.0.0        255.0.0.0       127.0.0.1       127.0.0.1        1
      224.0.0.0        224.0.0.0       10.10.3.1       10.10.3.1        1
 255.255.255.255  255.255.255.255       10.10.3.1       10.10.3.1        1
```

Notice that there are entries for two specific networks in this list. This system would act as a router between networks called 10.10.3.0 and 10.10.4.0. In this case the router is a static router, which is one of the two types of routers that you will deal with. (Routing tables are covered fully in the section "Viewing the Routing Table.")

STATIC AND DYNAMIC ROUTERS

As you now know, routers have built-in tables used to determine where to send a packet destined for a particular network. By default, any given router knows only about networks to which it is physically attached. This section will show you how routers find out about networks to which they are not physically attached—either through manual configuration or automatic (dynamic) configuration.

Static routers are not able to discover networks other than those with which they have a physical interface. For this type of router to be able to route packets to any other network, you need to manually enter a route. This can be done either by using a default gateway on the router or by editing the routing table.

Microsoft Windows NT can act as a static router. As has been discussed, this involves setting up multiple network cards and IP addresses and enabling routing. In a static router environment, new remote networks are not reflected in the routing tables on these routers.

Dynamic routers, on the other hand, use routing protocols that simply provide a language that routers can use to communicate with other routers about changes to their routing tables. In this way, routing tables are built dynamically, and the administrator does not have to manually edit route tables to bring up a new network segment.

The most popular routing protocols are the Routing Information Protocol (RIP) and Open Shortest Path First protocol (OSPF). RIP is a broadcast-based protocol used primarily on smaller networks. The more sophisticated OSPF protocol is used for medium and large networks. Microsoft Windows NT 4.0 supports the installation and use of RIP to provide dynamic routing for multihomed computers. OSPF is also available for NT; however, it is a third-party solution.

Again, using either routing protocol allows routing tables to be updated whenever any additions to a network occur. RIP or OSPF, if used in a routed environment, should eliminate most of the need to manually edit route tables in your environment. These protocols are described in detail later in the chapter.

The Static Routing Environment

In the simplest case a router connects two network segments (see Figure 6.1). In this case the system used to join the two segments needs to know only about these segments.

The routing table for router R1 in this case is simple; the following table shows its key routes:

Network Address	Netmask	Gateway	Interface
148.16.4.0	255.255.252.0	148.16.4.1	148.16.4.1
148.16.8.0	255.255.252.0	148.16.8.1	148.16.8.1

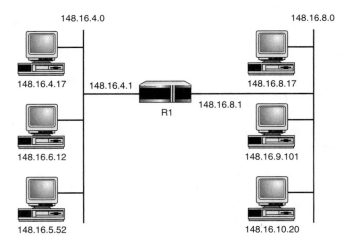

FIGURE 6.1
A simple network with two segments and a single router.

When the station at 148.16.6.12 attempts to communicate with the station at 148.16.10.20, IP performs the AND'ing process to determine two things: The local network ID is 148.16.4.0, and the destination network ID is not. This means, of course, that the destination host is not on the local network.

IP, therefore, is responsible for finding a route to the remote network, and it will consult the routing table. Here the local host will normally determine that the next step in the route is the default gateway, and it will send the packet to router R1.

Router R1 then receives the packet. After determining the packet is for another host and not the router itself, it checks the routing table. The router finds the route to 148.16.8.0 and sends the packet through the interface—and the system at 148.16.10.20 receives the packet.

This is a very simple route that takes only a single hop. However, when another network is added (as the number of hosts grows, or to accommodate physical or corporate structure), this simplicity is lost, and the systems on the most distant networks cannot communicate (see Figure 6.2).

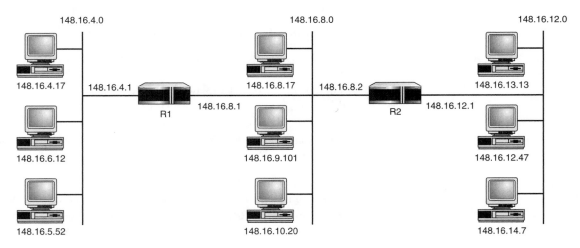

FIGURE 6.2
A network with three subnets forces you to configure static routes.

When the host at 148.16.5.52 wants to send data to the system at 148.16.12.47, the same steps will be followed as before. However, when the router receives the packet in this case, it cannot find a route to the remote network. The packet is discarded and an ICMP message indicating "destination host unreachable" is sent to the originating system.

You need to do one of two things to make routing work in this environment:

◆ Add a default gateway to the router's configuration.

◆ Add a manual entry in the router's internal table.

These two options are explained and compared in the following sections.

Static Routing Using a Default Gateway

The default gateway solution is simple and makes sense: Tell router R1 to send to R2 anything that it has no route for, and vice versa. Now there is a route when the system at 148.16.5.52 tries to communicate with 148.16.12.47. This is the default gateway that, if you remember from earlier, is entered as follows for router R1:

Network Address	*Netmask*	*Gateway*	*Interface*
0.0.0.0	0.0.0.0	148.16.8.2	148.16.8.1

This forces the router to send the packet to the next router, which in this case has a route to the destination network. Although this seems like a simple solution, you need to remember that a default gateway is not tied to a single card. This means that when more networks are added, there will be problems like the one presented in Figure 6.3.

In this case there are five networks connected by routers. At first glance you might be tempted to set the default gateway of router R1 to R2, and R2 to R3, and so on. This will work fine if all communications are one-way, because packets can travel left to right.

The problem is trying to get the packet back from right to left. For example, if a system on the 148.16.4.0 network PINGs a system on the 148.16.20.0 network, the following actions occur at the routers:

1. Router R1 forwards the packet to router R2.

2. Router R2 forwards the packet to router R3.

3. Router R3 forwards the packet to router R4.

4. Router R4 sends the packet to the system that attempts to respond.

5. Router R4 sends the packet to router R3.

6. Router R3 doesn't know the network and forwards the packet to R4—not R2.

The packet in this case will bounce between routers R3 and R4 until its time-to-live expires. What is required in a larger network function is that all routers need to be aware of the other networks.

Static Routing Using the ROUTE Command

Because the default gateway solution starts falling apart with more than two networks, you will probably need to be able to add routes to a system acting as a router. This will require that you use the ROUTE command to view and add routes.

Using the ROUTE Command

The ROUTE command has a number of switches that can be used to statically manage a route table. Up to this point, the ROUTE PRINT command is the only parameter that you have seen. To manage a route table, however, an administrator must be able to add,

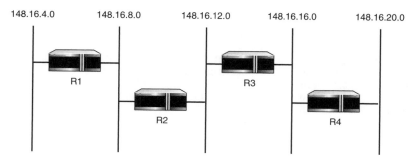

FIGURE 6.3

As the network grows, using the default gateway solution no longer works.

delete, change, and clear route table entries. Each of these options is available; the following table shows each respective command:

To Add or Modify a Static Route	*Function*
ROUTE ADD [net id] MASK [netmask][gateway]	Adds a route
ROUTE -p ADD [net id] MASK [netmask][gateway]	Adds a persistent route
ROUTE DELETE [net id]	Deletes a route
ROUTE CHANGE [net id][gateway]	Modifies a route
ROUTE PRINT	Displays route table
ROUTE -f	Clears (flushes) all routes

Notice the entry that uses a -p (persistent) before the ADD parameter. This parameter is required because the entries in the routing table are normally kept only in memory and are lost if you need to restart your system. The persistent entry switch writes route entries into the Registry so that they survive a restart of the machine.

Viewing the Routing Table

As you saw earlier, you can view the routing table of a Windows NT system using either of two utilities: the NETSTAT -r utility or the ROUTE command.

To view the route table using the ROUTE command, type **ROUTE PRINT**. This will give you a display similar to the one shown here:

```
Active Routes:

 Network Address          Netmask  Gateway Address       Interface  Metric
         0.0.0.0          0.0.0.0       10.10.3.1      10.10.3.200       1
      10.10.3.0    255.255.255.0     10.10.3.200      10.10.3.200       1
    10.10.3.200  255.255.255.255       127.0.0.1        127.0.0.1       1
 10.255.255.255  255.255.255.255     10.10.3.200      10.10.3.200       1
       127.0.0.0        255.0.0.0       127.0.0.1        127.0.0.1       1
       224.0.0.0        224.0.0.0     10.10.3.200      10.10.3.200       1
 255.255.255.255  255.255.255.255     10.10.3.200      10.10.3.200       1
```

The entries that are shown in this output are an example of the default routes in Windows NT 4.0. Following is an explanation of each:

◆ **0.0.0.0.** Assuming, of course, that a default gateway is specified, this entry identifies its IP address.

◆ **Local host (10.10.3.200).** This is used for self-reference purposes and points to the local loopback address as the gateway and interface.

◆ **Local network (10.10.3.0).** This is the identifier indicating the local network address. It indicates the gateway and interface and the machine's IP address, and it is used whenever a packet needs to be transmitted to a local destination.

◆ **Network broadcast (10.255.255.255).** This is a directed broadcast and is treated as a directed packet by routers. Most routers support the transmission of directed broadcasts: They forward them to the defined network, which broadcasts them to all machines on that network. In this case the entry specifies the IP address of your system for sending out network broadcasts to the local network.

◆ **127.0.0.1.** This is the local loopback address used for diagnostic purposes. It is used to make sure that the IP stack on a machine is properly installed and running.

◆ **224.0.0.0.** This is the default multicast address. If this machine is a member of any multicast groups, this and other multicast entries indicate to IP the interface used to communicate with the multicast network.

◆ **255.255.255.255.** This is a limited broadcast address for broadcasts destined for any machine on the local network. Routers that receive packets destined for this address may listen to the packet as a normal host, but they do not support transmission of these types of broadcasts to other networks.

To view your routing table, perform the following steps.

STEP BY STEP

6.1 Viewing Your Routing Table

1. Start a command prompt (Start, Run, and then type **CMD** and click OK).

2. Type **ROUTE PRINT** and press Enter.

Adding a Route

There are several reasons why you may need to enter a route for a host. However, the most common reasons involve either a network segment with multiple routers or a Windows NT system acting as a router.

Before you can add a route, you need to understand the parameters that you will need to include. These parameters are explained in the following list:

◆ **Network Address.** This is the network ID that the route is for. The system will use this after it ANDs the target IP address with the Netmask.

◆ **Netmask.** This subnet mask is used to determine how much of the IP address is used for the network ID and how much is used for the host. It is used with the target IP address to extract the network ID.

◆ **Gateway Address.** If you view TCP/IP routing as a series of steps (which it is), this indicates the next step that the packet must make on its way to the target. This could be another router; or, if the router is on the same subnet as the target, it is the router's local interface on that network.

◆ **Interface.** This is the interface or network card that the router uses to send the information to the next router or to the machine itself. (If the gateway and the interface are the same, the target is local.)

◆ **Metric.** This is used to determine the distance to the target host or network. The metric is the known number of routers that must be crossed to get to the remote system. If more than one route to a remote network is known, the one with the lowest metric is used.

Now that you have an understanding of the required values, you can add routes. To add a route, use the following steps.

STEP BY STEP

6.2 Adding a Route

1. Start a command prompt.

2. Enter this command:

   ```
   ROUTE -p ADD Network_ID MASK Netmask Gateway METRIC
   ➥Metric
   ```

3. Substitute the target Network_ID, Netmask, and Gateway. The Metric entry is optional.

4. Verify the entry using ROUTE PRINT.

Looking at Figure 6.4, you should now see that routes for the networks 148.16.12.0 and 148.16.16.0 need to be added to router R1. The following lines would handle this:

```
ROUTE -p ADD 148.16.12.0 MASK 255.255.252.0 148.16.8.2
➥METRIC 2
ROUTE -p ADD 148.16.16.0 MASK 255.255.252.0 148.16.8.2
➥METRIC 3
```

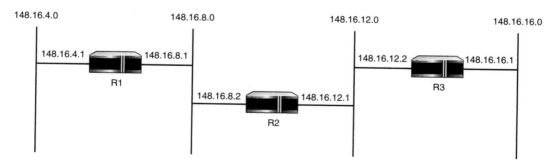

FIGURE 6.4
A network that requires static routes.

The -p is used so that the route will survive a restart. The metric indicates in each case the total number of routers that the packet must traverse.

Changing and Deleting Routes

The world is not a static place, and nowhere is this more true than in the world of routing. Therefore, you will occasionally need to change or even remove a route. By now you should be familiar with the parameters, so given here is the proper procedure.

To change a route, follow these steps:

STEP BY STEP

6.3 Changing a Route

1. Start a command prompt.

2. Use the ROUTE PRINT command to view the current route.

3. Enter this command to change the route:

   `ROUTE CHANGE Network_ID Gateway`

   Here Network is the network that already exists in the list, and Gateway is a new gateway (the metric can also be added).

4. Use the ROUTE PRINT command to verify the change.

To delete a route, use the following steps:

STEP BY STEP

6.4 Deleting a Route

1. Start a command prompt.

2. Use the ROUTE PRINT command to view the current route.

3. Enter this command to delete the route:

   `ROUTE DELETE Network_ID Gateway`

Here Gateway is required only if there is more than one route to the destination network.

4. Use the ROUTE PRINT command to verify the route has been deleted.

Dynamic Routing

The discussion to this point has focused on how to manually edit the route table to notify routers of the existence of networks they are not physically connected to. This would be an enormously difficult task on large networks, where routes and networks may change on a frequent basis.

Manually editing the route table also makes redundant pathways horribly complex to manage because you have to rely on each host to manage multiple default gateways and use dead gateway detection. Even using these features on the client side does not guarantee timely reactions to the failure of links between routers.

These problems have led to the development of routing protocols used specifically by routers to dynamically update each other's tables. Two of the most common protocols used by dynamic routers are RIP and OSPF. These protocols notify other routers that support these protocols about two things: the networks they are attached to, and any changes that occur due to disconnected links or too much congestion to efficiently pass traffic.

The characteristics of these protocols are discussed here because Windows NT can support either. However, because Windows NT does not support the OSPF protocol out of the box, the discussion of OSPF is informational only.

Routing Internet Protocol (RIP)

As you start to look at RIP, consider the sample networks that you have seen in this section. Look at the simple network in Figure 6.4, for example: When you add static routes, you are merely letting each router know about the networks that the other routers know about.

Knowing this, it makes sense that the RIP protocol was developed. RIP automatically lets the other routers know what networks they have in their routing tables. This is facilitated by causing the router to broadcast its routing table.

This might lead to problems: If a router broadcasts that it knows how to get to network 148.16.4.0, the next router will pick this up and add one to the metric (or hop count). The next router, however, will broadcast its table, including what it now knows about 148.16.4.0, which the original router will receive. If the original router updates its table and broadcasts this back, the other router will do the same—and back and forth. To prevent this, RIP will keep a route only if it doesn't have a better route.

By default, RIP routers exchange routing information every 30 seconds. The RIP broadcasts, which are sent out on all the routers' interfaces, contain a complete list of all network IDs that a router has routes to. The maximum number of networks that can be reported in a single RIP message is 25 networks. This means that in a larger network there will be many broadcasts, possibly to the point where the tables never completely synchronize.

Another problem concerning the broadcast nature of RIP could arise in a large, spread-out organization. As a router broadcasts, its routing table is picked up by the next router and is added to all the other routes it knows. All of this will be broadcast to the next router, which will add its routes and forward it. The sheer number of routes that could conceivably be sent by the time you reach router 50, for example, is overwhelming.

To borrow a maxim from chaos theory: If a router in China broadcasts its routing table, this will cause all the routers in New York to crash. To prevent this, routes that require you to traverse more than 15 routers are considered unreachable.

Even with these issues, RIP is a good protocol for smaller networks (fewer than a hundred subnets). To install RIP for Windows NT, use the following steps.

STEP BY STEP

6.5 Installing RIP for Windows NT

   1. Open the Network dialog box and choose the Services tab.

2. Click Add, and from the list choose RIP protocol for
   TCP/IP. Click OK.

3. Enter the path for your source files. Close the Network
   dialog box and restart the system when prompted.

Before installing RIP, you should consider its shortcomings:

◆ Because RIP keeps track of every route table entry, including
  multiple paths to a particular network, routing tables can
  become large rather quickly. This can result in multiple RIP
  packets having to be broadcast in order to send a complete
  route table to other routers.

◆ Because RIP can allow hop counts only up to 15 (with 16 representing an unreachable network), the size of networks on
  which RIP can be successfully implemented is restricted. Any
  large enterprise may need to achieve hop counts over 15.

◆ Broadcasts are sent by default every 30 seconds. This results in
  two fundamental problems. First, significant delays occur
  between the time when a route goes down and the time all
  routers in the environment are notified of this change in the
  network. If a network nine routers (hops) away goes down, it
  can take up to 4 1/2 minutes before that change makes it to
  the other end of the network. Meanwhile, packets sent in that
  direction can be lost and connections dropped. Secondly, on a
  LAN these broadcasts may not be significant in terms of bandwidth; but on a WAN, these broadcasts may become bother-
  some, especially if the network is stable and the route tables are
  large. These broadcasts transmit redundant route-table entries
  every 30 seconds without regard to whether it is necessary.

These problems should not discourage the administrator of a small-
to medium-sized network from using the RIP protocol. As long as
you understand the benefits and limitations of the protocol, you
should be able to use it quite successfully on a network.

Open Shortest Path First (OSPF)

As the size of networks grew, OSPF was developed to overcome the
problems that you encounter using RIP on a large network. This section provides only a brief overview of the OSPF protocol.

In OSPF the metric (hop count) becomes only part of the information that is used to determine a route. The status of the links between networks is also used. This allows OSPF to scale well to large networks.

Also, broadcasts are managed better in OSPF because your intranet is divided into smaller networks called *autonomous systems*. Furthermore, you can subdivide an autonomous system into smaller sections known as *areas*, each of which is assigned a unique number.

By developing a hierarchy, OSPF reduces the total amount of information that any one router needs to know. If data needs to be routed entirely within an area, all information for routing can be obtained from local routers.

Each OSPF router in an autonomous system maintains a network map known as the *link state database (LSDB)*. The LSDB is updated whenever a change to the network topology of an area occurs. The LSDB is evaluated every 10 seconds; if no changes have occurred to the area's topology, no changes are made to the LSDB.

The LSDB contains entries for each network that each router in an area is attached to. It also has an associated outgoing cost value assigned to each network interface of a router. This value measures the cost of sending traffic through that interface to the connected network. By assigning costs, router preferences can be set based on line cost or line speed.

The entries in the LSDB are built based on information sent in *link state advertisements (LSA)*. A network is in a converged state when the LSDB is the same for each router in the area. When the LSDB reaches this converged state, each OSPF router calculates the shortest path through the network for each network and router. A *Shortest Path First (SPF) tree* stores this information. The key is that every router maintains its own SPF tree.

After the SPF tree has been built, the routing table can be constructed by determining the lowest-cost route to each destination network. Routing tables are calculated locally at each router.

Static and Dynamic Router Integration

In some networks there will be a need to integrate the two types of routing. This will occur if you use static routing internally but use a dynamic router to connect to the Internet.

Integration is in fact simple. All you really need to do is add static routes to a dynamic router. Consider the network shown in Figure 6.5, in which a dynamic router is used to communicate with the Internet. The dynamic router knows about the routes it needs on the Internet and about 148.16.4.0 because it is connected to this network.

The dynamic router, however, does not know about 148.16.8.0 or 148.16.12.0; and because the other routers are static, they cannot tell the dynamic router about these networks. You can either install a routing protocol on all routers or inform the dynamic router about these other networks using static routes.

How this is done will depend on the dynamic router. However, if the router is a Windows NT system, you only need to add the routes to make this network function.

BUILDING A MULTIHOMED ROUTER

Windows NT allows an administrator to convert a machine to either a static or dynamic IP router. Static routers work well for extending a small network segment; dynamic routers using RIP work well on small

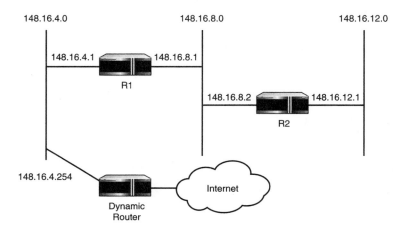

FIGURE 6.5

A combination of static and dynamic routing is used in this network example.

and medium networks. A multihomed computer would probably not work well on large networks, however, because of RIP's limitations and the significant overhead associated with maintaining large routing tables.

Generally, building a Windows NT router is easy to do. The first step is to install two or more network cards in the machine. Anyone who has ever tried to do this will tell you it sounds much easier than it is. Each network card has to have its own IRQ and I/O address to use on the machine.

The administrator then needs to decide whether the router will be static or dynamic. After IP forwarding is enabled, the router is a static router. If this is what is desired, no more configuration of the system is necessary. If the administrator wants to make this a dynamic router, the RIP protocol needs to be installed.

NOTE

Installation and Configuration Issues
See Chapter 2 for details on installing network adapter drivers and TCP/IP. Chapter 2 also discusses the configuration of TCP/IP addresses for the cards and enabling IP forwarding (or routing).

THE TRACERT UTILITY

Windows NT includes the TRACERT utility, which is used to verify the route a packet takes to reach its destination. To use this utility, simply go to the command prompt and type **tracert** *<IP address or host name>*.

The result of running this utility for a destination address will probably look similar to the following output:

```
Tracing route to www.ScrimTech.com [209.204.202.64]
over a maximum of 30 hops:

  1    220 ms    210 ms    211 ms   tnt01.magma.ca [204.191.36.88]
  2    311 ms    210 ms    210 ms   core1-vlan5.magma.ca [206.191.0.129]
  3    230 ms    221 ms    210 ms   border2-e3.magma.ca [206.191.0.9]
  4    221 ms    210 ms    240 ms   205.150.227.1
  5    231 ms    240 ms    220 ms   a10-0-0.102.bb1.ott1.a10-0-0.102.bb1.tor2.uunet.ca [205.150.242.89]
  6    250 ms    271 ms    260 ms   ATM11-0-0.BR2.TCO1.ALTER.NET [137.39.250.69]
  7    260 ms    281 ms    260 ms   112.ATM10-0-0.XR2.TCO1.ALTER.NET [146.188.160.94]
  8    250 ms    270 ms    261 ms   192.ATM3-0.TR2.DCA1.ALTER.NET [146.188.161.182]
  9    271 ms    280 ms    291 ms   101.ATM6-0.TR2.CHI4.ALTER.NET [146.188.136.109]
 10    271 ms    280 ms    280 ms   198.ATM7-0.XR2.CHI4.ALTER.NET [146.188.208.229]
 11    471 ms    580 ms       *     194.ATM8-0-0.GW1.CHI1.ALTER.NET [146.188.208.149]
 12    280 ms    280 ms    271 ms   napnet-gw.customer.ALTER.NET [137.39.130.174]
 13    281 ms    270 ms    361 ms   core0-a0-2.chi2.nap.net [207.112.247.130]
 14    261 ms    280 ms    291 ms   chi2-olm-ds3.axxs.net [207.112.240.142]
 15    271 ms    280 ms    281 ms   chi2-olm-ds3.axxs.net [207.112.240.142]
 16    280 ms    280 ms    280 ms   scrimtech.com [209.204.202.64]

Trace complete.
```

The result shows each router crossed to get to a destination, as well as how long it took to get through each particular router. The time it takes to get through a particular router is calculated three times, which is displayed for each router hop along with the IP address of each router crossed. If a Fully Qualified Domain Name (FQDN) is available, this is displayed as well.

The TRACERT utility is useful for two diagnostic purposes:

- ◆ It detects whether a particular router is not functioning along a known path. For instance, say a user knows that packets on a network always go through Sydney to get from Singapore to South Africa, but communication seems to be dead. A TRACERT to a South African address shows all the hops up to the point where the router in Sydney should respond. If it does not respond, the time values are marked with asterisks (*), indicating the packet timed out.

- ◆ The TRACERT utility also determines whether a router is slow and possibly needs to be upgraded or helped by adding additional routes on the network. You can determine this simply by looking at the time it takes for a packet to get through a particular router. If a particular router is deluged by packets, its return time may be significantly higher than that of any of the other hops, indicating that it should be upgraded or helped in some way.

CASE STUDY: ROUTING IN THE HEAD OFFICE

ESSENCE OF THE CASE

In this case there are only a couple simple considerations that you will need to address:

- Access to the Internet must be given to all the systems.

- Data must be able to move throughout the entire office.

- Some method will be required to let the dynamic router to the Internet know about the internal routes.

As you return to Sunshine Brewing Company, you can now look at the routing requirements for the organization. The first thing you will note is that they don't need to have any routing internally; all routing is external on the Internet. To give you a chance to investigate how the routing could be configured, this case study will look at the head office location and assume that Windows NT systems (instead of switched ethernet) will be used as routers.

SCENARIO

The basis of this scenario is that you have split the head office into three subnets connected by Windows NT systems acting as routers. The head office has been given a CIDR address of 198.53.8.0 with a subnet mask of 255.255.254.0, giving you a total of 510 addresses that you can work with.

The office takes up three floors of an office tower, each with around 50 users. There is a router between each set of floors, and the third-floor network also has a connection to the Internet through a Cisco 2500 (see Figure 6.6).

ANALYSIS

There are two approaches that could be taken here.

One approach is to simply install a routing protocol on the two Windows NT routers and allow the systems to discover each other. Because Windows NT ships with RIP as the default protocol, this could potentially increase the amount

CASE STUDY: ROUTING IN THE HEAD OFFICE

of network traffic for the RIP broadcasts that occur every 30 seconds.

Because this approach will increase the overall network traffic, and because there are only two internal routers, a better approach would be to configure the two internal routers and the dynamic router with static routes. This will require the following entries for each router.

Router A:

```
ROUTE -p ADD 0.0.0.0 MASK 0.0.0.0
➥198.53.8.130
```

```
ROUTE -p ADD 198.53.9.128 MASK
➥255.255.255.128 198.53.9.2
```

Router B:

```
ROUTE -p ADD 0.0.0.0 MASK 0.0.0.0 198.53.9.1
ROUTE -p ADD 198.53.8.128 MASK
➥255.255.255.128 198.53.9.1
```

Dynamic Router:

```
ROUTE -p ADD 198.53.9.0 MASK 255.255.255.128
➥198.53.8.129
ROUTE -p ADD 198.53.9.128 MASK
➥255.255.255.128 198.53.9.129
```

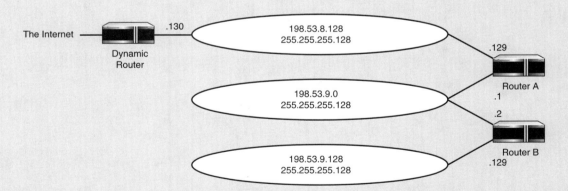

FIGURE 6.6
The head office network takes up three floors.

CHAPTER SUMMARY

KEY TERMS

- convergence
- dynamic routing
- OSPF
- RIP
- routing
- routing protocol
- routing table
- static routing

This chapter has covered the other half of routing and the protocols available in Windows NT. There will be questions on the exam about the differences between static and dynamic routing and about configuring the routing table. The following is a list of the key things that you will need to be able to do:

◆ You need to be able to use the ROUTE command.

◆ You will need to be able to create and configure static routers using Windows NT.

◆ You will need to understand what a dynamic router is (it has a routing protocol).

◆ You should understand the implementation of RIP that comes with Windows NT.

APPLY YOUR KNOWLEDGE

Exercises

The following exercises give you a chance to work with your routing table and try some of the knowledge you have gained.

6.1   Viewing the Routing Table

This exercise will help you view the routing table on your system:

1. From the Start menu, select Command Prompt.

2. Type **route print** at the command prompt.

6.2   Adding an Entry to Your Route Table

Now that you have verified that you have a routing table, you will add a route to it:

1. From the Start menu, select Command Prompt.

2. Type **route add 131.107.64.0 mask 255.255.224.0** *IP address of your current gateway*.

3. Type **route print** to observe the addition.

6.3   Using the TRACERT Utility

In this exercise you will use the TRACERT utility to view the route a packet takes to a remote network:

1. Open your connection to the Internet.

2. From the Start menu, select Command Prompt.

3. Type **tracert www.ScrimTech.com** at the command prompt. Note that you can choose any IP address or domain you wish.

4. Observe the results.

Review Questions

1. Describe the two types of routing.

2. What conditions must be met to allow Windows NT to act as a static or dynamic router?

3. How often does RIP broadcast? What does it broadcast?

4. If you have implemented the RIP protocol on a machine running Windows NT, what is the largest number of hops a route can involve before the network is considered to be unreachable?

Exam Questions

1. In your environment, you have a Windows NT machine that seems not to respond to PING requests using an IP address. You would like to make sure the machine's configuration is appropriate for the network. Which of the following options would you need to check?

   A. IP address

   B. Subnet mask

   C. Default gateway

   D. DNS

2. You've noticed a significant increase in the amount of time it takes to reach your remote offices across the network. You think one of your routers may not be functioning. Which utility would you use to find the path a packet takes to reach its destination?

   A. WINS

   B. DNS

APPLY YOUR KNOWLEDGE

C. TRACERT

D. Network monitor

3. You have a machine that seems to be able to communicate with other machines on its same local subnet; but whenever you try to reach destinations on a remote network, the communications fail. Which of the following could be the problem?

A. IP address

B. Subnet mask

C. Default gateway

D. WINS

4. You've set up a simple routed environment in which one router is central to three subnets, meaning that the router can see each of the three segments. No default gateway has been assigned because there doesn't seem to be any reason to do so. If a router doesn't know where to send a packet, and no default gateway has been assigned, what will the router do with the packet?

A. Drop the packet

B. Store the packet for later processing

C. Broadcast on the local network

D. Use ARP to locate another pathway

5. You want to have your Windows NT routers share information on the network so that you don't have to continually update the route tables manually. What protocol do you need to install to allow this to happen?

A. DNS

B. RIP

C. OSPF

D. WINS

6. Ten machines on your network have stopped communicating with other machines on remote network segments. When you check the router, you find that it seems to be working properly, but you want to make sure the route table itself has not been modified. What utilities can be used to view the route table on your Windows NT router?

A. ROUTE

B. NETSTAT

C. PING

D. RTTABLE

7. Your environment consists of both LAN and WAN connections spread out over five continents. You've begun an expansion that has added a number of routers to your already large organization. Your network currently uses RIP as the routing protocol; but as new network segments are being added, routers on either end of your network insist that they can't see each other and that they are unreachable. What could be the cause of this?

A. The routers aren't made by Microsoft.

B. The RIP protocol can't share routing tables.

C. The RIP protocol can't support more than 15 hops.

D. Routers aren't designed for WAN connections.

8. When installing and testing a brand-new NT router, you notice that the router routes packets to any network that it is physically attached to,

APPLY YOUR KNOWLEDGE

but drops packets intended for networks it is not attached to. There are seven of these networks that it can't seem to route packets to. What would be the easiest way to make sure the router performs its function for those other networks?

A. Disable IP routing.

B. Enable IP filtering on all ports.

C. Change the IP address bindings.

D. Add a default gateway.

9. You are the administrator of a network running on ethernet with 120 hosts. The response time is slow, and you intend to split up your network into smaller sections. You plan on using NT systems that are already connected to the network to route between the subnets that you will create. Currently, your organization uses a proxy server to access the Internet and will continue to do so. You intend to use the address 10.0.0.0 internally and create four subnets.

You decide to set the default gateway of each router to the next router in line and set the last router to default to the first. How does this solution work?

A. This is the best possible solution.

B. This is a good solution.

C. This solution works but is far from optimal.

D. This solution does not work.

10. Again you have the same situation as in question 9, but instead you decide to create static routes at each router for any networks that are not directly connected. How does this solution work?

A. This is the best possible solution.

B. This is a good solution.

C. This solution works but is far from optimal.

D. This solution does not work.

11. Again, you have the same situation illustrated in the previous two questions, but you decide to install RIP on all of the routers to allow them to update each other. How does this solution work?

A. This is the best possible solution.

B. This is a good solution.

C. This solution works but is far from optimal.

D. This solution does not work.

Answers to Review Questions

1. The two types of routing are: static, which does not exchange information with other routers and uses only its internal routing table; and dynamic, which learns about other networks automatically using one of several routing protocols, such as RIP or OSPF. See "Static and Dynamic Routers."

2. The system must have two network cards installed, each of which requires an IP address that is valid for the subnet that it is on. Then you need to check Enable IP Forwarding on the Routing tab of the TCP/IP Configuration screen. See "Building a Multihomed Router."

3. The RIP protocol will broadcast the routing table of a RIP-enabled router every 30 seconds. See "Routing Internet Protocol (RIP)."

4. The most distant network can be 16 networks away, or 15 hops; therefore, the largest metric possible in RIP routing is 15. See "Routing Internet Protocol (RIP)."

APPLY YOUR KNOWLEDGE

Answers to Exam Questions

1. **A, B,** and **C.** In this case the system is having a problem communicating with another host. The information given indicates only that it cannot communicate by IP address; therefore, the only listed item that we can ignore is DNS. If the systems were on the same subnet, the default gateway would also be eliminated. See "Introduction to Routing."

2. **C.** There are many reasons that the packet could be slow when it tries to reach the remote system. Name resolution could be slow if a DNS server or WINS server is down because the system will first have to time out while trying to use either of these. However, here you want to see the path the packet is taking, which of course you can do using the TRACERT utility. See "The TRACERT Utility."

3. **B** and **C.** The system is able to communicate locally. This means the IP address is correct and that name resolution is working. This leaves the subnet mask, which might be misleading IP into thinking a remote system is local; and the default gateway, which might not be configured correctly, giving the system no path to the remote network. See "Introduction to Routing."

4. **A.** If a system has a packet, but there is no route to which the packet can be sent, the packet is discarded. This is true for all systems and will cause the system to generate an ICMP message stating that the destination host is unreachable. See "Introduction to Routing."

5. **B** and **C.** Either the RIP or the OSPF protocol could be installed. Because RIP ships with the distribution files for NT, this would be the normal choice. See "Dynamic Routing."

6. **A** and **B.** There are two ways that you can see the routing table: You can either use ROUTE PRINT OR NETSTAT -r. See "Viewing the Routing Table."

7. **C.** Here you run into one of the limitations of RIP: the maximum hop count (or metric) that can be stored. With a network this size, there is a good possibility that the most distant networks are more than 15 hops away. See "Routing Internet Protocol (RIP)."

8. **D.** You need to assume that there is another router that knows about these networks to which you can forward the packets. The other choices here would be to add a route for each of the networks or to install RIP on all routers. See "Static and Dynamic Routers."

9. **C.** In this case it is possible for a packet to have to circle through three routers to get from one network to another. If, for instance, you labeled the networks A, B, C, and D and the routers AB (for the router between network A and B), BC, CD, and DA, the following would be true.

   The router BC knows about networks B and C. If you are trying to send from network B to network A, there could be a problem. Assume that systems on network B use router BC as a default gateway. If the packet is sent to router BC, it does not know about network A. If the default gateway at the router is set to router CD, the packet goes there.

   The router CD doesn't know about network A and forwards the packet to DA; this router does know the network A, and the packet is delivered— after three hops rather than one. If the original default gateway moves packets the other way,

Apply Your Knowledge

there will still be two hops. See "Static and Dynamic Routers."

10. **A.** This is the best way to configure a small routed network. There are no problems with multiple hops, and there is no additional traffic from RIP broadcasts. See "Static and Dynamic Routers."

11. **B.** This would be preferable in an environment that is likely to change frequently; however, in a static environment there is no need for a routing protocol, and this would only increase the general network noise. See "Static and Dynamic Routers."

Suggested Readings and Resources

1. Heywood, Drew. *Networking with Microsoft TCP/IP, Second Edition.* New Riders, 1997.

This chapter will help you prepare for the exam by covering the following objectives:

Install and configure Microsoft DNS server service on a Windows NT server.

▶ As with the other related objectives, you need to know what the service is and how to install and configure the server.

Integrate a DNS server with other name servers.

▶ This is included to ensure that you realize this is a standard DNS server and, therefore, it can be integrated with all other DNS servers. However, this is also a product of Microsoft, which was able to integrate it with WINS. This turns the DNS server into a dynamic DNS server.

Connect a DNS server to a DNS root server.

▶ If you will be using the DNS server on the Internet, you need to understand how it will integrate into the overall name space. This means understanding the purpose of the cache file.

Configure DNS server roles.

▶ Different DNS servers fill different roles. Some servers provide resolution to others, and some only to clients. The main roles are primary, secondary, and caching only.

CHAPTER 7

Microsoft Domain Name System (DNS)

As you read through this chapter, you should concentrate on the following key items:

▶ You need to know how to install the DNS server and how to have a client use it.

▶ You need to understand the structure of the DNS files and where you will use them.

▶ You need to know how to make a Microsoft DNS server a secondary for a UNIX DNS server, and vice versa.

▶ You need to know the roles that a DNS server can perform.

▶ You need to know the effect of configuring a caching-only server as a forwarder and slave.

▶ You need to know how to configure forward and reverse-lookup files.

▶ You need to know how to use NSLOOKUP to query a DNS server.

▶ You must know how to integrate the DNS server with a WINS server.

▶ You need to know what the settings in the SOA record are for.

▶ You need to understand the difference between an iterative query and a recursive query.

▶ You need to know how to configure Microsoft DNS to use the BIND files from an existing server.

The Domain Name System (DNS) was created to address the problem of locating computers by a friendly name. In non-Microsoft environments, host names are typically resolved through host files or DNS. In a Microsoft environment, WINS and broadcasts might be used if those methods can't resolve the name. DNS is the primary system used to resolve host names on the Internet. In fact, DNS had its beginning in the early days of the Internet.

In its early days, the Internet was a small network established by the Department of Defense for research purposes. This network linked computers at several government agencies with a few universities. The host names of the computers in this network were registered in a single HOSTS file located on a centrally administered server. Each site that needed to resolve host names downloaded this file.

Few computers were being added to this network, so the file, HOSTS.TXT, wasn't updated too often; the different sites had to download this file only periodically to update their own copies. As the number of hosts on the Internet grew, it became more difficult to manage all the names through a central file. The number of entries was increasing rapidly, changes were being made more frequently, and the different Internet sites trying to download a new copy were accessing the server with the central file more often.

DNS was created in 1984 as a way to resolve host names without relying on one central HOSTS file. With DNS, the host names reside in a database that can be distributed among multiple servers, decreasing the load on any one server and also allowing more than one point of administration for this name space.

The name space is based on hierarchical names in a tree-type directory structure. DNS allows more types of registration than the simple host-name-to-IP-address mapping used in a HOSTS.TXT file, and it also allows room for future defined types. Because the database is distributed, DNS can support a database much larger than can be stored in a single file. In fact, the database size is virtually unlimited because more servers can be added to handle additional parts of the database.

HISTORY OF MICROSOFT DNS

DNS was introduced in the Microsoft environment as part of the Resource Kit for Windows NT Server 3.51. In version 4.0, DNS was integrated with the Windows NT source files. DNS is not installed by default as part of a Windows NT 4.0 Server installation; however, you can specify that DNS be included as part of a Windows NT installation, or you can add DNS later just as you would any other network service.

Microsoft DNS is based on RFCs 974, 1034, and 1035. Another popular implementation of DNS is called Berkeley Internet Name Daemon (BIND), developed at the University of California, Berkeley, for its version of UNIX. However, BIND is not totally compliant with the DNS RFCs because it requires a boot file.

Some host-name systems, such as NetBIOS names, use a flat name space. With a flat name space, all names exist at the same level, so there can't be any duplicate names. These names are like phone numbers: Every person who has a phone must have a unique number.

DNS stores names in a hierarchical path like a directory structure. In a directory structure you can have a file called TEST.TXT in C:\ and another file called TEST.TXT in the C:\ASCII directory. Similarly, in a network using DNS, you can have more than one server with the same name, as long as each is located in a different path.

Domains in DNS

In order to make sense of DNS, you need to understand the Fully Qualified Domain Name (FQDN). Recall from Chapter 2, "Installing Microsoft TCP/IP," that the Host Name and Domain Name entries on the DNS tab of the TCP/IP configuration are combined to create the FQDN.

Normally, the domain entered there will have dots in it (for example, "ScrimTech.com"). The dots are used to separate the different levels in the FQDN; these levels are organized from the highest level down in the following list:

◆ **Root.** The root-level domain sits at the top of the DNS and doesn't normally show up in the FQDN; it is normally just assumed because all names begin here. If the root does need to be indicated, it will be the final period in a FQDN. Alone, the root domain is indicated by a dot (.).

◆ **Top-level domains.** These main divisions of the name space are used to group the type of systems together. There are many top-level domains, including .com and .edu (see Table

NOTE

DNS in Windows NT 5.0 Microsoft is planning major enhancements to DNS for Windows NT 5.0. The company is planning to introduce an X.500-type directory structure for its networks in version 5.0. This directory structure will use DNS as the means to organize and control the network name space. In DNS, an administrator will be able to see all the servers in the network (as well as their resources) in a particular hierarchy. This hierarchy will bring all the resources in the network together in a manner more logical than the current interface for trust relationships.

Microsoft is also planning a migration path to move existing trust relationships into DNS. Although administrators have been using DNS mostly to manage Internet or intranet connections, in the future administrators will use DNS to manage their entire network, both for local and Internet access.

7.1 for a partial list). Top-level domains must be known to the root-level domain so that inquires can be sent to the correct second-level server.

◆ **Second-level domains.** After specifying the type of system, you can get to the name of the company or organization. For example, in Microsoft.com the second-level domain is Microsoft. The top-level domains must know second-level domains, just as the root-level domain must know top-level domains.

◆ **Subdomains.** After the name space makes it to the second-level domains, the central control is long gone. In fact, this is where organizations (or their ISPs) begin to add records. In large organizations you may need to further break down the name space; therefore, the ability to create subdomains has been created.

◆ **Host name.** The name of the computer is the end of the FQDN, which will resolved to an IP address.

TABLE 7.1

A PARTIAL LIST OF TOP-LEVEL DOMAINS IN THE INTERNET

Name	Type of Organization
.com	Commercial organizations
.edu	Educational institutions
.org	Nonprofit organizations
.net	Networks (the backbone of the Internet)
.gov	Nonmilitary government organizations
.mil	Military government organizations
.num	Phone numbers
.arpa	Reverse DNS
.xx	Two-letter country code

In order to illustrate this further, look at the name `www.backoffice.microsoft.com`. Breaking this name down, you would find the elements in the following table:

www	*backoffice*	*microsoft*	*com*	
Host	Subdomain	Second-level domain	Top-level domain	Root (implied)

DNS Zone Files

If you think about the number of hosts that exist on the Internet, there is obviously no way that all the records can exist on one server. This is a central point to the DNS system: the database is distributed across many different servers. This means that you may have to refer to several servers to resolve a single name. However, there is no other way to hold the amount of information with any form of stability.

Because the database is distributed, there have to be several points in the DNS structure where you find a server that has the authority to say "This is the IP address for this name." Authority in DNS is given in the form of a zone file. All the parts of the DNS database are stored in these zone files.

With multiple zones, the load of providing access to the database is spread among a number of servers. Also, the administrative burden of managing the database is spread out because different administrators manage only the parts of the DNS database stored in their own zones. A zone can be any portion of the domain name space; it doesn't have to contain all the subdomains for that part of the DNS tree.

TYPES OF DNS SERVERS

A DNS server acquires information about part of the domain name space from a local copy of a zone file or by making queries to another DNS server. A name server can have more than one zone file installed on it. It could have the original copy of a zone, or it can have a copy of a zone file from another name server. If a name server has a copy of a zone file, it can provide an authoritative answer for queries related to the part of DNS stored in that file.

The three main types of name servers are primary, secondary, and caching-only servers. Each of these is described in the following sections.

Primary Servers

A primary server has the original copy of a zone file. Any changes made to the zone file are made to the copy on the primary server. When a primary server receives a query about a host name in its own zone, it retrieves the host resolution locally from its own zone files.

Secondary Servers

A secondary server gets a copy of zone files from another server. This zone file is a read-only copy of the original file from the primary server. Any changes made to the zone file are made at the primary server; then the changes are copied down to the secondary server through a zone transfer.

There are several reasons you should have a secondary server for each zone:

◆ A secondary server provides redundancy, enabling host names in the zone to be resolved even if the primary server goes down.

◆ A secondary server can also reduce the load on a primary server or reduce network traffic. For example, placing a secondary server on a remote site can reduce network traffic generated when clients cross the WAN link to resolve host names. With a secondary server at this remote site, client queries can be handled locally. The only traffic from DNS is generated when the zone file on the primary server changes and the secondary server downloads a new copy.

◆ Two servers are required to resolve names if you wish to register your domain with InterNIC.

◆ The primary server sees less activity because it communicates with only one host at the remote site (the secondary server) rather than resolving queries from all the clients at the site.

A server can have any number of zone files stored on it. The primary or secondary designation applies to each zone file rather than to the server itself. A server can be the primary for one zone (it has the original zone file for that zone) and a secondary for another zone (it gets a read-only copy of the zone file through a zone transfer).

Caching-Only Servers

A DNS server doesn't have to have any zone files, either as a primary or a secondary server. If a DNS server has no zone files, it is known as a caching-only server.

The only responsibility of a caching-only server is to respond to queries from a resolver (the part of your client application that resolves names) and return an answer. This result may require querying several servers (root, top-level, second-level) to obtain a resolution. This resolution is always cached.

Caching-only servers are not authoritative for any domains because they don't store copies of any zone files locally. When a caching-only server first starts, it does not have any DNS information stored; it builds information only when it caches results of queries made after the server starts.

After a caching-only server has resolved a query, a future query for the same information can be resolved locally from the cache. Local resolution eliminates the need to communicate across the network (at least until the cached entry expires). The time-to-live (TTL) of cached entries is determined by the server that provided the initial resolution. It returns a time-to-live for the query along with the name resolution.

RESOLVING DNS QUERIES

A client querying a DNS server is called a resolver, whereas a DNS server is generically called a name server. DNS servers and clients reside at the Application layer of the TCP/IP model and are both sockets applications. By working at this layer, DNS can more easily communicate with the client applications needing to resolve a host name.

DNS can use either UDP or TCP for its communications. DNS tries to use the more efficient UDP for better performance, but it will resort to TCP if it can't communicate properly through UDP.

A DNS server can receive several types of queries, which are described in the following sections.

Recursive Queries

Recursive queries force the DNS server to respond to the request with either a failure or a success response that includes the TCP/IP address for the domain name requested. Resolvers on the client computer typically make the recursive queries.

The local DNS server may contact many other DNS servers to resolve the request. When it receives a response from the other DNS servers, it sends an authoritative answer to the client. The DNS server is not allowed to pass the buck by simply giving the client the address of another DNS server that might be able to handle the request.

In addition to this type of query being made from a resolver (part of your application) on your client to a local DNS server, it can also be sent from a local DNS server to its forwarder—another name server configured to handle requests forwarded to it.

Iterative Queries

An iterative query is one in which a name server is expected to provide the best information based on what it knows from local zone files or from caching. If the name server doesn't have any information to answer the query, it simply sends a negative response. A name server makes this type of query as it tries to find names outside its local domain. It may have to query a number of outside DNS servers, starting with the root domain server and working down, in an attempt to resolve the name.

Figure 7.1 shows the entire query process with a DNS client making an initial query of a DNS server to resolve the name www.erudite.com. In this example the client makes a recursive query and expects to receive an answer without being referred to another server. The DNS server receiving the query can't resolve the host name with its own information (in the cache or zone files), so it makes an iterative query to a root-name server.

The root server sends back the address of the name server for the .com domain. The DNS server then sends an iterative query to the .com-domain name server. This server sends back the address of the name server authoritative for the erudite.com domain. The DNS server then sends a query for "www.erudite.com" to this server; the erudite.com name server finds a resolution for www and returns a reply.

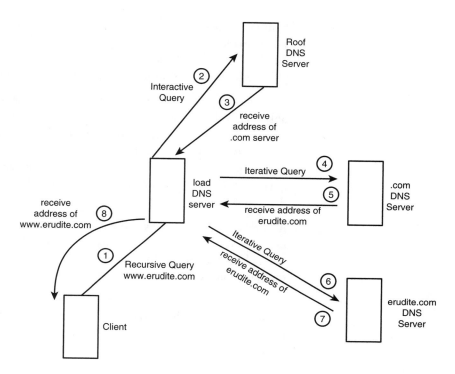

FIGURE 7.1
Resolving a name is a combination of recursive and iterative queries.

The local DNS server can finally respond to the client that made the original request for the name resolution. The client was kept on hold while the DNS server worked to find a response. Because the client sent a recursive query, the DNS server was forced to go through this extra work until it could obtain an answer.

Inverse Queries

A third type of query, an inverse query, is used when the client wants to know the host name of a specified IP address. A special domain in the DNS name space resolves this type of query; otherwise, a DNS server would have to completely search all the DNS domains to make sure it found the correct name. This special domain is called "in-addr.arpa." Nodes in this space are named after IP addresses rather than alphabetic host names.

Normal FQDNs start with the specific host and move to more general information. It may initially seem impossible to do this; however, the IP address does the same thing in reverse. The inverse query simply reverses the octets of the IP address to perform this resolution.

Inverse lookup queries are used when a client requests a service that only specified host names have been given permission to use. The server receiving the request knows only the IP address of the client, so the server must find out the host name to see whether the client is on the approved list. In this case, the server issues an inverse lookup query to find the host name matching the IP address of the client that requested the service.

A number of DNS servers also have zones for inverse lookups. The highest levels of zone files, for class A, B, and C networks, are maintained by InterNIC. Individual network address owners, however, can have zone files for subnets on their own networks.

A name server can return three types of responses to a query: a successful response with the IP address for the requested host name (or the host name for an inverse lookup), a pointer to another name server (only in an iterative query), or a failure message.

Time-to-Live (TTL) for Queries

A name server caches all the information it receives when it resolves queries outside its own zone files. These cached responses can then be used to answer queries for the same information in the future. But these cached entries don't stay on the DNS server forever; there is a time-to-live for the responses to make sure the DNS server doesn't keep information for so long that it becomes obsolete. The time-to-live for the cache can be set on each DNS server for each zone and for an individual resource record.

There are two competing factors to consider when setting the time-to-live. One is the accuracy of the cached information. If the TTL is short, the likelihood of having old information decreases considerably. If the TTL is long, the cached responses could become outdated, meaning the DNS server could give false answers to queries. The accuracy of the responses is also dependent on how stable your environment is. If names change often, a short TTL is necessary.

It is also important, however, to consider the load on the server and the network. If the TTL is large, the server can answer more queries from the cache and doesn't have to use local resources or network bandwidth to send out additional queries.

If a query is answered with an entry from the cache, the TTL of the entry is also passed with the response. This way, other DNS servers that receive the response know how long the entry is valid. Other DNS servers honor the TTL from the responding server; they don't set it again based on their own TTL. Thus, entries truly expire (instead of living forever) as they move from server to server with an updated TTL. Resolvers (clients) also have a cache and honor the TTL received from a name server that answered a query from its cache.

Forwarders and Slaves

When a client contacts a DNS server for name resolution, the DNS server first looks in its local files to resolve the request. If the DNS server is not authoritative for the zone pertaining to that request, it must look to another name server to resolve the request. When you are browsing the World Wide Web, resolving a domain name could involve either making a request of a name server maintained by your ISP or going on the Internet to contact a name server there.

You may not want all DNS servers in your organization to forward these requests. Microsoft DNS enables you to designate specific DNS servers as forwarders. In general, only forwarders can communicate outside your network; the other DNS servers are configured with the address of the forwarder.

The forwarder is much like a gatekeeper to which all outside requests are funneled. You can install firewall software or other protective measures only on the forwarder instead of all the DNS servers in your organization. Also, an entire server is designated as a forwarder; this is not done on a zone-by-zone basis.

When a forwarder receives a request to resolve a name, it accesses outside resources and returns the response to the DNS server that originated the request. If the forwarder can't answer the request, the originating DNS server may try to resolve the query itself. This can defeat the purpose of creating a server to be used as a forwarder, so there is an additional option to set the internal DNS servers as slaves.

Slaves, which are DNS servers configured to use forwarders only, return a failure message if the forwarder can't resolve the request. A slave does not try to contact other DNS servers if its designated forwarder can't handle the request. In other words, a slave makes a recursive query to a forwarder, and that's all.

STRUCTURE OF DNS FILES

Non-Microsoft name servers usually require manual editing of text files to create the zone files that comprise the domain name space. These files must be created with a specific syntax that can be read by DNS. Microsoft's DNS server includes DNS Manager, a graphical user interface (GUI) that displays the settings from these files and allows you to make entries in them via the interface rather than in the files themselves. DNS Manager also allows you to manage more than one DNS server from one location.

Although you can use DNS Manager to create or modify zone files even when you don't know their syntax, understanding the content and structure of the zone files is essential to your understanding of DNS. In fact, DNS Manager refers to many of the records in the zone file by their syntax name. So whether you use a text editor or DNS Manager to create and modify zone files, you must still understand what the different records are used for.

The zone file contains the resource records for the part of domain covered by the zone. These files in the NT structure are stored in the path C:\WINNT\SYSTEM32\dns for a default installation. A DNS server can use three types of files: zone files, a cache file, and a reverse-lookup zone file. You can also use a boot file to initialize the DNS server; however, a Microsoft DNS server is usually initialized from values stored in the Registry. The capability to initialize from a boot file is included in Microsoft DNS for compatibility with BIND-based DNS server files.

All these file types are covered in the next few sections.

Zone Files

Zone files have a .dns extension (for example, mcp.com.dns). A sample zone file called place.dns in the dns\samples directory can be manually edited and used as a zone file. Of course, you can use DNS Manager with its GUI interface to create zone files and the records within the zone.

You can use DNS Manager to create zone entries even when you do not know the syntax of the records. However, DNS Manager makes entries in zone files using the correct syntax for compatibility with other servers. It's important to know what each record is used for and what its parameters specify. The following sections examine the records that are usually found in a zone file.

Start of Authority (SOA) Record

Each database file starts with a start of authority (SOA) record for the file. This record specifies the zone's primary server—the server that maintains the read/write copy of this file. The syntax of this record follows:

```
IN SOA <source host><contact email><ser. No.><refresh
time><retry time><expiration time><TTL>
```

An example of the syntax follows:

```
@ IN SOA ns1.erudite.com. kwolford.erudite.com. (
101      ; serial number
10800    ; refresh [3 hours]
3600     ; retry [1 hour]
604800   ; expire [7 days]
86400 )  ; time to live [1 day]
```

The "@" symbol in this example indicates the local server; "IN" indicates an Internet record. The FQDN for the name server NS1 must end in a period. Note that the email address for the administrator must have a period instead of the "@" symbol. Also, if the SOA record is on more than one line, an open parenthesis must end the first line, and a close parenthesis must end the last line.

The following list explains the other parameters:

◆ **Source host.** The name of the host that has the read/write copy of the zone file.

◆ **Contact email.** The Internet email address of the person who maintains this file. This address must be expressed with a period instead of the "@" that is usually found in email addresses (for example, `kwolford.erudite.com` instead of `kwolford@erudite.com`).

◆ **Serial number.** A version number for the zone file. This number should be changed each time the zone file changes; it changes automatically if you use DNS Manager to change the zone file.

◆ **Refresh time.** The time, in seconds, that a secondary server waits before checking the master server for changes to the database file. If the file has changed, the secondary server requests a zone transfer.

◆ **Retry time.** The time, in seconds, that a secondary server waits before trying again if a zone transfer fails.

◆ **Expiration time.** The time, in seconds, that a secondary server keeps trying to transfer a zone. After the expiration time passes, the old zone information is deleted.

◆ **TTL.** The time, in seconds, that a server can cache resource records from this database file. The TTL is sent as part of the response for any queries that are answered from this database file. An individual resource record can have a TTL that overrides this value.

Name Server Record

The name server record specifies the other name servers for a domain. The syntax for a name server record follows:

```
<domain> IN NS <nameserver host>
```

An example of a name server record follows:

```
@ IN NS ns1.erudite.com
```

The "@" symbol indicates the local domain. The server NS1 in the domain erudite.com is the name server.

Local Host Record

The local host record is simply a regular host record using a special host name and the normal IP loopback address (the address used to direct, or "loop back," TCP/IP traffic to the host generating the traffic). For example, the following record maps the name "localhost" to the loopback address of 127.0.0.1:

```
localhost IN A 127.0.0.1
```

This record enables a client to query for `localhost.erudite.com` and receive the normal loopback address.

Host Record

The host record is the record that actually specifies the IP address for a host. All hosts that have static IP addresses should have an entry in this database. (Clients with dynamic addresses are resolved in other ways, such as through a WINS server.)

Most of the entries in a database file are host records. The syntax of this record follows:

```
<host name> IN A <ip address of host>
```

An example of some host records follows:

```
arthur      IN A 136.104.3.92
thomas      IN A 136.104.4.85
kathleen    IN A 136.104.1.38
```

In this example, three servers called "arthur," "thomas," and "kathleen" are registered with their corresponding IP addresses.

To add an address resource record in the DNS Manager, complete the following steps.

STEP BY STEP

7.1 Adding an Address Resource Record

1. Right-click on the name-lookup zone icon and choose New Host from the Object menu.

   or

   Right-click in the database area of the Zone Info pane and choose New Host from the menu.

2. In the New Host dialog box, enter the host name in the Host Name field.

3. Enter the host's IP address in the Host IP Address field.

4. If you want to create a record in the appropriate reverse-lookup database, check Create Associated PTR Record. The reverse-lookup zone must have been previously created.

5. Choose Add Host to create the database records.

6. Repeat steps 2 through 5 to enter additional address records as required.

7. Choose Done when you are finished.

CNAME Record

The CNAME (or canonical name) record is an alias, enabling you to specify more than one name for each IP address. The syntax of a CNAME record follows:

```
<alias name> CNAME <host name>
```

Using CNAME records, you can combine an FTP and a Web server on the same host, for example. The following example maps a server called "InetServer" to a TCP/IP address; then the names FTP and WWW are aliased to this server:

```
InetServer IN A 136.107.3.43
FTP CNAME InetServer
WWW CNAME InetServer
```

These records illustrate how easy it is to change the server on which services are provided while still allowing access to the new server for clients that refer to its original name. For example, if you want to move the Web server to another machine called New-Inet, you can modify the zone files to read as follows:

```
InetServer IN A 136.107.3.43
FTP CNAME InetServer
NewInet IN A 136.107.1.107
WWW CNAME NewInet
```

The only change required for access to the new server was to make entries at the DNS server; changes do not have to be made at the clients. Any clients querying the DNS server receive the updated address automatically in response to the query.

STEP BY STEP

7.2 Adding Resource Records

1. Right-click on the zone that is to contain the record.

2. Choose New Record from the Object menu to open the New Resource Record dialog box.

3. Select CNAME Record in the Record Type list.

4. Enter an alias in the Alias Name field.

5. Enter the FQDN, the actual name for the host, in the For Host DNS Name field. Include the trailing dot when entering the name.

6. Choose OK to add the record.

> **NOTE**
>
> **Adding other resource records** This same procedure can be used to add other types of records to the DNS server, such as mail exchange (MX) records.

Mail Exchange Record

The mail exchange (MX) record specifies the name of the host that processes mail for this domain. If you list multiple mail servers, you can set a preference number that specifies the order in which the mail servers should be used. If the first preferred mail server doesn't respond, the second one is contacted, and so on. The syntax of this record follows:

```
<domain> IN MX <preference> <mailserver host>
```

Using the Cache File to Connect to Root-Level Servers

There is a cache file included with DNS that has entries for root-level servers on the Internet. If a host name cannot be resolved from local zone files, the DNS checks the cache for the next server in the hierarchy. If no information is found, the DNS uses the cache file to look for a root-level DNS server to resolve the name. This file is called cache.dns and is located at \winnt\system32\dns.

Although this file rarely changes, it is possible that the file included with Windows NT will eventually become outdated. The latest version of this file can be downloaded from InterNIC at `ftp://rs.internic.net/domain/named.cache`.

If your organization only has an intranet without any Internet access, you should replace this file with one that lists the root-level DNS servers in your organization.

Arpa-127.rev File

The Arpa-127.rev file is included with every DNS server. It provides reverse lookup for the local host, which is known as the loopback.

Pointer Record

The reverse-lookup file has entries that enable IP addresses to be resolved to host names. Normally, DNS is used to resolve host names to IP addresses, so the opposite process is called reverse lookup. The files are named according the class of network, but with the octets in reverse order.

The following examples are zone filenames for certain class A, class B, and class C networks:

Network ID	Zone Filename
36.x.x.x	36.in-addr.arpa
138.107.x.x	107.138.in-addr.arpa
242.23.108.x	108.23.242.in-addr.arpa

Pointer records are the reverse-lookup entries. They specify the IP address in reverse order (like a DNS name, with the most specific information first) and the corresponding host name. The syntax for a PTR record follows:

```
<ip reverse domain name> IN PTR <host name>
```

An example of a pointer record follows:

```
43.3.107.136.in-addr.arpa. IN PTR InetServer.microsoft.com
```

This example is an entry for the server called InetServer with the IP address of 136.107.3.43.

BIND Boot File

The BIND boot file is necessary for migrations from a BIND server. It may also be used instead of allowing Windows NT to keep startup information in the Registry. This file controls the startup of the DNS server. The capability to use a BIND boot file is mainly provided for compatibility with BIND versions of DNS, which use boot files for startup. You can copy the files from these servers and, with some editing, use them to boot an NT DNS server.

The commands that control the boot process in the BIND boot file are explained in the following sections.

DIRECTORY Command

The DIRECTORY command specifies the directory where the DNS files, including the files referenced by the boot file, can be found. The syntax of the DIRECTORY command follows:

```
directory <directory>
```

An example of the DIRECTORY command follows:

```
directory c:\winnt\system32\dns
```

This example shows that the files are located in the normal path of DNS files, which is also where Windows NT is installed on C:\WINNT.

CACHE Command

The CACHE command specifies the cache file that is used to locate root servers for the domain. This command must be in the file. A cache file is part of Microsoft DNS. The syntax is as follows:

```
cache . <filename>
```

An example of the CACHE command follows:

```
cache . cache
```

This example shows the name of the cache file, which is "cache" by default. Remember that the path for this file is already specified with the DIRECTORY command.

PRIMARY Command

The PRIMARY command specifies zone files for which this server is authoritative. For example, this server has the primary file for the zone. There can be more than one primary record in a file because a server can be the primary server for any number of zones. The syntax is as follows:

```
primary <domain> <filename>
```

An example of the PRIMARY command follows:

```
primary erudite.com erudite.com.dns
primary training.erudite.com training.com.dns
```

In this example, the local server is primary for two zone files: erudite.dns and training.dns.

SECONDARY Command

The SECONDARY command specifies those zones for which this server is a secondary server. It downloads a copy of the zone file from the primary server for the zone. The command specifies the zone file and also the address of the server where the secondary server is to download the zone file. Remember that a server can download the zone file from the primary server or from another secondary server.

The filename specified identifies where the local copy of this file is to be stored. You can have more than one SECONDARY command in a file because a server can be the secondary server for any number of zones. The syntax is as follows:

```
secondary <domain> <hostlist> <local filename>
```

An example of the SECONDARY command follows:

```
secondary software.erudite.com 158.51.20.1 software.com.dns
```

In this example, the local server is secondary for the zone software.dns, which can be transferred from the DNS server with an IP address of 158.51.20.1 (which is its master server and can be either a primary or secondary name server).

FORWARDERS Command

The FORWARDERS command specifies a server that can help resolve recursive queries if the local DNS server cannot. The syntax is as follows:

```
forwarders <hostlist>
```

An example of the FORWARDERS command follows:

```
forwarders 158.51.20.100 158.51.20.101
```

In this example, two servers are configured as forwarders: 158.51.20.100 and 158.51.20.101.

SLAVE Command

If a SLAVE command is present, the local DNS server must use the forwarders to resolve queries; the local server can't resolve the query using its own resources. The SLAVE command must follow a FORWARDERS command.

In this example, the local server is slave to the two servers listed in the FORWARDERS command:

```
forwarders 158.51.20.100 158.51.20.101
slave
```

IMPLEMENTING MICROSOFT DNS SERVERS

Now that you have had a look at how DNS works and the files that are used, it is time to see how to implement DNS within Windows NT. This section deals with setting up and configuring DNS within Windows NT.

Installing the DNS Server

The first item of business is to install the DNS server. The system on which you install the DNS service must be running Windows NT Server and should have a static IP configuration (as seen in Chapter 1, "Introduction to Networking with TCP/IP").

Installing the DNS server is the same as installing any other network service. The steps are as follows.

STEP BY STEP

7.3 Installing the DNS Server

1. Open the Network dialog box.

2. On the Services tab, click Add and select the Microsoft DNS Server service (see Figure 7.2).

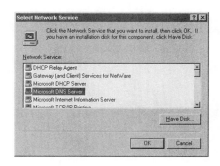

FIGURE 7.2
You add the DNS server service from the Select Network Service dialog box.

3. Click OK to add the service. When prompted, enter the directory in which your Windows NT source files are located.

4. Choose Close from the Network Settings dialog box and, when prompted, restart your system.

You have now installed the DNS service. To verify that the service is correctly installed, check the Services icon in Control Panel. Make sure the Microsoft DNS server is listed and has started.

Enabling DNS on the Client

Now that you have a DNS server, you need to have your clients use it. To enable Windows clients to use the DNS server, you can add its address to each station manually, or you can set the DNS server option on the DHCP server.

For Windows NT, you can use the following procedure to set the DNS server address (this process is similar for Windows 95):

STEP BY STEP

7.4 Setting the DNS Server Address

1. Open the Microsoft TCP/IP Properties dialog box. (Open the Network dialog box, and from the Protocol tab, double-click TCP/IP.)

2. On the DNS tab (see Figure 7.3), enter the required information. At the minimum, you need to enter the IP address of a DNS server. The other options on this tab were described in Chapter 2.

3. Click OK to close the TCP/IP settings.

4. Choose Close from the Network Settings dialog box and restart your system.

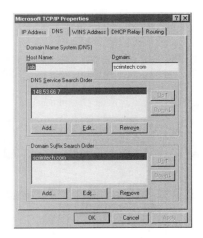

FIGURE 7.3
Configuring the DNS settings for the TCP/IP protocol.

You can also use the DNS server in addition to the WINS server for resolving NetBIOS names. To do this, you need to change the settings on the WINS tab in the TCP/IP configuration. Specifically, you need to select the option to use DNS to resolve NetBIOS names, as discussed in Chapter 2.

Using Existing BIND Files

If you already have a series of BIND files set up on an existing DNS server, you can use them to configure the Microsoft DNS server. Following are the steps you need to perform to configure the Microsoft DNS server to use the BIND files.

STEP BY STEP

7.5 Configuring the DNS Server to Use BIND Files

1. Install the Microsoft DNS service.

2. Stop the DNS service (from the Control Panel, choose the Services icon, click Microsoft DNS, and click the Stop button).

3. Copy all the BIND files, including the boot file, to the C:\WINNT\System32\DNS directory.

4. Start the DNS service (from the Control Panel, choose the Services icon, click Microsoft DNS, and click the Start button).

5. Use the DNS Manager to verify that your entries are there (see "The DNS Administration Tool").

Reinstalling the Microsoft DNS Server

There are a few things that you should know in case you need to reinstall the DNS server. When you start adding zones to a Microsoft DNS server, by default it switches to starting from the Registry rather than the DNS files discussed earlier, and it makes a note of this in the boot file. When you remove the server (before you reinstall), it does not remove this file; therefore, when you install the DNS server again, it assumes the boot file is valid and tries to read it. This creates several errors in the Event Log and causes the DNS server not to start.

Therefore, if you need to remove the DNS server, you should remove the boot file from the DNS directory. The original file is in the directory %winroot%\system32\dns\backup, and you can copy the files back from there; however, the server continues to boot from the Registry.

If you need to enable the system to start up from files, you must use the Registry Editor to open HKEY_LOCAL_MACHINE\SYSTEM\CurrentControlSet\Services\DNS\Parameters and change the data in the EnableRegistryBoot value to 1 (instead of the default of 0).

The DNS Administration Tool

Adding the DNS server also adds the DNS Administration tool, which makes configuring and maintaining the DNS server simple. It also provides single-seat administration for adding several DNS servers.

First, you need to add the DNS server that you want to manage, as follows.

STEP BY STEP

7.6 Adding a DNS Server

1. Start the DNS Manager by choosing Start, Programs, Administrative Tools, and then DNS Manager.

---

2. Right-click on the server list in the left pane of the DNS Manager (see Figure 7.4).

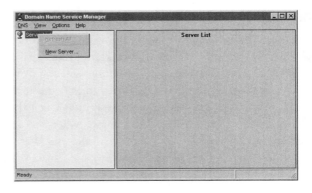

FIGURE 7.4
Adding a server to the DNS Manager.

3. Choose New Server from the menu.

4. In the DNS server box (see Figure 7.5), enter the name or IP address of the server you wish to add.

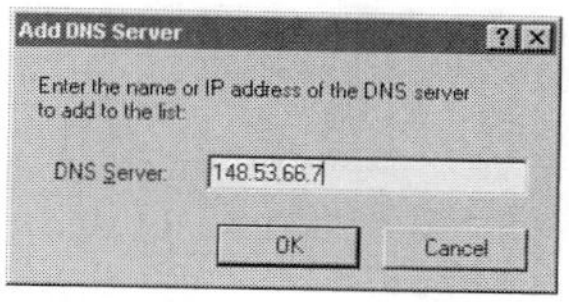

Now that you have added the server, you can configure it and add entries to its zone files.

FIGURE 7.5
Entering the IP address of the DNS server to add to the DNS Manager.

Configuring the Microsoft DNS Server

The roles that a DNS server can take on were discussed in the "Types of DNS Servers" section of this chapter. Included among the roles were primary, secondary, and caching-only servers. There also was a discussion of forwarders for caching-only servers.

The next few sections will focus on configuring a Microsoft DNS server for these different roles. The simplest role that a DNS server has is a caching-only server.

> **NOTE** **Master DNS Server** A master DNS server is a server from which a secondary server copies the zone file. This can be either a primary or secondary server.

Caching-Only Server

There is almost nothing you need to do to run a server as a caching-only server. As noted, this type of server does not host any zones. If this is all you need, you can stop here.

Forwarder

A forwarder is also a caching-only server; however, you need to configure it with the address of another Microsoft DNS server or any other DNS server, such as the one from your ISP. This configuration is fairly simple, and the only information you require is the IP address of the server to use.

Use the following steps to configure a forwarder.

STEP BY STEP

7.7 Configuring Forwarding

1. Right-click the server in the server list and select Properties.

FIGURE 7.6
Configuring forwarding on a Microsoft DNS
server.

2. On the Forwarders tab (see Figure 7.6), check the Use Forwarder(s) box.

3. If the server is only supposed to use the services of the other system, select Operate As Slave Server. (If you don't select this, the server attempts to resolve through the forwarder; however, it uses an iterative query if that fails.)

4. Enter the address or addresses of the DNS servers to which this one should forward queries.

5. If desired, set a time-out for the request.

6. Click OK to close the dialog box.

Creating a Primary Zone

The purpose of DNS is to resolve names to IP addresses. Therefore, you need to enter the addresses into the DNS server so that other users can find your hosts. You do this by creating a zone in the DNS server and entering the information that you want to make available to the world.

The following list covers the steps required to create a zone.

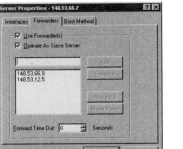

FIGURE 7.7
Choosing the type of zone to configure (primary or secondary).

STEP BY STEP

7.8 Creating a Zone

1. Right-click the server that hosts the zone in the server list.

2. Choose New Zone.

3. From the dialog box that appears, choose Primary (see Figure 7.7). Then choose Next.

4. Enter the name of the domain (or subdomain) for which you are creating a zone on the next screen (see Figure 7.8), and then press Tab. This automatically enters a zone file-name; if you are adding an existing zone file, enter the name of the file that has the information (it must be in

the %winroot%\System32\DNS directory). When the information is entered, click Next.

5. On the next screen, choose Finish.

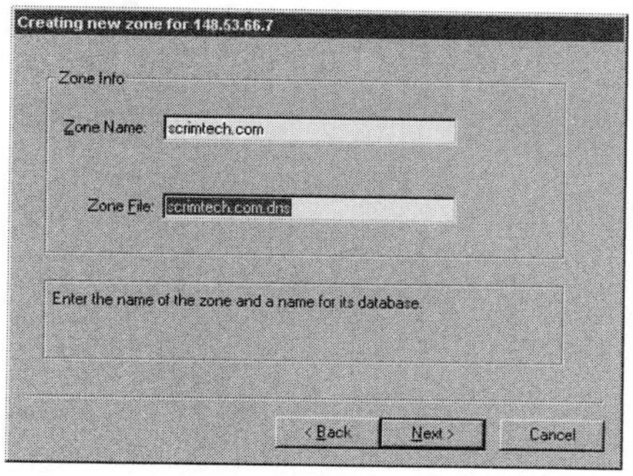

That is all there is to creating a zone. Now you can configure the zone and add the host and other records. When you have finished, the DNS Manager should look similar to Figure 7.9.

Setting Up and Reviewing the SOA Record

Configuring a zone is straightforward. Essentially, the information that you will enter here includes details for the SOA record and information about using WINS.

Setting up the information is easy. The following steps outline the process.

FIGURE 7.8
Enter the zone name and press Tab to enter the filename automatically.

STEP BY STEP

7.9 Configuring a Zone

1. Right-click the zone you want to configure. Choose Properties from the menu. The Properties dialog box should appear and present the basic zone information (see Figure 7.10).

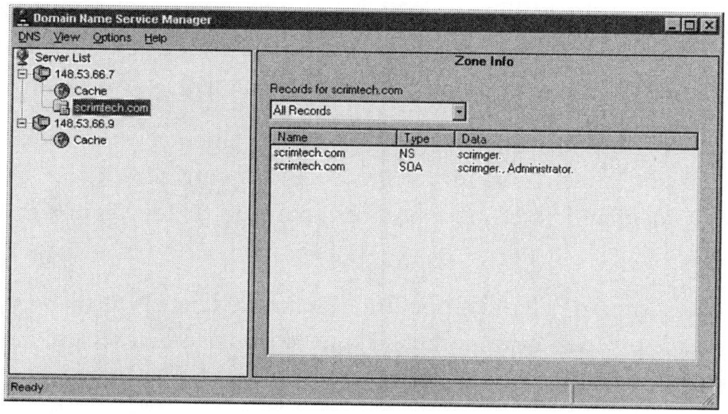

FIGURE 7.9
The DNS Manager with a primary zone configured.

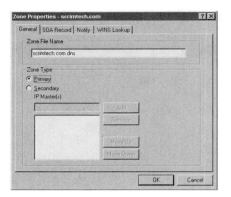

FIGURE 7.10
The zone information can be entered in this dialog box.

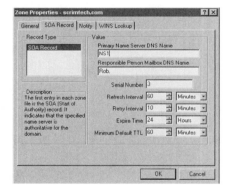

FIGURE 7.11
The SOA record should already be filled out.

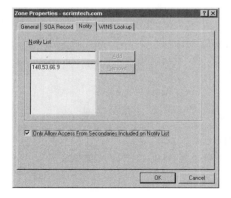

FIGURE 7.12
Configuring secondary notification.

2. Click on the SOA Record tab to bring up the information about the SOA (see Figure 7.11).

3. Edit the information in the SOA record. The fields that you can change were described previously; the defaults are fairly normal except for the following:

   • **Primary Name Server DNS Name.** This will contain the name of the primary name server for the zone. The DNS Manager will insert the FQDN of the local computer here (from the TCP/IP properties for the computer).

   • **Responsible Person Mailbox DNS Name.** This is the email address of the person controlling this zone. By default, the username logged in when the domain is created is used with the domain name entered in the TCP/IP properties.

4. Click the Notify tab (see Figure 7.12). Enter the IP address of secondary servers that should be notified when the zone file changes. If desired, you can also select the option only to allow access to these secondary servers.

5. Click OK to save the information.

Creating a Subdomain

Many organizations are broken down into smaller groups that focus on one area of the business. Or, perhaps the organization is dispersed geographically. In either case, the company may decide that it wants to break down its main domain into subdomains.

This is simple with Microsoft's DNS server. Choose the parent domain (scrimtech.com, for example), and then right-click. Choose New Domain and enter the subdomain name in the dialog box that appears.

If the subdomain is handled on another server, enter NS (name server) records for each of the other servers. If it is handled locally, simply add the records that are required.

Setting Up the Secondary Zone

After you configure your server, you may want to add a secondary server. Adding secondary servers provides redundancy and also splits the workload among the servers (you can have several secondary servers if you wish). The following list outlines the steps involved in adding a secondary zone.

STEP BY STEP

7.10 Adding a Secondary Zone

1. In the DNS Manager, right-click the server to be configured as a secondary server.

2. Choose New Zone from the context menu. From the New Zone dialog box, choose Secondary (see Figure 7.13).

   On this screen, you are asked for the zone name and the server from which to get zone files. A handy option is the ability (as seen in the figure) to drag the hand over another server listed in the DNS Manager to automatically pick up the information.

   If the primary DNS server is not a Microsoft DNS server, you will need to enter the information manually.

3. Click the Next button, and you can enter the information for the file. This should already be entered (see Figure 7.14), and you should click Next to accept the defaults.

4. The next screen asks you to identify the IP master for the zone. This should already be filled in for you (see Figure 7.15).

5. The last screen tells you that you are finished. Click Finish to close this screen.

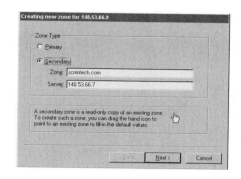

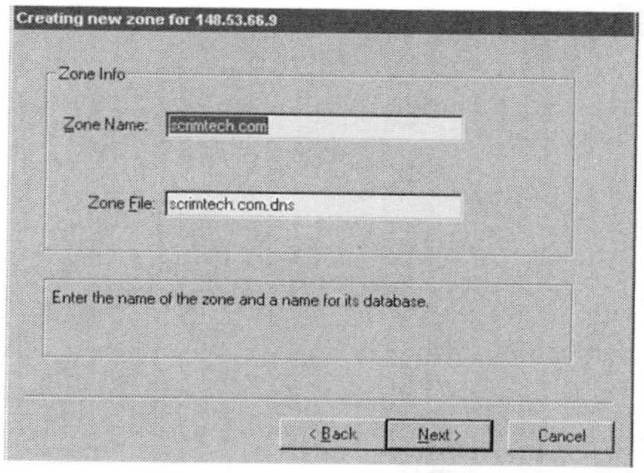

FIGURE 7.13
Configuring a secondary server for a zone.

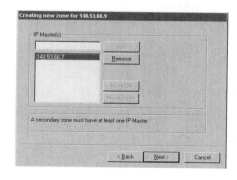

FIGURE 7.14
The file information for the secondary zone.

FIGURE 7.15
Configuring the IP master for a secondary zone.

Integration with WINS

When creating its DNS server, Microsoft followed the RFCs closely to ensure that the DNS you configure on Windows NT will be able to interact with existing DNS servers in your network and on the Internet. There is only one extension that has been added: the ability to integrate the DNS server with WINS.

As you should recall, the WINS server allows NetBIOS clients to dynamically register their names with a WINS server. This allows other systems to find their IP addresses even if they are DHCP clients whose addresses can change.

One of the major problems with DNS is the requirement to enter and update the host information for each host individually. This makes concurrent use of DHCP difficult because information in host records will be incorrect if the IP address changes for a host.

The simple extension that was added removes these problems. The DNS server can be configured to use a WINS server for name resolution. In essence, this provides a dynamic DNS for clients that can register with a WINS server.

To configure a DNS server to use a WINS server, you need to add the address of a WINS server to the zone configuration. The following steps outline how this is done.

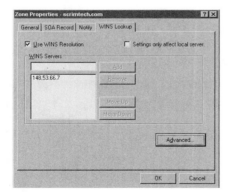

FIGURE 7.16
Adding WINS lookup to a DNS zone is simply a matter of adding the address.

STEP BY STEP

7.11 Configuring a DNS Server to Use a WINS Server

1. From the DNS Manager, choose the zone to which the systems should belong and choose Properties.

2. Click the WINS tab. Check the Use WINS Resolution box and add the IP address of a WINS server (see Figure 7.16).

3. Click OK.

NSLOOKUP

Along with the addition of a DNS server, Windows NT 4.0 also has a tool that enables you to test DNS to verify that it is working. The NSLOOKUP command line is shown here:

```
nslookup [-option ...] [computer-to-find ¦ - [server]]
```

You can use NSLOOKUP to query the DNS server from the command line (see Table 7.2 for a list of switches), or you can start an interactive session with the server to allow you to query the database. For the purposes of this section, look only at the command line.

TABLE 7.2

COMMAND-LINE SWITCHES FOR THE **NSLOOKUP** COMMAND

Switch	Description
-option	Allows you to enter one or more commands from the command line. (A list of the commands follows this table.) For each option you wish to add, enter a hyphen (-) followed immediately by the command name. Note that the command-line length needs to be less than 256 characters.
computer-to-find	The host or IP address you wish to find information about. It is processed using the default server (or a different server, if entered).

The following list provides the options that are available with the NSLOOKUP command.

- **-t *querytype*.** Lists all records of a given type. The record types are listed under querytype.

- **-a.** Lists all the CNAME entries from the DNS server.

- **-d.** Dumps all records that are in the DNS server.

- **-h.** Returns information on the DNS server's CPU and operating system.

- **-s.** Returns the well-known services for hosts in the DNS domain.

CASE STUDY: IMPLEMENTING DNS FOR THE SUNSHINE BREWING COMPANY

ESSENCE OF THE CASE

Here are some of the points that you should be considering in this scenario:

- You need to be able to control the entries in your DNS server.

- You have a limited amount of bandwidth and need to reserve as much as possible for your employees to reach resources on the Internet and in other offices.

- There will be a need for all internal employees, regardless of their branch, to be able to resolve names in your organization.

Looking back to the original requirements of your project with the Sunshine Brewing Company, you might remember that the company wanted to bring its Web page in-house. There will also be a need for Exchange clients to find the Exchange server that will be running POP3 (Post Office Protocol 3).

SCENARIO

As just noted, one of the elements required in this case is to bring the Web site in-house. This will mean creating a server and adding the correct entries for the DNS server. There will also be at least one Exchange server that will be used to receive mail; this server will also need the correct entry in the DNS name space.

There is also the matter of the other locations being able to connect to these servers (and others on the Internet). This means that they will require a local DNS server or have to traverse the Internet to the head office every time they need to resolve a name.

ANALYSIS

In this case, the requirements for DNS are very simple. There are three ways that you can approach the problem.

First, you could let the ISP used by the head office deal with the DNS servers. Typically, an ISP is happy to handle this function for a corporate customer and will sometimes not even charge for the updates to DNS that you make. This will provide two fast servers that will be able to resolve the names for your domain.

CASE STUDY: IMPLEMENTING DNS FOR THE SUNSHINE BREWING COMPANY

You can then add a caching-only server at each of the other locations. These will be able to cache the resolutions from the ISP's servers. This will actually be the case in whichever method you use because otherwise the zone transfer unnecessarily takes up the bandwidth that could be used by the employees.

Another way that you can set up the DNS servers is to choose to use systems in smaller offices (creating less traffic) and make them the DNS servers for the Internet. This will allow you to have total control over the DNS entries for your domain. The downside to this is the speed that will be available to people trying to resolve addresses who will need to enter your network. This also could present a security risk.

The last method allows you to control the information seen by the others on the Internet and still gives potential clients high speeds when resolving names to your network. This requires creating a primary server internally and arranging for your ISP to pick up the entries from your server and put them on two of their servers. This provides you with two servers on the Internet, and the only internal exposure is the SOA record. Furthermore, bandwidth is used only by the occasional zone transfer to the ISP's name servers.

CHAPTER SUMMARY

KEY TERMS

- BIND
- boot file
- cache file
- caching-only server
- CNAME record
- DNS
- forwarder
- host record
- iterative query
- master server
- MX record
- name server
- pointer record
- primary DNS server
- recursive query
- resolver
- reverse-lookup file
- secondary DNS server
- slave
- start of authority (SOA) record
- zone

This chapter has introduced you to the concept of name space. The DNS works with a name space that starts at the root servers and then breaks into more specific areas. The Domain Name System is probably the largest existing distributed database system in the world—and it grows every day.

From this chapter you should have gained the following knowledge:

- ◆ You need to know how to install the DNS service and configure the clients manually or using DHCP.

- ◆ You need to know how to create a primary zone and what the options in the SOA record are for.

- ◆ You need to know how to set up a server to act as a secondary server.

- ◆ You need to know what impact setting up WINS integration will have.

- ◆ You need to understand the recursive queries (resolver to DNS, DNS to forwarder, DNS to WINS).

- ◆ You need to understand iterative queries (for example: root, then .com, then microsoft.com, then www.microsoft.com).

- ◆ You need to understand that authority is given to the zone files; the SOA record could cover a second-level domain and one or more subdomains.

- ◆ You need to know that a secondary server obtains the zone file from a master server, which is either a secondary or a primary server itself.

- ◆ You need to know the difference between a forwarder and a forwarder slave.

- ◆ You should understand the construction and use of the DNS files (even the boot file).

- ◆ You need to know how to add domains, subdomains, and records to the name server.

- ◆ Specifically, you need to remember to reverse the network ID when creating a reverse lookup zone; also, you need to know why you would create it in the first place.

Exercises

The following exercises will give you a chance to try the Microsoft DNS server.

7.1   Installing the Microsoft DNS Server

First, you need to install the DNS server. This exercise assumes you have a network card in your system. If you do not, install the MS Loopback Adapter, which will enable you to do the following exercises. If the system you are working on is running DNS, make sure that you back up the files before you proceed, just in case.

Estimated Time: About 10 minutes.

1. Open the Network Settings dialog box. Choose the Protocols tab and double-click the TCP/IP protocol.

2. On the DNS tab, enter your IP address as the DNS server and click Add. Also, add the domain SunnyDays.com into the domain field.

3. Click the Services tab and choose Add. From the list that appears, choose the Microsoft DNS Server and click OK.

4. Enter the directory for the Windows NT source files.

5. Close the Network Settings dialog box and restart your computer.

7.2   Configuring a DNS Domain

Now that the server is up and running, you need to create the domains that you will use. The first domain to be created is the reverse-lookup domain. After that is in place, you will create the SunnyDays.com domain.

Estimated Time: About 10 minutes.

1. From the Start menu, choose Programs, Administrative Tools, DNS Manager.

2. From the menu, choose DNS, New Server. Enter your IP address and click OK.

3. To create the reverse-lookup domain, click your system's address. Choose DNS, New Zone.

4. Choose Primary and click Next.

5. For the Zone, enter **106.160.in-addr.arpa** and press Tab (the filename is filled in for you).

6. Click Next to continue, and then choose Finish.

7. Make sure "106.160.in-addr.arpa" is highlighted; then choose DNS, Properties from the menu.

8. On the WINS Reverse Lookup tab, check the box Use WINS Reverse Lookup. Enter **SUNNYDAYS.COM** as the host domain and choose OK. There should now be a new host record.

9. Select your DNS server's address, and then select DNS, New Zone from the menu.

10. Select Primary and choose Next. Enter **SUNNYDAYS.COM** as the zone name. Press Tab to have the system fill in the filename, and then choose Next. Click the Finish button.

11. Right-click the SunnyDays.com domain name. From the context menu that appears, select Properties.

12. Select the WINS Lookup tab.

13. Check the Use WINS Resolution box. Enter your IP address in the WINS Server space and choose Add.

APPLY YOUR KNOWLEDGE

14. Choose OK to close the dialog box. A WINS record should be in the SunnyDays.com domain.

7.3 Adding Records

Now that you have created the reverse-lookup domain and the SunnyDays.com domain, add some records to the database.

Estimated Time: About 20 minutes.

1. Right-click the SunnyDays.com domain and choose Add Host.

2. In the New Host dialog box, add **Rob** as the Host Name and **160.106.66.7** as the Host IP Address.

3. Check the Create Associated PTR Record to create the reverse-lookup record at the same time.

4. Choose Add Host. Now enter **Judy** as the Host Name and **160.106.66.9** as the Host IP Address.

5. Click Add Host. Then click the Done button to close the dialog box. You should see the two new records in the DNS Manager.

6. Click on the 106.160.in-addr.arpa domain and press F5 to refresh. Notice there is now a 66 subdomain.

7. Double-click the 66 subdomain. What new hosts are there? There should be PTR records for the two hosts you just added.

8. Select the SunnyDays.com domain again. Add the following hosts, making sure that you include the associated PTR records:

Mail1	160.106.92.14
Mail2	160.106.101.80
Mail3	160.106.127.14

Web1	160.106.65.7
Web2	160.106.72.14
FTP_Pub1	160.106.99.99
FTP_Pub2	160.106.104.255
DEV	160.106.82.7

9. Close the New Host dialog box. Verify that the records were added to the SunnyDays.com and reverse-lookup domains.

10. Highlight SunnyDays.com, and choose DNS, New Domain from the menu.

11. Enter **DEV** as the Name for the new domain and choose OK.

12. Right-click on the DEV subdomain, choose New Record, and select CNAME as the record type.

13. Enter **WWW** as the alias, and **web2.SunnyDays.com** as the Host. (This entry sets up WWW.DEV.SUNNYDAYS.COM to point to WEB2.SUNNYDAYS.COM.)

14. Click OK to add the record. (It should appear in the Zone Info window.)

15. Create the CNAME entries from the following table in the SunnyDays.com domain. Right-click SunnyDays.com, each time choosing New Record.

Alias	Host
WWW	web1.SunnyDays.com
FTP	FTP_PUB1.SunnyDays.com
DEV_FTP	FTP_PUB2.SunnyDays.com

16. Create a new record in the SunnyDays.com domain. This time, choose MX as the Record Type.

APPLY YOUR KNOWLEDGE

17. Leave the Host blank for this record, and enter **mail1.SunnyDays.com** as the Mail Exchange Server DNS Name. Enter **10** as the Preference.

18. Choose OK to add the record. Add a second MX record for the SunnyDays.com using **mail2.SunnyDays.com** as the Mail Server and **20** as the Preference.

19. Now add the MX record for dev.SunnyDays.com. To do this, right-click on SunnyDays.com and choose New Record; again, this is an MX record.

20. The difference is that you include the host name. Enter **DEV** as the Host, **mail3.SunnyDays.com** as the Mail Exchange Server DNS Name, and **10** as the preference.

21. Ensure that all the records appear to be in place, and then close the DNS Manager.

7.4 Testing the DNS Server

This exercise gives you a chance to test the information you entered and to check that everything is working correctly.

Estimated Time: About 20 minutes.

1. Start a command prompt.

2. Type the command **NSLOOKUP 160.106.101.80** and press Enter. What response did you get? (The response should show that 160.106.101.80 is mail2.SunnyDays.com. Here you have done a reverse lookup on the IP address.)

3. Using the NSLOOKUP command, find out what responses the following entries give you:

   160.106.66.7
   160.106.99.99

www.SunnyDays.com

www.dev.SunnyDays.com

ftp.SunnyDays.com

The results should be:

160.106.66.7	rob.SunnyDays.com
160.106.99.99	ftp_pub1.SunnyDays.com
www.SunnyDays.com	160.106.65.7 (web1.SunnyDays.com)
www.dev.SunnyDays.com	148.55.72.14 (web2.SunnyDays.com)
ftp.SunnyDays.com	160.106.99.99 (ftp_pub1.SunnyDays.com)

4. Start an interactive session with the name server by typing **NSLOOKUP** and pressing Enter.

5. Try the following commands:

```
ls SunnyDays.com

ls -t mx SunnyDays.com

ls -d

q=soa

SunnyDays.com

q=mx

SunnyDays.com
```

6. Press Ctrl+C to exit the interactive query.

7. Close the command prompt.

Review Questions

1. What is an FQDN?

2. What is the purpose of a CNAME record?

APPLY YOUR KNOWLEDGE

3. What is the difference between a recursive query and an iterative query?

4. What purpose does a forwarder serve?

5. For what two main roles can a DNS server be configured?

6. What four main files are used to configure a DNS server?

7. What is required to configure a Microsoft DNS server to act as a dynamic DNS server?

8. What does reverse lookup provide?

9. Which type of applications use a DNS server?

10. How do you configure Windows NT to use DNS to resolve NetBIOS names?

Exam Questions

1. Your organization primarily uses Microsoft operating systems, and you want to be able to provide DNS lookup for the hosts in your organization for servers on the Internet. Your organization uses DHCP to assign IP addresses. What do you need to do to provide reverse-lookup capabilities?

   A. Reserve a DHCP address for each client and enter this information into the DNS server.

   B. Set up the clients to use DNS for WINS resolution.

   C. Add a WINS record in the DNS database.

   D. This is not possible.

2. Your organization wants to be able to control the entries that are in your DNS server. You currently have a domain registered with InterNIC, and your ISP is providing your DNS resolution. You have a 128Kbps link to your ISP and don't want to use all the bandwidth resolving DNS queries. Which of the following would best suit your needs?

   A. Increase your line speed to a T1 and set up two DNS servers.

   B. Set up a DNS server in your organization and arrange for your ISP to transfer your zone to its servers.

   C. Have your ISP continue to handle DNS for your organization.

   D. Use WINS to handle all name resolution.

3. Which of the following are roles that you can configure your DNS server for?

   A. Primary

   B. Tertiary

   C. Backup

   D. Forwarder

4. You installed Microsoft DNS Server and tested the configuration. Later you removed and reinstalled the service in preparation for configuring the DNS server with the real information. What must you do to make sure the DNS server starts cleanly?

   A. Remove the files from the %winroot%\system32\dns directory.

   B. Reinstall Windows NT.

   C. Remove and reinstall the WINS server.

   D. Nothing—the configuration will work fine.

APPLY YOUR KNOWLEDGE

5. Your organization currently uses a UNIX server for DNS. The server is fully configured using BIND files. In which two ways can you configure your Microsoft DNS server so you will not need to re-enter any information?

   A. Set up Microsoft DNS as the primary server and transfer the zone to the UNIX system.

   B. Set up Microsoft DNS as the secondary server and transfer the zone from the UNIX system.

   C. Configure the Microsoft DNS server as a forwarder.

   D. Configure the Microsoft DNS server as a caching-only server.

6. Which of the following statements about DNS are true?

   A. DNS resolves NetBIOS names to IP addresses.

   B. DNS resolves host names to IP addresses.

   C. DNS resolves IP addresses to hardware addresses.

   D. DNS resolves IP addresses to host names.

7. You have a computer called WEBSERVER with an IP address of 148.53.66.45 running Microsoft Internet Information Server. This system provides the HTTP and FTP services for your organization on the Internet. Which of the following sets of entries should you configure in your database file?

   A. www IN A 148.53.66.45

      ftp IN A 148.53.66.45

   B. www IN A 148.53.66.45

      ftp IN A 148.53.66.45

      webserver CNAME www

   C. webserver IN A 148.53.66.45

      www CNAME webserver

      ftp CNAME webserver

   D. 45.66.53.148 IN PTR webserver

8. Which of the following is not part of a Fully Qualified Domain Name?

   A. Type of organization

   B. Host name

   C. Company name

   D. CPU type

9. Your organization uses a firewall with five subnets. You intended to provide a DNS server on each subnet, but you want them to query the main DNS server that sits outside the firewall. What configuration should you choose for the DNS servers that you will put on each subnet?

   A. Configure the DNS server outside the firewall to use a WINS server on each local subnet; then configure the DNS servers on the local subnets to use WINS resolution.

   B. Set up the DNS servers on the local subnets as IP forwarders to the DNS server outside the firewall.

   C. Create a primary zone on each of the DNS servers inside the firewall and configure the DNS server outside the firewall to transfer each zone.

   D. This is not possible.

APPLY YOUR KNOWLEDGE

10. When you are configuring your DNS server, where do you set the length of time that an entry will be cached on your server?

    A. Set the TTL in the DNS Manager Properties on your server.

    B. Set the TTL in the cache file on the remote server.

    C. Set the TTL in the Registry under HKEY_LOCAL_MACHINE\SYSTEM\ CurrentControlSet\Services\TCPIP\Parameters.

    D. Set the TTL from the remote server in the SOA record.

11. Which of the following will enable a client computer to use a DNS server for NetBIOS name resolution?

    A. Configure the WINS server to use DNS lookup.

    B. Do nothing; this will happen automatically.

    C. On the WINS configuration tab, enable DNS for NetBIOS Name Resolution.

    D. Add a DNS entry in the LMHOSTS file.

12. Which of the following NSLOOKUP commands will provide a list of all the mail servers for the domain nt.com?

    A. NSLOOKUP -t MX nt.com

    B. NSLOOKUP -a MX nt.com

    C. NSLOOKUP -h nt.com

    D. NSLOOKUP -m nt.com

13. In which of the following scenarios will a recursive query not be used?

    A. Your system querying the DNS server

    B. Your DNS server querying the root-level servers

    C. Your DNS server querying the WINS server

    D. Your DNS server querying when configured as a forwarder

14. You are at a computer named PROD172. The IP address of the computer is 152.63.85.5, and the computer is used to publish to the World Wide Web for the domain gowest.com. Which entries should you find in the database file?

    A. prod172 IN MX 152.63.85.5

    B. www IN cname 152.63.85.5

    C. prod172 IN A 152.63.85.5

       www IN CNAME 152.63.85.5

    D. prod172 IN A 152.63.85.5

       www IN CNAME prod172

15. Which of the following files is not required for compliance with the DNS RFCs?

    A. The cache file

    B. The database file

    C. The boot file

    D. The reverse-lookup file

16. Which of the following best describes the order in which you should configure the DNS server?

    A. Install the server, create the zone, enter all the records, create the reverse-lookup zone, and add the WINS records.

    B. Install the server, create the reverse-lookup zone, and add the zone information followed by the WINS lookup records and the other hosts.

C. Create the DNS server database files using a text editor, install the server, and verify the information.

D. Install the DNS server and then transfer the zone from the WINS server.

17. What information is contained in an MX record?

A. A Preference entry.

B. The mail server name.

C. The WWW server name.

D. There is no such record.

18. What is the purpose of the cache file?

A. It stores the names of hosts that your server has resolved.

B. It allows you to enter commonly used hosts that will be loaded to the cache.

C. It stores the addresses of root-level servers.

D. It is used to temporarily build the DNS server information as the server starts.

Answers to Review Questions

1. An FQDN, or Fully Qualified Domain Name, is a combination of the host name and the name of the domain it belongs to within the Domain Name Space. See "Resolving DNS Queries."

2. A CNAME record is an alias within the DNS server that allows one record (a CNAME record) to point at another (a host record). See "CNAME Record."

3. A recursive query demands a definitive answer from the server it is sent to, whereas an iterative query requests a best answer in an effort to find an authoritative answer. Normally, a recursive query is from a resolver to a DNS server and an iterative query is from one DNS server to another. See "Resolving DNS Queries."

4. An IP forwarder is a server to which a DNS server forwards requests for resolutions. This allows several internal servers all to point to a single external DNS server so that the internal servers do not need to go out of the local network. See "Forwarders and Slaves."

5. The two main roles of a name server are as a primary or secondary server for a zone file, or resolving addresses only (as with a caching-only server). See "Types of DNS Servers."

6. The files that are used to configure a server include the cache file, which lists the root servers and the zone files that contain the records for the local domain. This is also the reverse-lookup file that is used to resolve an IP address to a host name, and the boot file that is used by a BIND-compatible server to hold the startup parameters. See "Structure of DNS Files."

7. To create a dynamic DNS server in a Microsoft environment, you need only configure the zone (and the reverse-lookup zone to use a WINS server to resolve names they do not have). See "Integration with WINS."

8. Reverse lookup provides the ability to resolve an IP address to a host name. This can be used by a server to obtain the host name for a client that is connecting. See "Inverse Queries."

APPLY YOUR KNOWLEDGE

9. DNS is used for standard sockets applications. This includes such services as FTP and HTTP. See "Resolving DNS Queries."

10. On the WINS Address tab of the TCP/IP Properties, you need to select Use DNS for NetBIOS Name Resolution. See "Enabling DNS on the Client."

Answers to Exam Questions

1. **C.** By adding a WINS record to the DNS server, the server will be able to use the WINS server to resolve name queries for which it has no entry. See "Integration with WINS."

2. **B.** Because the Microsoft DNS Server is compliant with the RFCs, you can use the ISP's servers as a secondary. This will allow you to control the addresses in your organization yet leave name resolution to the servers located at your ISP. See "Creating a Primary Zone" and "Setting Up the Secondary Zone."

3. **A.** There are three roles for which a server can be configured: primary, secondary, and caching only. See "Types of DNS Servers."

4. **A.** As was discussed in the chapter, the boot file (and other files) are not removed along with the service when DNS is removed. You will need to remove these files before reinstalling the DNS server. See "Reinstalling Microsoft DNS Server."

5. **B** and **C.** Either of these methods will allow you to access the information on the UNIX server without re-entering the information. If you configure the system as a secondary server, it will

resolve the addresses locally; as a caching-only forwarder, the UNIX server will provide the resolution. Configuring as a caching-only server may work but would require that you use external servers to provide part of the resolution. See "Types of DNS Servers."

6. **B** and **D.** DNS does not work with NetBIOS names, which are assigned by a flat method. DNS can also use reverse lookup to resolve the host name from the IP address. ARP resolves IP addresses to MAC addresses. See "Resolving DNS Queries."

7. **C.** These entries provide the resolution for ftp and www to the correct server: webserver. Although the answer given in D is correct, this is for the reverse-lookup file, not for the database file. See "Structure of DNS Files."

8. **C** and **D.** Neither the company name nor the CPU type is by definition part of the FQDN. The type of organization is normally given by the top-level domain, and the host name is the first part of the FQDN. See "Resolving DNS Queries."

9. **B.** By configuring the local DNS servers to forward resolution requests to the DNS server outside the firewall, you will be able achieve this. See "Forwarders and Slaves."

10. **D.** The server that resolves the query will return the length of time you can cache the address entry along with the address. Therefore, you do not configure it on the local system but rather on the remote DNS server. See "Resolving DNS Queries."

11. **C.** Because name resolution is initiated by the client, this configuration must be done on the

APPLY YOUR KNOWLEDGE

client. Therefore, the correct answer is C. See "Resolving DNS Queries."

12. **A.** When using NSLOOKUP to find a type of record, you use the -t option. This and the type of record you are looking for will be required along with the domain to look in. See "NSLOOKUP."

13. **B.** The only query listed in the question that is not recursive is trying to find a definitive answer for a host-name query. These queries almost always start at the root-level or top-level domains as the first iteration. See "Resolving DNS Queries."

14. **D.** These entries include a resolution of the regular computer name to an IP address and the alias of www pointing to the computer name in a CNAME record. See "Structure of DNS Files."

15. **C.** The boot file is part of the BIND name server implementation. The boot file is used to point to

all the other files that are required to bring the server up. See "BIND Boot File."

16. **B.** The server will need to be installed. Then you will create a reverse-lookup file so the entries can be added along with the host records. Now you can create the zone and host information and add a WINS lookup record. See "Implementing Microsoft DNS Servers."

17. **B.** The MX records are used to store mail exchange records, which are used to tell other servers where to send mail. More than one MX record can exist; however, the servers will be tried in order of preference (lowest number to highest). See "Mail Exchange Record."

18. **C.** The cache file is used to store the records that point to the root-level servers. Zone files store host names. See "Using the Cache File to Connect to Root-Level Servers."

Suggested Readings and Resources

1. Masterson, Michael. *Windows NT DNS*. New Riders, 1998.

2. *Windows NT 4.0 Resource Kit, Networking Guide*: Chapter 9 "Managing MS DNS Servers."

3. Albitz, Paul, and Cricket Liu. *DNS and BIND, Third Edition*. O'Reilly, 1998.

This chapter will help you prepare for the exam by covering the following objective:

Configure HOSTS and LMHOSTS files.

▶ Here you will need to know the general configuration for the HOSTS and LMHOSTS files, and the tags that are available for the LMHOSTS.

CHAPTER 8

Name Resolution

STUDY STRATEGIES

As you read through this chapter, you should concentrate on the following key items:

▶ You need to understand why the HOSTS and LMHOSTS files are used.

▶ You need to know how to configure each file.

▶ You need to know how to configure a centralized LMHOSTS file.

One of the big problems with using TCP/IP is that the addressing is unusual and difficult for humans. Most people have problems remembering a few phone numbers; therefore, remembering thousands of IP addresses is out of the question.

For this reason, hosts on a TCP/IP intranet have assigned names in addition to IP addresses that you can use to connect to them. This sure makes it easier for humans; however, this adds a great deal of complexity for TCP/IP. IP already needs to know the IP address to determine if a host is local or remote. Furthermore, the Network Access layer needs the MAC address to actually send the data.

You have already seen in Chapter 1, "Introduction to Networking with TCP/IP," the address resolution protocol (ARP), which uses a simple broadcast to resolve an IP address to a MAC address. This works because all the IP addresses ARP works with are on the local subnet. And if an IP address is remote, an ARP on a router somewhere else is used to find the MAC address of the final destination.

When you attempt to understand name resolution, you should realize that the name you are looking for may not be on the local network—it might be for a system across the hall or halfway around the world. This means that name resolution needs to use something other than broadcasts.

The whole issue of name resolution is made even more complex when you add NetBIOS on top of TCP/IP because the NetBIOS session created over TCP/IP will need to use the configured NetBIOS name of the remote host.

This chapter will look at two aspects of name resolution: resolution of hostnames and resolution of NetBIOS names.

HOSTNAME RESOLUTION

Most sockets applications use hostnames interchangeably with IP addresses. This includes applications such as File Transfer Protocol (FTP) and Internet Explorer (IE), which can use either the IP address or hostname of the user, but always uses the IP address in actual communications.

The best way to think of a hostname is that it is a pointer or alias to an IP address. After the IP address is known, the hostname is no longer required. Therefore, hostname resolution is the process by which hostnames are mapped to IP addresses. You can do this in a number of ways, listed here in the order of use:

◆ Local hostname

◆ HOSTS file

◆ Domain Name System (DNS) servers

Later in this chapter, you will see that there are also different methods used to resolve NetBIOS names. Windows NT will use those methods as a backup to the methods of hostname resolution just given.

These are the NetBIOS name resolution methods that can be used for hostname resolution:

◆ WINS servers

◆ Local broadcast

◆ LMHOSTS files

Again, the NetBIOS name resolution methods will be saved for later in the chapter. In the next few sections, the methods that are used primarily for hostname resolution will be discussed.

The Local Host

The first item that will be checked when trying to resolve a hostname is the local hostname. This prevents traffic from going to the network in a case in which you are attempting to connect to your own system.

The local hostname is set on the DNS tab of the TCP/IP configuration, as discussed in Chapter 1. This name is normally the same as the NetBIOS name in Windows NT, but it can be different.

As discussed previously in this book, a Fully Qualified Domain Name (FQDN) is a combination of the hostname and the domain name. This name is viewed using the HOSTNAME utility. To determine the local hostname, do the following:

STEP BY STEP

8.1 Checking the Local Hostname

1. Start a command prompt.

2. Type **HOSTNAME** and press Enter.

The HOSTS File

If the system that you're attempting to connect to is not your local system, your application will then look at the HOSTS file for a resolution of the name.

The HOSTS file is a simple text file that resides in the *winnt_root*\system32\drivers\etc directory. The file can be edited using any standard text editor. However, you must not save the file as unicode or with an extension.

A sample HOSTS file might look like the following:

```
209.206.202.64        www www.scrimtech.com  scrimtech.com
➥# corporate web server
199.45.92.97          sparky sparky.leanrix.ca learnix.ca
➥# learnix server
127.0.0.1             localhost
```

As you look at the sample, you will notice that there are basically three components to each line:

◆ **IP address.** This is the IP address that will be returned for the name given to the right.

◆ **Name or names.** After the IP address, you leave at least one space and enter the name or names that map to this IP address. Note that more than one name can be added, each separated by a space.

◆ **Comments.** The last portion allows you to add comments. These are not required, but they make the file easier to read by providing more information about the entries. Comments start with a pound sign (#) and a space. Everything after a space is ignored by Windows NT.

Names in the HOSTS file are limited to 255 characters and are not case sensitive. The HOSTS file must reside on each host, and the file is read from top to bottom. As soon as a match is found for a hostname, the application stops reading the file. For that reason, when there are duplicate entries, the latter ones are always ignored, and the names used most often should be near the top of the file.

DNS Servers

Because it would be impractical to keep a list of all the servers that you ever connect to in the HOSTS file, Windows NT then tries using a DNS server. A recursive query is generated and sent to the DNS server that is configured in the TCP/IP properties. The system may have to send more than one query to find the hostname that it is trying to resolve. The queries will be sent until you get a resolution or a negative response.

The following list describes the queries sent:

1. The name queried is appended with the domain name configured in the DNS tab of the TCP/IP Properties. For example, if Windows NT is configured with the domain "ScrimTech.com," and you PING "tomorrow," Windows NT will send a query for "tomorrow.ScrimTech.com."

2. The system will query on the name you entered. In the previous example, you would query for "tomorrow."

3. The system will continue sending queries by appending each entry from the domain suffix search order to the hostname until all entries are tried or a resolution is found.

NETBIOS NAME RESOLUTION OVER TCP/IP

Now that hostname resolution has been discussed, it is time to look at NetBIOS name resolution. NetBIOS names are registered for each service running on the system that you are working on.

The NetBIOS name for a service is made up of two parts: the name you enter (up to 15 characters), and a sixteenth character to identify the service that is registering the name. If this sounds a lot like sockets, it is not surprising because they both serve the same purpose: providing an endpoint for communications.

Just like a socket tells TCP which port to give received data to, the service number tells NetBIOS which service to give data to. This seems to be, and is, a duplication of effort. Recall that NetBIOS was not designed for use with TCP/IP and cannot rely on the transport protocol to route the data to the correct service.

Just like the way regular TCP/IP communications require a full socket number, NetBIOS communications require the full service name. This means that NetBIOS names cannot use aliases; NetBIOS will not have the alias registered and cannot pass the data. This is the same as how TCP cannot pass data up to a socket that is not open.

Because of this requirement, you can see how the need for name resolution systems has evolved. You can generally resolve NetBIOS names in one of three ways: using broadcasts, the services of a NetBIOS name server, or an LMHOSTS file.

In any case, there are three main functions required by the NetBIOS:

- ◆ **Name Registration.** As mentioned, NetBIOS registers the names for the local computer (primarily to prevent duplicate names). Broadcasting a NetBIOS name registration on the local network or sending the registration to a NetBIOS name server (such as WINS) can accomplish this.

- ◆ **Name Resolution.** This is the process of resolving the computer name to an IP address. A NetBIOS name query is broadcast on the network or sent directly to a NetBIOS name server.

- ◆ **Name Release.** As you shut down your system, a name release request is broadcast on the wire or sent to a NetBIOS name server. This informs other hosts you are communicating with that you are shutting down. This primarily releases your username and makes it available so you can log on to other hosts.

It should be noted that if a broadcast is used, the NetBIOS name is resolved (or registered) only on the local segment. In most multisegment networks, a WINS server is used to provide enterprisewide name registration and resolution services.

Just like with hostname resolution, there are different methods of name resolution for NetBIOS. The following list outlines the methods available in the default order in which they are tried:

◆ NetBIOS name cache

◆ LMHOSTS file

◆ Broadcast

◆ NetBIOS name server

◆ HOSTS file

◆ DNS server

NetBIOS Node Types

A key issue in NetBIOS name resolution is the order in which the various methods are tried. Using the wrong order might cause the system to sit, appearing to be hung, as some methods time out.

The NetBIOS node type determines the order of Resolution. This can be set by configuring services, editing the Registry, or using a Dynamic Host Configuration Protocol (DHCP) server.

You should note that Windows NT defaults to a broadcast node type (enhanced b-node)—unless a WINS server address is entered, in which case it defaults to a hybrid node type (h-node).

The node types are as follows:

◆ b-node (broadcast)

◆ p-node (point-to-point)—Uses an NBNS

◆ m-node (mixed)—First tries b-node, then p-node

◆ h-node (hybrid)—First tries p-node, then b-node

Remember that this is the resolution order for NetBIOS names only. Resolving hostnames uses the order shown earlier.

b-node

The simplest way to resolve a name on the network is to ask every system on the network if a name belongs to it. Obviously, this is

NOTE

Microsoft's LMHOSTS File Windows NT defaults to a node type of enhanced b-node as defined in RFCs 1001/1002. Because Microsoft already had an LMHOSTS file that had been used successfully with LAN Manager (hence, the name **LM**HOSTS), Microsoft included the searching of this file in all forms of NetBIOS name resolution.

done as a broadcast (hence, broadcast node, or b-node) to the local network with every host on the network evaluating it.

NetBIOS name queries that are broadcast can take up a significant amount of bandwidth on the network. It can also take CPU time from every host on the network as the query is passed fully up the stack to be processed at the Application layer. This causes the overall network performance not only to seem slower, but to actually be slower. Windows NT attempts three times to resolve the name using a broadcast, waiting 7.5 seconds between each attempt.

The steps that an enhanced b-node system goes through to resolve a NetBIOS name are as follows:

1. Checks the NetBIOS name cache.

2. Broadcasts a NetBIOS name query.

3. Checks the LMHOSTS file.

4. Checks a HOST file.

5. Checks with a DNS server.

p-node

As you saw, there are better ways to resolve a NetBIOS name than broadcast. The best way is to ask a central system that has a list of every host's IP address and NetBIOS name, as well as special entries for systems from run services such as Netlogon.

P-node (peer node) still uses a NetBIOS name query that is sent on the network. However, rather than being sent as a broadcast, the query is sent directly to an NBNS. In this way, the resolution is made quicker, and no CPU time is taken up on the other hosts on the network. Like the b-node, p-node makes three attempts to contact an NBNS if it does not respond, but it waits 15 seconds each time.

If more than one NBNS (such as WINS) is configured, the system will try each one in order if a previous NBNS server does not respond. The order of resolution for p-node is the following:

1. NetBIOS name cache

2. NetBIOS name server

3. HOSTS file

4. DNS

m-node

An m-node (mixed) system tries every method of resolution. This and h-node (hybrid) are combinations of the b-node and p-node systems. The only difference is the order in which Windows NT resolves the names.

For m-node, the order of resolution is the following:

1. NetBIOS name cache

2. Broadcast

3. LMHOSTS file

4. NetBIOS name server

5. HOSTS file

6. DNS server

h-node

The hybrid node, as stated, is a combination of the p-node and b-node resolution methods. Unlike m-node, h-node reduces broadcast traffic on your network by first consulting the NBNS before attempting a broadcast.

If you put a WINS address into the TCP/IP configuration, Windows NT automatically defaults to h-node. The order of h-node resolution is as follows:

1. NetBIOS name cache

2. NetBIOS name server

3. Broadcast

4. LMHOSTS file

5. HOSTS file

6. DNS server

Viewing and Setting the Node Type

Because the node type is important to the performance of the system you are using, you can change it if a better method is available.

To check the current node type, use the command IPCONFIG /all, which you have seen in previous chapters. In the following output from this command, note that the node type is broadcast (also note that no WINS server is listed):

```
Windows NT IP Configuration

        Host Name . . . . . . . . . : scrimger.ScrimTech.
➥com

        DNS Servers . . . . . . . . : 10.10.1.50
        Node Type . . . . . . . . . : Broadcast
        NetBIOS Scope ID. . . . . . :
        IP Routing Enabled. . . . . : No
        WINS Proxy Enabled. . . . . : No
        NetBIOS Resolution Uses DNS : No

Ethernet adapter NDISLoop1:

        Description . . . . . . . . : MS LoopBack Driver
        Physical Address. . . . . . : 20-4C-4F-4F-50-20
        DHCP Enabled. . . . . . . . : No
        IP Address. . . . . . . . . : 10.10.3.200
        Subnet Mask . . . . . . . . : 255.255.255.0
        Default Gateway . . . . . . : 10.10.3.1
```

By default, Windows NT uses enhanced b-node resolution. However, if you enter the IP address of a WINS server, Windows NT will default to h-node. If you need to use a different node type, you have to edit the Registry or assign the node type using a DHCP server. The entry is under the following subkey:

```
HKEY_LOCAL_MACHINE\SYSTEM\CurrentControlSet\Services\NetBT\
➥Parameters
```

The entry is NodeType, which you will normally need to add (if it is there you should check whether a WINS server is installed on the system). The values you can set are listed here:

◆ **0x1 (hex)**—b-node

◆ **0x2 (hex)**—p-node

◆ **0x4 (hex)**—m-node

◆ **0x8 (hex)**—h-node

On most networks, you automatically set the node type by using the DHCP server. The DHCP options that you set are 044

(WINS/NBNS Server) and 046 (WINS/NBT Node Type). This enables an administrator to set the node type for all machines that use DHCP.

Resolution Methods

Now that you have seen the order in which the resolution methods are used, the next few sections are dedicated to explaining these methods.

NetBIOS Name Cache

The NetBIOS name cache is an area of memory containing a list of NetBIOS computer names and the associated IP address. An address in the name cache can get there in one of two ways: you resolve that address or it is preloaded from the LMHOSTS file (see "The LMHOSTS File" later in this chapter). The NetBIOS name cache provides a quick reference to frequently used IP addresses.

The NetBIOS name cache, however, cannot keep every address on your network. The cache (like ARP) keeps entries for a short period of time—ten minutes by default. The exceptions are preloaded entries, which remain in the cache until you clear them.

You cannot directly modify the NetBIOS name cache. However, you can add preloaded entries using the LMHOSTS file. If you want to do this, use `nbtstat -R` to purge and reload the name cache. If you want to view the resolved names, you can use NBTSTAT -r. If you want to view the name cache, type NBTSTAT -c. The switches for NBTSTAT are case sensitive.

There are several Registry entries that affect the way the name cache works. The entries are found under the following Registry key:

```
HKEY_LOCAL_MACHINE\SYSTEM\CurrentControlSet\Services\NetBT\
➥Parameters
```

The entries are as follows:

- ◆ **Size**—the number of names kept in the name cache. The settings are small (1—maintains only 16 names), medium (2—maintains 64 names), and large (3—maintains 128 names). The default is 1, which is sufficient for most client stations.

◆ **CacheTimeout**—The time, in milliseconds, that an entry will remain in the NetBIOS name cache. The default is 927c0 (hex) or 600,000 (decimal) milliseconds, which is ten minutes.

Broadcast

If the name cannot be found in the NetBIOS name cache, the system may attempt to find it using a broadcast on the local network. A broadcast is a necessary evil: it takes up bandwidth, but in many cases is the simplest way to find a system.

NetBIOS uses UDP (port 137) to send a name query to every computer on the local network. Every computer must then take the packet and pass it all the way up the protocol stack to NetBIOS so the name can be checked against the local name table.

Two problems with using a broadcast are increased network traffic and wasted CPU time on all the systems as the request is passed to NetBIOS to check names that don't exist. (Fortunately, you are going to see two methods that enable you to resolve names without broadcast traffic.) You should note that broadcasts are a throwback to the early days of networks, when computers were slower, networks tended to be single segments, and the bandwidth of networks was more than enough to cover the occasional broadcast.

You can use a couple Registry entries to customize the broadcast function. These are under the following Registry key:

```
HKEY_LOCAL_MACHINE\SYSTEM\CurrentControlSet\Services\NetBT\
➡Parameters
```

The entries are as follows:

◆ **BcastNameQueryCount**—the number of times the system retries the broadcast for the name. The default is three times.

◆ **BcastQueryTimeout**—the amount of time to wait before retrying the name query broadcast. The default is 750ms.

The LMHOSTS File

The LMHOSTS file dates back to the days of LAN Manager. This predecessor of Windows NT was jointly developed by Microsoft and IBM. Originally, the design goals called for a departmental-size network (that is, a single segment), and NetBEUI was developed as the protocol for LAN Manager.

Several companies, however, required a protocol that was routable. TCP/IP was eventually included as an alternative protocol, and NetBIOS over TCP/IP was introduced. This also meant that names needed to be resolved for systems on remote subnets—a job for which LAN Manager was not intended.

The solution was relatively easy: create a list of the systems to which the computer would have to communicate. Given that peer-to-peer networking had not become "in vogue," only a limited number of computers to communicate with existed anyway. In this list you could have the IP address and NetBIOS name of the systems you needed to communicate with.

This list was put in the file LMHOSTS (no extension), located in the c:\winnt\system32\drivers\etc directory by default. However, in some situations, the client did not know which particular system it needed to communicate with; instead, it would be looking for any computer with a particular service (the Netlogon service is a good example).

The solution to the problem of finding a system running a particular service rather than a particular computer was to include tags. Microsoft introduced several tags that enabled systems to send a request to all the computers that had a particular service running. For example, the #DOM tag tells your system that a particular system should be running the Netlogon service.

The result was a system that could communicate across routers even though it internally used NetBIOS—a workable compromise, sort of. As time went on, the amount of time that was spent updating the LMHOSTS file increased. In addition, the task became even more difficult because this file needed to be located on every host.

Tags were a good solution once, and again they proved to be able to resolve the issue. Microsoft added new tags that enabled computers to read a central LMHOSTS file. The client computer still needed a local LMHOSTS file so the system would know where and how to find the central one. However, this reduced the required number of lines from 70 or 80 or more to 5 or 6.

Windows NT supports and uses several tags. The following table describes the available tags.

Tag	*Use*
#PRE	Tells the computer to preload the entry to the NetBIOS name cache during initialization or after the NBTSTAT -R command has been issued. Entries with the #PRE tag have a life of –1 (static), meaning they are always in cache.
DOM	Indicates to the system that the computer is a domain controller, along with the domain that it controls. This enables Windows NT to handle domain functions, domain logon, and browsing services across routers.
#NOFNR	Prevents the use of NetBIOS-directed name queries in the LAN Manager for a UNIX environment.
INCLUDE	Tells the computer the location of a central LMHOSTS file. The file is specified using a UNC (Universal Naming Convention) name, such as \\MIS\Information\LMHOSTS. The computer name must be included in the local LMHOSTS file as a preloaded entry.
#BEGIN_ALTERNATE	Used in conjunction with the INCLUDE tag, marks the beginning of a list of alternative locations for the centralized LMHOSTS file that can be used if the first entry is not available. Only one central LMHOSTS file is used.
#END_ALTERNATE	Ends the list of alternative locations for a central LMHOSTS file. Between the two entries, add as many alternatives as you like; Windows NT tries each in sequence (remember, the names must preloaded).
#MH	Lets the system know that this is a case where it should not ignore other entries in the list with the same NetBIOS name (because multihomed computers may appear in the LMHOSTS file more than once).

The LMHOSTS file is scanned from top to bottom. Therefore, the servers accessed most frequently should be listed first. Any entries to preload a name should be at the bottom because they will already be in the NetBIOS name cache.

Each of the tags is preceded with a pound sign (#PRE, for example). There cannot be a space between the pound sign and the tag name—the pound sign followed by a space indicates a comment.

The following is an example of what an LMHOSTS file might contain:

```
152.42.35.2      victoria1     #PRE #DOM:MYCORP
152.42.160.45    ottawa8       #PRE
152.42.97.56     houston4      #PRE
#INCLUDE \\victoria1\INFO\LMHOSTS
#BEGIN_ALTERNATE
#INCLUDE \\ottawa8\INFO\LMHOSTS
#INCLUDE \\houston4\INFO\LMHOSTS
#END_ALTERNATE
```

This file would preload the computers victoria1 (which is a domain controller), ottawa8, and houston4. In addition, the file points at a central LMHOSTS stored on a share called INFO on victoria1, with copies on ottawa8 and houston4.

Of course, nothing in this world is perfect, so you need to keep the following facts in mind when using the LMHOSTS file:

◆ If the IP address is wrong, your system resolves an incorrect IP address. However, you cannot connect. Normally this shows up as a Network Name not Found error.

◆ If the NetBIOS name is spelled wrong in the LMHOSTS file, Windows NT can do nothing to resolve it (note that the names are not case sensitive).

◆ If the LMHOSTS file has multiple entries, the address for the first one is returned. If that entry is wrong, the result is the same as having a wrong IP address.

The LMHOSTS file is no longer required, and you can control its use from the WINS Address tab of the TCP/IP configuration. To change the Enable LMHOSTS setting, perform the following steps:

STEP BY STEP

8.2 Changing the Enable LMHOSTS Lookup Option

1. Open the Network dialog box.

2. Select the Protocol tab and open the Properties for TCP/IP.

3. On the WINS Address tab, ensure there is a check in the Enable LMHOSTS Lookup check box to enable the LMHOSTS file. Clear the check box to disable it.

4. Close the TCP/IP Settings dialog box and the Network Settings dialog box.

5. Restart your computer.

NetBIOS Name Server

The LMHOSTS file has some limitations; even using a central LMHOSTS file requires a great deal of updating. If you don't use a central LMHOSTS file and you attempt to update a host's address, you must visit every station on your network. In addition, the LMHOSTS file does not reduce broadcast traffic unless every entry is preloaded (meaning the system never has to perform a NetBIOS name query broadcast).

As the size of networks around the world began to increase, another method of name resolution had to be found. The method had to be able to reduce broadcast traffic and to update itself without intervention.

TCP/IP already had a simple DNS service that computers could query to find the IP address for a given hostname. The problem with DNS is that it resolves only the basic hostname, and you are not able to find services (such as Netlogon) that you sometimes seek. In addition, DNS requires a large, centralized file to be kept with a listing of all the IP-address-to-host-name mappings (the zone file). Of the three functions of NetBIOS naming—registration, resolution, and release—the DNS service fit only one of the criteria.

So a new type of name service had to be built that would enable systems to register their own IP addresses and could respond to these systems' queries about the IP addresses of others. The system that emerged was the NetBIOS Name Server (NBNS). Windows NT implements this in the form of a WINS server, as discussed in Chapter 5, "Windows Internet Name Service (WINS)."

Using an NBNS such as WINS for name registration, resolution, and release has some major advantages if you use TCP/IP as your networking protocol with Windows products. The advantages include the following:

◆ Reduces broadcast traffic

◆ Reduces administrative overhead for maintenance

◆ Facilitates domain activity over a WAN

◆ Provides browsing services across multiple subnets

You can customize several Registry entries for the WINS server. These are under the following subkeys:

```
HKEY_LOCAL_MACHINE\SYSTEM\CurrentControlSet\Services\NetBT\
➥Parameters
```

◆ **NameServerPort.** The UDP port used for NetBIOS name queries going to the NBNS. The default is 137 (89 hex).

◆ **NameSrvQueryCount.** Indicates the number of times your system should try each NBNS. The default is three times.

◆ **NameSrvQueryTimeout.** Indicates how long your computer should wait for a response from the NBNS. The default is 15 seconds (5dc milliseconds hex).

HOSTS File and DNS Server for NetBIOS Name Resolution

If the previous methods cannot resolve the name, the system will automatically look at the HOSTS file, if there is one. This provides backup for NetBIOS name resolution, but there will be a delay as the other methods time out; thus, the HOSTS file should not be the main method of resolution.

If your system has an entry for the DNS server, you can configure your system to use the DNS as a backup method for NetBIOS name resolution. This is not automatic; you will need to complete the following steps to configure this.

STEP BY STEP

8.3 Configuring Your System to Use the DNS as a Backup Method for NetBIOS Name Resolution

1. Open the Network dialog box and choose the Protocol tab.

2. Double-click the TCP/IP protocol and choose the WINS Address tab.

3. Click Enable DNS for Windows Resolution.

4. Click OK, and then close the Network dialog box.

5. Restart the computer.

CASE STUDY: ADDING LMHOSTS AT SUNSHINE BREWING COMPANY

ESSENCE OF THE CASE

In Chapter 5 we left off with the following solutions to the name resolution problems.

- To facilitate the local connections, you will establish a WINS server in each of the local offices. Then you will set up all the hosts to use the WINS server. Then you could create a static entry for the servers that users connect to in the head office (which will need to be updated if the IP addresses change). This will allow for the connection to the head office without having to perform replication.

- The Exchange server problem can also be eliminated using the same strategy. The domain activity simply requires that you create a domain group on each of the WINS servers; this should list all the domain controllers that are likely to become the PDC.

- The problem still remains, though, of the laptop users having to connect to their home server. This could force you to use replication (which is not bad, but can use up the bandwidth to the Internet). The other solution is the LMHOSTS file, which lists the IP address and name of NetBIOS servers. You could configure each laptop, therefore, with an LMHOSTS file that lists the users' home server and IP address.

- This is not necessarily the best solution. However, as was stated, you will refine this scenario after you gain a better understanding of the entire name resolution issue.

You may recall from the case study in Chapter 5 that most of the name resolution will be handled by WINS servers at Sunshine Brewing Company. There were a couple of cases, however, that pointed to the LMHOSTS file.

SCENARIO

Here is a recap of the information from Chapter 5. As you look at the network you are working with here, there are basically four types of offices that you will address. These include:

- **Head office.** This is the largest of the offices, with resources that all users will require access to. This includes a SQL server (configured for TCP/IP on port 1433) and a series of newsgroups on an IIS 4.0 server.

- **Regional offices.** These offices use the resources of the head office servers, including the SQL server. It also has file and print servers for the local users.

- **Production centers.** These offices will need to connect to the head office SQL server to receive the orders for production. Other than this, there is the normal need to provide local file and print services.

- **Sales offices.** These centers will need to be able to connect to the head office SQL server to post orders, and they will need local file and print services.

continues

CASE STUDY: ADDING LMHOSTS AT SUNSHINE BREWING COMPANY

continued

ANALYSIS

In this case, the analysis is primarily done. The work completed previously leads us to the need for the LMHOSTS file on the laptops. The only point that really needs to be added is that the entries in the LMHOSTS files should have the #PRE tag to ensure that they are loaded to the NetBIOS name cache.

It might be tempting to add an LMHOSTS file to several other servers with the #PRE tag to reduce the amount of network traffic and time required for name resolution. This can be a problem, however, if you ever need to change an IP address, and it would not be advisable in a scenario where this might happen. In this case, there is always the possibility that an ISP will go out of business or be bought out, and you would need to change IP addresses at one of the 61 locations.

CHAPTER SUMMARY

KEY TERMS

- b-node
- h-node
- HOSTS
- LMHOSTS
- m-node
- name query
- name registration
- name release
- NBT
- NBTSTAT
- NetBIOS name cache
- NetBIOS node type
- NetBT
- p-node

A key issue in any networked environment is the capability to connect to other systems. This requires that you identify the system to which you wish to connect, which can be done using the reference that is used by the system (the IP address). However, it is easier for humans to use a name.

Name resolution, therefore, is critical to the use of networked computers—and an important exam topic. Some of the key facts to keep in mind are listed here:

- ❖ You need to understand that name resolution breaks down into two main groups: hostname resolution and NetBIOS name resolution.

- ❖ You need to know what the six methods of name resolution are, and in what order they will be used.

- ❖ You need to know that by default Windows NT systems will use b-node, unless they have been configured with a WINS server address, in which case they will use h-node.

- ❖ You need to know where the HOSTS file is located and how to configure it (IP address, aliases, comments).

CHAPTER SUMMARY

◆ You need to know where the LMOHSTS file is and how to configure it.

◆ You need to know the tags that can go in the LMHOSTS file, notably #PRE, #DOM, and #INCLUDE.

◆ You will need to know how to configure a client to use WINS, both manually and using DHCP.

◆ You will also need to know how to configure a client to use the DNS for NetBIOS name resolution and how to use an LMHOSTS file.

APPLY YOUR KNOWLEDGE

Exercises

These exercises will concentrate on the LMHOSTS file. Because the HOSTS file is, in essence, a subset of the LMHOSTS, this will cover the basics for both.

8.1 Reviewing the Sample LMHOSTS

In this exercise, you will look at the sample LMHOSTS file that comes with Windows NT.

Estimated Time: About 10 minutes.

1. Start a command prompt.

2. Change to the \%winroot%\system32\drivers\ etc directory.

3. Edit the LMHOSTS.SAM (**EDIT LMHOSTS.SAM**).

4. Review the file.

8.2 Creating a Simple LMHOSTS File

In this exercise, you will create a simple LMHOSTS file based on a sample network. This exercise assumes all hosts on the network will use the same LMHOSTS file.

Estimated Time: About 10 minutes.

> **NOTE**
>
> **Back up the LMHOSTS file** If you are currently using an LMHOSTS file, please back it up before proceeding.

1. Review the sample network presented in Figure 8.1.

2. If we assume that only the SQL server, Windows NT servers, or domain controllers will provide network services, which systems will these be?

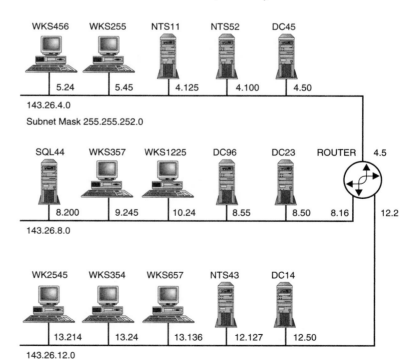

FIGURE 8.1
This is the sample network that you will use to create an LMHOSTS file.

APPLY YOUR KNOWLEDGE

The following systems provide network services:

System Name	IP Address
DC14	143.26.12.50
DC23	143.26.8.50
DC45	143.26.4.50
DC96	143.26.8.55
NTS11	143.26.4.125
NTS43	143.26.12.127
NTS52	143.26.4.100
SQL44	143.26.8.200

3. Think about the entries required in the LMHOSTS file. Which ones will require tags?

   The domain controllers will require tags to facilitate user logon. Also, the Windows NT servers and SQL server will need to be included to allow the users from remote subnets to access them.

4. After you create the LMHOSTS file, it should look like the following:

```
143.26.12.50     DC14    #DOM:ScrimTech
143.26.8.50      DC23    #DOM:ScrimTech
143.26.4.50      DC45    #DOM:ScrimTech
143.26.8.55      DC96    #DOM:ScrimTech
143.26.4.125     NTS11
143.26.12.127    NTS43
143.26.4.100     NTS52
143.26.8.200     SQL44
```

5. Add the #PRE tag to all the entries. Save the file as \%winroot%\system32\drivers\etc\lmhosts without an extension on the file.

6. Run another command prompt.

7. Check the names in your NetBIOS name cache by executing NBTSTAT -c. (Note: -r shows names that are resolved, and -c shows all names in cache.)

8. Now purge and reload the cache with NBTSTAT -R.

9. Check the names again. What did you get? You should have this:

```
C:\>nbtstat -c

Node IpAddress: [160.106.96.135] Scope Id: []

        NetBIOS Remote Cache Name Table

 Name          Type      Host Address    Life
                                         [sec]
-------------------------------------------------
 SQL44  <03>   UNIQUE    143.26.8.200    -1
 SQL44  <00>   UNIQUE    143.26.8.200    -1
 SQL44  <20>   UNIQUE    143.26.8.200    -1
 DC96   <03>   UNIQUE    143.26.8.55     -1
 DC96   <00>   UNIQUE    143.26.8.55     -1
 DC96   <20>   UNIQUE    143.26.8.55     -1
 DC45   <03>   UNIQUE    143.26.4.50     -1
 DC45   <00>   UNIQUE    143.26.4.50     -1
 DC45   <20>   UNIQUE    143.26.4.50     -1
 DC23   <03>   UNIQUE    143.26.8.50     -1
 DC23   <00>   UNIQUE    143.26.8.50     -1
 DC23   <20>   UNIQUE    143.26.8.50     -1
 DC14   <03>   UNIQUE    143.26.12.50    -1
 DC14   <00>   UNIQUE    143.26.12.50    -1
 DC14   <20>   UNIQUE    143.26.12.50    -1
 NTS52  <03>   UNIQUE    143.26.4.100    -1
 NTS52  <00>   UNIQUE    143.26.4.100    -1
 NTS52  <20>   UNIQUE    143.26.4.100    -1
 NTS43  <03>   UNIQUE    143.26.12.127   -1
 NTS43  <00>   UNIQUE    143.26.12.127   -1
 NTS43  <20>   UNIQUE    143.26.12.127   -1
 NTS11  <03>   UNIQUE    43.26.4.125     -1
 NTS11  <00>   UNIQUE    143.26.4.125    -1
 NTS11  <20>   UNIQUE    143.26.4.125    -1
```

APPLY YOUR KNOWLEDGE

10. What entries would be required if all Windows clients had peer networking enabled (that is, file and print sharing)?

    All the stations would need to be listed in the LMHOSTS file.

11. If you were to install a WINS server and configure all clients to use it for name resolution, what would be required in the LMHOSTS file?

    Nothing, WINS would handle all NetBIOS name resolution for you.

Review Questions

1. What is the sixteenth character in the NetBIOS name used for?

2. Which Winsock port is used for name services?

3. What are the three NetBIOS name functions?

4. What are the six methods of NetBIOS name resolution over TCP/IP?

5. What is the command used to see which names your system has resolved on the network?

6. When is an LMHOSTS file required?

7. What do the #BEGIN_ALTERNATE and #END_ALTERNATE tags do in the LMHOSTS file?

8. What does the #PRE tag do?

Exam Questions

1. Which of the following utilities will use NetBIOS name resolution?

    A. FTP

    B. NT Explorer

    C. Internet Explorer

    D. net.exe

2. What settings are available for the size of the NetBIOS name cache?

    A. Big

    B. Large

    C. Small

    D. Tiny

3. On a network with one segment, what benefit can be gained by using WINS?

    A. WINS can aid in the resolution of hostnames.

    B. WINS will facilitate interdomain browsing.

    C. WINS may reduce network traffic.

    D. All of the above.

4. In using the #INCLUDE statement, what is required for the server that contains the central LMHOSTS file?

    A. The server is listed in the LMHOSTS file with a #DOM tag.

APPLY YOUR KNOWLEDGE

B. The server is listed in the LMHOSTS file with a #PRE tag.

C. The server is listed in the LMHOSTS file with no tags.

D. The server is on the local subnet.

5. At what point in b-node resolution is the LMHOSTS file checked?

A. Second

B. Third

C. Fourth

D. Fifth

6. What pair of methods can be used to register a name on the network?

A. Broadcast and the LMHOSTS file

B. The LMHOSTS file and the HOSTS file

C. Broadcast and an NBNS server

D. The name is registered on the network when the computer is installed.

7. If your organization uses WINS, how many hosts need to be configured with an LMHOSTS file?

A. The WINS server only

B. Domain controllers only

C. All non–WINS-capable workstations

D. None

8. What are the three main functions of name management?

A. Name resolution, renewal, and release

B. Name queries, release, and renewal

C. Name registration, renewal, and release

D. Name registration, query, and release

9. By default, how long does a NetBIOS name remain in the name cache?

A. 2 minutes

B. 5 minutes

C. 10 minutes

D. 1 day

Answers to Review Questions

1. The sixteenth character is used to identify the server that registered the name on the network. See "NetBIOS Name Resolution over TCP/IP."

2. The NetBIOS name service runs on UDP port 137. See "NetBIOS Name Resolution over TCP/IP."

3. The NetBIOS name functions are name registration, name query, and name release. See "NetBIOS Name Resolution over TCP/IP."

APPLY YOUR KNOWLEDGE

4. The methods that Microsoft TCP/IP can use include NetBIOS name cache, NetBIOS name server, broadcast, the LMHOSTS file, the HOSTS file, and a DNS server. See "Resolution Methods."

5. The command is NBTSTAT -r; this will list all resolved names in the cache. See "The LMHOSTS File."

6. LMHOSTS is required if you will require services from remote hosts when no WINS server is available. See "Resolution Methods."

7. These tags will surround a list of alternative sites where your system can find a copy of the central LMHOSTS file. There would be one or more #INCLUDE lines between them. See "The LMHOSTS File."

8. This tells NetBIOS over TCP/IP to load the entry into your name cache when in initializes or if the cache is reloaded using NBTSTAT -r. See "The LMHOSTS File."

Answers to Exam Questions

1. **B** and **D.** Of the listed utilities, these are the only NetBIOS clients. A simple rule of thumb is that if a utility can use an IP address, it uses hostname resolution; otherwise, it uses NetBIOS name resolution. See "NetBIOS Name Resolution over TCP/IP."

2. **B** and **C.** The NetBIOS name cache can be set to one of three sizes: small, medium, or large. See "NetBIOS Name Cache."

3. **D.** There are many benefits that you can gain using WINS, including reduction of broadcast traffic, resolution of hostnames if hostname resolution fails, and easier interdomain browsing. See "NetBIOS Name Server."

4. **B.** The server name must already be resolved to an IP address to use #INCLUDE; this means that it must be included in the LMHOSTS file and given the #PRE tag to preload it. See "The LMHOSTS File."

5. **B.** If your system is using b-node resolution, it will use the resolution methods in the following order: NetBIOS name cache, local broadcast, LMHOSTS, HOSTS, and then DNS. See "NetBIOS Node Types."

6. **C.** Names can be registered on the network using a broadcast or name server. The LMHOSTS and HOSTS files can be used only to resolve names. See "NetBIOS Name Resolution over TCP/IP."

7. **D.** There is no need to use an LMHOSTS file if your network uses a WINS server. This is one of the key advantages of WINS: it is dynamic. See "Resolution Methods."

8. **D.** The functions that are required include name registration, name resolution (queries), and name release (the "3 Rs" of NetBIOS names). See "NetBIOS Name Resolution over TCP/IP."

9. **C.** The default life for a NetBIOS name in the name cache is 10 minutes. See "NetBIOS Name Cache."

APPLY YOUR KNOWLEDGE

Suggested Readings and Resources

1. Siyan, Karanjit. *Windows NT Server 4, Professional Reference, Second Edition.* New Riders, 1997.

2. Heywood, Drew. *Networking with Microsoft TCP/IP, Second Edition.* New Riders, 1997.

3. TechNet (from Windows NT 3.5 training material)

- Windows Internet Naming Service (WINS)
- Using LMHOSTS File to Find Computers and Services
- Host Name Resolution

This chapter will help you prepare for the exam by covering the following objective:

Configure a Windows NT Server computer to support TCP/IP printing.

▶ One of the benefits of using Windows NT is that it can interact with other operating systems. This objective is included to ensure that you are able to set up TCP/IP printing to share printers with the UNIX world.

CHAPTER 9

TCP/IP Printing Services

O**UTLINE**

S**TUDY** S**TRATEGIES**

As you read through this chapter you should concentrate on the following key items:

▶ You will need to know how to set up the TCP/IP printing services.

▶ You will need to know how to connect to UNIX printers.

▶ You will need to know how to share your printers with UNIX stations.

One of the goals in designing Windows NT was to create an operating system that could interact with the many different environments that already existed. This meant having the capability not only to work with the file systems and servers from other operating systems, but also to share printers with them.

For a long time, TCP/IP has been associated with the UNIX world and mainframe computers. To share printing services with these systems, Windows NT has to have the ability to work with a Line Printer Daemon (LPD) on a foreign system using the Line Printer Remote (LPR) utility or the LPR Print Monitor.

In order to share printers with the UNIX world, Windows NT itself must be able to act as an LPD. This is required only if you need to allow non-Microsoft systems to use the print services of Windows NT. When Microsoft networking clients attempt to print, they use the server service (NetBIOS).

One of the most common problems you will run across is a user that can't print. There are many reasons for this, many of which have nothing to do with TCP/IP in particular—too many, in fact, to cover in this text.

This chapter will cover the basics of printing from Windows NT. After that, TCP/IP printing services will be discussed. These services fall into two pieces: using a remote LPD server and setting Windows NT up as an LPD server. Remember that LPD is a Line Printer Daemon normally used with UNIX platforms.

PRINTING WITH WINDOWS NT

This section is an overview of the printing process in Windows NT. Although many users will already be familiar with printing from Windows NT and creating printers, this section also talks about the actual underlying process used to print from Windows NT.

The Print Process

When you print from Windows NT, you normally choose File, Print from the menu for the application you are working with. For many users, this is the extent of their knowledge of the Windows NT printing process. But there are many different components at work in the background that are needed to move the bytes of data from your system to the page.

The following list provides an overview of the printing process:

1. The user starts the printing process by choosing File, Print from the application he or she is working with.

2. If the system uses a network printer, the next step involves verifying the version of the driver that is stored locally. With Windows NT, the system is able to retrieve the driver from the print server, ensuring that the current and correct driver will always be used when printing. The local system checks the version of the driver with the version on the print server; if that one is newer, the local system retrieves a copy.

3. The generic portion of the print driver (the three parts of a print driver are covered shortly), in conjunction with the GDI (Graphics Device Interface), creates an enhanced metafile (EMF). An EMF file is a simple file similar in concept to an HTML document. For example, when the printer needs to turn the bold feature on, a generic bold code is used. When it should be turned off, another generic code is used. The EMF format is common to both Windows NT and Windows 95; this allows Windows 95 systems to send print jobs to a Windows NT print server in this format—saving the local system the resources that would be needed to complete the rendering process.

4. As the GDI and printer drivers build the EMF file, it moves to a spool file on the local system. The local spooler contacts the spooler on the print server and creates a remote procedure call (RPC) to that system. The local spooler sends the print job to the print server over this connection. Obviously, this does not occur if the user is printing to a local printer.

5. On the print server, the spooler service receives the print job and stores it to disk. It also lets the print processor know the file is there.

6. The print processor checks the type of data that the file contains and completes the rendering of the print job to the data format the printer expects.

7. The print processor works with the print driver to complete the rendering process. This involves removing all the codes that the system put into the file in step 3 and replacing them with the actual codes that are required by the physical printer to perform the given function.

8. Another processor generates a separator page and adds it to the beginning of the file. The file is now ready to be copied to the printer.

9. A port monitor moves the file from the spool file to the printer. (The port monitors are the link between the logical printers and the physical printer.)

10. Finally, the job prints from the physical printing device.

As you can see, there are many different parts to the printing process in Windows NT. The four main parts are the printer driver, the print spooler, the print processor, and the port monitors. If any of the parts fail, the whole printing process will fail. The next few sections will look at each of these parts.

Print Drivers

The print drivers in Windows NT are broken down into three sections: the graphics driver, printer interface, and characterization data files. All three of these need to function together to allow Windows NT to print.

Graphics Driver

The graphics driver is the part of the print driver that works with the GDI to create the EMF file. The graphics driver knows about the type of printer you are printing to.

There are three main types of printers: raster, PostScript, and plotters. For each of these types of printers there is a different graphics driver that knows how each type of printer prints. The following are the three graphics drivers:

❖ **RASDD.DLL.** This file will be used for the most common form of printer—the raster printer. A raster printer creates an image with a series of dots—most evident with the older, dot-matrix printers. The same method is also used by most of the laser printers that are available. RASDD.DLL can call on other files, when required, to complete the process; HPPCL.DLL, for example, is called on by RASDD.DLL with most HP LaserJet printers.

◆ **PSCRIPT.DLL.** Systems with a PostScript printer use this graphics driver. These printers use a programming language to describe the page and how it will look using vectors. Vectors use a starting point, direction, and distance to build your page out of a series of lines. A common example of a PostScript printer is the Apple LaserWriter.

◆ **PLOTTER.DLL.** As you might guess from the name, this driver is used with plotters. Plotters create a page just like we do: they move a pen across the paper (or the paper across the pen), lifting the pen and lowering it to start and stop marking.

Printer Interface

The printer interface is just that—an interface to the settings of the printer you are working with. Just as there are three types of printer drivers for the three main types of printers, there are also three types of printer interface files:

◆ **RASDDUI.DLL**—used for raster printers.

◆ **PSCRPTUI.DLL**—used for PostScript printers.

◆ **PLOTUI.DLL**—used with plotters.

The printer interface reads information from the characterization file so that it knows what options are available on the printer; then it allows you to set the options.

Characterization Data File

Nearly every printer that Windows NT supports has its own characterization data file (in some cases, several printers share a common characterization file). These files are the key to putting the whole thing together. They provide the information for the printer interface so that it knows what the capabilities are; they also contain the codes used to transform the EMF file to a printer-ready state.

Print Spooler

The print spooler is responsible for storing the print jobs on the hard disk and moving them through the various stages on the way to the printing device. It runs as a service on Windows NT and can be seen in the Services icon in the Control Panel.

> **NOTE**
>
> **Stopping and Restarting the Spooler Service**   If your printer seems to be jammed, you can sometimes fix it by stopping and restarting the spooler service.

Print Processor

When you print from a Windows application, your file ends up as an EMF; if you print from a DOS application it becomes raw text or formatted printer data; with a Macintosh system a PSCRIPT1 file is created. In any case, the printer needs to see the data as formatted printer data if it is to actually print the file.

The print processor (WINPRINT.DLL) converts the data types mentioned in the previous paragraph to the data type the printer requires. If it is a print server, the processing is handled on the server, not the client. In this way, the burden is moved off of the client computer, leaving more processing power for the applications on that computer.

Port Monitor

As stated previously, the port monitor is the link between the logical printer the users will connect to and the physical printer the paper will come out of. There are many different port monitors that support the various types of connections that can be used for printers. The following list covers some of the port monitors that are available:

- ◆ **LOCALMON.DLL.** This file handles any printer that is connected locally to the computer (LPT1, COM1, and so on) and any printers that you have created a connection to (for example, NET USE LPT3: \\server\printer).

- ◆ **LPRMON.DLL.** This file, the reason for this discussion, allows you to connect to and use the services of an LPD server.

- ◆ **HPMON.DLL.** This is used to communicate with Hewlett-Packard JetDirect printers.

- ◆ **SFMMON.DLL.** This monitor allows Windows NT to share files with a Macintosh printer on the network.

◆ **DECPSMON.DLL.** This monitor works with Digital Equipment Corporation network interface printers.

◆ **LEXMON.DLL.** This is the monitor for Lexmark Vision network printers.

◆ **PJLMON.DLL.** This monitor is used for any printers that follow the Printer Job Language communications standards.

The separation of the logical and physical printers has allowed Microsoft to add extra functionality to the printing process. First, there is the ability to link several different logical printers to a single physical printer (many network operating systems do this). This means that you can have different settings on the logical printers but use the same printing device. An example would be creating a logical raster printer and a logical PostScript printer that both print to the same multimode physical printer.

Another function is the unique ability to connect several physical printers to the same logical printer, creating a printer pool. Many different printing devices will all accept jobs from one logical printer; this works well in areas with high demand and a long queue. Creating a printer pool increases the number of pages per minute you can process without having to purchase expensive, high-end printers.

Installing a Printer

The process of installing a printer is straightforward—there is a wizard to walk you through the entire process. The steps will vary slightly depending on the type of printer you are installing and the type of port it will attach to. However, the general steps are listed here.

STEP BY STEP

9.1 General Steps Involved in Installing a Printer

1. Double-click the My Computer icon, and then double-click the Printers icon.

2. Double-click the Add Printer icon.

3. Choose either My Computer if the print driver will be installed on the local computer, or Network Print Server if it will not.

4. If you select My Computer, you will be asked to tell the system which port the printer is connected to. (If you choose Enable Print Pooling, you may choose more than one port.) If required, click Add Port or Configure Port.

5. Choose the manufacturer from the list on the left side and the model from the list on the right side. (If the printer is not listed but you have a driver disk, click Have Disk.) Then choose Next.

6. Name the printer anything you want to (up to 31 characters), and choose whether it will be the default printer. Click the Next button to continue.

7. If you want to share the printer, choose Shared and enter the share name and the platforms of the users that will connect to it. This will tell NT to add the drivers for these other platforms so the clients will be able to retrieve the driver from your server. Choose Next.

8. Try the printer by printing a test page. Click Finish when done.

This section has provided you with the basics of printing. There are many other things that could be discussed about printing from NT; however, this is a book about TCP/IP, and this chapter should concentrate on TCP/IP printing services.

INSTALLING TCP/IP PRINTING SERVICES

The installation and configuration of the services for TCP/IP printing support are simple. However, you must first have TCP/IP installed and functioning correctly. Also, if you use hostnames, you must have some method of resolving them.

Assuming you have met these criteria, the following steps describe how to install the services.

STEP BY STEP

9.2 Installing the TCP/IP Printing Services

1. Open the Network dialog box.

2. On the Services tab, choose Add.

3. Highlight Microsoft TCP/IP Printing and choose OK.

4. Enter the directory for your source files.

5. Select Close from the Network dialog box. Then choose Yes to restart your computer.

That is all there is to adding the service. Now you can configure your system to either become or make use of an existing LPD server.

CONNECTING TO AN **LPD** SERVER

A monitor handles the process of moving print files from the queue to the physical printing device in Windows NT. There are many different monitors available to allow you to print to the many different types of printers.

When you want to connect to an LPD server, you have to create a printer (unless you simply want to redirect an existing printer). You have already seen how to install a printer under Windows NT and now should concentrate on the LPR (Line Printer Remote) port monitor. The following steps outline how to configure a printer to access a remote LPD server.

FIGURE 9.1
The Ports tab on a Printer Properties sheet.

STEP BY STEP

9.3 Configuring a Printer to Access a Remote LPD Server

1. Open the Printers folder using Start, Settings, Printers. Right-click on a printer, and then choose Properties from the pop-up menu. Choose the Ports tab (see Figure 9.1).

2. Click the Add Port button, and then from the Printer Ports dialog box (see Figure 9.2) choose LPR Port and click New Port.

3. In the Add LPR compatible printer dialog box (see Figure 9.3), enter the IP address and printer name for the LPD printer.

4. Click OK, and the system will attempt to connect to the server to verify the printer. You may get an error message (see Figure 9.4) if the printer is not available.

5. Click Close on the Add Port dialog box and close the Printer Properties.

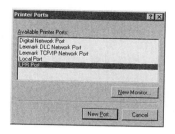

FIGURE 9.2
The Printer Ports dialog box.

If everything worked correctly, you now have another port in the list of available ports. This is the connection to the LPD server.

FIGURE 9.3
The IP address and printer name are entered here.

SHARING YOUR PRINTER USING LPD

As stated, Windows NT can also act as an LPD server. The LPD server, like most other servers, is implemented as a service. There are basically two steps involved in sharing your printer using LPD services.

First, you need to share your printer normally. You should keep the name simple; not all platforms that support LPR also support long share names. After you have shared the printer, you need only start the LPD service in the Services icon of the Control Panel. The printer is now available to other users, including those using the other platforms that support the LPR standards.

If you want to have the service start automatically every time you start your system, select the Startup button for the service and change the Startup Type to Automatic. (This can be found using the Server Manager by choosing the system where the LPD is installed and then selecting Computer, Services from the menu.)

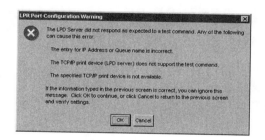

FIGURE 9.4
If the LPD cannot be located, you will receive an error message.

COMMAND-LINE UTILITIES

There are two command-line utilities that can be used to print to a TCP/IP printer: LPR (to send a job) and LPQ (to check on your job). An example LPQ output follows:

```
Windows NT LPD Server
                          Printer TCP_TEST (Paused)

Owner   Status            Jobname          Job-Id   Size   Pages   Priority
-------------------------------------------------------------------------
Scrim   (152. Waiting     \autoexec.bat    2        48     0       1
```

Both require the IP address or hostname and the name of the printer. These are covered in Chapter 11, "Heterogeneous Environments."

CASE STUDY: TCP/IP PRINTING IN THE PRODUCTION FACILITIES

ESSENCE OF THE CASE

There are only a few facts that need to be considered in this part of the network planning:

- You need to be able to handle print pooling, which you can do easily on Windows NT.

- The reports are being printed to a system that is running an LPD server.

- There will need to be a connection between the two networks to allow this to happen.

- The reports currently take around 23 hours a day to print; if there is a problem, data is lost.

In this part of the case study, there is not much that will apply. For practice, however, consider the production facilities. In these locations there are both Microsoft and Solaris systems.

SCENARIO

In the production facilities, the Solaris systems that control the equipment currently send reports to a single printer. You want to be able to use the services of print pooling to speed up the printing process rather than adding several printers to the Solaris network.

CASE STUDY: TCP/IP PRINTING IN THE PRODUCTION FACILITIES

ANALYSIS

In this case, there is really only one way to go: Create a printer on Windows NT with three or four printing devices in a printer pool. You will then want to add a network card to the system that has the Microsoft TCP/IP printing service so that it can access the Solaris network.

For security reasons, you would not enable IP forwarding on the Windows NT system. You would, however, set the Microsoft TCP/IP printing service to start automatically. All that is left to do is add the Windows NT system to the HOSTS file on the Solaris systems and set them up to print to the NT system.

CHAPTER SUMMARY

The chapter covered three main areas: printing from Windows NT, accessing an LPD server on the network, and becoming an LPD server. As you have seen, TCP/IP printing is simple as long as the underlying transport is in place. Accessing a remote LPD server is a matter of adding an LPR port, and becoming an LPD server is simply a matter of starting the service.

These are some of the important facts you will need to know:

◆ You need to know that a printer is a logical driver, and a printing device is a physical device.

◆ You need to understand that the LPD is a service that you install, and when it is started, your printers are available to the TCP/IP world.

◆ You need to know that you can use the command-line utilities.

◆ You need to know how to create an LPR printer by adding an LPR port to the printer setup.

KEY TERMS

- LPD
- LPQ
- LPR
- LPR Print Monitor
- printer
- printing device

APPLY YOUR KNOWLEDGE

This section will give you a chance to apply the knowledge that you have gained in this chapter.

Exercises

Now it's time to put what you have learned in this chapter to good use. The following exercises use the information in this chapter in real-world ways.

9.1 Installing the TCP/IP Printing Service

In this lab you will create an LPD printer and send a job to it. You will also connect (virtually) to an LPD printer using an LPR port.

Estimated Time: About 10 minutes.

1. Open the Network dialog box (right-click on Network Neighborhood).

2. On the Services tab, choose Add.

3. Highlight Microsoft TCP/IP Printing and choose OK.

4. Enter the directory for your Windows NT source files.

5. Choose Close from the Network Setting dialog box. When prompted, restart your system.

6. When restarted, open the Control Panel and double-click the Services icon.

7. Scroll down and verify that TCP/IP Print Server is listed.

9.2 Creating a Demonstration Printer

In this exercise, you will create a printer that you can use for demonstration purposes, so as not to destroy the setting for your real printer.

Estimated Time: About five minutes.

1. From the Start menu, choose Settings, Printers.

2. Double-click the Add Printer icon.

3. By default, My Computer should be selected; if it is not, select it and click Next.

4. For the port, choose LPT3: and click Next.

5. From the list, choose any printer that you like and click Next.

6. In the Printer Name box, enter **TCP_TEST**. Do not set this up as the Windows default printer. Choose Next.

7. Select Shared, and click Next. Choose No for the Test Page and click Finish.

8. Enter the location of your source files.

9.3 Turning on the TCP/IP Print Server

Now that you have a printer, it's time to turn on the TCP/IP print server.

Estimated Time: About five minutes.

1. In the Control Panel, open the Services icon.

2. Choose TCP/IP Print Server and click Start.

9.4 Printing to the TCP/IP Printer

Now you can print to the TCP/IP printer.

Estimated Time: About 10 minutes.

1. From the Start menu, choose Settings and Printers (this dialog box may still be open).

2. Right-click the TCP_TEST printer and choose Pause Printing from the pop-up menu.

3. Close the Printers dialog box.

4. Start a command prompt (Start, Programs, Command Prompt).

5. Enter the following:

```
LPR -Scomputername -PTCP_TEST
c:\autoexec.bat
```

> **NOTE**
>
> **Command-line options**   The -S and the -P are case sensitive. If you do not have an autoexec.bat, you can use a text file. Substitute your computer name for *computername*.

6. To verify that the printing worked, type the following command:

```
LPQ -Scomputername -PTCP_TEST
```

The output should look like the LPQ output in the section "Command-Line Utilities."

9.5   Hooking Up to the LPD Service

Finally, you can hook up to an LPD service from the printer created in Exercise 9.2.

Estimated Time: About five minutes.

1. Open the Printers dialog box. Right-click on the TCP_TEST printer and choose Properties.

2. On the Ports tab, choose Add.

3. Click LPR Port in the list; then click the New Port... button.

4. If you are asked, enter the source file location.

5. Enter your computer name in the Name or Address box. Then enter **TCP_TEST** as the printer name.

6. Click OK to add the port and Close to return to the Printer Properties box.

You should notice that the printer's properties are different. There is a new port that is listed, and it is checked. You can now delete the printer and remove Microsoft TCP/IP printing.

Review Questions

1. What do the TCP/IP printing services do?

2. What does LPD stand for?

3. How will an LPR port appear in the Printer Ports dialog box?

4. At the command prompt, type **LPR /?** and read the information that appears. Then type **LPQ /?** and read about it. What is each used for?

Exam Questions

1. A user at a Windows NT computer running the TCP/IP protocol wishes to send a print job to an LPD printer on a remote host system. Which methods enable the user to send the print job to the remote host?

   A. Using the LPD command-line utility from the Windows NT system, and specifying the hostname, printer name, and filename

APPLY YOUR KNOWLEDGE

B. Using the LPR command-line utility from the Windows NT system, and specifying the hostname, printer name, and filename

C. Creating an LPR printer in Control Panel/Printers, and specifying the hostname and printer name required for the creation of an LPR port

D. Creating an LPR printer in Control Panel/Printers, and specifying the hostname and printer name required for the creation of an LPD server on the Windows NT computer

2. Which procedure requires the fewest steps to enable a remote UNIX computer to send a print job to a Windows NT printer?

A. Creating an LPR printer on the Windows NT computer, sharing the printer, and running the LPR command from the remote host system specifying the required information.

B. Creating the LPD printer on the Windows NT computer, and running the LPR command from the remote host system specifying the required information.

C. Running the LPR command on the remote system—Windows NT automatically routes the print job to the printer with no further configuration on the Windows NT computer.

D. Running the LPD command from the remote host—the LPD command spawns a copy of the LPDSVC command on the Windows NT computer whether or not TCP/IP printing support is installed.

3. Which of the following procedures allows a Windows NT computer to act as a print gateway to an LPD printer on a remote host?

A. Creating an LPR printer on the Windows NT computer, sharing the printer, and connecting to the newly created printer from any other computer on the network.

B. Creating an LPR printer on the Windows NT computer, and installing an LPR printer on every other computer on the network (because Windows NT computers cannot act as print gateways to LPR printers).

C. Creating an LPR printer on the Windows NT computer, and installing the LPDSVC service on every other computer on the network.

D. None of the above—Windows NT automatically routes print jobs to any printer, including LPR, without any configuration.

4. Which parameters are required when using the LPR command on a Windows NT computer to send a print job to a remote LPD host?

A. The remote hostname

B. The username and password for the remote system

C. The remote printer name

D. The name of the file to be printed

E. The remote system's SMB server name

5. You are the administrator of a network that contains both Microsoft clients and Solaris clients. You want to be able to share printers between all the clients.

You decide that you will install a printer on a share Solaris station and create a Windows NT printer using the LPR Port Monitor. You then will share the Windows NT printer so the

APPLY YOUR KNOWLEDGE

Microsoft systems can also print to the printer. How good a solution is this?

A. This is the best possible solution.

B. This is a good solution.

C. This solution works but is far from optimal.

D. This solution does not work.

6. Some of the users on your network are complaining that it takes a long time for a print job to finish. You currently have four printers available: two are always busy, and two are normally idle. Your network has a mix of DOS, Windows for Workgroups, Windows 95, Windows NT Workstation, Macintosh clients, and Linux systems. You want to be able to print from all the workstations and control the printer.

You decide that you will install a printer on a share Solaris station and create a Windows NT printer using the LPR Port Monitor. You then will share the NT printer so that all the Windows NT client systems can also print to the printer. How good a solution is this?

A. This is the best possible solution.

B. This is a good solution.

C. This solution works but is far from optimal.

D. This solution does not work.

Answers to Review Questions

1. TCP/IP printing services allow you to print to and accept jobs from all types of TCP/IP hosts, such as a UNIX workstation. See "Installing TCP/IP Printing Services."

2. LPD stands for Line Printer Daemon. Daemon is the name given to a service running on a UNIX system. See "InstallingTCP/IP Printing Services."

3. The standard is `host_name:printer_name`. See "Connecting to an LPD Server."

4. LPR, or Line Printer Remote, is used to send a job to a Line Printer Daemon. LPQ, or Line Printer Query, is used to view the jobs on the printer. See "Command-Line Utilities."

Answers to Exam Questions

1. **B** and **C.** Using the LPR command-line utility from the Windows NT system, and specifying the hostname, printer name and filename; and creating an LPR printer in Control Panel/Printers, and specifying the hostname and printer name required for the creation of an LPR port. See "Command-Line Utilities."

2. **B.** Creating the LPD printer on the Windows NT computer, and running the LPR command from the remote host system specifying the required information. See "Sharing Your Printer Using LPD."

3. **A.** Creating an LPR printer on the Windows NT computer, sharing the printer, and connecting to the newly created printer from any other computer on the network. "Sharing Your Printer Using LPD."

4. **A, C,** and **D.** The remote hostname, the remote printer name, and the name of the file to be printed. See "Command-Line Utilities."

APPLY YOUR KNOWLEDGE

5. **A.** In this case, putting the printer on a remote system is not a great concern and will unload some of the processing from the Windows NT system. All the Windows NT clients will still be able to print to the printing device because of the distinction between the two. See "Sharing Your Printer Using LPD."

6. **D.** In this case, the solution does not provide the required results. It does work for most clients; however, for the Linux clients to be able to print, you will need the Microsoft TCP/IP printing service installed (the LPD server). You also would need Services for Macintosh. Also, users at the remote station where the printer resides could prevent you from accessing it. (You should—as you may have guessed—create a printer pool in this case.) See "Sharing Your Printer Using LPD."

Suggested Readings and Resources

1. *Windows NT 4 Resource Kit*: Resource Guide, the Overview of the Printing Process and TCP/IP Print Service (LPD).

This chapter will help you prepare for the exam by covering the following objective:

Configure SNMP.

▶ The Simple Network Management Protocol (SNMP) service provides two major capabilities for Windows NT: the capability to remotely manage systems and, more importantly, the capability to use the Performance Monitor counters.

CHAPTER 10

Implementing the Microsoft SNMP Service

STUDY STRATEGIES

As you read through this chapter, you should concentrate on the following key items:

▶ You need to know how to install and configure the service.

▶ You need to understand that TCP/IP Performance Monitor counters don't work without SNMP.

▶ You need to understand the security of SNMP.

▶ You need to know what a MIB is and which ones are available.

▶ You should know what commands are available and how they work.

SNMP enables network administrators to remotely troubleshoot and monitor hubs, routers, and other devices (see Figure 10.1). Using SNMP, you can find out information about remote devices without having to be physically present at the device itself.

SNMP can be a useful tool if understood and used properly. You can obtain various amounts of information on a wide variety of devices, depending on the type. Some examples of information accessible using SNMP include the following:

◆ The IP address of a router

◆ The number of open files

◆ The amount of hard drive space available

◆ The version number of a Windows NT host

SNMP uses a distributed architecture design to facilitate its properties. This means that various parts of SNMP are spread throughout the network to complete the task of collecting and processing data to provide remote management.

Because SNMP is a distributed system, you can spread out the management of it in different locations so as not to overtax any one system, and for multiple management functionality (see Figure 10.2).

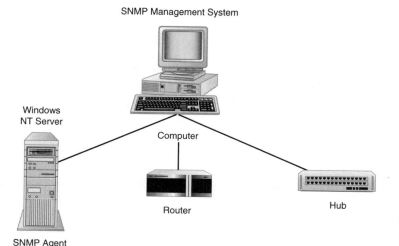

FIGURE 10.1

An SNMP management system manages devices as well as computers.

FIGURE 10.2

A simple network using SNMP.

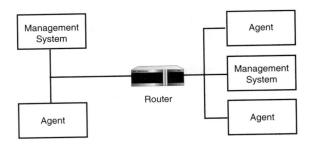

The SNMP provided by Microsoft enables a machine running Windows NT to be able to transfer its current condition to a computer running an SNMP management system. However, this is only the agent side, not the management tools.

This chapter's exercises use SNMPutil.exe, a basic command-prompt utility—not a full-blown management program. Various third-party management utilities are available, including the following:

- IBM NetView

- Sun Net Manager

- Hewlett-Packard OpenView

This chapter focuses primarily on the SNMP protocol rather than the management utilities; the management utilities are third-party products and, as such, are not included in Microsoft Windows NT.

SNMP AGENTS AND MANAGEMENT

There are two main parts to SNMP: the management station and the agent.

- The management station is the centralized location from which you can manage SNMP.

- The agent resides in the piece of equipment from which you are trying to extract data.

Each part is discussed in the following sections.

The SNMP Management System

The management system is the key component for obtaining information from the client; you need at least one to even be able to use the SNMP service. The management system is responsible for "asking the questions." As mentioned earlier, there are a certain number of questions it can ask each device, depending upon the type of device. The management system is, of course, a computer running one of the various software packages mentioned earlier (see Figure 10.3).

There are also certain commands that can be given specifically at the management system. These are generic commands not directly specific to any type of management system:

- ◆ **get**—requests a specific value. For example, it can query how many active sessions are open.

- ◆ **get-next**—requests the next object's value. For example, you can query a client's ARP cache and then ask for each subsequent value.

- ◆ **set**—changes the value on an object that has the properties of read-write. This command is not often used because of security considerations and the fact that the majority of objects have a read-only attribute.

Usually, you have only one management system running the SNMP service per group of hosts. This group is known as a community. Sometimes, however, you may want to have more. Following are some reasons for wanting more than one management station:

- ◆ You may want to have multiple management systems monitoring different parts of the same agents.

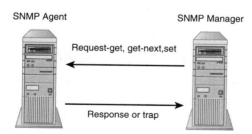

SNMP Agent   SNMP Manager

Request-get, get-next,set

Response or trap

FIGURE 10.3

Most of the communications between an agent and a management station are started from the management station.

◆ There might be different management sites for one community.

◆ As the network grows and becomes more complex, you may need to help differentiate certain aspects of your community.

The SNMP Agent

You have seen so far what the SNMP management side is responsible for and can specifically do. For the most part, the management side is the active component for getting information.

The SNMP agent, on the other hand, is responsible for complying with the requests and responding to the SNMP manager accordingly. Generally, the agent is a router, server, or hub. The agent is usually a passive component responding only to a direct query.

In one particular instance, however, the agent is the initiator, acting on its own without a direct query. This special instance involves a *trap*. A trap is set up from the management side on the agent; however, the management system does not need to go to the agent to find out if the trap information has been tripped. The agent sends an alert to the management system telling it that the event has occurred.

MANAGEMENT INFORMATION BASE

Now that you've learned a little about the management system and agents, you can delve into the different databases that you can query.

The data that the management system requests from an agent is contained in a Management Information Base (MIB). This is a list of values the management system can ask for. (The list of values depends on what type of device it is asking.) The MIB is the database of information that can be queried against.

A variety of MIB databases can be established. The MIB is stored on the SNMP agent and is similar to the Windows NT Registry in its hierarchical structure. These MIBs are available to both the agents and management system as a reference from which both can pull information.

The Microsoft SNMP Service supports the following MIB databases, by default:

◆ Internet MIB II

◆ LAN Manager MIB II

◆ DHCP MIB

◆ WINS MIB

These databases are discussed in the following sections.

Internet MIB II

Internet MIB II defines 171 objects for fault identification and troubleshooting on the network and configuration analysis. It is defined in RFC 1212, which adds to and supersedes the previous version, Internet MIB I.

LAN Manager MIB II

LAN Manager MIB II defines about 90 objects associated with Microsoft Networking, such as

◆ Shares

◆ Users

◆ Logon

◆ Sessions

◆ Statistical

The majority of LAN Manager MIB II's objects are set to read-only mode because of the limited security of SNMP.

DHCP MIB

The DHCP MIB identifies objects that can monitor the DHCP server's actions. It is set up automatically when a DHCP server service is installed and is stored in a file called DHCPMIB.DLL. It has

14 objects that can be used for monitoring the DHCP server activity, including items such as the following:

- The number of active leases
- The number of failures
- The number of DHCP discover requests received

WINS MIB

WINS MIB (WINSMIB.DLL) is a Microsoft-specific MIB relating directly to the WINS server service. It is automatically installed when WINS is set up. It monitors WINS server activity and has approximately 70 objects. It contains information such as the following:

- Number of resolution requests
- Successful queries
- Failed queries
- The date and time of last database replication

MIB Structure

As mentioned previously, the name space for MIB objects is hierarchical. It is structured in this manner so that each manageable object can be assigned a globally unique name. Certain organizations have the authority to assign the name space for parts of the tree design.

The MIB structure is similar to TCP/IP addresses: you get only one address from the InterNIC and then can subnet it according to your needs, and you do not have to contact InterNIC for each address assignment. The same applies for MIB name space, except you receive the number from the International Standards Organization (ISO).

Organizations can assign names without consulting ISO for every specific assignment. For example, the name space assigned to Microsoft's LAN Manager is 1.3.6.1.4.1.77. More recently, Microsoft has been assigned 1.3.6.1.4.1.311; any new MIB would then be identified under that branch. Figure 10.4 illustrates the hierarchical name tree.

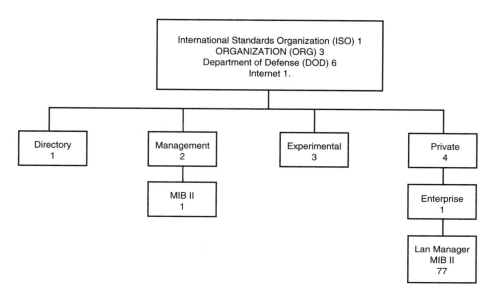

FIGURE 10.4
MIBs all start with the International Standards Organization and branch from there.

The object identifier in the hierarchy is written as a sequence of labels beginning at the root and ending at the object. It flows down the chart, starting with the ISO and ending with the object MIB II. Labels are separated by periods. Following are examples of this labeling technique.

The object identifier for the Internet MIB II:

Object Name	Object Number
Iso.org.dod.internet.management.mibii	1.3.6.2.1

The object identifier for LAN Manager MIB II:

Object Name	Object Number
iso.org.dod.internet.private.enterprise.lanmanger	1.3.6.1.4.77

MICROSOFT SNMP SERVICE

The SNMP service is an additional component of Windows NT TCP/IP software. It includes the four supported MIBs; each is a dynamic-link library and can be loaded and unloaded as needed. It provides SNMP agent services to any TCP/IP host running SNMP management software. It also performs the following:

◆ Reports special happenings, such as traps, to multiple hosts

◆ Responds to requests for information from multiple hosts

◆ Sets up counters in Performance Monitor that can be used to monitor the TCP/IP performance

◆ Uses hostnames and IP addresses to recognize which hosts it receives and requests information

SNMP Architecture

The MIB architecture can be extended to allow developers to create their own MIB libraries called extension agents. Extension agents expand the list of objects that an MIB can report on, making it not only more expansive, but also directed to be specifically related to network setup and devices. Figure 10.5 illustrates the SNMP architecture.

Although the Microsoft SNMP service doesn't include management software, it does have a Microsoft Win32 SNMP Manager API that works with the Windows Sockets. The API can then be used by developers to create third-party SNMP management utilities.

The Microsoft SNMP uses User Datagram Protocol (UDP port 161) to send and receive messages and IP to route messages.

SNMP Communities

A community creates a management group for a set of hosts running the SNMP service. These usually consist of a management system and multiple agents. Figure 10.6 illustrates SNMP communities.

Communities are given a community name just like an NT group. This name is case sensitive and, by default, all SNMP agents respond to any manager requests from the community name "public." By using unique community names, however, you can provide basic security and segregation of hosts.

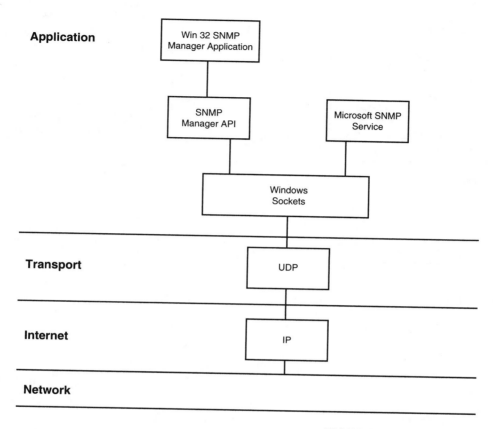

FIGURE 10.5
The SNMP architecture.

Agents do not accept requests or respond to hosts that are not from their configured community. Agents can be members of multiple communities at the same time, but they must be explicitly configured as such. This enables them to respond to different SNMP managers from various communities.

In the example in Figure 10.6, two separate communities are defined: CommA and CommB. Only the managers and agents that are members of the same community can communicate.

◆ Agent1 can send and receive messages to and from Manager1 because they are both members of the CommA community.

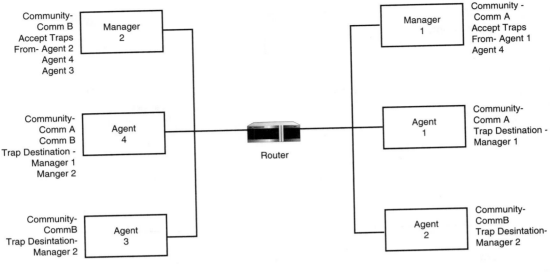

FIGURE 10.6
A network example showing SNMP communities.

◆ Agent2 and Agent3 can send and receive messages to and from Manager2 because they are all members of the CommB community.

◆ Agent4 can send and receive messages to Manager1 and Manager2 because Agent4 is a member of the CommA and CommB communities.

Security

There really is no established security with SNMP. The data is not encrypted, and there is no specific setup to stop someone from accessing the network, discovering the community names and addresses used, and sending fake requests to agents.

A major reason most MIBs are read-only is so that unauthorized changes cannot be made. The best security you can have is to use unique community names. Choose Send Authentication Trap and specify a trap destination, and choose Only Accept SNMP Packets from these Hosts.

You might also set up traps that let you know whether the agents receive requests from unspecified communities or addresses. This way, you can track down unauthorized SNMP activity.

INSTALLING AND CONFIGURING SNMP

The SNMP Service can be installed for the following reasons:

◆ You want to monitor TCP/IP with Performance Monitor.

◆ You want to monitor a Windows NT–based system with a third-party application.

The following steps for installing the SNMP service assume that you already have TCP/IP installed and set up, and that you have administrative privileges to install and use SNMP.

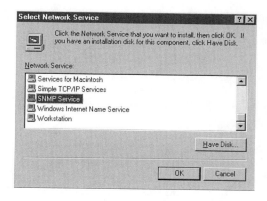

FIGURE 10.7
Installing the SNMP service.

STEP BY STEP

10.1 Installing the SNMP Service

1. Open the Network dialog box and, from the Services tab, click Add.

2. The Select Network Service dialog box appears (see Figure 10.7). Choose the SNMP service and click OK.

3. Specify the location of the Microsoft Windows NT distribution files.

4. After the files are copied, the Microsoft SNMP Properties dialog box appears (see Figure 10.8). Here you should enter the Community Name and Trap Destination.

5. Choose OK to close the SNMP Properties dialog box. Then choose Close to exit the Network dialog box; when prompted, click Yes to restart your computer.

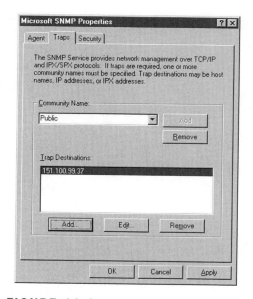

FIGURE 10.8
Entering the basic SNMP configuration.

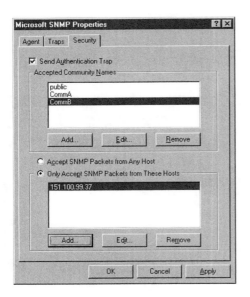

FIGURE 10.9
Configuration tab for SNMP security.

SNMP Security Parameters

There are several options that you can set that affect the security of the SNMP agent (see Figure 10.9). By default, the agent will respond to any manager using the community name "public." Because this can be inside or outside your organization, you should at the very least change the community name.

The following are available security options:

◆ **Send Authentication Trap**—sends a trap to the configured management station if an attempt is made to access SNMP from a manager that is not from the same community or that is not on the Only Accept SNMP Packets From list.

◆ **Accepted Community Names**—a list of community names that the agent will respond to. When a manager sends a query, a community name is included.

◆ **Accept SNMP Packets from Any Host**—responds to any query from any management system in any community.

◆ **Only Accept SNMP Packets from These Hosts**—responds to only the hosts listed.

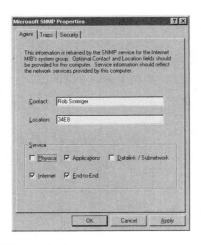

FIGURE 10.10
The Agent configuration tab.

SNMP Agent

In some cases you will configure other aspects of the SNMP agent (see Figure 10.10). These settings set the type of devices that you will monitor and who is responsible for the system.

The options available are as follows:

◆ **Contact.** This is the contact name of the person you want to be alerted about conditions on this station—generally the user of the computer.

◆ **Location.** This is a descriptive field for the computer to help keep track of the system sending the alert.

◆ **Service.** The items in this box identify the types of connections and devices this agent will monitor. These include the following:

   • **Physical.** This should be used if this system is managing physical devices such as repeaters or hubs.

- **Applications.** Set this if the Windows NT computer uses an application that uses TCP/IP. This should always be selected.

- **Datalink/Subnetwork.** Selecting this indicates this system is managing a bridge.

- **Internet.** This should be selected if the Windows NT computer acts as an IP router.

- **End-to-End.** Set this if the Windows NT computer uses TCP/IP. Obviously, this should always be selected.

Any errors with SNMP will be recorded in the system log, which records any SNMP activity. Use Event Viewer to look at the errors and to find the problem and possible solutions.

USING THE SNMP UTILITY

The SNMP utility does not come with Windows NT, but it is included in the Windows NT Resource Kit (SNMPUTIL.EXE). Basically, it is a command-line management system utility. It checks that the SNMP service has been set up and is working correctly; you can also use it to make command calls. You cannot do full SNMP management from this utility; but, as you will see, you would not want to because of its complex syntax.

The following is the general syntax structure:

```
snmputil command agent community object_identifier_(OID)
```

The following are the commands you can use:

- ◆ **WALK**—moves through the MIB branch identified by what you have placed in the object_identifer.

- ◆ **GET**—returns the value of the item specified by the object_identifier.

- ◆ **GETNEXT**—returns the value of the next object after the one specified by the get command.

To find out the time the WINS server service began, for example, (providing WINS is installed and the SNMP agent is running) query the WINS MIB with the following command:

```
c:\>snmputil getnext localhost public
.1.3.6.1.4.1.311.1.1.1.1
```

In this example, the first part refers to the Microsoft branch: .1.3.6.1.4.1.311 (or iso.org.dod.internet.private.enterprise.microsoft). The last part of the example refers to the specific MIB and object you are querying: .1.1.1.1 (or .software.Wins.Par.ParWinsStartTime). A returned value might look like the following:

```
Value = OCTET STRING - 01:17:22 on 11:23:1997.<0xa>
```

CASE STUDY: SETTING UP FOR PERFORMANCE MONITORING

ESSENCE OF THE CASE

There are several important aspects that you will need to look at in this case. Most notably, you will be attempting to cause a protocol you are installing not to work. The following are important points to remember:

- The SNMP protocol provides next to no security.

- The default community name, "public," is just that: public knowledge.

- The systems will have Internet access, and this could leave you open to attack.

- You need to enable the protocol so the Performance Monitor counters will work.

- You know that SNMP uses UDP port 161 and 162.

- You don't actually have any management software.

In this case, there is no need to run SNMP. The network that you are designing does not have a great number of routers or bridges that need to be remotely monitored (which is what SNMP is mostly used for).

SCENARIO

You will want to be able to use the Windows NT Performance Monitor to check the performance of all servers on your network. Because the SNMP agent needs to installed to enable these counters, this case study will look at how SNMP can be installed without compromising the security of the network.

In this case, you will be installing the SNMP agent on all the servers that will be located in the remote offices, and you will be using the Internet connection to reach them remotely using the Performance Monitor.

CASE STUDY: SETTING UP FOR PERFORMANCE MONITORING

ANALYSIS

In this case, things might look hopeless. However, with some simple precautions you can enable the protocol without great exposure.

Before you even install the SNMP agent on the servers, you should set up the routers coming into your network so they do not forward UDP ports 161 and 162. This will reduce the threat of attack greatly.

Now you can install the SNMP agent. You should configure the community name to something other than "public." In this case, because the protocol will never be used, you can generate a sequence of random characters with a different sequence for each server. This will make it more difficult for internal hackers; they might get the community name for one server, but they won't have the name for all the agents.

Next you should add an IP address for a management station (any address will do) and set the agent to accept SNMP commands only from that address. Again, a different address could be used for each server.

CHAPTER SUMMARY

KEY TERMS

- Management Information Base (MIB)
- SNMP
- SNMP agent
- SNMP community
- SNMP Manager

This chapter has covered Simple Network Management Protocol. As you have seen, SNMP is a very simple protocol that can be used to look at the information stored in a Management Information Base. This allows management software (such as HP's OpenView) to read information from a Windows NT system.

If you intend to use SNMP, you must purchase SNMP management software (you could use SNMPUTIL, but you would need to memorize all the numbers, which is not realistic). SNMP can be installed whether you are using it directly or not; this is done to allow the Performance Monitor counters to function correctly.

The following list summarizes the key points in this chapter:

◆ You need to understand that the SNMP agent is only an agent, and only an SNMP Manager API (no software) is provided.

◆ You need to know the three commands that a manager can send an agent: set, get, and get-next.

◆ You need to know what a trap (event notification) is, and that this is sent from the agent.

◆ You need to know the five areas the agent can monitor and where each is used: physical, applications, datalink/subnetwork, Internet, and end-to-end.

◆ You need to know how to install the agent.

◆ You need to know how to configure an authentication trap.

◆ You need to know how to configure the community names and the addresses of the stations that will be acting as managers.

◆ You need to understand the structure of a MIB and which four MIBs come with Windows NT: LAN Manager MIB II, Internet MIB II, DHCP MIB, and WINS MIB.

◆ You need to know that the SNMP agent must be installed to enable the Performance Monitor counters.

APPLY YOUR KNOWLEDGE

Exercises

This set of exercises covers use of the SNMP agent. The lab uses SNMPUTIL, which is available in the Windows NT Resource Kit and from various sites on the Internet.

10.1 Installing the Protocol

The first step in working with SNMP is to install the protocol. In this exercise, you will install the SNMP agent.

Estimated Time: About 10 minutes.

1. Open the Network dialog box, and click the Services tab.

2. Choose Add, select the SNMP Agent, click OK, and enter the source directory.

3. Choose Close on the Network Setting dialog box and restart your system when prompted.

10.2 Using SNMPUTIL to Test SNMP

In this lab, you will need a copy of the SNMPUTIL, which can be found in the Windows NT Resource Kit. If you do not have the Resource Kit, you can also find SNMPUTIL on the Internet (however, the Windows NT Resource Kit is recommended).

Estimated Time: About 15 minutes.

You will want to increase the number of lines in the command prompt for this lab. To do this, click the Control Menu box in the upper left corner of the window and select Properties. On the Layout tab, change the height value to a higher number, such as 300.

1. Start a command prompt.

2. Enter the following commands:

```
SNMPUTIL get 127.0.0.1 public
.1.3.6.1.4.1.77.1.2.2.0
SNMPUTIL get 127.0.0.1 public
.1.3.6.1.4.1.77.1.2.24.0
```

3. Verify the numbers that you received. To verify the first number, open the Services icon in the Control Panel and count the number of services that are started. (Or type **NET START** from the prompt and count the services listed.)

   To verify the second number, open the User Manager for Domains and count the number of users.

4. In User Manager for Domains, add a test user. Switch to the Command Prompt, and enter the second SNMPUTIL command again (use the up arrow to repeat the command).

5. Verify that the user you added increased the number, and then enter the following command:

```
SNMPUTIL walk 127.0.0.1 public
.1.3.6.1.4.1.77.1.2.25
```

   This should list the names of all the users.

6. Open the Services icon from the Control Panel again. Stop the Server service. It will warn you that this will also stop the Computer Browser service—this is fine.

7. Re-enter the command:

```
SNMPUTIL get 127.0.0.1 public
.1.3.6.1.4.1.77.1.2.2
```

   The number should be two fewer than before.

8. Verify that the services are not running, and then enter the following command:

```
SNMPUTIL walk 127.0.0.1 public
.1.3.6.1.4.1.77.1.2.3.1.1
```

APPLY YOUR KNOWLEDGE

The services that are running will be listed. Server and Computer Browser should not be included on the list.

> **Why It Still Works** You are still able to access this information using the sockets interface even though the server service is stopped. Remember that the server service is a NetBIOS server. Because you are communicating over sockets directly, you are able to use the SNMP agent, which uses UDP port 161 directly.

9. Restart the server service and the Computer Browser service.

10. You can enter the following optional command, which will give you a list of all the information in the LAN Manager MIB:

```
SNMPUTIL walk 127.0.0.1 public
.1.3.6.1.4.1.77
```

Review Questions

1. What three things will you gain if you install the SNMP agent?

2. For an SNMP Manager to be able to request information from an agent, what conditions must be true?

3. There are four commands in the SNMP protocol. What are they? Which system will initiate the command?

4. What MIBs does Windows NT use?

Exam Questions

1. Which of the following commands are you able to implement on the management system side when making requests to the agents?

   A. get, set, go

   B. walk, get, get-next

   C. get, get-next, trap

   D. set, get-next, get

2. Where are the set of manageable objects that SNMP works with stored?

   A. MIIB

   B. Management Information Base

   C. MHB

   D. Management Internet Information Base

3. A community is a group of hosts running SNMP, to which they all belong, and respond to requests from a management system. The default community name for all communities is _____.

   A. punic

   B. comm

   C. community

   D. public

4. When setting up an SNMP management system on a Windows NT host machine, what MIBs are supported by default under Windows NT 4.0?

   A. Internet MIB I, LAN Manager MIB II, WINS MIB, DHCP MIB

   B. Internet MIB II, LAN Manager MIB I, WINS MIB, DHCP MIB

APPLY YOUR KNOWLEDGE

    C. Internet MIB II, LAN Manager MIB II, WINS MIB, DHCP MIB

    D. Internet MIB II, LAN Manager MIB II, WINS MIB I, DHCP MIB

5. Which SNMP operation does the agent instead of the management system institute?

    A. walk

    B. set

    C. trap

    D. get

Answers to Review Questions

1. With the SNMP agent you will get an SNMP agent and the SNMP Management API, and the TCP/IP Performance Monitor counters will be added. See "Microsoft SNMP Service."

2. The agent and manager must at least share a common community name. See "Microsoft SNMP Service."

3. The manager will send the get, get-next, and set commands. The agent will respond to those commands and will also send traps when significant events occur. See "SNMP Agents and Management."

4. There are four MIBs that come with Windows NT: Internet MIB II, LAN Manager MIB II, DHCP MIB, and WINS MIB. See "Management Information Base."

Answers to Exam Questions

1. **D.** There are three commands that can be issued by a management station. The three are get, get-next, and set. See "The SNMP Management System."

2. **B.** The MIB, or Management Information Base, contains the set of manageable objects for a service. There can be multiple MIBs installed at the same time on Windows NT. See "Management Information Base."

3. **D.** The default community name is "public." This should be changed to increased security even if you are only installing SNMP to activate the Performance Monitor counters. See "SNMP Communities."

4. **C.** The four MIBs available from Windows NT are Internet MIB II, LAN Manager MIB II, WINS MIB, and DHCP MIB. See "Management Information Base."

5. **C.** Of the four commands that can be issued, the only one that the SNMP agent will initiate is the trap command. See "The SNMP Agent."

Suggested Readings and Resources

1. *Windows NT 4 Resource Kit*: Networking Guide. Chapter 11, "Using SNMP for Network Management."

PART

CONNECTIVITY

This chapter helps you prepare for the exam by covering the following objectives:

Given a scenario, identify which utility to use to connect to a TCP/IP-based UNIX host.

▶ This is a general-knowledge objective. Here you will be tested on your use of the various utilities to ensure that you know how to connect to remote systems.

CHAPTER 11

Heterogeneous Environments

STUDY STRATEGIES

As you read through this chapter you should concentrate on the following key items:

▶ You will need to know how to transfer files using FTP and what TFTP can be used for.

▶ You need to know how to work in a Telnet session.

▶ You will need to know what the three Berkeley R-utilities—REXEC, RSH, and RCP—are used for.

▶ You should know how to use Internet Explorer.

It is common to have different operating systems and platforms within a network. One way to achieve connectivity between platforms is to use the TCP/IP protocol. TCP/IP is available as a transport protocol on most network operating systems, including Windows NT, Novell NetWare, almost all UNIX operating systems, and many more.

This chapter examines ways to connect different systems using the TCP/IP protocol. Although you can connect them without using TCP/IP, this protocol provides a large number of utilities and services that are not available with other protocols:

- **Connectivity using Microsoft networking.** Remote host systems that support the requirements of NetBIOS networking (that is, systems that provide NetBIOS services) can easily be accessed by other client computers. This is not exactly provided by TCP/IP, but it is supported under TCP/IP.

- **Remote execution.** Using standard utilities provided with Windows NT, you can execute certain commands on remote computers. These utilities—which include RSH (remote shell) and REXEC (Remote Execute)—require TCP/IP to operate.

- **File transfer.** When direct connectivity using Microsoft networking is impossible, file-transfer utilities are available to transmit and receive files to or from a remote host system. These utilities—which include FTP (File Transfer Protocol) and RCP (Remote Copy Protocol)—require TCP/IP to operate.

- **Printing.** Integration between Microsoft Windows NT and print subsystems on a remote host system can be achieved using standard utilities and services available with Windows NT. These utilities—which include LPR (Line Printer Request), LPQ (Line Printer Query), and the LPD (Line Printer Deamon) service—require TCP/IP to operate. (TCP/IP printing was covered in detail in Chapter 9, "TCP/IP Printing Services.")

You will experience varying degrees of connectivity and transparency depending on your requirements and the TCP/IP options your other systems can support. The following sections will look at the utilities that provide connectivity using TCP/IP.

COMMUNICATING OVER TCP/IP

The TCP/IP suite offers a transport protocol; it does not, in and of itself, provide network services. Instead, it provides to the Application layer services that allow connectivity. You can use standard NetBIOS commands, such as the NET USE command or Windows NT Explorer, to connect to remote hosts over TCP/IP if the following requirements are met:

❖ Your computer and the remote host must be using the same transport protocol (such as TCP/IP, IPX/SPX, or NetBEUI).

❖ The remote host must provide a NetBIOS (SMB) server. The Workstation service in Windows NT can then communicate using the SMB (server message block) server process.

Effectively, connectivity using Microsoft networking is available when the remote host can provide the equivalent of a NetBIOS server service. To connect to resources on a remote system, you don't need to change the configuration of the Windows NT system; however, the remote computer needs to be configured to act as a NetBIOS server on a protocol used by your Windows NT system.

This option provides the greatest degree of integration between Microsoft client computers and remote host systems. Many systems support connectivity through Microsoft networking, including LAN Manager for OS/2, LAN Manager for UNIX, DEC PATHWORKS, and IBM LAN Server for OS/2. In cases where this connectivity is impossible, you have other options.

MICROSOFT TCP/IP UTILITIES

Windows NT includes TCP/IP utilities that provide many options for connecting to foreign systems, even when it is impossible to connect to remote host systems using NetBIOS networking. These utilities allow Microsoft clients to perform remote execution, data transfer, and much more. The following sections examine these utilities in more detail.

Remote Execution Utilities

Windows NT includes a series of remote execution utilities that enable a user to execute commands on a remote host system. These utilities provide varying degrees of security.

Any of these utilities that require passwords transmit the password as plain text; unlike with the Windows NT logon sequence, the logon information is not encrypted before being transmitted. Any unscrupulous user with access to network-monitoring software could intercept the username and password for the remote host. If you use the same username and password on the remote host as you do on your Windows NT system, your Windows NT account could be compromised.

> N O T E   **Utilities**   Note that varying subsets of these utilities are available with Windows NT Server and Workstation. The resource kit includes all of these utilities.

The REXEC Utility

REXEC enables a user to start a process on a remote host system using a username and password for authentication. If the host authenticates the user, REXEC starts the specified process and terminates. The REXEC command line is shown here, with its options in the following table:

```
REXEC host -l username -n command
```

Option	Purpose
host	Specifies the remote host on which to run the command (indicated by hostname or IP address)
-l *username*	The logon name to pass to the remote host (required by most systems)
-n	Redirects the input from the REXEC to NULL (this option is normally not used)
command	The command that the remote system should run for you

After REXEC connects to the specified host, it asks for a password. If the host authenticates the user, the specified command is executed and the REXEC utility exits. REXEC can be used for command-line programs; interactive programs such as text editors would not be usable with REXEC.

This utility provides a reasonable degree of security because the remote host authenticates the user. The downside is that the username and password are not encrypted prior to transmission.

The RSH Utility

Remote Shell (RSH) provides basically the same function as REXEC, but it handles user authentication differently. Unlike with REXEC, you do not need to specify a username with RSH. The only validation performed by RSH is to verify that the username is in a hidden file (.rhosts) on the UNIX system.

If the remote host is configured to allow any user to use RSH, no username needs to be provided. However, because it is extremely unlikely a system would be configured in this way, the RSH utility provides the logged-on username if no username is provided. This can be overridden if desired.

On UNIX systems, the .rhosts and the hosts.equiv files are used for authentication. Because these files can be used to grant access to all or some users on a computer, use it carefully. Refer to *Internet Firewalls and Network Security* (New Riders Publishing) for the formatting and contents of these files and related security issues.

The RSH command is run from a command prompt using the following syntax (its options are described in the succeeding table):

```
RSH host [-l username] [-n] command
```

Option	Purpose
host	Specifies the remote host on which to run the command (indicated by hostname or IP address)
-l *username*	The logon name to pass to the remote host (required by most systems)
-n	Redirects the input from the REXEC to NULL (this option is normally not used)
command	The command that the remote system should run for you.

After you start RSH, it connects to the remote system's RSH daemon (UNIX-speak for a service). The RSH daemon on the remote UNIX system ensures that the username is in its .rhosts file; if authentication succeeds, the specified command is executed.

Like REXEC, RSH provides a certain degree of security in that the remote host validates the access.

The Telnet Utility

You may be surprised that there are still many times that you are required to connect to another system using terminal emulation. Using Telnet might cause you to see your (expensive) computer as a dumb terminal.

The Telnet screen is very simple (see Figure 11.1). For all intents and purposes, it is a dumb terminal that you run under Windows. Many versions of Telnet are available, including several that are shareware or freeware. However, the supplied version functions just fine for most purposes.

Some of the Telnet configuration parameters that you can adjust are explained in the following sections.

Connecting to a Remote Host

Obviously, one of the main capabilities you will require is to connect to the remote host. This is fairly easy, as the following steps indicate.

STEP BY STEP

11.1 Connecting to the Remote Host

1. Start the Telnet client. This can be done from the Start menu by choosing Run and typing **Telnet**.

FIGURE 11.1

A Telnet window, which is essentially a dumb terminal running under Windows.

FIGURE 11.2
The Telnet Connection dialog box.

2. From the menu, choose Connect, Remote System (see Figure 11.2).

3. Enter the name or IP address of the system that you wish to connect to in the Host Name box. (If required, specify a port in the Port box.)

4. From the TermType drop-down box, select the type of terminal that you want Telnet to emulate. When the settings are correct, click OK.

When you are finished with the remote host, you can disconnect from it by choosing Connect, Disconnect.

Setting the Terminal Preferences

There are several options that you can configure in Telnet. The following steps outline how to set them.

STEP BY STEP

11.2 Configuring Telnet Options

1. Choose Terminal, Preferences from the menu (see Figure 11.3).

2. Choose the emulation by clicking VT-52 or VT-100. Normally, you should try the VT-100 emulation first because it has more features.

3. Set the other options as required (see the following list for details).

4. Click OK when you are finished.

FIGURE 11.3
The Terminal Preferences dialog box is used to configure the Telnet session.

The following list defines the other settings in the Terminal Preferences dialog box:

◆ **Local Echo.** Normally, the characters that are displayed in the terminal window come from the remote system. This option tells the system to show what you are typing directly.

- ◆ **Blinking Cursor.** This will set the cursor type to a blinking cursor. This is normally chosen to make it easier to find the cursor.

- ◆ **Block Cursor.** This will set the cursor type to a block cursor instead of the default underscore.

- ◆ **VT100 Arrows.** This enables the use of the arrow keys. This is not available in VT-52 emulation mode.

- ◆ **Buffer Size.** This will allow you to increase the number of lines of text that will be in memory. Setting this number to a higher value lets you scroll up through the data that is already there.

Logging a Telnet Session

Occasionally, you will want to record the Telnet session so you can later review the session. To do this, you will need to turn on the Telnet log. To create a Telnet log, complete the following steps.

STEP BY STEP

11.3 Creating a Telnet Log

1. Choose Terminal Logging.

2. Enter the filename and path where you wish to keep the file. (If the file you enter already exists, the old file will be overwritten.)

3. When you have captured the data that you wanted, select Terminal, Stop Logging.

Data Transfer Utilities

Several utilities are available to allow file transfer between Windows NT systems and remote hosts. As with remote execution utilities, the same caveat applies when dealing with usernames and passwords. These utilities are examined in greater detail in the following sections. In addition to the clients, an FTP and an HTTP server are available for Windows NT from the Internet Information Server or Peer Web Server.

The RCP Utility

The Remote Copy Protocol (RCP) command copies files from a Windows NT system to a remote host and handles authentication in the same way as RSH. To communicate with the RCP daemon on the remote system, the username provided must be in the remote host's .rhosts file. The following command line is used for RCP:

```
RCP -a -b -h -r host.user:source  host.user:path\destination
```

The following table describes the options available with the RCP utility:

Option	Purpose
-a	Specifies ASCII transfer mode, in which the end-of-line characters are converted to a carriage return for UNIX and a carriage return/line feed for personal computers. This is the default transfer mode.
-b	Sets the binary image transfer mode, in which translation is not made for the end-of-line character. When transferring executables and other binary files, this mode must be used.
-h	Indicates that hidden files should also be transferred.
-r	Tells TCP to recurse subdirectories (that is, to copy the contents of all subdirectories). In this case, the destination must be a directory.
host	The local or remote host. If the host is given as an IP address, you must specify the user.
.user:	Specifies a username to use if it is not the current user.
source	The file or files you want to copy.
path\destination	Specifies the path relative to the logon directory on the remote host. Use the escape characters (\ , ", or ') in remote paths to use wildcard characters on the remote host.

As with RSH, RCP provides security by matching the username provided with a username in the .rhosts file. Unlike RSH, RCP does not prompt for a password.

The FTP Utility

File Transfer Protocol (FTP) transfers files to and from a computer running an FTP server service. FTP is an interactive system, however, you can also add switches at the command line so the transfer can be scripted.

The FTP client that comes with Windows NT is a character-based client (so that it can be scripted). The basic command is as follows:

```
FTP hostname
```

This will open an interactive FTP session. In Figure 11.4 you can see such a session in which the help commands have been brought up onscreen.

The full command line that includes the options required for scripting is shown here, with options explained in the succeeding table:

```
ftp -v -d -i -n -g -s:filename -a -w:windowsize computer
```

Switch	Purpose
-v	Turns off the display of remote host responses (verbose mode).
-n	Disables automatic login upon initial connection.

continues

FIGURE 11.4
An interactive FTP session with help commands displayed.

continued

Switch	Purpose
-i	Turns off prompting during multiple file transfers.
-d	Turns on debugging mode, which will display all commands passed between the client and server.
-g	Turns off filename globbing. This will permit the use of wildcard characters in local filenames and pathnames, which permits the use of filename extensions.
-s:*filename*	Tells FTP to use the specified text file as a script; the commands will automatically run after FTP starts.
-a	Directs FTP to use any local network card when creating the data connection.
-w:*windowsize*	Allows the use of a window size other than the default transfer buffer size of 4096.
computer	Tells FTP the computer name or IP address of the remote host that it should connect to.

Interactive FTP Commands

Most of the time you will use the FTP client in interactive mode. There are several commands that you should be aware of when you are in this mode. The following table lists all the valid FTP commands for the Microsoft FTP client.

Command	Purpose
!	**Usage: !** *command.* Specifies a command that should be run on the local computer. If *command* is left out, the local command prompt is opened.
?	**Usage: ?** *command.* Displays the help descriptions for FTP commands. If a command is entered, help about that command will be displayed; otherwise, general help comes up.
append	**Usage: append** *local_file remote_file.* Tells FTP to transfer the local file and append it to the remote file. If the remote filename is not given, FTP will use the same filename as the local filename. If this does not exist, FTP will create it.

Command	Purpose
ascii	**Usage: ascii.** Converts the end-of-line character between UNIX hosts and PC. ASCII is the default in this mode, end of line conversion will take place.
bell	**Usage: bell.** Toggles the bell on or off. The bell is off by default; when turned on, it will ring after each file transfer.
binary	**Usage: binary.** Changes the mode to binary from ASCII (see above). This must be done whenever you transfer a file so that character conversion will not take place on executable or compressed files, which would make them unreadable.
bye	**Usage: bye.** Closes the FTP session and the window (equivalent to CTRL+C).
cd	**Usage: cd _directory_name_.** Changes the working directory on the FTP server (same as the Windows NT cd command).
close	**Usage: close.** Closes the FTP session with the remote host, but keeps you in FTP.
debug	**Usage: debug.** Enters the debug mode. In this mode all commands that are sent between the two hosts will be echoed to the local printer. Normally this is off.
delete	**Usage: delete _filename_.** Tells FTP to delete the file from the remote host.
dir	**Usage: dir _directory filename_.** Provides a listing of the directory you specify from the remote system. The output can be directed to a file by entering a filename. Neither option is required. If the filename is omitted, the list will only be displayed; if the directory name is omitted, the contents of the current directory are displayed.
Disconnect	**Usage: disconnect.** Performs the same function as close.
get	**Usage: get _remote_file local_file_.** Retrieves a file from the remote host. The local_file entry is optional; if it is not given, the same name will be used as the remote_file.

continues

continued

Command	Purpose
glob	**Usage: glob.** Toggles the glob setting on or off. Globbing permits the use of wildcards in filenames. By default, this is turned on, restricting the use of filename extensions.
hash	**Usage: hash.** Turns the display of hash marks (#) on or off. A hash mark will be displayed for every block (2,048 bytes) of data that is transferred. The default setting for hash is off; however, on large transfers this can be used to ensure the session is active.
help	**Usage: help *command*.** Has the same function as the "?".
lcd	**Usage: lcd *directory*.** Changes the directory you are currently in on the local machine. If you do not include a directory name, the current directory is displayed.
literal	**Usage: literal *parameter*.** Sends a literal string to the remote FTP host. Normally, a single reply code will be returned.
ls	**Usage: ls *directory filename*.** This command has the same function as the dir command.
mdelete	**Usage: mdelete *filename filename filename*.** Multiple delete, works in the same manner as the delete command, only it will accept multiple filenames.
mdir	**Usage: mdir *dirname dirname dirname*.** Multiple directory, displays a listing of filenames that match the patterns given.
mget	**Usage: mget *filename filename filename*.** Multiple get, retrieves more than one file. If you use mget or mput, you should set the prompt off.
mkdir	**Usage: mkdir *dirname*.** Creates a new directory of the given name on the remote host.
mls	**Usage: mls *filename filename filename*.** Same as the mdir command.
mput	**Usage: mput *filename filename filename*.** Multiple put, places the series of files you specify on the remote system.

Command	Purpose
open	**Usage: open** *hostname port.* Opens an FTP session with the host given. The port number to open the connection can be given if the server uses something other than the default (21).
prompt	**Usage: prompt.** Turns on or off the prompting for each file as you use mget or mput. The option is on by default.
put	**Usage: put** *local_filename remote_filename.* Opposite of the get command, places the local filename on the FTP server. If the remote filename is not given, the system will use the current filename.
pwd	**Usage: pwd.** Displays the name of the present working directory from the FTP server.
quit	**Usage: quit.** Same as the bye command, closes the connection and the FTP software.
quote	**Usage: quote** *parameter.* Same as the literal command.
recv	**Usage: recv** *remote_filename local_filename.* Same as the get command.
remotehelp	**Usage: remotehelp** *command.* Works in the same way as help or "?"; however, it will list the specific commands that are supported on the remote system.
rename	**Usage: rename** *old_filename new_filename.* Just like the NT ren command, will rename a file.
rmdir	**Usage: rmdir** *directory_name.* The same as the rd command from NT, will remove the given directory.
send	**Usage: send** *local_filename remote_filename.* Same as the put command.
status	**Usage: status.** Returns the current status of your FTP connections.
trace	**Usage: trace.** Toggles on or off the display of each packet that is being sent or received. This is off by default.
type	**Usage: type binary/ascii.** Switches between the two data modes.

continues

continued

Command	Purpose
user	**Usage: user *username password*.** Logs you on to the remote FTP server. It should be noted that this type of logon is not secure, and that the username and password will be sent to the remote host as clear text.
verbose	**Usage: verbose.** Toggles the verbose mode on or off. In verbose mode, more information is displayed.

The FTP client will, of course, have to talk to an FTP server. FTP uses TCP to handle communications and will create a session between the two hosts. FTP is different than many other protocols in that it will use two ports. FTP uses TCP port 21 as the control port over which the interactive part of the connection will flow. FTP also uses TCP port 20 to actually transfer the files.

The TFTP Utility

Trivial File Transfer Protocol (TFTP) provides similar functions as FTP. Unlike FTP, TFTP uses the connectionless communication features of UDP/IP. The features available in FTP are complex; those in TFTP are simpler. Unlike FTP, TFTP can be used only in a command-line mode. The command-line options are given here and explained in the succeeding table:

```
TFTP -i host GET PUT source destination
```

Option	Purpose
-i	Specifies binary image transfer mode (also called octet). In binary image mode, the file is moved byte by byte. Use this mode when transferring binary files.
host	Specifies the local or remote host.
GET	Transfers the file destination on the remote host to the file source on the local host.
PUT	Transfers the file source on the local host to the file destination on the remote host.
source	Specifies the file to transfer.
destination	Specifies where to transfer the file.

There is no TFTP server included with Windows NT. However, third-party TFTP servers are available.

Many network devices, such as routers and concentrators, use an operating system stored in firmware. As such, upgrades are usually handled using TFTP; the process is known as a firmware update.

Internet Explorer

As we look at Internet Explorer 4.0, we should consider what is really happening when we are surfing on the Web. Essentially, all the Web sites that you have visited are simple text files that are written in HTML. It is, in fact, possible to use Notepad or Edit or even VI (a common text editor on UNIX) to create a home page.

Essentially, browsing builds into a simple file-transfer utility a way of describing the types of files, where they are put on the screen, and where to go if a user clicks—this is the magic that is the World Wide Web. Here is an example of a text file that came from a Web site:

```
<HTML>
<HEAD>
   <TITLE>Welcome to LCBO</TITLE>
</HEAD>

<BODY  background="/images/newerbg.gif" TEXT="#00353A" BGCOLOR="#FFFFCC" LINK="#613730"
➥ALINK="#D5D78D" VLINK="#13280E" >


                  <MAP NAME="map1">
<!-- #$-:Image Map file created by Map THIS! -->
<!-- #$-:Map THIS! free image map editor by Todd C. Wilson -->
<!-- #$-:Please do not edit lines starting with "#$" -->
<!-- #$VERSION:1.20 -->
<!-- #$DATE:Tue May 26 17:41:25 1998 -->
<!-- #$PATH:images/ -->
<!-- #$GIF:menu.gif -->
<AREA SHAPE=RECT COORDS="192,260,317,284" HREF=http://www.vintages.com target="_blank">
<AREA SHAPE=RECT COORDS="193,290,318,315" HREF=mainframe_ht.html?content=sitemap.html>
<AREA SHAPE=RECT COORDS="168,143,317,166" HREF=mainframe_ht.html?content=programs services/index_main
➥ht.html>
<AREA SHAPE=RECT COORDS="181,173,320,195" HREF=mainframe_ht.html?content=products_stores/index_
➥pr_ht.html>
<AREA SHAPE=RECT COORDS="194,114,320,138" HREF=mainframe_ht.html?content=about/index_main_ht.html>
<AREA SHAPE=RECT COORDS="191,229,322,254" HREF=mainframe_ht.html?content=events/index_main_ht.html>
<AREA SHAPE=RECT COORDS="161,201,322,226" HREF=mainframe_ht.html?content=social_resp/index_main_
➥ht.html>
</MAP>
```

```
            <MAP NAME="OnlineOrdering">
                    <AREA SHAPE=CIRCLE COORDS="51,60,46" HREF=/ordering/>
            </MAP>

<CENTER><TABLE BORDER=0 HEIGHT="90%">
    <TR>
        <TD ALIGN="TOP" ROWSPAN="2" NOWRAP><IMG SRC="leaf.gif" WIDTH=111 HEIGHT=120 ALT="" BORDER="0"
➥USEMAP="#OnlineOrdering"
                ><IMG SRC="images/1.gif" WIDTH=23 HEIGHT=77 ALIGN=bottom
                ><BR
                ><img src="images/menu.gif" width=331 height=346 border=0 usemap="#map1">


        </TD>
        <TD VALIGN="TOP" HEIGHT="150" NOWRAP>
                <IMG SRC="images/1.gif" WIDTH=1 HEIGHT=150 ALIGN=bottom
                ><IMG SRC="images/3.gif" WIDTH=269 HEIGHT=77 BORDER=0 ALT=""
                ><BR
                ></TD>
    </TR>
    <TR>

        <TD VALIGN="TOP">
        <BLOCKQUOTE><B><I>The LCBO is continually improving itself in every way
    possible - by offering Sunday shopping, AIR MILES <font size="-1">&#174;</font> Travel
        Miles, credit and debit payment options, value-adds and
            Limited-Time-Offer discounts. We're also offering
    bottle-your-own bulk wine in Toronto on a pilot basis. Find
        out more about the LCBO today, and the LCBO of the
                            future.</I></B></BLCOKQUOTE>
        </TD>
    </TR>
</TABLE>
</CENTER>
</BODY>
</HTML>
```

NOTE

**Viewing Source HTML in Internet
Explorer** If you want to see the
source HTML listing for a site in
Internet Explorer, choose View, Source
from the menu.

When you open the site by typing www.ScrimTech.com into the File, Open dialog box or into the Address box, you will see the site as it is meant to be viewed (see Figure 11.5).

A complete discussion of the Internet Explorer is far outside the scope of this text; however, in the next few sections some of the basic operations will be reviewed.

Opening a Page

Of all the functions that you will perform in the Internet Explorer, the most basic (and most common) is to open a Web page. This can be done using Start, Run and typing the full name of the page (for example, http://www.metacrawler.com or http://www.microsoft.com/train_cert); or you can use File, Open from the menu to see the Open Site dialog box.

FIGURE 11.5
A sample home page on the Internet.

Subscribing to a Site

Now that you have made it to a site, you may wish to remember where the site is. This is easy to do, and all Web browsers will allow you to do it. Microsoft, however, has added the capability not only to add a site to a list of your favorites, but also subscribe to a site (see the following steps).

STEP BY STEP

1.4 Subscribing to a Site

1. Open the Internet Explorer and locate the site you want to subscribe to.

2. From the menu, choose Favorites, Add to Favorites. This will bring up the dialog box shown in Figure 11.6.

3. Choose the option you want and click OK.

The options you may choose are as follows:

◆ **No, just add the page to my favorites.** This will add the page to the favorites list so you can get there using Favorites and choosing the site name from the menu.

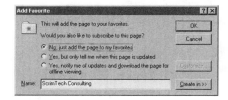

FIGURE 11.6
When you add a site to your favorites list, you have three options on what to do if the site is updated.

NOTE

Speed Considerations Choosing either of the Yes options will use more bandwidth and make Internet Explorer slower to open. Choose these options only if you have a fast Internet connection.

◆ **Yes, but only tell me when this page is updated.** This will check the page whenever you are in the Internet Explorer and let you know if it has been modified.

◆ **Yes, notify me of updates and download the page for offline viewing.**

Using a favorite is as simple as choosing Favorites from the menu and the site name from the menu.

Configuring the Internet Explorer

Finally, this section will cover the basic configuration of the Internet Explorer. Again, this is only an overview of the configuration of a browser that has grown to be one of the most comprehensive on the market today.

To view the configuration choose View and Options (this will actually be Internet Options in most cases and will be the last item on the menu).

The General Tab

The first tab that you come across is the General tab (see Figure 11.7). This allows you to configure only very basic information; the options available are described in the following list:

◆ **Home page.** This is the page that you will see when you open the Internet Explorer

◆ **Temporary Internet files.** This sets how much space can be used on your system by temporary Internet files.

◆ **History.** This tells the system how long to keep a list of the sites that you visited

◆ **Colors.** Set the colors that you want IE to use.

◆ **Fonts.** This will let you set the fonts that IE will use.

◆ **Languages.** This tells the system which languages you will view a site in if multiple languages are posted.

◆ **Accessibility.** This will override the settings from the site designer for font and color settings.

FIGURE 11.7
The General options that can be set in the Internet Explorer.

The Security Tab

Before you begin the configuration, you need to understand that the Internet Explorer treats each site differently. Four categories of sites may be configured on your system.

◆ **Local Intranet zone.** These are servers that are configured as part of your internal network.

◆ **Trusted sites zone.** These are servers that you have specifically.

◆ **Internet zone.** These settings will be used for most servers on the Internet unless they are added to the Trusted sites or Restricted sites.

◆ **Restricted sites zone.** These are sites that you will not trust or download programs and applets from.

You should first choose the zone that you wish to configure, and then you can set the other options in the Security tab (see Figure 11.8).

The following list describes the options available on the Security tab:

◆ **Add Sites.** This will allow you to add sites to the Trusted sites or the Restricted sites.

◆ **Set the security level for this zone.** This will set the level of security for the site.

The Content Tab

The Content tab (see Figure 11.9) provides you with a chance to limit the content that will be viewed by users on the system. It also allows you to customize the settings for the current user for certificates (which are a security mechanism) and personal information.

There are three areas available on this tab:

◆ **Content Advisor.** This will allow you to add a content-filtering system that will read the information placed on a page that describes the content (this is voluntary on the part of the Web designer).

◆ **Certificates.** This contains information that will positively identify you or the systems you communicate with. These normally include a public key to allow communications to be performed using private key/public key encryption.

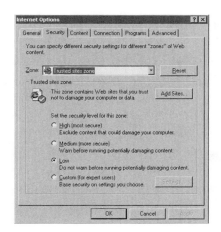

FIGURE 11.8
The Security options set what programs and applets can be downloaded from a site.

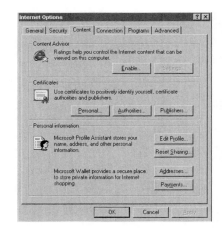

FIGURE 11.9
The Content tab can be used to set information about the user and the content they wish to view.

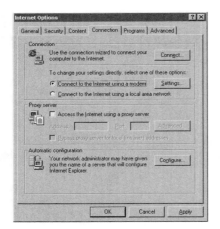

FIGURE 11.10
The Connection tab will configure the connection to your intranet or the Internet.

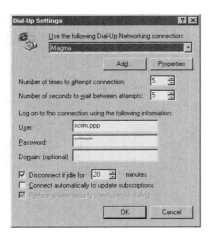

FIGURE 11.11
Select the dial-up connection that the Internet Explorer should use.

◆ **Personal information.** This will allow you to configure your settings for the Internet Explorer; this allows several users to share a computer and still keep their own settings. In this area you can also configure Microsoft Wallet with your credit card information for making payments to some sites.

The Connection Tab

Obviously, if you are going to surf the Internet, you will need to *connect* to the Internet. This can be done using your local network, a proxy server, or even a modem. The Connection tab (see Figure 11.10) will allow you to configure the type of connection you are using.

The options available on the Connection tab include the following:

◆ **Connection.** In this area you will choose the type of connection you are using. You can choose to create a new dial-up account using the Connect button, or use your existing network or dial-up connection. When you choose to connect using a modem, you should click the Settings button and configure the connection (see Figure 11.11).

◆ **Proxy server.** A proxy server will forward the requests that you want to send to the Internet. This allows an organization to use fake addresses internally and to use a small number of real addresses externally. This area will allow you configure how the proxy server is used and where it is. Using the advanced button, you will be able to configure a different proxy for each service.

◆ **Automatic configuration.** This will tell your computer that it can retrieve the connection (and other configuration) from another system on the network. This will allow an administrator to control the IE settings using the Internet Explorer Administration Kit.

The Programs Tab

The next tab that you will see is the Programs tab (see Figure 11.12). On this tab you can tell the Internet Explorer which external programs to use for various functions.

This tab is broken down into these sections:

◆ **Messaging.** Here you can tell the Internet Explorer which mail system you are using. This will be used when you hit a "mail to" spot on a Web page.

◆ **Personal information.** This lets the Internet Explorer know which calendar systems and address book to use.

◆ **Internet Explorer should check to see whether it is the default browser.** This option will check to see if IE is the default browser when starting. If it is not, a dialog box will appear asking if you want to make it so.

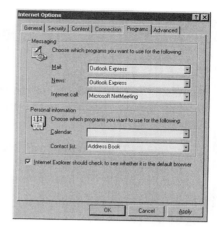

FIGURE 11.12
The Programs tab helps to integrate the Internet Explorer with the other programs that you use.

The Advanced Tab

The last tab, Advanced (see Figure 11.13), allows you to set various individual options that affect the way your system will work. There are too many options to go into here, especially because this is a book on TCP/IP, not the Internet Explorer.

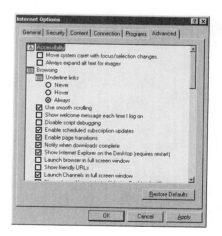

FIGURE 11.13
The Advanced tab has many different options that can be set as required.

CASE STUDY: UTILITIES IN USE AT SUNSHINE BREWING COMPANY

ESSENCE OF THE CASE

There will be only a few things to consider as you look at the use of TCP/IP clients in this network:

- The use of these utilities will require that you are able to resolve the names of the systems on the production network.

- The utilities that you might need are FTP and Telnet.

- You will be able to use Telnet to connect to the Solaris systems and control them from the one workstation.

- You may occasionally need to copy files to or from these stations using FTP.

For this chapter, there is not much new that will need to be added to the scenario that you have been reading about. The utilities in this chapter will be in use in the production facilities, but only to a limited degree.

SCENARIO

As you might recall from the initial chapters, there are only six locations—the production facilities—that have UNIX-based stations. In Chapter 9, we connected a Windows NT system to the network that has these systems on it to allow them to print to the Windows NT system. These systems will be the only ones that will be able to gain access to the UNIX workstations.

ANALYSIS

There are only a couple of things that you will need to check on here. First, you will need to ensure the Solaris workstations are running FTP and Telnet daemons. This will allow the utilities from Windows NT to connect.

You will also want to use a HOSTS files on the Windows NT system; this will allow you to locate the systems on the production network.

CHAPTER SUMMARY

This chapter has looked at some of the utilities that come with Windows NT. These utilities fall into two main categories: remote execution and file transfer.

This topic on the exam will be fairly straightforward, as long as you are comfortable with the following:

◆ You need to understand that FTP is the most common method of transferring files. You should know how to use it.

◆ You need to know what RCP and TFTP are and the requirements for them.

◆ You need to know that FTP is connection-oriented and TFTP is not.

◆ You need to know that TFTP is used primarily for diskless workstations (and other devices) to receive boot code.

◆ You need to know how to set up, start, and end a Telnet session.

◆ You should know the Internet Explorer connects to HTTP servers, such as the Internet Information Server.

◆ You should know how to open a World Wide Web page.

◆ You should know the differences between RSH and REXEC, including the security and output differences.

KEY TERMS

- Berkeley .rhost file
- File Transfer Protocol Utility (FTP)
- Internet Explorer
- Remote Copy Protocol Utility (RCP)
- Remote Execution Utility (REXEC)
- Remote Shell Utility (RSH)
- Terminal Emulation Utility (Telnet)
- Trivial File Transfer Protocol Utility (TFTP)

APPLY YOUR KNOWLEDGE

Exercises

The following lab will give you a chance to try the FTP command that you have seen here. These exercises require that you have networking and the Internet Information Server installed.

11.1 Using the FTP Command to Move Files

In this exercise, you will work with the FTP command to move some files around. Reference here is to the standard locations; if you have installed components in other locations, please substitute them.

Estimated Time: About 15 minutes.

1. Copy a group of files into the C:\INETPUB\FTPROOT directory.

2. Start an FTP session on your system by using FTP 127.0.0.1.

3. Log in as "anonymous," and enter anything for the password.

4. Attempt to list the files on the FTP server (use **ls -l**). Can you see the files you copied? (You should be able to.)

5. Exit the FTP session (press Ctrl+C).

6. Go to the C:\WINNT\SYSTEM32\ DRIVERS\ETC directory and copy SERVICES to SERVICES.GOOD.

7. Edit the SERVICES file and delete the line that has the FTP entry (leave the FTP_DATA entry).

8. Save the file, and shut down and restart your computer.

9. Go to the Internet Service Manager and double-click the FTP service. Change the port from 21

to 9999. Ensure that Allow Only Anonymous is not selected.

10. On the Directories tab, double-click the Home directory; then ensure that both the Read and Write check boxes are selected.

11. Click OK. You should receive a warning that the changes will not take effect until you restart the service.

12. Stop and restart the FTP service.

13. Attempt again to connect using FTP 127.0.0.1. Were you able to? (No, the FTP client attempts to connect to port 21 by default.)

14. Start an FTP session, type **FTP**, and press Enter.

15. Try to open your site using **OPEN 127.0.0.1 9999**. Does this work? (This should allow you to connect.)

16. Start another DOS prompt. Enter the **NETSTAT** command and observe the connection to port 9999.

17. Switch back to the DOS session where the FTP client is running. Enter your administrator account and password to log on.

18. Switch to binary by typing **BINARY**.

19. Enter the command **ls -l**. You should receive a listing of the files that you put in the directory.

20. Choose a file and type **GET *filename.ext*;** the file should transfer to the current directory. Type **! DIR** to check.

21. Rename the local filename using **! ren filename.ext filename.RJS**.

22. Put a copy back on the FTP Server: **PUT *filename*.RJS**.

APPLY YOUR KNOWLEDGE

23. Verify by using **ls -l**.

24. Close the FTP session using **BYE**.

You will want to change the port and security back to their original state. Also, be sure to copy SERVICES.GOOD over top of the SERVICES file.

Review Questions

1. What utilities can be used to copy files?

2. What is the main difference between FTP and TFTP?

3. When using the RSH and RCP commands, where must your name be listed?

4. What two emulation modes will Telnet support? Which is more common?

5. In the case of a REXEC command, which CPU will actually run the instructions?

Exam Questions

1. In most cases, how will a remote execution utility transfer a password?

   A. Encrypted text

   B. Plain text

   C. LAN Manager–compatible

   D. RS232 strings

2. In which two ways can the REXEC utility specify a host?

   A. Hostname

   B. ARP address

   C. MAC address

   D. IP address

3. You need to connect to an IBM mainframe and interactively run an application. Which utility is best suited to this purpose?

   A. RCP

   B. Telnet

   C. FTP

   D. REXEC

4. Given that REXEC and RSH work in a similar manner, what is the main area of difference?

   A. Availability to system resources

   B. System overhead

   C. Permissions

   D. Authentication

5. What two files can be used on a UNIX system to grant all or some users access for remote authentication?

   A. /passwd

   B. /dailup

   C. .rhosts

   D. hosts.equiv

6. Which of the following items are required for a Telnet session to be established?

   A. Port

   B. Service

   C. Terminal type

   D. Hostname

APPLY YOUR KNOWLEDGE

7. By what method does Telnet authenticate the user?

   A. Username

   B. Password

   C. Username and password

   D. .rhosts file

8. You need to be able to transfer a group of files from your Windows NT Workstation to a UNIX server running Apache Web server. Which of the following would be the best utility to script this transfer?

   A. REXEC

   B. Telnet

   C. FTP

   D. RCP

9. In order to establish an FTP session, which of the following criteria must be met? (Select all correct answers.)

   A. Both systems must be running TCP/IP.

   B. NetBEUI must be used to broadcast service availability.

   C. The remote system must be running an FTP host service.

   D. The client system must be running FTP client software.

10. You are the administrator of a network that uses a combination of Windows NT computers and UNIX workstations. The UNIX workstations are used to control equipment running a milling

process. You need to be able to easily transfer files between the UNIX workstations and the Windows NT systems.

You decide to use FTP as the transfer protocol and install the Peer Web Server on the Windows NT Workstations. You are already running an FTP Daemon on the UNIX workstations. How good a solution is this?

   A. This is the best possible solution.

   B. This is a good solution.

   C. This solution works but is far from optimal.

   D. This solution does not work.

Answers to Review Questions

1. Three utilities can be used to copy files: FTP, TFTP, and RCP. See "Data Transfer Utilties. "

2. FTP is a connection-oriented file-transfer utility that uses TCP as the transport protocol; TFTP is connectionless and uses UDP as a transport protocol. See "Data Transfer Utilties."

3. In using these commands, your name must be listed in the .rhosts file on the system that you are communicating with. See "The RSH Utility."

4. Telnet will work with both VT100 and VT52 emulation, but the VT100 is more common. See "The Telnet Utility."

5. The CPU on the remote host will run the instructions. See "The REXEC Utility."

APPLY YOUR KNOWLEDGE

Answers to Exam Questions

1. **B.** Remote execution utilities transmit passwords as plain text, creating a security weakness. See "The REXEC Utility."

2. **A** and **D.** REXEC can specify a host by its IP address or hostname. See "The REXEC Utility."

3. **B.** In this case, the best answer is Telnet. RCP and FTP are for moving files, and REXEC doesn't provide the same level of interaction as Telnet. See "The Telnet Utility."

4. **D.** RSH works like REXEC but is not as stringent on authentication. See "The REXEC Utility" and "The RSH Utility."

5. **C** and **D.** The .rhosts and hosts.equiv files can be used on UNIX systems for authentication of remote users. See "The RSH Utility."

6. **A, C,** and **D.** Terminal type, port, and hostname (or IP address) are required information you must supply for a Telnet session. See "The Telnet Utility."

7. **C.** Telnet authenticates users by username and password. See "The Telnet Utility"

8. **C.** In this case, you would want to use FTP because it provides better scripting options than RCP. Telnet and REXEC are not file-transfer utilities. See "The FTP Utility."

9. **A, C,** and **D.** NetBEUI is not used with FTP; all other choices are correct. See "The FTP Utility."

10. **A.** The FTP protocol is easy to use and efficient. Because both platforms support both the client and server, this solution makes sense. See "Data Transfer Utilities" and "The FTP Utility."

Suggested Readings and Resources

1. Hare, Chris, and Karanjit Siyan. *Internet Firewalls and Network Security, Second Edition.* New Riders, 1996.

2. *Windows NT 4.0 Resource Kit, Networking Guide.* Appendix A, "TCP/IP Utilities Reference."

This chapter helps you prepare for the exam by covering the following objectives:

Configure a RAS server and Dial-Up Networking for use on a TCP/IP network.

▶ This objective is included to ensure that you know how to configure Remote Access Service and Dial-Up Networking. You will need to know how to configure both ends of a connection.

CHAPTER 12

Remote Access Service and TCP/IP

STUDY STRATEGIES

As you read through this chapter, you should concentrate on the following key items:

▶ You need to understand the Dial-Up Networking configuration for TCP/IP.

▶ You need to understand the basics of SLIP and PPP.

▶ You should know how to configure RAS to accept dial-in calls.

▶ You should know what PPTP is and where it can be used.

One of the cornerstones of TCP/IP is the ability to handle wide-area communications. This obviously must extend into the world of serial (modem) communications.

In this chapter, you will learn about the configuration of the Remote Access Service as it relates to TCP/IP. Specifically, you will see how to configure the client to dial into RAS (or other communications server) and how to configure RAS to accept connections.

To wrap up the chapter, you will learn about PPTP, which can be used to secure connections across the Internet. This allows organizations that use laptops or have telecommuters to securely access the Internet using a local Internet service provider (ISP). This saves money in long-distance charges and in setting up and maintaining a modem pool.

CONFIGURING RAS TO DIAL OUT

There are several areas that you need to configure in order to allow users to dial into a server using RAS. First, you need to configure RAS to allow you to dial out, and you must tell the service which protocols you wish to use to do so. Configuring RAS in the Networking Settings dialog box, as described in the following steps, accomplishes this.

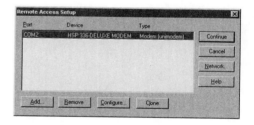

FIGURE 12.1
From this dialog box you can configure the modems and other devices used for the Remote Access Service.

STEP BY STEP

12.1 Configuring Remote Access Service

1. Open the Network dialog box, and on the Services tab double-click the Remote Access Service. The Remote Access Setup dialog box will appear (see Figure 12.1). If you have not added the service yet, click Add and choose Remote Access Service.

2. Select the modem you want to dial out with and click the Configure button. Choose either Dial Out Only or Dial Out and Receive Calls (see Figure 12.2). Click OK to close the Configure Port Usage dialog box.

FIGURE 12.2
Configuring the port usage for the RAS configuration.

FIGURE 12.3
Setting the dial-out network protocols.

3. Click the Network button; the Network Configuration dialog box appears (see Figure 12.3). Make sure TCP/IP is selected in the Dial Out Protocols section, and then click OK to close the dialog box.

4. Click Continue to close the Remote Access Setup dialog box, and then click OK to close the Network dialog box.

DIAL-UP NETWORKING

Now that the configuration for the RAS has been completed, you need to add entries to Dial-Up Networking, which is actually where you will keep the information about each of the locations that you will dial into. Dial-Up Networking is found in My Computer.

Dial-Up Networking allows you to dial out to an Internet access provider using either the Point-to-Point Protocol (PPP) or the Serial Line Interface Protocol (SLIP). SLIP is an older, simpler protocol that performs well, but provides few amenities. PPP is a newer protocol that provides more-reliable communication and a number of options that automate session configuration and logon. Because of the advantages of PPP, it is the preferred protocol for the majority of ISPs.

Adding Phonebook Entries

The Dial-Up Networking application is used to manage your dial-up configurations and to connect to remote locations. The first time you start Dial-Up Networking, you see the message The phone book is empty. Press OK to add an entry. When you choose OK, you are shown the New Phonebook Entry Wizard. You need to configure at least one Phonebook entry to use Dial-Up Networking.

The following list describes the information that is required by the wizard:

◆ A name for the new Phonebook entry

◆ Whether you are calling the Internet

◆ Whether it is okay to send your password in plain text if requested by the server

◆ If you are calling a non-Windows NT server, whether the server expects you to enter login information after connecting

◆ The phone number (and alternative phone numbers, if available)

◆ Whether the Phonebook entry will use telephony dialing properties

The following list will step you through creating an entry using the New Phonebook Entry wizard.

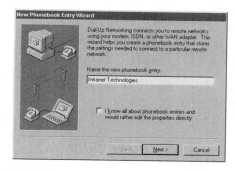

FIGURE 12.4
The first screen of the New Phonebook Entry Wizard.

STEP BY STEP

12.2 Creating a Phonebook Entry

1. Enter a name in the initial box and click Next (see Figure 12.4).

2. You are asked what type of system you are calling and whether your password should be sent as clear text (see Figure 12.5).

3. You are then asked for the phone number (see Figure 12.6). Here you also may enter alternative phone numbers if you wish; this will allow your system to try all the numbers and use whichever one works.

4. After you click the Next button, the system will tell you that you are finished. Click the Finish button.

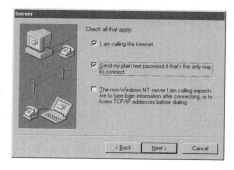

FIGURE 12.5
On the next screen of the wizard, you are asked for the type of server you are dialing.

When the Phonebook entry is completed, it will resemble what you see in Figure 12.7.

From this screen you will be able to perform any of several options, including the following:

◆ **New**—creates a new phone entry using the same wizard you just saw.

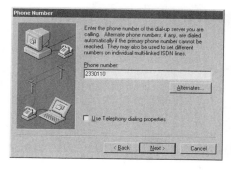

FIGURE 12.6
On this screen you can enter the all-important phone numbers.

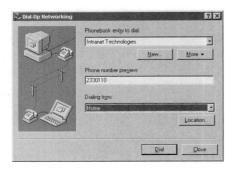

FIGURE 12.7
The RAS Phonebook, showing the entry that was just added.

FIGURE 12.8
There are several options that are available from the More drop-down menu.

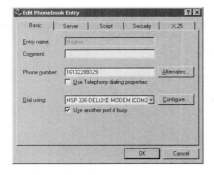

FIGURE 12.9
Editing a Phonebook entry is done using this dialog box.

◆ **More**—drops down a menu with several options (see Figure 12.8), which are explained in the following list:

- **Edit entry and modem properties.** Using this option, you will be able to change the properties for this dial-up entry.

- **Clone entry and modem properties.** If you add another dial-up service similar to an existing one, you can use this to copy the one that you already have working.

- **Delete entry.** This removes the entry.

- **Create shortcut to entry.** This will add an icon to your desktop that can be used to connect to the entry.

- **Monitor status.** This will open the Dial-Up Networking Monitor.

- **Operated assisted or manual dialing.** In some cases, you will need to dial the number yourself; this will allow you to do so. If you choose this option, dialing will still be done normally. However, you will see a dialog box that will tell you when to dial.

- **User preferences.** This is used to view or set your preferences for dialing.

- **Logon preferences.** This will set your logon preferences.

◆ **Phone Number**—changes the phone number; if you change the number, it is saved.

◆ **Dialing from**—allows you to choose the telephone location that you are dialing from.

◆ **Locations**—allows you to temporarily change the dialing prefix and/or suffix that is used to dial the number.

Editing Phonebook Entries

There are two ways that you can edit a Phonebook entry: you can return to Dial-Up Networking, or you can right-click a shortcut on the desktop and choose Edit Entry and Modem Properties. In either case, you will see the dialog box in Figure 12.9.

The Server tab (see Figure 12.10) defines the protocols that are used to communicate with the server. Options in this tab are as follows:

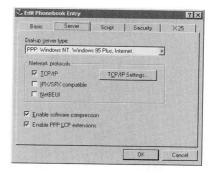

FIGURE 12.10
The Server tab allows you configure the type of dial-in server and the TCP/IP settings.

- ◆ **Dial-up server type.** In this field you have three choices that will determine the type of line protocol that you will use. A line protocol essentially replaces the frames that you find on a local area network; that is, it will be used to move the data between hosts. These are the three choices:

  - • **PPP: Windows NT, Windows 95 Plus, Internet.** The Point-to-Point Protocol (PPP) is the protocol used most commonly for TCP/IP dial-up services. This is the default and the best all-around choice. PPP can be used with all supported protocols.

  - • **SLIP: Internet.** The Serial Line Internet Protocol (SLIP) is an older Internet protocol that is losing popularity. SLIP is less reliable and has fewer features than PPP, but it is more efficient and provides somewhat better performance. When SLIP is selected, only TCP/IP is available as a protocol option.

  - • **Windows NT 3.1, Windows for Workgroups 3.11.** This option selects an older RAS protocol that is not usable on the Internet.

- ◆ **Network protocols.** You must check TCP/IP in this box to enable TCP/IP support.

- ◆ **Enable software compression.** This option is checked by default and configures the communication software to compress and decompress communications data. It is unproductive and unnecessary to enable both hardware (modem) and software (protocol) compression. Typically, software compression is more efficient, particularly on higher-end computers; however, it is not supported by the SLIP protocol.

- ◆ **Enable PPP LCP extensions.** This check box enables newer PPP features and should be cleared only if you are having problems connecting.

After TCP/IP has been checked, the TCP/IP Settings button can be used to access the TCP/IP Settings dialog box. The contents of the dialog box depend on whether you have selected PPP or SLIP.

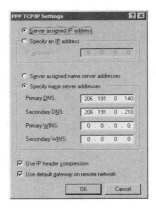

FIGURE 12.11
The TCP/IP settings for a PPP connection.

Figure 12.11 shows the PPP TCP/IP Settings dialog box, which has the following options:

◆ **Server assigned IP address.** Check this option if the PPP dial-in server will assign an IP address to you. This is the most common situation.

◆ **Specify an IP address.** Select this option and specify an IP address in the IP address field if the PPP server does not assign an IP address.

◆ **Server assigned name server addresses.** Select this option if the PPP dial-in server adds the address of a DNS server to your configuration when you dial in. This is chosen less often than automatic IP address assignment.

◆ **Specify name server addresses.** Select this option to manually specify the IP addresses of DNS and WINS name servers.

◆ **Use IP header compression.** Header compression—also known as Van Jacobson IP header compression or VJ header compression—is almost always used to reduce the amount of traffic. Check with the manager of the dial-in server to determine if header compression is used.

◆ **Use default gateway on remote network.** This option applies to computers that are connected to local networks at the same time they are dialing remotely. When this option is checked, packets that cannot be routed to the local network are routed to the default gateway on the remote network.

Figure 12.12 shows the SLIP TCP/IP Settings dialog box, which might be used when connecting to an ISP. You must complete the following fields:

◆ **IP address.** SLIP cannot supply an IP address, so you must specify one here.

◆ **Primary DNS.** SLIP cannot supply a DNS server address, so again you will need to supply one. Optionally, you can supply a secondary DNS server address.

◆ **Force IP header compression.** Check this option if the SLIP server uses header compression.

◆ **Use default gateway on remote network.** This option applies to computers that are connected to a local network at the same

FIGURE 12.12
Configuring TCP/IP for a SLIP connection is similar to configuring it for a PPP connection.

time they are dialing remotely. When this option is checked, packets that cannot be routed to the local network are routed to the default gateway on the remote network.

◆ **Frame size.** This value determines the size of frames that will be used. Adjust this value, if required, for the SLIP server. Frame sizes of 1006 and 1500 can be selected.

DIALING WITH A PHONEBOOK ENTRY

After you have created a Phonebook entry, you will be able to dial the number—the easiest part. In the simplest case, all you need to do is perform the following steps.

STEP BY STEP

12.3 Dialing

1. Select an entry in the Phonebook Entry to Dial field, and then click Dial or double-click the shortcut.

2. Enter the requested information in the Connect To dialog box (see Figure 12.13). If you are dialing an ISP, you should leave the domain blank unless otherwise informed. Click OK to dial.

If you click on the Save Password option, you will not be prompted to enter the Connect To information again. This will make dialing very simple, and it lets the system use this Phonebook entry automatically for some programs (such as Outlook Express).

When you first connect to an ISP, you will be given a dialog box telling you that the connection was successful; from here you can choose one of these options:

◆ **Close on dial.** If this box is checked, the Dial-Up Network application will be closed when a connection is established.

◆ **Do not display this message again.** If this box is checked, you will not see this message in the future when a connection is completed.

FIGURE 12.13

When you first dial an entry, you will be prompted for the logon information.

When you have finished, right-click the Dial-up Networking icon on the task bar, and then choose Hang Up and the name of your ISP.

CONFIGURING A RAS SERVER

When RAS is installed, setting up the system to act as a RAS server is simply a matter of configuration. There are two places where you will need to change the configuration:

◆ **RAS Setup.** You will need to set up the port to receive calls, and the Network Settings for inbound connections.

◆ **User Manager for Domains.** This optional setting allows you to grant dial-in permissions using the User Manager for Domains.

RAS Setup

The first thing you need to do in the RAS Setup dialog box is to set the port usage to at least receive calls. To do this, follow these steps.

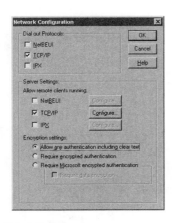

FIGURE 12.14
Here the Network Configuration dialog box includes the settings for dial-in and dial-out.

STEP BY STEP

12.4 Setting the Port Usage to Receive Calls

1. Open the Network dialog box, and on the Services tab double-click the Remote Access Service.

2. Choose the port (or ports) that you will use as dial-in ports and click Configure.

3. Select either Receive Calls or Dial Out and Receive Calls.

4. Click OK to close the Port Usage dialog box.

Now you need to configure the way that the network will work with systems that dial in. This is handled in the Network Configuration dialog box (see Figure 12.14).

Configuring TCP/IP on the Dial-In Server

The configuration for TCP/IP is fairly easy. After you have selected TCP/IP as a protocol, click the Configure button to its right. You will now see the RAS Server TCP/IP Configuration dialog box (see Figure 12.15). Following are the options available in this dialog box:

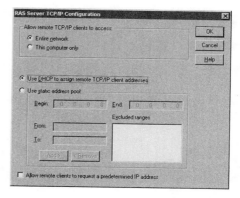

FIGURE 12.15
The RAS Server TCP/IP Configuration dialog box lets you set the properties that dial-in clients will get.

- **Allow remote TCP/IP clients to access.** The two options you can configure here are fairly simple: clients can communicate only with this system or with your whole network.

- **Use DHCP to assign remote TCP/IP client address.** This will tell the dial-in server to use the DHCP server to allocate TCP/IP addressing and configuration to the remote client. (You will be able to identify these leases in the DHCP server by the small telephones on the icons.)

- **Use static address pool.** Here you can enter a fixed series of addresses that will be given out to clients. This is all the configuration the client will get, so you will need to configure the name servers and such.

- **Allow remote clients to request a predetermined IP address.** This may be required in some environments. However, it will require a good deal more planning because the IP must be for the correct subnet.

Assigning Dial-In Permissions

Now that the server is configured, you will need to permit users to dial in. This is a matter of assigning dial-in permissions, which can be done from the Remote Access Admin program or from the User Manager. To grant dial-in permissions from the User Manager, follow these steps.

STEP BY STEP

12.5 Granting Dial-In Permissions

1. Open the User Manager (or User Manager for Domains).

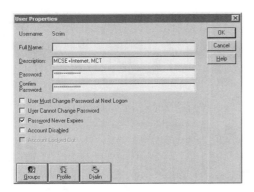

FIGURE 12.16
From the User Properties dialog box you will be able to access the dial-in permissions.

FIGURE 12.17
The Dial-In Information is simple to enter.

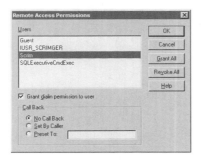

FIGURE 12.18
Setting permissions from the Remote Access Permissions dialog box is also simple.

2. Select the user or users you wish to grant dial-in permissions to.

3. Choose User, Properties from the menu. This will bring up the User Properties dialog box (see Figure 12.16).

4. Click the Dial-In icon; this opens the dial-in properties for the user (see Figure 12.17).

5. Select the Grant Dial-In Permission to User check box and, if desired, set the call-back security.

6. Click OK to close the Dial-In Information, and click OK again to close the User Properties dialog box.

To grant the permissions in the Remote Access Admin program, you can follow these steps.

STEP BY STEP

12.6 Granting Permissions in the Remote Access Administration Program

1. Open the Remote Access Admin program (Start, Programs, Administrative Tools, Remote Access Admin).

2. Choose Users, Permissions from the menu to bring up the Remote Access Permissions dialog box (see Figure 12.18).

3. Click on the user and then grant permissions by checking the Grant Dial-In Permissions to User box. You can also set a call-back mode here.

4. Click OK when done.

When the permissions are set, the user will be able to dial in to the server to connect to your network.

USING THE POINT-TO-POINT TUNNELING PROTOCOL

Using RAS, you can construct a dial-in server that enables clients to access your network from anywhere in the world. RAS works well and provides a high level of security; however, RAS is not always the perfect solution. For example, over long distances there can be big problems with line quality—and, of course, high costs. In addition, you would need to install and upgrade a large number of modems, all of which require phone lines.

The solution is to use the Internet as part of your corporate backbone. Until recently, security issues prevented this from being a possibility. However, with Windows NT 4 came the introduction of PPTP.

The Point-to-Point Tunneling Protocol (PPTP) is a new feature in Windows NT 4. PPTP uses tunneling to enable packets for one protocol to be carried over networks running another protocol. For example, NWLink packets can be encapsulated inside IP packets, enabling the IPX packets to be transported through the TCP/IP world of the Internet. PPTP has the added benefit of enhancing security because it works hand-in-hand with the encryption capability of RAS.

In a scenario in which both the RAS client and the RAS server are directly connected to the Internet, a PPTP tunnel between the client and the server can established, providing a secure communication channel between them. The use of PPTP enables the client and server to connect via the Internet without a need for the client to dial in to RAS through a switched connection. While communicating, RAS encrypts traffic between the client and server, providing a secure communications data stream.

Microsoft refers to PPTP tunnels as virtual private networks (VPNs) because they establish a logical private network that runs over the public network infrastructure. PPTP configuration is not difficult; the following sections show how to configure PPTP support on the RAS server and client.

Configuring PPTP

PPTP must be enabled for each RAS server or client that will use it. To enable PPTP, perform the following steps.

STEP BY STEP

12.7 Enabling PPTP

1. Using the Network dialog box, install the Point-to-Point Tunneling Protocol in the Protocols tab.

2. After the protocol is copied from the installation disks, the PPTP Configuration dialog box is displayed (see Figure 12.19). Number of Virtual Private Networks specifies the number of PPTP connections that will be supported.

3. You should see a message that the RAS setup will be invoked. Click OK to start the RAS setup utility. Then add the virtual ports that support the VPNs you wish to establish.

4. Choose Add to open the Add RAS Device dialog box shown in Figure 12.20. In the example, the RAS Capable Devices list is open, showing the virtual ports that correspond to the VPNs specified in step 2. Select an entry and choose OK.

5. In the Remote Access Setup dialog box, select each new entry and choose Configure to open Configure Port Usage. Select one of the options for port usage. (For a PPTP client, at least one VPN port must be configured to permit dial-out; for a PPTP server, at least one VPN port must be configured to permit receiving calls.)

6. Repeat steps 4 and 5 for each VPN device you want to add.

7. When all virtual devices have been added, choose Continue. When you see the Protocols tab, choose Close. Restart the computer.

FIGURE 12.19
The PPTP Configuration dialog box configures the number of VPNs you will support.

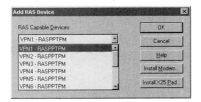

FIGURE 12.20
Adding VPN devices as RAS ports.

Enabling PPTP Filtering

After PPTP is installed, the RAS server will support both PPTP and non-PPTP connections—creating a potential security hole. If you want, you can enable PPTP filtering, disabling support for any traffic except PPTP.

To enable PPTP filtering, follow these steps.

STEP BY STEP

12.8 Enabling PPTP Filtering

1. Select the Protocols tab in the Network dialog box.

2. Select TCP/IP Protocol and choose Properties.

3. Select the IP Address tab.

4. Select a network adapter for which PPTP filtering is to be enabled.

5. Click Advanced.

6. Check Enable PPTP Filtering.

7. Repeat steps 4 through 6 for each interface that will support PPTP filtering.

8. Restart the computer to activate the changes.

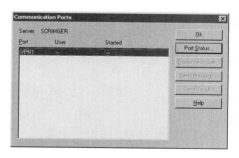

Monitoring Server PPTP Support

You can monitor the PPTP ports in the Remote Access Admin utility by choosing the Communication Ports command from the Server menu. As shown in Figure 12.21, VPN ports are listed with modem ports and can be managed in the same way. Ports will appear only if they are configured to receive calls; ports configured only to dial out will not be listed.

FIGURE 12.21
The Communication Ports dialog box showing a VPN port.

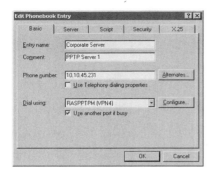

FIGURE 12.22
A PPTP connection entry from Dial-Up Networking.

Enabling Client PPTP Support

When a client is dialing into the Internet, establishing a PPTP tunnel to the RAS server involves two steps:

◆ The client establishes a dial-up connection to the Internet through an Internet access provider.

◆ The client establishes a PPTP connection to the RAS server.

When a client is directly connected to the Internet, it is unnecessary to establish a dial-up connection. The procedure for starting a PPTP connection to the RAS server remains the same, however.

To establish a PPTP connection, you need to create a special entry in the Dial-Up Networking Phonebook. This entry, an example of which appears in Figure 12.22, has two distinguishing characteristics:

◆ The Dial Using field is configured with one of the VPN devices that were added to the RAS configuration when PPTP was installed. VPNs will appear in this list only if they have been configured to support dial-out.

◆ The Phone Number field is completed with the DNS name or the IP address of the PPTP server.

Creating a dial-up connection to PPTP also involves two steps:

◆ In Dial-Up Networking, run the Phonebook entry that connects to your ISP using a telephone number and a modem.

◆ After the connection is established, run the Phonebook entry that connects to the PPTP tunnel using a DNS host name or IP address.

If the client is directly connected to the Internet, it is necessary only to run the Phonebook entry that creates the PPTP tunnel.

CASE STUDY: SETTING UP SECURE DIAL-IN

ESSENCE OF THE CASE

The basic problem here then is how to create a secure network connection that you can access from any location and still make the system cost-effective. There are several points that you need to consider as you look at this problem:

- You need to secure the transmission of data.

- You will be using the Remote Access Service of Windows NT.

- You want to avoid long-distance charges.

- You don't want to have to set up your own modem pool and the additional phone lines required for them, if it's possible to avoid them. (This saves a significant amount of money.)

- Laptop users will dial in at all hours and for varying lengths of time.

- There are ISPs in all the locations where your sales staff (the laptop users) will be working.

One of the key elements of the case we are looking at for Sunshine Brewing Company is the ability to provide a secure dial-in environment for the laptop users. Furthermore, because you will be using the Internet for the backbone, you might also consider how to create a secure connection between offices.

SCENARIO

As you look at the various connections, you should realize that not a single one in the organization is secure. In a real-world scenario, you would set up each office with an internal and external network and use a server, such as Microsoft Proxy Server, to connect them. This would give you a single point of contact and allow you to use the Routing and RAS extensions in Windows NT to establish PPTP links to the other offices.

To keep this scenario based strictly on TCP/IP (and, therefore, within the content of the text), that solution has not been implemented here. Consider, though, as you think about the laptop connections that you will look at, how easy it would be to extend this to include the connections between the offices to actually allow you to use the Internet as a backbone.

Here, as noted, you should concentrate on the laptop dial-in issue. Obviously, a brewing company, like any other company, would prefer to keep orders and other internal information internal. Thus, it would present a problem if you were to simply have the laptop users dial in to the Internet from anywhere and start sending information to the servers at the office.

continues

CASE STUDY: SETTING UP SECURE DIAL-IN

continued

ANALYSIS

Given the criteria, there are two ways you can attack this problem. In the first approach, you will actually incur the cost of the lines and the modem pool (and the maintenance and operation costs that go with it). This would allow users to dial directly into your network and would provide some level of security. However, you would need to set up the laptops with several different Phonebook entries, one for each location they will dial into. Furthermore, the users would need to decide which is the best to dial into. There is

also a good deal of long-distance communication involved in this case.

The other choice is to use PPTP. This will allow the users to connect to a local provider (both the Microsoft Network and the IBM Network are worldwide). After they are connected, they can use the Internet as the transport for the PPTP protocol to run on top of. They can connect to any office easily, meaning they could be configured to always connect to their home office (which makes name resolution worries disappear).

CHAPTER SUMMARY

KEY TERMS

- Dial-Up Networking (DUN)

- Integrated Services Digital Network (ISDN)

- modem (Modulating/Demodulating Device)

- Point-to-Point Protocol (PPP)

- Point-to-Point Protocol–Multilink Protocol (PPP–MP)

- Point-to-Point Tunneling Protocol (PPTP)

- Public Switched Telephone Network (PSTN)

- Remote Access Service (RAS)

- Serial Line Internet Protocol (SLIP)

- virtual private network (VPN)

In this chapter, you were introduced to the Remote Access Service and to configuring RAS and Dial-Up Networking to function with TCP/IP. There are two types of connections that you can create using RAS—normal connections and PPTP virtual private networks (VPNs).

The following list highlights the key facts that you need to be aware of for the exam:

- ◆ You need to know that the RAS can use a communications port to dial in, receive calls, or both.

- ◆ You need to know that there are two line protocols that you can use on the dial-in side: PPP and SLIP. Windows NT, however, acts as a PPP server when others connect to your system.

- ◆ You need to know the difference between PPP and SLIP. PPP can transfer multiple protocols and supports IP address and option assignment. SLIP does not, requiring you to configure this information and the frame size.

- ◆ You need to know how to create a Phonebook entry; this is how you dial out.

CHAPTER SUMMARY

◆ You need to know the ways a server can be configured to assign addresses: DHCP or a local scope. You also need to be aware that there is an override to allow the remote host to choose its own IP address.

◆ You need to know how to assign dial-in permissions for users from both the User Manager and from the Remote Access Admin tool.

◆ You need to know how to see what sessions are available in the Remote Access Admin utility.

◆ You need to understand the purpose of Point-to-Point Tunneling Protocol (PPTP) and how it can be used to form a VPN.

APPLY YOUR KNOWLEDGE

This section will give you a chance to apply the knowledge that you have gained in this chapter.

Exercises

In this series of exercises, you will install the Remote Access Service. If you have already done this, you can skip to Exercise 3. If you do not have a modem, you can follow the instructions in Exercise 1, which will install a false modem.

12.1 Adding a Null Modem

In this exercise, you will install a null modem that will allow you to proceed through some of the remaining exercises without a modem.

Estimated Time: About five minutes.

1. Open the Control Panel and double-click the Modems icon.

2. Click the Add button; this will bring up the modem installer.

3. Choose Don't Detect My Modem, I Will Select it From a List, and then click Next.

4. The list of manufacturers and models will appear. From the Standard Modem Types, choose Dial-Up Networking Serial Cable Between 2 PCs and click Next.

5. Choose any available port and click Next. Windows NT will install your modem. When the next screen appears, choose Finish.

6. Finally, choose OK to close the modem installer.

12.2 Installing Remote Access Service

In this exercise, you will install the Remote Access Service. If you already have this installed, skip to Exercise 3.

Estimated Time: About 10 minutes.

1. Open the Network dialog box. From the Services tab, choose Add.

2. From the list, choose the Remote Access Service. Click OK and, when prompted, enter the source file's directory.

3. Choose Close on the Network dialog box. When prompted, select the null modem or the modem you already had installed.

4. From the RAS Setup dialog box choose Configure, and select Dial Out from the dialog box that appears. Click OK to return to the RAS Setup dialog box.

5. Click the Continue button.

6. When prompted, restart your system.

12.3 Creating Phonebook Entries

You will now create a new Phonebook entry. This will walk you through all the steps that would be required to create a real Phonebook entry.

Estimated Time: About 10 minutes.

1. Open the My Computer icon and double-click Dial-Up Networking.

2. If this is the first time that you have run Dial-Up Networking, you will be informed the Phonebook

APPLY YOUR KNOWLEDGE

is empty and asked to add a new entry. (If you have already used Dial-Up Networking, you can click the New button and you will be in the same position.)

3. For the name, enter **Test Entry Number 1**, and then click Next.

4. Select the first (I am calling the Internet) and third (The non-Windows NT server) check boxes. Then select Next.

5. Enter **555-3840** as the phone number and click Next.

6. Select PPP as the protocol and click Next.

7. Choose Use a Terminal Window from the next screen; then click Next.

8. Assuming the server provides you an address, click Next.

9. Enter **148.53.66.7** as the DNS server and click Next.

10. Now you have entered all the information. Click Finish.

12.4 Editing Phonebook Entries

In this exercise, you will work with editing a Phonebook entry and the preferences.

Estimated Time: About five minutes.

1. To create a shortcut to the entry, open Dial-Up Networking from the My Computer icon and choose More, Create a Shortcut to the Entry.

2. Accept the default name (Test Entry Number 1.rnk).

3. Close the Dial-Up Networking dialog box.

4. On the Desktop, right-click the icon and choose Edit Entry and Modem Properties.

5. Add the alternate numbers **555-9930** and **555-6110**. To do this, click the Alternates button, type the first number in the New Phone Number field, and click Add. Do the same for the second number.

6. Click OK to save the changes.

7. You have created a script for this entry and wish to use it. Right-click the icon on the desktop and choose Edit Entry and Modem Properties.

8. Select the Script tab and click Run this Script.

9. From the drop-down list, choose PPPMENU.SCP.

10. Click on the Server tab and Enable Software Compression.

11. Click OK to save the changes.

12.5 Configuring RAS as a Server

In this exercise, you will set up the Remote Access Service to act as a RAS server; this will allow others to dial into your machine.

Estimated Time: About 15 minutes.

1. Open the Network Settings dialog box and choose the Services tab.

2. Click on the Remote Access Service, and then click the Properties button.

3. In the dialog box that appears, select the null modem cable (or the modem you are using) and select Configure.

4. Click the Dial Out and Receive Calls option, and then click OK to close the dialog box.

5. Click the Network button. Ensure that TCP/IP is configured in the Server Settings.

6. Click the Configure button next to TCP/IP, and then choose Use Static Address Pool.

7. Enter **148.53.90.0** as the begin address and **148.53.90.255** as the end address. Click OK to close the dialog box, and OK again to close the server settings.

8. Click Continue to return to the Network Settings dialog box, and then choose close.

9. You will need to restart your computer.

12.6 Assigning Permissions

You will now provide your users with dial-in permissions and review the Remote Access Admin program.

Estimated Time: About 10 minutes.

1. Start the User Manager for Domains (User Manager will work fine in this case).

2. Choose User, New user and enter the following information:

Username:	**Bilbo**
Full name:	**Bilbo Baggins**
Description:	**Burglar**
Password:	**Blank**

3. Click the Dial-In icon and check the Grant Dial-In permission.

4. Click OK to close the dial-in screen and OK to add the user.

5. Close User Manager for Domains.

6. Open the Remote Access Admin program from the Administrative Tools group.

7. Choose Users, Permissions from the menu. Click on Bilbo's name in the list. Notice that he has dial permissions.

8. Choose the account you logged on with. If you do not have dial-in permission, grant it to yourself.

Review Questions

1. What service does RAS provide?

2. When a user dials in, can he talk to just the system that he dialed into?

3. What are the three options that can be set for port usage?

4. Can you enter more than one phone number per Phonebook entry?

Exam Questions

1. Where can you enable a log that will record all the communications between the modem and the system?

   A. In the Telephony API advanced options

   B. In the RAS Administration tool under Advanced Options

   C. In the Modem advanced properties

   D. In the Port Settings Advanced dialog box

APPLY YOUR KNOWLEDGE

2. How do you create a shortcut to a Phonebook entry?

   A. By using the RAS administrator

   B. By using Dial-Up Networking

   C. By using the User Manager for Domains

   D. By using Drag-and-Drop

3. What do you have to change in order to use a different DNS for a Phonebook entry?

   A. The Dial-Up Networking properties

   B. The TCP/IP properties

   C. The settings in RAS administrator

   D. Dial-Up Networking will always use the default

4. What protocol requires you to select a frame size?

   A. PPP

   B. PPTP

   C. SLIP

   D. CSLIP

5. If your dial-in server requires you to log on, but this cannot be scripted, what can you do?

   A. Use Windows NT logon.

   B. Bring up a terminal window.

   C. Use Client Services for NetWare.

   D. You will not be able to dial in.

6. Where can you grant a user dial-in permissions?

   A. From the command prompt

   B. From the User Manager

   C. From the Remote Access Admin

   D. From Server Manager

7. Where does the IP address for a client come from?

   A. From the client

   B. From the DHCP server

   C. From a scope of addresses on the RAS server

   D. All of the above

8. What is the major benefit of PPTP?

   A. New form of the PPP protocol

   B. Allows tuned connections

   C. Allows secure connections across the Internet

   D. Enables the user to dial in using more than one line

9. How does PPTP show up in the Remote Access Admin?

   A. RPN

   B. VPN

   C. SPN

   D. DPN

Answers to Review Questions

1. RAS provides dial-in networking for Windows NT Workstation and Server. See "Configuring RAS to Dial Out" and "Configuring a RAS Server."

APPLY YOUR KNOWLEDGE

2. Depending on the configuration of the protocol that he used to dial in, he will be allowed to see either the one computer he dialed into, or he will be able to see the entire network. See "Configuring TCP/IP on the Dial-In Server."

3. A port can be used for Dial Out, Receive Calls, or both. See "Configuring RAS to Dial Out" and "Configuring a RAS Server."

4. Yes—using the Alternates button on the General tab of an entry's property sheet allows you to enter as many phone numbers as you like. See "Adding Phonebook Entries."

Answers to Exam Questions

1. **C.** You can set the system to record a log of the communications between the modem and the system in the Advanced Settings for the modem. See "Configuring RAS to Dial Out."

2. **B.** Creating an icon can be done while you are in the Dial-Up Networking icon. To do this, choose More, Create Shortcut. See "Editing Entries."

3. **B.** One of the choices that you have in the TCP/IP properties for a Dial-Up Networking entry is the entry of two DNS servers and two

WINS servers. See "Adding Phonebook Entries."

4. **C.** The only time you will need to set the frame size is when you use the older SLIP protocol. See "Adding Phonebook Entries."

5. **B.** You can always bring up a terminal window, which will allow you to log on to a server in a normal manner. See "Adding Phonebook Entries."

6. **B** and **C.** You can grant dial-in permissions from either the User Manager or the Remote Access Admin package. See "Assigning Dial-In Permissions."

7. **D.** The address can be configured to come from the client requesting the address, the DHCP server, or from the pool of addresses on the RAS server. See "Configuring TCP/IP on the Dial-In Server."

8. **C.** Because PPTP can create a VPN, you are able to perform secure communications across the Internet. See "Using the Point-to-Point Tunneling Protocol."

9. **B.** PPTP connections show up as a virtual private network (VPN) and act exactly like a modem. See "Configuring PPTP."

Suggested Readings and Resources

1. Microsoft Windows NT Server Manuals, Network Supplement Manual

   - Chapter 5—Understanding Remote Access Service

This chapter helps you prepare for the exam by covering the following objectives:

Configure and support browsing in a multiple-domain routed network.

▶ One of the philosophies that Microsoft has held for years is that you should have "information at your fingertips." The browser service is part of this and appears on all the operating system exams. In this case you need to understand the problems that may be encountered as routers are added to a Microsoft networking solution.

CHAPTER 13

The Browser Service and TCP/IP

STUDY STRATEGIES

As you read through this chapter, you should concentrate on the following key items:

▶ You need to understand the impact of routers on the Microsoft browser service.

▶ You need to understand the process of building and distributing the browse list.

▶ You need to know how to use the LMHOSTS file and the WINS service to aid in browsing and domain functions.

▶ You need to know the difference between browsing and name resolution.

You already know that Microsoft uses NetBIOS as its Application layer networking protocol. NetBIOS uses broadcast traffic for many of the functions it performs. This causes problems with running Microsoft networking over the TCP/IP protocol stack because NetBIOS broadcasts do not get forwarded by routers.

This chapter looks at these problems and how they are overcome. There are two primary solutions: LMHOSTS and WINS. You will see how these two methods of name resolution allow the use of the browser services and how they work to support domain activity over TCP/IP—even though both of these methods are broadcast-based.

THE BROWSING PROCESS

When you double-click on the Network Neighborhood, you receive a list of computers available on your network. This list includes any system that has the ability to provide services to the network (that is, any system that has a server service).

The next section will look at the process of starting a server service, and how this server ends up in the list you see in the Network Neighborhood. At the end of the section is a discussion of problems that might arise and how to get around them.

The Basics of the Microsoft Browser Service

In Figure 13.1, you see that a server is starting up. This computer, named NTS99, announces itself to the network as it initializes the server service. The actual name announced on the network is NTS99(0x20)—the 0x20 indicating the server service.

The server announces its presence to the network every minute for the first five minutes that it is up and running. After the initial period, the server continues to announce its presence every 12 minutes. These announcements are made over the NetBIOS datagram service port, which is port 138.

FIGURE 13.1
A server starts up and announces its presence
to the network.

Obviously, if a server announces itself to the network, there should
be a system listening to the announcements. In Microsoft networking, this system is the master browser. In Figure 13.2, you can see
that the master browser is also on the network. This browser maintains a list of any servers that announce themselves.

The master browser now has a copy of all the servers on the network. You will notice that in Figure 13.2 the master browser is also
included in the list (computer name NTS5). When another computer (in this case, NTS3) comes up on this network, it announces itself
because it also has a server service (see Figure 13.3).

The system NTS3 will act as a backup browser and will be marked
as a special system in the master browser list (browser roles will be
discussed shortly). As a backup browser, NTS3 will retrieve a copy of
the list of servers that the master browser has been building.

The backup browser retrieves a new copy of the browse list from the
master browser every 15 minutes. In this way the list of servers is
always updated.

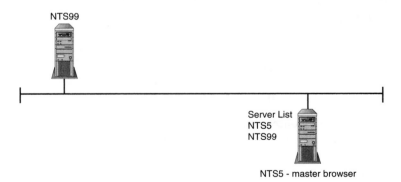

FIGURE 13.2
The master browser adds to its list all servers
that announce themselves.

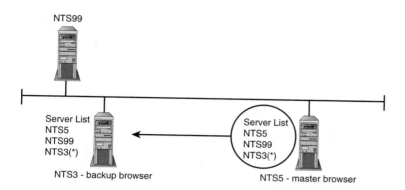

FIGURE 13.3
A backup browser is added to the network.

At this point, all the basics of the browser service are in place. All that is needed is a workstation; so in Figure 13.4, a station called WKS454 (running Windows 95 with file and print sharing) is added to the network. The user at this workstation wants to get a file from a share that is on NTS99.

If the workstation has not yet attempted to connect to another station over the network, it will need to retrieve a list of backup browsers—that is, a list of all the specially marked systems in the browse list. From then on, the client computers will always connect to the backup browser; if they all talked to the master browser, they would overload the resources on that system.

There is a problem here, though: the client does not know who the master browser is. Because of this, the master browser will register an additional NetBIOS name—_MBROWSE—on the network. The

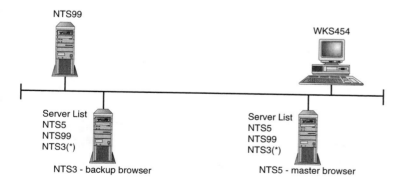

FIGURE 13.4
Finally, a client is added to the network.

client, therefore, needs only to find this name to retrieve the list (see Figure 13.5).

Now that the client has a list of backup browsers, it will not have to talk to the master browser again unless the client restarts or if none of the backup browsers respond. The client now retrieves a list of servers from one of the backup browsers on the list the master browser gave it (see Figure 13.6).

The client now has a list of all the servers present on the local subnet. (Remember, the announcements cannot cross routers; therefore, only local systems are included.) Next, the client system displays the list for the user. As the users choose the system they want to connect with, their system contacts that computer directly (see Figure 13.7). Included will be the user's credentials so that only appropriate resources will be shown.

The user can now access the resource normally. Sometimes when you click on a system name in the Network Neighborhood, you will receive an error explaining that the name cannot be found on the

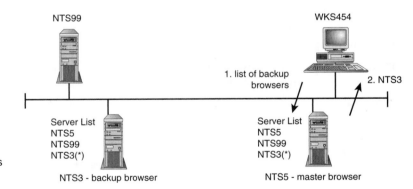

FIGURE 13.5
The client retrieves the list of backup browsers from the master browser.

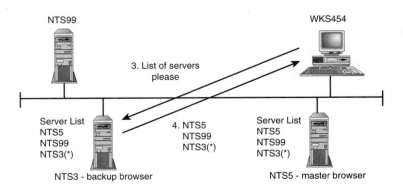

FIGURE 13.6
The client retrieves the browse list from the backup browser.

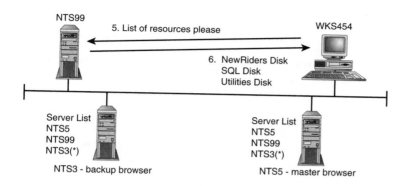

FIGURE 13.7
The client obtains a list of resources directly from the server.

network. This will happen if the system is down. But if it is down, why is it in the list?

One of the main problems with this method of sharing names is that updating the information is not instantaneous. The master browser will keep an entry in its list until that entry has missed three announcement periods. That could be as long as 36 minutes (three periods of 12 minutes each). Furthermore, because the backup browser retrieves a new copy of the list every 15 minutes, the lag time can be extended from 36 to 51 minutes.

This means that a system that shuts down abnormally (crashes) could remain in the list for up to 51 minutes. However, if it closes down normally (if the user shuts the system down from the Start menu rather than the power button), the name is removed from all lists (the NetBIOS name release).

Configuring Browsers

So far you have heard about the master browser and the backup browser; yet there are other types of browsers that will appear on the network. This section will look at the different types of browsers and then explain how they are configured.

Types of Browsers

The following list describes the different types of browsers:

◆ **Domain master browser.** This is the master browser responsible for an entire domain. The primary domain controller (PDC) for a domain automatically becomes the domain master browser

(DMB). The DMB coordinates the browse lists from all the network segments so you can see all computers in your domain.

◆ **Master browser.** As you saw in the preceding discussion, the master browser is the system that builds the browser list and distributes it to the backup browsers when they request it. On the subnet where the PDC is located, the DMB handles these functions; on other domains, this is normally a BDC. However, this could be nearly any system if there is no BDC such as Windows for Workgroups, Windows 95, Windows NT Workstation, or Windows NT Server installed as a server.

◆ **Backup browser.** In the domain model, this is just about always the BDC. However, just like the master browser, this could be very nearly any version of Windows. The backup browser retrieves a copy of the browse list from the master browser every 15 minutes and provides it to clients on request.

◆ **Potential browser.** This is a system that can act as a browser, but does not currently. Most systems fit into this category.

◆ **Nonbrowser.** You can configure a system not to participate in browsing (this is described in the next section). If you do this, the system is a nonbrowser.

Configuring the Browser Type

The configuration of the browser service on a particular computer depends on the operating system. For Windows NT and Windows 95, the configuration is performed in the Registry. The key is as follows:

```
HKEY_LOCAL_MACHINE\System\CurrentControlSet\Services\
➡Browser\Parameters
```

There are two settings in this key that you can set to configure the browser service:

◆ **IsDomainMaster**—tells the system to attempt to become the master browser. On the subnet that contains the PDC, this setting only ensures that the system becomes a backup browser (the PDC always "wins"). The setting can be either TRUE or FALSE (the default is FALSE).

◆ **MaintainServerList**—tells your system whether to keep the browse list. There are three settings for this entry: Yes, No, and

Auto. For the vast majority of systems, you should leave this as the default of Auto. If you choose Yes, the system will normally become a backup browser; if you have a system that is more powerful on a particular subnet, you could consider setting this to Yes. Setting this to No will ensure that this system does not participate in browsing; use this setting for workstations that absolutely need every ounce of performance.

Browser Elections

The process of choosing the master browser is handled in a democratic fashion: the computers on a subnet hold an election. The election process is simply a broadcast that determines the new master browser. Unlike a regular election, systems don't vote for each other—they all vote for themselves. The first one to cast the ballot wins.

There are two main criteria in determining how long a system will wait before casting its ballot:

◆ **Current browser role.** The backup browser will win over a potential browser.

◆ **Operating system and version.** Windows NT 4.0 will win over 3.51, and both will win over Windows 95. Windows 95 will win over Windows for Workgroups.

This, of course, means that there could be a tie at times, but there are methods for tie-breaking. A tie will be decided by the following:

◆ **Time up.** The system that has been up longer will win.

◆ **Computer name.** If the systems have been up an equal amount of time, the system with the first name alphabetically will win.

So now you should be familiar with what the browser service does and the election process. The next item to look at is when an election is held. Three reasons for an election are listed here:

◆ **Master browser shuts down.** If the master browser shuts down in a normal fashion, the last thing it does is call an election to determine its replacement.

> **WARNING**
>
> **Windows for Workgroups conflict**
> The original networking components of Windows for Workgroups contained code that became invalid when Windows NT 3.5 was released. There is a path on the Windows NT Server CD that corrects this; it should be applied to any stations running Windows for Workgroups.

◆ **Backup browser fails to update its copy of the browse list.**
If a backup browser attempts to contact the master browser to
update the browser list but cannot, it will call an election.

◆ **A client fails to contact the master browser.** If a client
attempts to get a list of backup browsers and fails, the client
will call an election.

Calling an election is simply the process of sending a broadcast to
the network. All the systems will receive the broadcast, and the system with the highest criteria will be the first to broadcast a reply,
hence becoming the master browser.

Browsing Workgroups and Domains

There is one last concept to cover before you look at how TCP/IP
gets involved in the browsing process. You need to understand that
the browsers and clients that talk to each other all have to be in the
same domain or workgroup. If there is more than one domain or
workgroup on the same network, each will have its own master and
backup browsers.

There will always be only one master browser for each domain or
workgroup per subnet. In the case of the domain model, this will be
the PDC on the subnet that has the PDC, and it will normally be a
BDC on the other networks.

In a domain model, the backup browsers will be BDCs. You can have
up to three BDCs acting as backup browsers on each subnet, but not
more. This might seem restrictive; however, the PDC and BDCs have
to be able to talk to each other anyway to allow for domain activity.
Because of this, they are able to exchange the browse list. The other
consideration in using the BDCs as the backup browser is simple:
they tend to be more powerful machines; therefore, they are able to
better handle the extra load of being a backup browser.

The workgroup model is different: there are no systems that always
act in a main role. This is where the election process becomes very
important and common. In this scenario, though, you do not know
what sort of systems will be acting as the backup browsers; therefore,
there is no guarantee they will have enough resources to be able to
handle the requests.

In order to relieve this, Microsoft designed the system so the master browser chooses one backup browser for every 32 active systems. Therefore, if you have 78 systems on the network, there will be one master browser and three backup browsers. This way, no one system will be overloaded with requests for information.

SUPPORTING DOMAIN ACTIVITY

Before discussing the issues of the browser service and multiple subnets, let's take a look at the other big issue that needs to be addressed when routers are used with Windows NT domains.

Windows NT is normally configured as a domain controller or a server in a domain model. Working in the domain model has many advantages over the workgroup model, most of which deal with the centralized security that Windows NT Directory Services provides. However, in a network that spans multiple subnets, there is still a need to be able to communicate between domain controllers, even over routers (which don't pass the NetBIOS broadcasts that domain activity relies on).

A Quick Review of NT Directory Services

In the domain model, Windows NT works with a PDC and usually one or more BDCs. The advantage of using this model is that there is a single user database, meaning that all the user accounts are handled at a central level. This also means that for any one user there is only one account—and that the user will be validated not by a single server, but by the domain giving the user access to any system they have privileges on in the entire domain.

In order for this to happen, the domain controllers have to be able to share a single user-accounts database that will always be on the PDC. Therefore, all changes made to the accounts database will have to be made on the PDC, whether it is an administrator adding an account or a user changing a password.

The BDCs have a copy of the accounts database, which allows them to validate user logons as well. Therefore, a process has to be in place that will keep the copy of the accounts database on each BDC in synchronization with the actual accounts database on the PDC. This process is the NETLOGON service that runs on all the domain controllers. The NETLOGON service provides three basic functions:

◆ **Logon validation.** The actual user logon, this process creates an access token that establishes the user's security level.

◆ **Pass through authentication.** In a multidomain model, this passes the user logon request to the trusted domain that contains the user's account. (Trust relationships are covered in other books such as *MCSE Training Guide: Windows NT Server 4 Enterprise.*)

◆ **Synchronization.** This is the process of synchronizing all the BDCs with the PDC.

All these processes depend on the ability of the systems to be able to locate each other. This requires NetBIOS name resolution and, therefore, broadcasts.

User Logon

The process that occurs when a user attempts a logon also uses NetBIOS broadcasts. In designing the network system, Microsoft decided that users should not have to be validated by a particular server; instead, any domain controller should be able to handle the request. This makes sense because if a server goes down or is busy, the users will still be able to log on to the domain.

You must remember, however, that because this is a broadcast, it is unable to pass a router. This would be a problem if the user were located on a subnet with one domain controller and that controller were to go down. The user in that case would be unable to be validated on the network and, therefore, unable to function.

BROWSING MULTIPLE SUBNETS

The problems of both the browser service and domain activity can be resolved in one of two ways: you can use the LMHOSTS file discussed in Chapter 8, "Name Resolution"; or you can use a NetBIOS name server such as WINS, which was discussed in Chapter 5, "Windows Internet Name Service (WINS)."

The rest of this chapter will cover how these methods of NetBIOS name resolution can be used to resolve the problems that have been described.

Using LMHOSTS

Domain activity is easily handled using the LMHOSTS file. If you remember, a series of tags can be included in the LMHOSTS file to handle various requirements. One of the tags, #DOM:*domain_name*, handles the problem of domain activity over a routed network.

In the sample network shown in Figure 13.8, you can see that there are three subnets. On each subnet is a domain controller that is able to handle the domain validation.

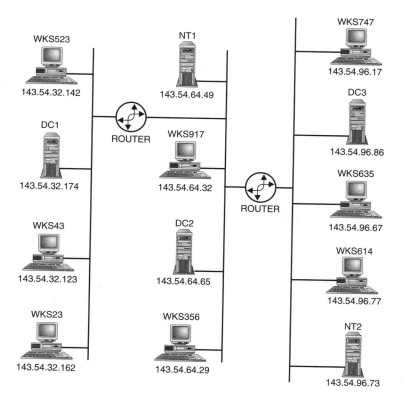

WKS523
143.54.32.142

DC1
143.54.32.174

WKS43
143.54.32.123

WKS23
143.54.32.162

NT1
143.54.64.49

ROUTER

WKS917
143.54.64.32

DC2
143.54.64.65

WKS356
143.54.64.29

ROUTER

WKS747
143.54.96.17

DC3
143.54.96.86

WKS635
143.54.96.67

WKS614
143.54.96.77

NT2
143.54.96.73

FIGURE 13.8
A sample network with three subnets, each of which has a domain controller.

In this case, the three domain controllers are unable to communicate with each other because they don't know each other's location. There is no way the broadcast is able to pass the router; therefore, the domain is unable to synchronize.

This creates some situations that you should be aware of. The users that reside on the subnets 148.53.32.0 and 148.53.64.0 are unable to make changes to the accounts database because they are unable to contact the PDC. This means the users are unable to change their passwords.

For the domain controllers to be able to synchronize with each other, they need to be added to an LMHOSTS file that is placed on each of them. The file should give the address of the controllers and, using the #DOM tag, identify the system as a domain controller. The file looks like this:

```
148.53.32.174      DC1      #PRE #DOM:training
148.53.64.65       DC2      #PRE #DOM:training
148.53.96.86       DC3      #PRE #DOM:training
```

Without this file there is no way that any domain activity could take place. Notice that all three controllers are listed and that the PDC is not specifically marked as such. This is because the PDC may change from time to time, and the controllers all have to be able to talk to each other.

This same file should be placed on each of the user's stations. In this way, if the local domain controller were to fail, the users would still be able to log on to one of the other domain controllers. This would also allow the user to contact the PDC no matter which system was acting in the role of PDC.

Browsing with LMHOSTS

As stated earlier, the browser broadcast travels only on the local subnet. Even the LMHOSTS file doesn't change that fact. Solving this problem requires expansion of the browsing services.

First, there is only one master browser for a domain on each subnet. Because you know that the PDC is the master browser, looking at the network in Figure 13.8 you might assume that the browse list would contain only the systems on subnet 148.53.96.0. Because this is not the case, something else has to come into play.

In this case, the PDC takes on the role of the domain master browser. Acting in this role, the PDC coordinates the browser lists from each master browser and creates a complete browser list. Then it can send the list to each master browser on each subnet, which will then give the list to the backup browsers. In this way, a host on any subnet will be able to see all the resources available on the entire network.

There is still the problem, however, of how the master browsers and the domain master browser all find each other. Because it is normally a BDC that becomes the backup browser, if the BDC is on a different subnet it will also become the master browser for that subnet.

Because you have already seen the LMHOSTS file and know that it allows domain activity over the routed network, it makes sense now to use the BDCs as the master browsers for the other subnets because they already have a way to find the domain master browser—the PDC. So in addition to enabling domain activity, the #DOM tag tells the systems where the other master browsers are. Now, every 15 minutes, the master browser for each subnet is able to exchange lists with the domain master browser.

There is still a small problem, though. Again, look at Figure 13.8. Say that the user at WKS23 wants to connect to a file share on the system NT2. Looking at the steps that would take place, you would find the following:

1. When the system NT2 starts up, it announces itself.

2. The master browser for that subnet (here, the domain master browser) hears the broadcast and adds NT2 to its list.

3. The domain master browser exchanges lists with the master browser on the remote subnet.

4. The backup browsers on that subnet call the master browser and retrieve the browse list.

5. The client WKS23 starts and contacts the master browser for a list of backup browsers.

6. From the list of backup browsers, the client chooses and contacts one, asking for the browse list.

7. The client displays the browse list for the user who clicks on the NT2 system in that list.

8. Client WKS23 attempts to contact the server. However, the client's LMHOSTS file has no mapping for NT2, there is no WINS server, and the NT2 system is on a different subnet; therefore, the client cannot resolve the name.

9. The client station gives the user an error.

Obviously, the browse list is only part of the problem. The client still is unable to work with the server because there is no way for it to resolve the name that it received to an IP address. If the client needs to talk to the remote hosts, the LMHOSTS file needs to be modified. The new file would look like the following listing:

```
148.53.32.174      DC1      #PRE #DOM:training
148.53.64.65       DC2      #PRE #DOM:training
148.53.96.86       DC3      #PRE #DOM:training
148.53.96.73       NT2
```

This, however, only solves this particular problem. If the client station WKS635 wants to talk to the server NT1, it will go through the same steps just outlined and will be unable to resolve the name. The process will be further aggravated if file and print sharing is enabled for all the Windows workstations on the network.

PROBLEMS CREATED BY ENABLING FILE AND PRINT SHARING

Unless there is a very good reason for it, file and print sharing should generally be turned off. If you think about it, every system that has a server service installed will broadcast to announce its presence every 12 minutes (over each protocol installed). This means that if you have 100 stations on a segment, there will be 100 broadcasts every 12 minutes.

There is also the problem of the size of the browse list. If every station on your intranet has file and print sharing enabled, they are servers that will be listed in the browse list. If you have 10 or 15 systems, this is not a problem; but if you have 1,000 or 1,500 systems in your network, each one will be in that list, and you might get to the point where the list runs out of space.

The amount of CPU time used to coordinate the list, and the time spent transmitting the list every 15 minutes between the domain master browser and the master browser on each subnet. In addition to the extra time, sending the list from the master browsers to the backup browser (three possibly on each subnet) reduces the performance of your network considerably. There is also the problem of the user attempting to find a system in a list of 1,500.

So as a rule of thumb, don't enable file and print sharing unless you absolutely have to. If you must, there are two Registry entries that you should be aware of that control browser service announcements on Windows NT. Both of the entries are under `HKEY_LOCAL_MACHINE\ MACHINE\System\CurrentControlSet\Services\LanmanServer\ Parameters`. The first, Announce (REG_DWORD), sets the period between announcements in seconds. The other, Hidden (case sensitive REG_DWORD), stops browser announcements if it is set to 1, thus hiding the system from the browse list.

If you wish to allow all the systems on all the networks to be able to see every server, you need to change the LMHOSTS file. You should include every system that will be able to share files using a NetBIOS server service (all Microsoft-based systems). In the case of the example network, that means the LMHOSTS file needs to look like this:

```
143.54.32.142      WKS523
143.54.32.174      DC1        #PRE #DOM:training
143.54.32.123      WKS43
143.54.32.162      WKS23
143.54.64.49       NT1
143.54.64.32       WKS917
143.54.64.65       DC2        #PRE #DOM:training
143.54.64.29       WKS356
143.54.96.68       WKS747
143.54.96.86       DC3        #PRE #DOM:training
143.54.96.77       WKS635
143.54.96.67       WKS614
143.54.96.73       NT2
```

This file should be located on every system in the network, or you could use a central LMHOSTS file as discussed earlier. In either case, if you add another host that will be able to share files, or if you move a system from one network to another, you need to update the file.

Obviously, this is not the solution to sharing NetBIOS resources across a routed network.

Using WINS

As you have seen, there are potentially many problems that can be associated with using NetBIOS networking over routed networks. These problems led (in the days of LAN Manager) to many hours of laborious work for the system administrators of those networks. Thankfully, you can solve these problems using WINS.

You should recall that WINS is a NetBIOS name server. This means that it handles the resolution of a NetBIOS computer name to a TCP/IP address. Even if that were all it did, that would solve a great portion of the problem. However, it does more than that.

WINS helps you get around the problem of domain activity and also aids the browsing service. As you know, when a station starts up, it registers its names with the WINS server. Because the WINS server can register all NetBIOS name types, it is able to register the services running on a computer as separate entries in the WINS database.

The WINS database contains a special group called the domain name group. This group is used to register domain controllers that are close to the WINS server. There is space for up to 25 IP addresses in a domain group; this includes the PDC and up to 24 BDCs.

When a client computer needs to authenticate a user, it can now ask the WINS server for the domain group, which provides the list of IP addresses for logon. The PDC is specially marked to differentiate it so the change requests (for example, password changes) can be sent to it directly.

This will also allow the BDCs to find the PDC in the same way, thus permitting the NETLOGON service to handle the synchronization of the domain.

Browsing with WINS

The WINS server also aids in the browsing process. Obviously, the ability to resolve the computer names in the browse list plays an important part. Also, the registration of the domain controllers as members in the domain group allows the master browsers to talk easily with the domain master browser.

However, in addition to the parts of browsing you have already seen, the domain master browser makes a domain announcement every 15 minutes. This would normally be done by a local broadcast; however, the domain master browser is registered with the WINS server (as the PDC of the domain), and the domain master browser can look up the domains and their PDCs in the WINS server.

Because the domain announcement contains the domain name and the address of the domain master browser, this use of WINS removes the requirement for domain announcement broadcasts.

CASE STUDY: PLANNING FOR EFFECTIVE BROWSER SERVICES

ESSENCE OF THE CASE

Looking back at the previous sections dealing with NetBIOS over TCP/IP, you might pick up on the following facts:

- The head office, the largest of the offices, maintains resources that all users will require access to. This includes a SQL server (configured for TCP/IP on port 1433) and a series of newsgroups on an IIS 4.0 server.

- The regional offices use the resources of the head office servers, including the SQL server; it also has file and print servers for the local users.

- The production centers will need to connect to the head office SQL server to receive the orders for production. Other than this, there is the normal need to provide local file and print services.

- The sales offices need to be able to connect to the head office SQL server to post orders and will need local file and print services.

- The company operates as a single domain model; therefore, you will need to be able to perform name resolution between domain controllers to facilitate the synchronization of the domain accounts database. This also means that every system will need to be able to find the primary domain controller so that they will be able to change passwords.

- There are a good number of laptop users who will need to be able to find the resources from their local network regardless of where they travel.

- All users will need to be able to connect to the Microsoft Exchange network to collect and send email.

As you look back at the Sunshine Brewing Company, you might remember that concerns about the ability to resolve names was covered in the chapters on Windows Internet Name Service (WINS) (Chapter 5) and Name Resolution (Chapter 8).

SCENARIO

If you review Chapter 5, you will note that two issues were identified:

- How many servers are there and who has to connect to them?

- Where are the systems physically located?

What you will need to decide here is who will be able to see these systems and how they will be able to get to them. In the case at hand, you are dealing with a single domain that is cut up into 61 subnets. Do users need to be able to see all the servers in these locations? If so, do they need to be able to connect?

In this case study, you will look at the effect of the decisions made earlier on the current situation, and what needs to be done to allow all users to access all the main servers. In this case, you will assume ownership of the network.

So far, the planned solution includes the following:

- To facilitate the local connections, you will establish a WINS server in each of the local offices. Then you will set up all the hosts to use the WINS server.

- You will create a static entry in each WINS server for the servers that users connect to in the head office. (This entry will need to be updated if the IP addresses change.)

continues

CASE STUDY: PLANNING FOR EFFECTIVE BROWSER SERVICES

continued

- The Exchange server problem can also be eliminated using the same strategy. The domain activity simply requires that you create on each of the WINS servers a domain group that lists all the domain controllers that are likely to become the PDC.

- The needs of the laptop users will be addressed by a local LMHOSTS file. Entries will be added for the servers outside the head office that the users require; these entries will include the #PRE tag to ensure that they are loaded to the NetBIOS name cache.

ANALYSIS

In this case, you need to look at what effect the settings of name resolution will have on the browser service and decide if these are acceptable.

Given that all the systems on any network (other than the production Solaris system) are registered with the local WINS server, all the server services will also be registered with the master browser for that subnet. The BDC at each location will act as the master browser; each has a method of finding the PDC (in this case, the domain master browser). This means that every server will be listed in the browse list from all of the 61 locations.

This means that there will be cases when a user will click on a server in location X and not be able to resolve the name. To prevent this, you can use the logon scripts to connect to the servers. All you need to do is resolve the name for the local file and print server. They do not need, therefore, to be in the browser list, and you can use the Hidden value in the Registry to stop them from appearing. This leaves the systems in the head office, for which users can resolve names using the static entries in the local WINS server.

The net effect is a clean browse list with only the entries that are needed. There would be a problem if a user started sharing directories; therefore, you should also disable this function on the local machines (which can be done using policies).

CHAPTER SUMMARY

This chapter started by introducing the browser service and the requirements for domain activity (account synchronization). Although this might seem like a minor topic, there are often hard questions dealing with this because you need to know Windows NT before you move to networking with TCP/IP and Windows NT.

There are several key items to bear in mind about this topic:

◆ The master browser builds a list of available servers within the domain on a subnet.

◆ The backup browser retrieves a copy of the browse list from the master browser every 15 minutes.

◆ Servers announce their presence every minute for the first five minutes, and then every 12 minutes, by default.

◆ The domain master browser coordinates the browse lists of the various subnets. This is the PDC.

◆ The master browser is chosen by an election process that occurs on each subnet.

◆ A server is any system that has a server service installed.

◆ Routers don't propagate NetBIOS broadcasts; therefore, server announcements don't cross routers.

◆ Domain activity includes synchronizing the domain accounts database and making changes to the accounts database.

◆ A LMHOSTS file or a WINS server can be used to let the browsers find each other.

◆ In addition to being able to see the computer in the browse list, a client must be able to resolve the name to an IP address.

◆ Users need to be able to locate a domain controller to facilitate user authentication.

◆ There are several types of browsers: domain master browser, master browser, backup browser, potential browser, and non-browser.

◆ A browser will have a server service.

KEY TERMS

- backup browser
- browser election
- browser service
- domain master browser
- master browser
- NETLOGON service
- nonbrowser
- potential browser

APPLY YOUR KNOWLEDGE

Exercises

13.1 Implementing WINS

The following exercise shows how WINS works across routers. You need a network with a router, and on each side of the router should be at least one master browser, a few WINS-capable clients, and a WINS server (see Figure 13.9).

Estimated Time: About 30 minutes.

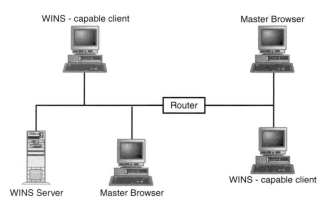

FIGURE 13.9
Setup required for Exercise 13.1.

The first thing you need to do is disable the WINS server. This does not mean, however, uninstalling it:

1. Go to Control Panel and double-click on the Services icon.

2. Click on Windows Internet Name Service, click Stop, and choose Yes to stop the WINS service.

3. Click on Startup, and then select Manual.

4. Click OK and close all windows.

The next thing you need to do is make certain the clients are not enabled to access WINS. Use the following steps on each client:

1. Go to Control Panel and double-click on the Network icon.

2. Select Protocols, TCP/IP, Properties.

3. Click on WINS Address.

4. Remove any WINS server address by highlighting the address listed and pressing the Delete key.

5. Close the windows by clicking OK, and then restart your system.

6. After Windows NT reboots, use the Windows NT Explorer to find out who you see on the network.

With WINS disabled and no LMHOSTS, you should only see what is on your local subnet (although you might have to wait for the next server announcement). It may help to draw a diagram of your network design so that you can identify what systems you should be able to see. It may take a few minutes of updating before everyone appears on the browsing list in your subnet; have patience and keep refreshing or do a direct search.

Now that you have isolated your subnets, the next step is to set up WINS and watch it work. If you had WINS set up prior to the beginning of this exercise but disabled it, all you need to do now is go back into Services (Control Panel, Services) and enable the WINS service (change the Startup to automatic and Start the service). You also need to ensure that all clients are using WINS.

APPLY YOUR KNOWLEDGE

With WINS newly enabled or installed, go to Network Neighborhood and browse the network; you should now see resources on both sides of the router. Sometimes WINS takes a minute to update its database, so again keep refreshing before assuming you did something wrong.

Review Questions

1. What system do you receive a list of servers from?

2. In a workgroup model, how many backup browsers are there?

3. What are the three functions of NETLOGON?

4. Which system has to be in the LMHOSTS file if no WINS server is used?

5. What tag in the LMHOSTS file allows domain activity over TCP/IP?

6. A user clicks on a system in the Network Neighborhood, but the system responds that the network name could not be found. What could be the cause of this?

7. How often does the server service announce itself?

8. When are systems removed from the browse list?

9. What type of group do domain controllers register in with the WINS server?

10. Which systems require an LMHOSTS file to allow the user-accounts database to remain synchronized?

11. How do other domains become visible in the Network Neighborhood?

12. How many domain controllers can register in a domain group?

13. What types of computers make browser announcements?

Exam Questions

1. What enables users to search for available network resources without knowing the exact location of the resources?

   A. Browsing through Network Neighborhood

   B. The NET USE command

   C. The NETSTAT command

   D. The NET VIEW command

2. If a server name doesn't appear on the browse list, what are some possible causes?

   A. The server is on a different domain.

   B. The server does not have a NetBIOS server enabled.

   C. The master browser hasn't updated the backup browser.

   D. The master browser hasn't updated the server.

3. You are running a Windows NT 4.0 server that is currently the PDC, and you have a multiple-domain network. What browser role or roles does the server have?

   A. Backup browser

   B. Master browser

   C. Potential browser

   D. Domain master browser

APPLY YOUR KNOWLEDGE

4. Which one of these situations is true regarding master browser-to-backup browser synchronization?

   A. The master browser copies the updates to the backup.

   B. The backup browser copies the updates to the master.

   C. The master browser copies the updates from the backup.

   D. The backup browser copies the updates from the master.

5. If you have a domain set up with two Windows 95 computers, three Windows NT Workstation computers, three Windows NT server computers, and four Windows for Workgroup computers, what is the third backup browser for this domain?

   A. Windows 95.

   B. Windows for Workgroups.

   C. Windows NT Workstation.

   D. None of these will fill this role.

6. What is in charge of continually updating the browse list and managing the database of network servers, domains, and workgroups?

   A. Backup browser

   B. Master browser

   C. Potential browser

   D. Domain master browser

7. If a server stops sending announcements, how long could it be before the server is removed from the browse list?

   A. 30 minutes

   B. 36 minutes

   C. 42 minutes

   D. 51 minutes

8. Which of the following NetBIOS services use broadcasts?

   A. Logging in and passwords, PDC-to-PDC replication

   B. DNS zone transfers and TFTP

   C. User authentication

   D. Logging in and passwords, PDC-to-BDC replication

9. If a domain spans 15 subnets connected by routers that do not forward NetBIOS broadcasts, how many master browsers will there be?

   A. 1

   B. 14

   C. 15

   D. 16

10. Your users are having a problem changing their passwords. What does this indicate?

    A. The users are not allowed to change their passwords.

    B. The users are not successfully logging onto the domain.

C. The users are unable to resolve the IP address of the local BDC.

D. The users are unable to resolve the IP address of the PDC.

11. If your subnet does not have a BDC, what systems could act as the backup browser?

A. Windows NT server acting as a member server

B. Windows NT server installed in a workgroup

C. Windows 95 system without file and print services

D. Windows 95 system with file and print services

12. The administrator of a local area network, you are setting up the network to facilitate browsing. Your company does not want to use the WINS service because of the network overhead, but it does want to ensure that all the systems are able to communicate with servers on all subnets.

You decide to create an LMHOSTS file that contains the name of each domain controller marked with the #PRE and #DOM tags and place a copy on each system in the network. How well does this solution work?

A. This is the best possible solution.

B. This is a good solution.

C. This solution works, but is far from optimal.

D. This solution does not work.

13. You are in the same situation as in the previous question. However, you decide to create an LMHOSTS file that contains the name and IP

address of every domain controller and server in the organization. You will include the #PRE and #DOM tags for the domain controllers and the #PRE tag for the key servers. You will store this on the PDC and replicate it to all the BDCs. On the clients, you will increase the size of the NetBIOS name cache and create an LMHOSTS file that includes the #INCLUDE tag and #BEGIN ALTERNATE tag, which points at the local domain controller and one or more other domain controllers. The file will also include the resolution for all domain controllers with the #PRE and #DOM tags. How well does this solution work?

A. This is the best possible solution.

B. This is a good solution.

C. This solution works, but is far from optimal.

D. This solution does not work.

Answers to Review Questions

1. The list of servers comes from the backup browser. See "The Browsing Process."

2. There is one backup browser for every 32 systems in the workgroup. See "Browsing Workgroups and Domains."

3. The functions that NETLOGON handles include user validation, pass through authentication, and user-account database synchronization. See "Supporting Domain Activity."

APPLY YOUR KNOWLEDGE

4. The LMHOSTS file needs to provide address resolution for any system that registers a server service. See "Using LMHOSTS."

5. The #DOM:domainname tag facilitates domain activity over a TCP/IP network. See "Using LMHOSTS."

6. The system either could not resolve the NetBIOS name to an IP address, or the system crashed. See "The Browsing Process."

7. The server service announces its presence every minute for the first five minutes, and every twelve minutes after that. See "The Browsing Process."

8. If a system shuts down correctly, it broadcasts a name release. This removes it from the browse list. The other case in which a system is removed is if it misses three announcements. See "The Browsing Process."

9. The domain controllers register in the domain group. See "Using WINS."

10. Every domain controller requires an LMHOSTS file. See "Using LMHOSTS."

11. This is handled by the domain announcements that the domain master browsers make every 15 minutes. See "The Browsing Process."

12. The PDC and up to 24 BDCs can register in the domain group. See "Using WINS."

13. All systems that have a server service installed make announcements. This includes Windows for Workgroups, Windows 95, and Windows NT. See "The Browsing Process."

Answers to Exam Questions

1. **A** and **D.** If you are looking for resources and are unsure what server they are on, you can use the Network Neighborhood to locate it. The net view command can be used to view the list of servers as well by using the /DOMAIN command. See "The Browsing Process."

2. **B** and **C.** If the server has recently started up (within 15 minutes), it is possible that the master browser knows about it but has not updated the backup browser. It is also possible that the system does not have a NetBIOS server but rather some other type, such as a SPARC station, in which case the system won't show up in the browse list. See "The Browsing Process."

3. **D.** Even if it acts as the master browser for the subnet it resides on, the PDC is still the domain master browser. See "Types of Browsers."

4. **D.** The backup browser obtains the list of servers for a domain from the master browser every 15 minutes. See "The Browsing Process."

5. **C.** In this case, the system with the next-highest priority is the Windows NT Workstation. See "Browser Elections."

6. **B.** The master browser is in charge of building the list of servers, domains, and workgroups available on each local subnet. These are shared with the domain master browser to build a complete picture of all network resources. See "The Browsing Process."

7. **B.** The server is removed from the browse list after missing three announcements. Because announcements are spaced 12 minutes apart, the

APPLY YOUR KNOWLEDGE

system will be remove after 36 minutes. It may take up to 15 minutes more before the backup browser updates its copy of the browse list and the server disappears from view. See "The Browsing Process."

8. **C.** User authentication uses a broadcast to locate a domain controller to validate the logon. See "Supporting Domain Activity."

9. **B.** There are 14 master browsers, one for each subnet. Other than the one where the PDC is located, the PDC acts as the domain master browser on that subnet, handling the functions of the master browser and coordinating all the master browsers. See "The Browsing Process."

10. **D.** The only read/write copy of the domain accounts database is the one on the primary domain controller. This means the users need to be able to locate this system to change their password. If they can't change their password, this indicates a problem with name resolution. See "Supporting Domain Activity."

11. **A** and **D.** If the Windows NT system is installed as a member server, it can act as a browser in the domain. The Windows 95 station requires file and print services to act as a browser because the code from this function is included in the file and print services. The Windows NT server installed in a workgroup may act as a browser if the workgroup name is the same as the domain. However, it would not coordinate with the domain master browser; therefore, only systems on the local subnet would be visible. See "Browser Elections."

12. **D.** This solution does provide your domain controllers the ability to perform domain functions, and it provides your users with a list of the systems available within the entire domain. However, users will not be able to connect to systems on other subnets because they will not be able to resolve the names to IP addresses. See "The Browsing Process."

13. **A.** If you need to run without a WINS server, this would be the best possible solution. You would need only to update the LMHOSTS in one place in most cases (unless you change the IP address of a domain controller); the clients would have multiple locations where they would be able to obtain the central LMHOSTS file. Using a larger NetBIOS name cache would let the clients cache more names, and you would probably also increase the life span. See "The Browsing Process."

Suggested Readings and Resources

1. *Windows NT Resource Kit, Networking Guide.* Chapter 3, "Windows NT Browser Service."

2. Sirockman, Jason. *MCSE Training Guide: Windows NT Server 4 Enterprise.* New Riders, 1997.

MONITORING AND OPTIMIZATION

This chapter helps you prepare for the exam by covering the following objectives:

Given a scenario, identify which tool to use to monitor TCP/IP traffic.

▶ This objective is included to ensure that you know how to monitor TCP/IP and, specifically, which tool is used to monitor what.

CHAPTER 14

Monitoring and Optimizing TCP/IP

STUDY STRATEGIES

As you read through this chapter, you should concentrate on the following key items:

▶ You will need to understand how TCPWindowSize is used by the TCP/IP stack.

▶ You need to know what each of the tools is used to monitor.

▶ You should know how to work with Performance Monitor and Network Monitor.

The monitoring and optimization of the TCP/IP protocol in Windows NT is fairly simple. Optimization is achieved by setting TCPWindowSize to the optimum size for the network topology that you are using. This setting determines the size of the sliding window used to stream communications.

To determine whether you have achieved an increase in traffic, or even just to figure out how much traffic you are dealing with, you need to monitor the TCP/IP counters in the Performance Monitor or use Network Monitor to view the packets as they move across the network. In addition, you may need to watch the steps involved in the establishing and tearing down of sessions using NETSTAT or NBTSTAT.

In the next few sections you will be introduced to these tools and given an overview of how they work. You need to practice using these tools before you will be able to use them effectively.

Understanding TCP Sliding Windows

TCP uses the concept of sliding windows for transferring data between machines. Each machine has both a send window and a receive window that it uses to buffer data and make the communication process more efficient.

A window represents the subset of data that is currently being sent to a destination machine and the amount of data that is being received by the destination machine. At first, this seems redundant, but it really isn't: not all data that is sent is guaranteed to be received, so it must be kept track of on both machines. With a sliding window, a sending machine can send the window data in a stream without having to wait for an acknowledgment for every single packet.

A receiving window allows a machine to receive packets out of order and reorganize them while it waits for more packets. This reorganization may be necessary because TCP uses IP to transmit data and IP does not guarantee the orderly delivery of packets. By default, window sizes in Windows NT are a little more than 8KB in size, representing eight standard ethernet frames. Standard ethernet frames are a little more than 1KB apiece.

Unfortunately, packets do not always make it to their destination. However, TCP has been designed to recover in the event that packets are lost along the way, perhaps by busy routers. TCP keeps track of the data that has been sent out; if it doesn't receive an acknowledgment that the data was received by the destination machine in a certain amount of time, the data is re-sent. In fact, until acknowledgment for a packet of data is received, further data transmission is halted completely.

Setting the TCPWindowSize

The Microsoft TCP/IP protocol is designed to be self-tuning in most cases. Rather than using a hard-coded window size, TCP adjusts the size to even increments of the maximum segment size (MSS)—the largest block of data that can be transferred on the underlying network—that is negotiated during connection startup.

Setting the receive window to an even increment of the MSS increases the number of full-sized TCP segments used during data transmission. Windows NT uses a default size of 8KB for the window, which it automatically increases to the nearest full MSS multiple. Furthermore, Windows NT ensures that there are at least 4 times the MSS; if not, it will adjust the window size to 4 times the MSS to a maximum size of 64KB.

This means that for ethernet the window is normally set to 8760 bytes (8192–8KB, and then rounded up to six 1460-byte segments); for token ring or FDDI it is about 16KB. These values are optimal for most networks, and it's generally not advisable to alter them.

To set the TCPWindowSize, you need to edit the Registry and add the value to the following key (it is not there, by default):

```
HKEY_LOCAL_MACHINE\SYSTEM\CurrentControlSet\Services\TCPIP\
➥Parameters
```

> **NOTE**
>
> **Maximum TCP Windows Size** The window size limit is 64KB because the length field in the TCP header is 16 bits in length. In RFC 1323 there is a description of a TCP window scale option used to obtain larger receive windows; currently, Microsoft TCP/IP does not implement this option.

Effects of Window Size

The effects of TCPWindowSize vary depending on the size that you set. Again, you should always make sure that you set it to an even multiple of the MSS.

If you set the window size too small, you lose the advantages of streaming data. This means that you will have to transfer a few packets and then wait for the target system to acknowledge their reception.

On the other hand, if the window size is too large, you will send too many packets. In this case the likelihood of some of the packets being lost in transit or timing out is increased. This means they will have to be retransmitted.

UTILITIES FOR MONITORING AND OPTIMIZING PERFORMANCE

The rest of this chapter will look at the utilities that you can use to monitor your system and determine how it is performing. In this section are four tools used for monitoring as well as for troubleshooting system problems.

NETSTAT

The NETSTAT command is useful for determining the types of connections that you have made through the TCP/IP stack. It shows all connections, including the ones made using NetBIOS over TCP/IP. The full syntax of this command is as follows:

```
netstat [-a] [-e] [-n] [-s] [-p protocol] [-r] [interval]
```

Table 14.1 summarizes the command-line switches that are available with NETSTAT.

TABLE 14.1

COMMAND-LINE SWITCHES FOR THE NETSTAT COMMAND

Switch	Description
-a	Shows every connection as well as the listening ports, which are normally not displayed.
-e	Displays network card statistics. This can be combined with the -s option.
-n	Shows the information using the IP addresses rather than host names.

continues

TABLE 14.1	*continued*

COMMAND-LINE SWITCHES FOR THE NETSTAT COMMAND

Switch	Description
-s	Shows statistics on a per-protocol basis. Normally, statistics are given for TCP, UDP, ICMP, and IP; the -p switch can be used to select a subset of these.
-p *protocol*	Displays connections for only the protocol given in the switch. Normally, this can be TCP or UDP; however, in conjunction with -s switch, you can specify TCP, UDP, ICMP, or IP.
-r	Shows the content of the routing table.
interval	Continues to show statistics, updating the display at the interval given.

The information that is displayed by NETSTAT might look like the following:

```
Active Connections

  Proto  Local Address          Foreign Address        State
  TCP    godzilla:1026          0.0.0.0:0              LISTENING
  TCP    godzilla:1028          0.0.0.0:0              LISTENING
  TCP    godzilla:1030          0.0.0.0:0              LISTENING
  TCP    godzilla:1031          0.0.0.0:0              LISTENING
  TCP    godzilla:1032          0.0.0.0:0              LISTENING
  TCP    godzilla:1033          0.0.0.0:0              LISTENING
  TCP    godzilla:1034          0.0.0.0:0              LISTENING
  TCP    godzilla:135           0.0.0.0:0              LISTENING
  TCP    godzilla:135           0.0.0.0:0              LISTENING
  TCP    godzilla:1025          0.0.0.0:0              LISTENING
  TCP    godzilla:1025          LOCALHOST:1026         ESTABLISHED
  TCP    godzilla:1026          LOCALHOST:1025         ESTABLISHED
  TCP    godzilla:1028          ftp.microsoft.com:ftp  ESTABLISHED
  TCP    godzilla:1030          www.genet.dfait-maeci.gc.ca:80   ESTABLISHED
  TCP    godzilla:1031          www.genet.dfait-maeci.gc.ca:80   ESTABLISHED
  TCP    godzilla:1032          www.genet.dfait-maeci.gc.ca:80   ESTABLISHED
  TCP    godzilla:1033          www.genet.dfait-maeci.gc.ca:80   ESTABLISHED
  TCP    godzilla:1034          lxotta.learnix.ca:telnet   ESTABLISHED
  TCP    godzilla:137           0.0.0.0:0              LISTENING
  TCP    godzilla:138           0.0.0.0:0              LISTENING
  TCP    godzilla:nbsession     0.0.0.0:0              LISTENING
  UDP    godzilla:135           *:*
  UDP    godzilla:nbname        *:*
  UDP    godzilla:nbdatagram    *:*
```

The following list explains all the different types of information that you might see, except for the routing table (which was explained in Chapter 6, "IP Routing").

◆ **Foreign Address**—the IP address or host name and socket number of the remote host that you are communicating with. If the port is initializing, an asterisk (*) will be displayed.

◆ **Local Address**—your computer's IP address or host name and the socket number that you are using to connect to the remote host.

◆ **Proto**—the name of the protocol being used for the connection.

◆ **State**—displays the state of TCP connections that you are viewing. The possible states are explained in the following list:

   • **CLOSED.** The TCP session has been closed.

   • **FIN_WAIT_1.** The connection is being closed.

   • **SYN_RECEIVED.** A session request has been received.

   • **CLOSE_WAIT.** The connection is being closed.

   • **FIN_WAIT_2.** The connection is being closed.

   • **SYN_SEND.** A session is being requested.

   • **ESTABLISHED.** A session currently exists between the systems.

   • **LISTEN.** A service has performed a passive open on a port.

   • **TIMED_WAIT.** The session is currently waiting for activity from the other computer.

   • **LAST_ACK.** Your system has made a last acknowledgment.

NBTSTAT

The NBTSTAT diagnostic command displays protocol statistics and current TCP/IP connections using NBT (NetBIOS over TCP/IP). This will allow you to check the status of connections made using tools such as the Network Neighborhood. The full syntax of this command is as follows:

```
nbtstat [-a remotename] [-A IP address] [-c] [-n] [-R]
➥[-r] [-S] [-s] [interval]
```

The switches that you can use on this command are listed in Table 14.2.

TABLE 14.2

SWITCHES FOR THE **NBTSTAT** COMMAND

Switch	Description
-a *remotename*	Lists the names that another host has registered on the network. *Remotename* is the computer name of the other host.
-A *IP address*	The same as the previous command, except you can specify the IP address rather than the name.
-c	Displays all the names in the NetBIOS name cache and the IP address they map to.
-n	Lists all the names that your computer has. If they have been registered, they will be marked as such.
-R	Purges and reloads the NetBIOS name cache. The cache will be reloaded from the LMHOSTS file, if one exists, using the entries marked with #PRE.
-r	Lists all the names your computer has resolved and the IP addresses for them. The difference from the -c switch is that preloaded names are not listed when using the -r switch.
-S	Lists all current sessions that have been established with your computer. This includes both client and server sessions.
-s	The same as the -S switch, except that the system will attempt to resolve the IP addresses to a host name.
interval	The interval, in seconds, at which the computer should update the information on the screen.

The output of the NBTSTAT command with the -s switch may look like this:

```
NetBIOS Connection Table

Local Name              State     In/Out  Remote Host          Input   Output
- - - - - - - - - - - - - - - - - - - - - - - - - - - - - - - - - - - - - - - - -
GODZILLA      <00>  Connected   Out   H6848402      <20>   91B     432B
GODZILLA      <03>  Listening
GODZILLA      <03>  Listening
SCRIM         <03>  Listening
SCRIM         <03>  Listening
```

The column headings generated by the NBTSTAT utility have the following meanings:

◆ **Input**—the number of bytes of information that have been received.

◆ **Output**—the number of bytes of information that have been sent.

◆ **In/Out**—the direction in which the connection was made (OUT means to the other computer, IN means from it).

◆ **Life**—the time remaining before the cache entry is purged.

◆ **Local Name**—the local name that was used for the session.

◆ **Remote Host**—the name on the remote host being used in this session.

◆ **Type**—the type of name that was resolved.

◆ **State**—the state of the connection. Possible states are explained in the following list:

  • **Connected.** A NetBIOS session has been established between the two hosts.

  • **Associated.** Your system has requested a connection and has resolved the remote name to an IP address. This is an active open.

  • **Listening.** This is a service on your computer that is currently not being used. This is a passive open.

- **Idle.** The service that opened the port has since paused or hung. No activity will be possible until the service resumes.

- **Connecting.** At this point your system is attempting to create a NetBIOS session. The system is currently attempting to resolve the name of the remote host to an IP address.

- **Accepting.** A service on your system has been asked to open a session and is in the process of negotiating the session with the remote host.

- **Reconnecting.** After a session has dropped (often due to timing out), your system is trying to reconnect.

- **Outbound.** The TCP three-way handshake is in process. This will establish the Transport layer session that will be used to establish the NetBIOS session.

- **Inbound.** This is the same as outbound, except that a connection is being made *to* a service on your system.

- **Disconnecting.** The remote system has requested a session be terminated, so the session is being shut down.

- **Disconnected.** Your system is requesting a session be terminated.

Performance Monitor

To tune or optimize Windows NT, you will need to be able to look at the performance of the server on many different levels. Windows NT contains an integrated tool, Performance Monitor, that provides information about your system on many different levels.

Before you can use the Performance Monitor to work with TCP/IP counters, you need to have the SNMP service installed. Covering all the capabilities of the Performance Monitor is truly beyond the scope of this text; however, the next few sections will cover the basics of working with this tool. In addition, a list of available TCP/IP-related counters is given in Appendix E, "Performance Monitor Counters."

Using Performance Monitor

When you open Performance Monitor, you will see a screen similar to the one shown in Figure 14.1. This is one of the four views that can be used in Performance Monitor.

The Chart view shown in Figure 14.1 allows you to monitor real-time or logged activity on the computer. Although empty at the moment, it is easy to add items to the chart. To do this, choose Edit, Add to Chart from the menu. The dialog box shown in Figure 14.2 will appear.

There are many options available in this dialog box. The following list explains them:

◆ **Computer.** Using this option, you will be able to select the computer you wish to monitor. In this way, you will be able to get a better view of what is really happening because the monitoring process does not have to run on the system you will be monitoring. To select a different computer, click the ellipsis button at the end of the computer field; you will get a list of the computers in your workgroup.

◆ **Object.** After you have chosen the computer that you wish to monitor, you should choose the object. Objects represent the categories or areas that can be monitored.

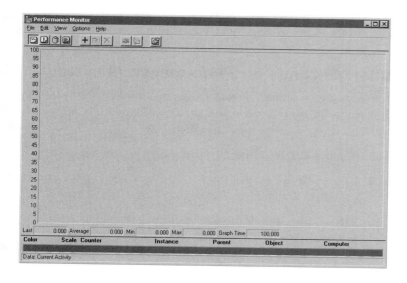

FIGURE 14.1

The starting screen for the Performance Monitor.

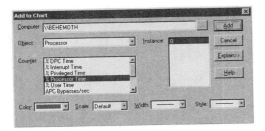

FIGURE 14.2
Adding to the Performance Monitor chart.

◆ **Counter.** Within each of the different objects is a series of counters that measure some aspect of the object's performance.

◆ **Instance.** With some objects, you are able to choose which instance of the object you wish to look at. For example, if your system has more than one processor, you may wish to look at each of them individually; you can do this by choosing the instance. The same would apply to the hard disks in your system and the processes that are currently running.

MORE ON PERFORMANCE MONITOR

This book is not about Performance Monitor. However, there are a couple of quick points that should be passed on. First, the disk objects (Logical Disk and Physical Disk) will not report any information unless you turn on disk-performance monitoring. To do this, type **diskperf -y** at the command prompt and restart your system. (If you are using RAID, use **diskperf –ye**.)

You should also note that there are two separate objects for the processors in the system: the Processor object allows you to see each individual processor and report on it; the System object combines all the processors and treats them as a single object.

Finally, there is no need to memorize the Performance Monitor counters because their descriptions are available. You only need to be aware of what types of counters are available.

Figure 14.3 shows an example of a chart with a few options enabled.

Chart Settings for Performance Monitor

There are several settings that affect the way the chart works. To set preferences for the chart, choose Option, Chart from the menu. You will see a dialog box like the one in Figure 14.4.

The options available are as follows:

◆ **Legend**—turns on the display of the legend at the bottom of the chart.

◆ **Value Bar**—controls the display of the information at the bottom of the graph. This includes the following categories:

　• **Last**—the last recorded value

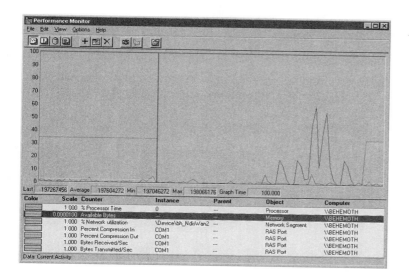

FIGURE 14.3
The Performance Monitor with objects selected.

- **Average**—the average of the values for the period given in Graph Time

- **Min/Max**—the minimum and maximum values that have been recorded in this session

- **Graph Time**—the period of time shown on the graph

◆ **Vertical Grid**—displays vertical gridlines.

◆ **Horizontal Grid**—displays horizontal gridlines

◆ **Vertical Labels**—controls whether the list of values is shown down the side.

◆ **Gallery**—allows you switch between a regular graph and a histogram.

◆ **Vertical Maximum**—sets the top value of the graph scale.

◆ **Update Time**—tells Performance Monitor how often to update the graph.

FIGURE 14.4
You can change the way a chart looks using the chart options.

The Log Setting

The Chart view of the Performance Monitor is good for watching the current data. However, you will frequently want to view the activity over a longer period of time. To do this, you can create a log file (see Figure 14.5) that contains the counters for all instances of

FIGURE 14.5
The Log view of the Performance Monitor lets you capture data over a period of time.

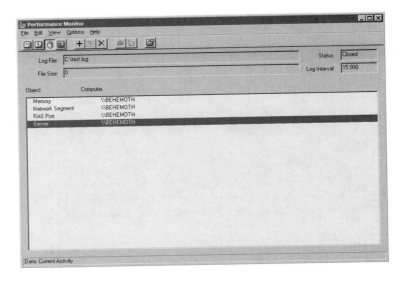

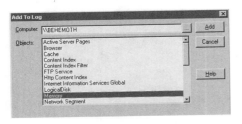

FIGURE 14.6
From this dialog box you can add objects to the log.

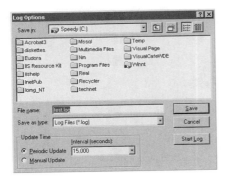

FIGURE 14.7
Setting the location for the log.

the objects you select. This information, when collected, can be viewed in either the Chart view or the Report view (the Report view is not covered in this text).

Creating a log is fairly simple, as illustrated in the following steps.

STEP BY STEP

14.1 Creating a Log

1. Choose View, Log from the Performance Monitor menu.

2. Choose Edit, Add to Log. A dialog box appears asking which objects you wish to log (see Figure 14.6).

3. Select the items you wish to log from your system, any other system, or the network that you have administrator privileges for.

4. Click Cancel when everything that you want to log is listed.

5. Choose Options, Log from the menu. This will bring up a dialog box (see Figure 14.7) in which you can enter information about where to store the log.

6. Enter the log filename and check the Periodic Update value (if you intend to log a long period, do not make this value too small). Then click Start Log.

7. When you have finished logging, go back to Options, Log on the menu and choose Stop Log.

WARNING

Log File Size Log files can grow very rapidly if you are not careful. Make sure the Periodic Update value is sufficiently high so that your log will not fill your disk. You will be able to see the size of the log on the log screen.

Using a Log File

After you have created a log file, you will want to view the contents. This will normally be handled by the Chart view. To use the information in a log, perform these steps.

STEP BY STEP

14.2 Opening a Log in Chart View

1. Go to the Chart view of the Performance Monitor.

2. Choose Options, Data From; a dialog box appears (see Figure 14.8).

3. Choose Log File and enter the name of the file. Then click OK.

As before, you can now add the counters and instances to the chart (Edit, Add to Chart). However, you will only be able to add to the chart for objects that you logged.

One of the advantages of logging is that you are able to zoom in on a particular time period. This can be done by following these steps.

STEP BY STEP

14.3 Zooming In on a Time Period

1. Add to the chart the items you wish to view.

FIGURE 14.8

Selecting a data source for the chart view.

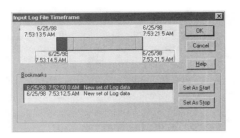

FIGURE 14.9
The Input Log File Timeframe dialog box lets you zoom in on a period of time.

Systems Management Server   To monitor the entire network from a single computer, you need Microsoft's Systems Management Server (SMS), which includes a more powerful version of Network Monitor. SMS can monitor network traffic associated with any computer that is running a Network Monitor Agent. (Agents are proxy programs that collect data and forward them to another computer for analysis.) The Network Monitor Agent is included with Windows NT 4.0.

2. Choose Edit, Time Window. A dialog box appears (see Figure 14.9) that allows you to choose the period of time you want to view.

3. Slide the handles along the time window until you have the period you wish to view. You will see black bars on the chart in the background that tell you where you are.

4. Click OK, and the display is updated.

Network Monitor

Network Monitor extends your ability to manage the network by enabling you to capture network data for detailed examination. You can look inside the frames to perform a detailed analysis of the network's operation.

Network Monitor is equipped with a wide variety of protocol parsers, which are modules that examine network frames to decode their contents. Among the 62 or so included protocol parsers are many you will recognize from discussion in this book, including ethernet, token ring, IP, TCP, and PPP. However, a complete discussion of the protocol parsers is beyond the scope of this book.

As shipped with Windows NT 4.0, Network Monitor has one significant limitation: It can capture only those frames that originate from or are delivered to the computer on which Network Monitor is running, including broadcast and multicast frames. You cannot use Network Monitor to monitor frames associated with other computers on the network.

Installing Network Monitor

The following steps detail how to install the Network Monitor:

STEP BY STEP

14.4 Installing Network Monitor

1. Open the Network dialog box.

2. Choose the Services tab and click the Add button.

3. Choose either the Network Monitor Agent or the Network Monitor Tools and Agent. The following is a brief description of the choices:

   • **Network Monitor Agent.** Choose this option if this computer will be monitored by another computer running the Network Monitor.

   • **Network Monitor Tools and Agent.** Choose this option if this computer will be used to collect and analyze network data. This option also installs the Network Monitor Agent, which enables Network Monitor to monitor this computer remotely.

4. Choose OK to add the Service. When prompted, enter the source files directory.

5. Click OK to close the Network dialog box and restart the system.

Network Monitor is added to the Administrative Tools group of the Start menu. Network Monitoring Agent is added to the Control Panel as the Monitoring Agent utility. The computer must be restarted to activate Network Monitor.

Capturing Network Frames

The Network Monitor Capture window, shown in Figure 14.10, contains the following four panes:

◆ **Graph.** This pane includes bar charts that dynamically display current activity. The five bars in this pane are % Network Utilization, Frames Per Second, Bytes Per Second, Broadcasts Per Second, and Multicasts Per Second. You can display or hide this pane by clicking the Toggle Graph Pane button. A line in the % Network Utilization bar designates the highest utilization encountered during the current capture (this has also been added as a counter in the Performance Monitor). The numbers at the right ends of the other bars describe the highest measurement encountered.

FIGURE 14.10

The Network Monitor Capture window is where you will start grabbing network data.

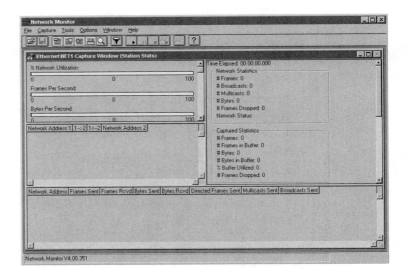

◆ **Total Statistics.** This pane displays cumulative network statistics summarizing network traffic in five areas: Network Statistics, Capture Statistics, Per Second Statistics, Network Card (MAC) Statistics, and Network Card (MAC) Error Statistics. You can display or hide this pane by clicking the Toggle Total Statistics Pane button.

◆ **Session Statistics.** This pane displays statistics about sessions that are currently operating on the network. You can display or hide this pane by clicking the Toggle Total Session Statistics Pane button.

◆ **Station Statistics.** This pane displays statistics about sessions in which this computer is participating. You can display or hide this pane by clicking the Toggle Total Station Statistics Pane button.

When capturing is active, network frames are captured into a buffer that is limited in size. When the buffer is full, older data are discarded to make room for new entries.

You can control the capturing of data using five options in the Capture menu: Start, Stop, Stop and View, Pause, and Continue. These functions can also be controlled using buttons in the toolbar.

If you want, you can focus on the activity in one of the panes. Simply select the pane and click the Zoom Pane button in the toolbar. The pane you select will expand to fill the available space. To return to normal display, click the Zoom Pane button again.

Saving Captured Data

After you are finished capturing data, choose Stop in the Capture menu to stop the capture. The data in the capture buffer can now be analyzed as required, or it can be saved for future study.

Creating an Address Database

When you first capture data in Network Monitor, most devices are identified by their MAC addresses. Because it is easier to associate a name with a computer rather than having to memorize MAC addresses, Network Monitor includes a feature that identifies the NetBIOS names of computers from which data are captured.

To build the address database, start capturing data on the network and let Network Monitor continue to collect data for an extended period of time. As traffic is generated, computers will be added to the Session Statistics and Station Statistics panes, identified by their network addresses.

After capturing a large number of frames, stop capturing. Then select the Find All Names command in the Capture menu. The frames in the capture buffer will be scanned and the names will be added to the address database. During future capture operations, computers will be identified by name.

Examining Captured Data

After frames have been captured, you can examine them in considerable detail. To examine captured frames, do one of the following:

◆ When capturing is active, click the Stop and View Capture toolbar button. Choose the Stop and View option in the Capture menu, or press Shift+F11.

◆ When capturing is stopped, click the Display Captured Data toolbar button, choose the Display Captured Data option in the Capture menu, or press F12.

> **NOTE**
>
> **Capturing Frames That Include Computer Names**   A bit of luck is required to capture frames that include computer names. Each time you capture data, collect names and add them to the database until the list is complete. You can save the names so they will remain after Network Monitor is closed. Whenever you close the Network Monitor, it will prompt you to save the names so you don't forget.

Any of these actions opens the Capture dialog box shown in Figure 14.11. At first, this dialog box includes one pane, which lists all frames currently in the capture buffer.

The capture consists of a single PING event in which the host running Network Monitor PINGed another host. As you may have determined from the Description column, the sequence begins with a DNS query to determine the IP address of the remote host together with a response from the DNS server. Finally, a series of ICMP Echo and Echo Reply datagrams comprise four repeated PINGs.

To examine details for a frame, double-click on its entry. In Figure 14.12, an ICMP Echo datagram has been opened. The panes are as follows:

◆ **Summary Pane**—includes a one-line summary of each frame in the capture buffer.

◆ **Detail Pane**—displays the contents of the frame, organized by protocol layer.

◆ **Hex Pane**—displays the data in the pane in hexadecimal and ASCII characters. The highlighted bytes are associated with the protocol section highlighted in the Detail Pane.

The following sections discuss the Summary and Detail Panes.

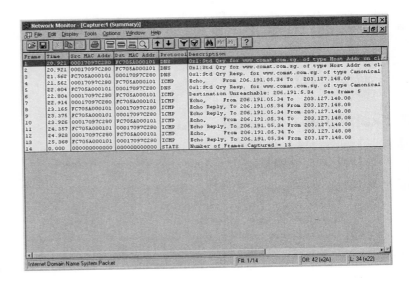

FIGURE 14.11
The Capture window showing captured frames.

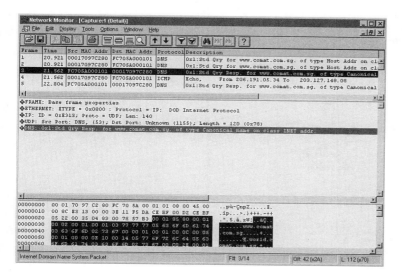

FIGURE 14.12
Here a packet has been open so the contents
can be examined.

The Summary Pane

The Summary Pane briefly describes each frame that is held in the
capture buffer. To open a frame for detailed analysis, select the entry
for that frame in the Summary Pane.

The source and destination computers are identified by the Src
MAC Address and Dst MAC Address fields. If a name database has
been created, names will appear in place of hexadecimal physical
addresses.

The Protocol field describes the protocol associated with the frame.
As you can see, the entries in the Description column can be reason-
ably clear (for example, "Echo Reply, To 200.190.50.01"), but they
can also be downright obscure. To decode the descriptions, you will
need to learn the operational details of the protocols being analyzed.

The Detail Pane

Unless you are knowledgeable enough to undertake a byte-by-byte
analysis of the data, the Detail Pane will probably be the pane that
occupies most of your analytical effort. This pane translates the data
from the various header layers into a more legible form.

As can be seen in Figure 14.13, selecting the pane and clicking the
Zoom Pane button expands the Detail Pane.

FIGURE 14.13
Zooming in on a packet that was captured.

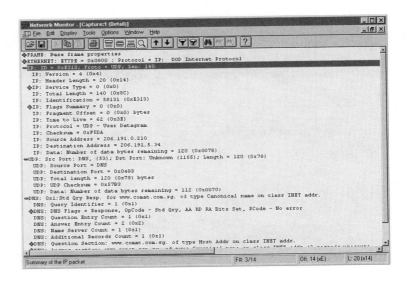

The frame represented in Figure 14.13 is an ICMP Echo frame. Notice that each entry is tagged with a plus sign (+) to the left, indicating that the entry can be expanded by clicking the plus key to show greater detail.

Versions of Network Monitor

There are two versions of the Network Monitor: the basic version that comes with Windows NT and the full version that comes with SMS. Both versions allow you to capture the packets that are flowing into and out of your computer. The full version that comes with SMS will allow you extra functionality, such as the ability to capture all packets on the local network or on remote networks, edit those packets, and derive statistics about protocols and users on the network.

CASE STUDY: MONITORING RESOURCES AT SUNSHINE BREWING COMPANY

ESSENCE OF THE CASE

As you look at the network that has been evolving over the chapters, you might consider some of the following areas as the weak links in the chain:

- The Internet connections for each of the offices must be available or the office will be isolated.

- The systems will need to be able to connect to the PDC for changes to the accounts database; this involves connectivity and name resolution.

- Almost all the users will need to connect to the SQL server; therefore, this system is critical.

- The laptop users will need to be able to connect to their offices using PPTP; this means the RAS servers running PPTP must be available.

- In the larger offices, you need to ensure that sufficient bandwidth is available for the local networks.

- All the users need to be able to retrieve their mail, and the mail server must be available at all hours for incoming SMTP traffic.

In this section you will look at the network you have been designing and decide what parts of it require monitoring, what tool to use, and how much monitoring will be required.

As a starting point, you will be using Network Monitor (full version) and Performance Monitor to look at your network because the NETSTAT and NBTSTAT utilities are used primarily for troubleshooting.

SCENARIO

Part of designing a network is to design the maintenance requirements for it. Looking at this network you will need to determine the key areas that require monitoring and determine the best way to monitor them. This will mean looking at the network as a whole and anticipating where the failures might occur, and where these failures will have a profound effect on productivity.

ANALYSIS

In this case the analysis is really a matter of choosing the correct counters and determining the upper and lower limits acceptable for performance in at least the key areas just noted.

The Internet connections, for example, you will monitor with both Performance Monitor and Network Monitor. The system will be monitored for the % Network Utilization statistic to determine what percent of the available bandwidth is used; here you would like to see 40–80 percent utilization, with only occasional peaks going higher. The Network Monitor will be used to determine what protocols are being used and

continues

CASE STUDY: MONITORING RESOURCES AT SUNSHINE BREWING COMPANY

continued

who is using them; this will guide you in setting Internet surfing policies.

Monitoring the various servers will be handled by using the Performance Monitor to look at the counters that come with the servers. You will also look at the % Network Utilization to determine if the server is on too busy a subnet, and you will look at the bytes in total for the network

interfaces to ensure the load on the server can be accommodated.

Monitoring the local area networks in the larger offices is simply a matter of looking at the % Network Utilization for the various networks and seeing how busy they are. Network Monitor will then be used to determine what the source of traffic is if a network should reach saturation.

CHAPTER SUMMARY

KEY TERMS

- capturing
- Chart view
- counter
- instance
- Log view
- Network Monitor
- Network Monitor Agent
- Network Statistics Utility (NETSTAT)
- object
- Performance Monitor
- sliding windows

This chapter looked at the monitoring tools available for Windows NT, notably when running TCP/IP. The exam will ask you in which situations to use each type of tool and what the tools can do.

Before you take the exam, make sure you are comfortable with the following issues:

- ◆ You should know that NBTSTAT looks at NetBIOS over TCP/IP, specifically the name resolution and session state.

- ◆ You need to know that NETSTAT is used to look at TCP/IP networking. It can view single protocols and connections and even display the routing table.

- ◆ You need to understand the Object/Counter/Instance relationship in the Performance Monitor.

- ◆ You need to know that the Performance Monitor can view live data or log data to view later.

- ◆ You should be aware of the ability to set alerts in the Performance Monitor.

- ◆ You should understand that Network Monitor looks at the traffic on the network and not necessarily at a single system.

- ◆ You should know that there are two versions of the Performance Monitor: the basic version that comes with Windows NT and the full version that comes with SMS.

APPLY YOUR KNOWLEDGE	

Exercises

14.1 Monitoring Real Time Performance

In this exercise you will use the Performance Monitor to monitor real-time performance. You will work with FTP to generate statistics and see how heavy the load is.

Estimated Time: About 15 minutes.

1. First, you need to create a log file, which can be done using the Performance Monitor. Open the Performance Monitor and choose View, Log.

2. Choose Edit, Add to Log. Select the first object in the list, and then Shift+click on the last object. Click Add, Done.

3. From Options, Log enter the name **C:\INETPUB\FTPROOT\TEST.LOG** (if you installed the FTPROOT directory elsewhere, use that directory). Set the Periodic Update to 1 second. Then choose Start Log.

4. When the log reaches 2MB in size, choose Options, Log from the menu and click Stop Log. (This should only take one or two minutes.)

5. Switch back to the Chart view (View, Chart) and add the following objects and counters to the chart (Edit, Add to Chart):

   IP—Datagrams/sec

   ICMP—Received Echo Reply/sec

   ICMP—Sent Echo/sec

   ICMP—Received Time Exceeded

   TCP—Connections Established

   TCP—Segments/sec

   UDP—Datagrams/sec

6. Set the vertical maximum for the chart to 30. You can do this using Options, Chart and entering the value in the Vertical Maximum field.

7. Start a DOS prompt and log into your FTP server (FTP 127.0.0.1). Observe that the number of sessions in the Performance Monitor increased.

8. List the files that are on the FTP server.

9. Switch to binary mode and retrieve the file you created (test.log). As you do this, observe the activity in the Performance Monitor.

10. Close the FTP session.

14.2 Logging TCP/IP Activity

In this exercise you will observe and log the information created during a TRACERT. The Performance Monitor should still be running with the same settings as before.

Estimated Time: About 15 minutes.

1. Start a command prompt.

2. Ensure you are connected to the network, and then issue the following command:

   TRACERT www.ScrimTech.com

   There is a small increase in the traffic, and the ICMP:Received Time Exceeded increases steadily. This is because the TRACERT command sends a series of ICMP echo requests. With incrementing time-to-live values, there should be an increase in traffic. Because the packets being sent are intended to time out, there should also be a steady increase in the ICMP:Received Time Exceeded.

3. Change the scale so that 2 is the top. Select the ICMP:Received Time Exceeded and press Delete

APPLY YOUR KNOWLEDGE

to remove it. Also remove the TCP:Connections Established.

4. Perform the trace again. After the trace, note the values shown and click on each of them. Notice the number of echo replies: There is only one set (the value will probably read less than this). This represents the last echo request sent, which did eventually reach the host. All the other requests timed out.

5. Switch to the log view (View, Log). Add the ICMP object to the log using Edit, Add to log. (You can clear any existing items using File, New Log Settings.)

6. Set the Options, Log so the file is captured to ICMP.log and the Periodic Update is 0.1.

7. Start the log and repeat the trace once more. Stop the log when you are finished. (This file could be over 1MB in size.)

8. Switch to the Chart view and select Options, Data From. Enter the filename for the log you just created.

9. Add the following to the chart:

    ICMP—Received Echo Reply/sec

    ICMP—Sent Echo/sec

10. Select the ICMP:Received Echo Reply/sec. Multiply the value by the time in the Graph Time.

    The received value will vary. However, the calculated value will be around 3 (probably a little less). If you think about the TRACERT command, it always shows three values; this is because it always sends three echo requests.

11. Verify the number of hops. Take the average of ICMP:Echo Sent/sec and multiply this by the Graph Time value. Divide the result by three. You should get approximately the number of hops.

14.3 Installing Network Monitor

In this exercise you will install the Network Monitor and Agent. You will need, at the very least, to have a functioning network card in your system for this.

Estimated Time: About 10 minutes.

1. Open the Network dialog box, and from the Services tab choose Add.

2. Select the Network Monitor and Agent from the list and click OK.

3. Enter the directory for your Windows NT source files.

4. Click OK to close the Network Settings dialog box.

5. When prompted, restart your system.

14.4 Viewing an ARP Broadcast

In this exercise you will look at a simple ARP broadcast using the Network Monitor.

Estimated Time: About 10 minutes.

1. Start a command prompt and Network Monitor.

2. In the Network Monitor, choose Capture, Start.

3. Switch to the command prompt and PING your default gateway.

4. Switch back to the Network Monitor. Choose Capture, Stop and View.

APPLY YOUR KNOWLEDGE

5. A list is presented showing the packets that have been sent or received by your system.

6. One of the first packets should be an ARP:Request. Double-click on it.

7. Expand the packet completely (click the plus signs so that all of the packet is in view).

8. In the packet, find the target MAC and IP addresses. This should be the IP address of the router.

9. If the PING worked on your system, look in the Summary Pane at the top of the screen. The next packet should be an ARP:Reply.

d. An application that you are developing uses UDP as the transfer protocol. You have tested the application on several machines. However, one of them will not respond. You suspect that the application has not bound to the port correctly.

e. You implemented a Windows NT system as an IP router. Your clients are complaining that their network access is slower now.

f. You want to watch the counters that are used for TRACERT.

5. What can the Network Monitor that comes with Windows NT capture?

Review Questions

1. Which utility allows you to see all the IP-type connections to your system?

2. What command can you use to purge and reload the NetBIOS name cache?

3. What are the steps for creating a log file using Performance Monitor?

4. Using the information in Appendix B, "Overview of the Certification Process," choose the object and counter that you would use in the Performance Monitor in each of the following situations:

   a. You want to know how much data is sent using NetBIOS networking.

   b. You are having problems transferring files using NetBIOS networking. You suspect that there are transmission problems.

   c. FTP is running slowly, but the file eventually gets to the destination.

Exam Questions

1. You are using Performance Monitor, but very few TCP/IP statistics are available. How can you increase the number of TCP/IP objects and counters to monitor?

   A. Install a promiscuous mode adapter card.

   B. Configure the correct default gateway in Performance Monitor.

   C. Bind TCP/IP to the Performance Monitor service.

   D. Install the SNMP service.

2. Executing NETSTAT with what parameter will display all connections and listening ports, even those ports not currently involved in a connection?

   A. -a

   B. -s

   C. -p

   D. -?

3. Optimization changes are made primarily through what tool?

   A. Performance Monitor

   B. Network Monitor

   C. ARP

   D. Regedt32

4. Performance Monitor uses statistical measurements called _____.

   A. counters

   B. baselines

   C. benchmarks

   D. objects

5. The Network Utilization counter for your local network is sitting at 92 percent most of the time and occasionally climbing to 100 percent. Which tool will allow you to see what is causing this?

   A. NETSTAT

   B. NBTSTAT

   C. Performance Monitor

   D. Network Monitor

6. A team from your research and development facility has asked to analyze a piece of software. They need to know on what ports the software is used for incoming connections. Which tool will allow you to determine this?

   A. NETSTAT

   B. NBTSTAT

   C. Performance Monitor

   D. Network Monitor

7. You want to profile the network usage for a process that your R&D team is working on to assess the impact it will have on the network. You want to know which protocols are going to be used and whether the information is secure when it is being transmitted. Which tool will allow you to see what is causing this?

   A. NETSTAT

   B. NBTSTAT

   C. Performance Monitor

   D. Network Monitor

8. You are the administrator of a local area network. You have noticed that network response for a server is particularly slow. You need to figure out what is causing the poor response time.

You decide to monitor the traffic moving into and out of the server using the Network Monitor. You intend to track the traffic over a four-hour period and then review the information in the capture. How good a method is this for determining the cause of the problem?

   A. This is the best possible solution.

   B. This is a good solution.

   C. This solution works but is far from optimal.

   D. This solution does not work.

APPLY YOUR KNOWLEDGE

Answers to Review Questions

1. You can use NETSTAT -a. This will display all connections for clients and services that are using Winsock.

2. The NBTSTAT -R command will perform this function.

3. If you wish to create a log file in Performance Monitor, do the following:

   Open Performance Monitor and choose View, Log.

   Choose Edit, Add to Log and choose the objects you want to log.

   Choose Options, Log and give the log a name and update frequency. Then choose Start log.

   Choose Options, Log, and then Stop Log when you have finished the log.

4a. Log the Bytes Sent/sec from the NBT connection. When the log is complete, multiply the average for this counter by the total time of the log.

4b. There are several counters that can be used from the ICMP object to handle this. The key one is Messages Received/sec; this will let you know if you are receiving messages from ICMP (which handles error reporting). This will help determine if the problem is with the network.

4c. Again, you can use the ICMP object; however, you would also want to look at TCP—Segments Retransmitted/sec. Because FTP uses the TCP protocol, slowness is usually a result of lost packets or packets with an expired retransmit timer.

4d. In this case, the object is obvious: UDP. The counter that will allow you to test the theory is the Datagrams No Ports/sec. This will allow you

to see the number of times that a UDP datagram was sent but there was nothing there to listen.

4e. You would want to look at the IP object for this because routing takes place at the IP layer. Some of the counters that you might look at are Datagrams Received/sec (total incoming traffic), Datagrams Forwarded/sec (the number that need to be forwarded), Datagrams Outbound Discarded (the number of datagrams that timed out and such), Datagrams Outbound No Route (tells you that your router needs more routing information), and Datagrams Received Address Errors (the number discarded because the address is wrong). One other counter you could look at is Fragmentation Failures. However, this is caused by the Do Not Fragment flag that would be set by the client.

4 f. When you look at the TRACERT, you would need to look at ICMP counters, specifically Sent Echo/sec, Received Echo Reply/sec, and Received Time Exceeded.

5. The Network Monitor that comes with Windows NT will only be able to capture packets sent to or from your system. The version that comes with SMS can capture packets from any system that has the monitor agent installed.

Answers to Exam Questions

1. **D.** The SNMP service must be installed to collect TCP/IP statistics.

2. **A.** NETSTAT -a displays all connections and listening ports, even those ports not currently involved in a connection.

APPLY YOUR KNOWLEDGE

3. **D.** Optimization changes are made primarily through the Registry Editor (Regedt32.exe).

4. **A.** Performance Monitor uses statistical measurements called counters.

5. **D.** In a case like this you will want to capture and then review a sample of traffic from your network. For this you will use the Network Monitor.

6. **A.** In this case the answer is to use the NETSTAT -a utility, which allows you to view all the ports in use on your system (including listening ports, which you are looking for here).

7. **D.** Here you could use the Performance Monitor for some of the information (and you would, probably, to determine CPU and memory usage and the like). However, what you are really interested in is network traffic; therefore you should use the Network Monitor. In this case, of course, you should perform the testing on an isolated network segment.

8. **B.** This is a good strategy; however, you would first look at the Task Manager to determine if any of the processes are using too much memory or CPU. If this is not the case, you would want to involve Network Monitor and also the Performance Monitor. (Note that a single service using all resources on a system is a sign of a denial of service attack; you will want to use NETSTAT to see if you can find the offender and then shut down the attached service.)

Suggested Readings and Resources

1. Sirockman, Jason. *MCSE Training Guide: Windows NT Server 4 Enterprise.* New Riders, 1997.

2. *Windows NT Server Manuals: Concepts and Planning Manual.* Chapter 8, "Monitoring Performance," and Chapter 10, "Monitoring Your Network."

PART

V

TROUBLESHOOTING

This chapter helps you prepare for the exam by covering the following objectives:

Diagnose and resolve IP addressing problems.

▶ The most common errors in working with TCP/IP are configuration errors. This objective is included to ensure that you know how to resolve this type of problem.

Use Microsoft TCP/IP utilities to diagnose IP configuration problems.

Identify which Microsoft TCP/IP utility to use to diagnose IP configuration problems.

▶ You need to be able to use the PING and IPCONFIG utilities to determine the current configuration of TCP/IP. You will need to be able to tell what is wrong with the configuration based on information gathered using these utilities.

Diagnose and resolve name resolution problems.

▶ This objective covers a large number of problems, including failed or slow connections.

CHAPTER 15

Troubleshooting
Microsoft TCP/IP

As you read through this chapter you should concentrate on the following key items:

▶ You need to know what problems occur at each layer.

▶ You should understand the configuration of TCP/IP.

▶ You need to know how to isolate a problem in a logical manner.

▶ You should know what tools are available for troubleshooting TCP/IP configuration errors.

▶ You need to understand the uses of Performance Monitor and Network Monitor.

▶ You will need to understand NETSTAT and NBTSTAT and what they can tell you.

Troubleshooting in TCP/IP follows the same logic as troubleshooting in any computer system. First, you must understand what should be happening, and then you can trace the data path and see where the problem is occurring.

In the case of TCP/IP, the transportation of data from one system to another involves a whole series of events occurring throughout a number of different layers. As data moves from one level of the TCP/IP networking model to the next, different areas of the TCP/IP configuration can cause problems with communications.

Throughout this text you have seen the various parts and pieces of the TCP/IP implementation under Microsoft Windows NT. The key element in making Microsoft TCP/IP work is running NetBIOS networking over the top of the TCP/IP stack. Unfortunately, this adds yet another layer to the complexity of troubleshooting TCP/IP.

A number of steps are involved in a connection between two systems using NetBIOS over TCP/IP. The following list provides a general outline of the process, which will be followed by a look at ways to troubleshoot problems along the way:

1. You request a network resource from a remote system.

2. Your computer (the NetBIOS Helper service) creates a NetBIOS name query and broadcasts it on the local network or sends it to a WINS server.

3. The name query is sent to UDP port 137 (the nbNameService port), encapsulated in a UDP datagram.

4. UDP passes the datagram and a pseudo-header to IP.

5. IP determines if the address is a local or remote address; if it is a remote address, it also determines if there is a route to the network. Assuming a route is found, the IP header is added to the datagram and the IP datagram is created.

6. The address resolution protocol (ARP) is asked to resolve the IP address to a MAC address. In the case of a local system, this will be the machine's MAC address; if the address is remote, it will be the address of the gateway that was found in the routing table; and in the case of a broadcast, it will be the topology's broadcast address.

7. The request is sent from the system to the address the ARP finds using the network adapter configured with the IP address indicated by the interface in the routing table. Now the machine waits.

8. Eventually, a reply packet is either sent directly to the system or is received as a broadcast. In either case, the packet is received by the network adapter and is passed up to IP. IP strips the header off the packet and passes it to the protocol specified in the header.

9. In this case, UDP receives the packet and strips off the UDP header. This tells UDP which port to use; in this case, it's 137.

10. The NetBIOS Helper service receives the packet and examines its information, which should include the address of the system that contains the resource you requested in step 1.

11. The NetBIOS helper service determines if it has a session with the remote system; if not, it will begin to create one.

12. If a new session is required, NetBIOS requests a session from TCP using the nbSessionPort (TCP 139). TCP then begins a three-way handshake to create the session.

13. The handshake starts by creating a TCP segment. In this segment, which contains your system's current sequence number, the SYN (synchronize) flag is turned on; this indicates that the remote system should set the acknowledgment numbers to the sequence number in the segment.

14. TCP passes the segment and a pseudo-header to IP, which will determine whether the system is local or remote.

15. IP encapsulates the TCP segment in an IP datagram and requests that ARP locate the appropriate MAC address.

16. The network adapter is used to send the packet to the remote host. Your system then waits. (In reality, this is only one of a number of different connections that will be active at any given time.)

17. A packet is sent to your system and passed to the IP layer.

18. IP strips the header and passes the packet up to the correct protocol (TCP in this case).

19. TCP strips off its header. In this case the packet contains an ACK (acknowledgment) flag and a request for your system to synchronize sequence numbers with the remote system. This is a function that can be handled at the TCP layer; therefore, a reply is formulated at this layer. The ACK number is checked to verify that the other system has correctly synchronized its acknowledgment numbers to your system's sequence numbers. The sequence number from the remote system is used to create an acknowledgment number (the next number your system expects to see), which is placed in the header of the reply. The ACK flag is set in the TCP header (there is no actual data at this point).

20. TCP passes the segment and a pseudo-header to IP, which determines whether the system is local or remote.

21. IP encapsulates the TCP segment in an IP datagram and requests that ARP locate the appropriate MAC address.

22. The network adapter is used to send the packet to the remote host. This completes the three-way handshake; now the nbSessionPort is informed that communications can begin.

23. The NetBIOS Helper sends a NetBIOS session request to the remote system using the TCP session that was just established. The information includes a request to create a session and the name of the local and target systems.

24. The information is passed through port 139 to the TCP and is encapsulated in a TCP segment.

25. TCP passes the segment and a pseudo-header to IP, which determines whether the system is local or remote.

26. IP encapsulates the TCP segment in an IP datagram and requests that ARP locate the appropriate MAC address.

27. The network adapter is used to send the packet to the remote host. The system waits for the TCP acknowledgment that the data was received.

28. Eventually, the ACK is received; however, this only acknowledges the receipt of the data. The system continues to wait for a reply.

29. The other system sends a positive NetBIOS session response. This arrives at your system's network adapter and is passed to IP.

30. IP strips the header and passes it to TCP, which strips its header and passes the data to port 139. Now the NetBIOS Helper has created a session and begins to negotiate the SMB (server message block) protocol that will be used.

31. The NetBIOS Helper suggests an SMB protocol and sends the suggestion to the remote system.

32. The information is passed through port 139 to the TCP, encapsulated in a TCP segment.

33. TCP passes the segment and a pseudo-header to IP, which determines whether the system is local or remote.

34. IP encapsulates the TCP segment in an IP datagram and requests that ARP locate the appropriate MAC address.

35. The network adapter is used to send the packet to the remote host. The system waits for the TCP acknowledgment that the data was received.

36. Eventually, the ACK is received; however, this only acknowledges the receipt of the data. The system continues to wait for a reply.

37. The other system accepts or rejects the SMB protocol; this arrives at your system's network adapter and is passed to IP.

38. IP strips the header and pass it to TCP, which strips its header and passes the data to port 139. Assuming the protocol was accepted, you can now send or receive information using SMB (NetBIOS) networking.

You should be aware that the steps shown here are the actions performed on only one of the systems. Furthermore, this is just the establishment of a simple NetBIOS session over TCP/IP—other functions will be more involved.

The key here is to isolate the steps that are not being completed so that you can quickly locate the components that don't work. It is best to organize your troubleshooting efforts by following the data flow through the network layers.

THE NETWORK INTERFACE LAYER

Although there doesn't seem to be much at this layer, it is possible for things to go wrong at the bottom of the stack. There are basically four problems you might run into at this level.

◆ **Physical connectivity.** As with all networking, TCP/IP works better if it is plugged in. All networks require that the system be connected to the network—so always check the cable.

◆ **No IP address was assigned to the DHCP client.** This should be obvious to the user because a large message appears. However, you should always verify that an IP address is assigned by using the IPCONFIG utility.

◆ **ARP problems.** If the address resolution protocol is not functioning properly, you will not be able to resolve an IP address to a MAC address. The ARP utility, described in the next section, allows you to verify the ability to resolve addresses.

◆ **Duplicate IP addresses are on the network.** Another problem that you can run into occurs when two systems on the network share the same IP address. This is not suppose to happen; but if it does, your system may resolve the MAC address to one system at first and to the other the next time.

The only case in which you should have a problem with the ARP is if a static resolution is added to the ARP cache, which may be done for performance purposes. However, if the network adapter is changed in the system for which the IP address was entered, the mapping will cause problems. You can check for this problem using ARP.

ARP

The address resolution protocol (ARP) utility can be used to see the entries in the ARP table, which stores mappings of MAC addresses to IP addresses. You can check the table for the IP addresses you believe should be there, and whether they are mapped to the appropriate computers.

Usually, you do not know the MAC addresses of the hosts on your network. However, if you cannot contact a host, or if a connection is made to an unexpected host, you can check this table with the ARP command to isolate which host is actually assigned an IP address.

Primarily, you need to check for entries that are marked as static. If an entry is marked as static for the IP address you are trying to communicate with, remove it. The basic structure of the ARP command is shown here, followed by an explanation of its options:

```
ARP -s inet_addr eth_addr [if_addr]
      OR
ARP -d inet_addr [if_addr]
      OR
ARP -a [inet_addr] [-N if_addr]
```

Option	Purpose
-a	Displays the ARP cache. If you specify an inet_addr, the IP and physical addresses for only that system are displayed.
-g	For compatibility, and functions the same as -a.
inet_addr	Specifies an Internet address.
-N if_addr	Displays only the ARP entries for the network interface specified by if_addr.
-d	Deletes the host specified by inet_addr.
-s	Adds a static mapping for the host and associates the Internet address inet_addr with the physical address eth_addr. The physical address is given as six hexadecimal bytes separated by hyphens. The entry remains until the system is restarted.
eth_addr	Specifies a physical address.
if_addr	If present, specifies the Internet address of the local interface whose address translation table should be modified. If not present, the first applicable interface is used.

IPCONFIG

Another utility, IPCONFIG, can be used to verify that an address has been obtained from the DHCP server along with the current configuration of the computer. IPCONFIG should also be used to verify the parameters, which will be used by the system whenever it attempts to communicate over TCP/IP. Remember that a parameter entered locally will override the one from the DHCP server.

This is the structure of the IPCONFIG command (followed by an explanation of its options):

```
ipconfig [/all ¦ /renew [adapter] ¦ /release [adapter]]
```

Switch	*Description*
/all	Provides the full details on the configuration for the system. This will often fill more than one screen; however, you can pipe the command with this to display the output one screen at a time, as such: IPCONFIG /ALL ¦ MORE.
/renew [*adapter*]	Renews the IP lease for a specific adapter (if one is given) in the computer. With no parameter, it will renew the lease for all adapters with the DHCP server.
/release [*adapter*]	Releases the IP lease that was granted by the DHCP server. This should be done before powering down a system that will move to a different subnet.

Displaying Information

To display concise TCP/IP information about the local host, type **ipconfig** at a command prompt. This entry displays the IP address, subnet mask, and default gateway for each network interface card on the local host that uses TCP/IP.

The following is an example of output displayed after IPCONFIG is typed from a command prompt:

```
C:\>ipconfig

Windows NT IP Configuration
Ethernet adapter NDISLoop1:
IP Address. . . . . . . . . : 200.20.1.30
Subnet Mask . . . . . . . . : 255.255.255.0
Default Gateway . . . . . . : 200.20.1.1
```

For more detailed information, you can run the IPCONFIG /all command from a command prompt. This will list the following bits of information for each network interface card on the local host that is bound to TCP/IP:

◆ The domain name service (DNS) hostname appended to the DNS domain name, if one is configured

◆ The IP address of any configured DNS servers

◆ The NetBIOS name resolution node type, such as broadcast (b-node), hybrid (h-node), peer-to-peer (p-node), or mixed (m-node)

◆ The NetBIOS scope ID

◆ Whether IP routing is enabled between two network interface cards (if on a multihomed computer)

◆ Whether this host acts as a WINS proxy agent for non-WINS clients

◆ Whether NetBT on this host uses DNS for NetBIOS name resolution

Also, IPCONFIG /all displays the following information about each network interface card bound to TCP/IP on the host:

◆ A description of the type or model

◆ The hardware or physical address

◆ Whether DHCP is enabled for automatic IP address configuration

◆ IP address

◆ Subnet mask

◆ Default gateway

◆ The IP address for the primary WINS server, if configured

◆ The IP address for the secondary WINS server, if configured

The following example shows output after you type IPCONFIG /all at a command prompt:

```
C:\>ipconfig/all

Windows NT IP Configuration
Host Name . . . . . . . . . : binky.gopherit.com
DNS servers . . . . . . . . : 200.20.16.122
```

```
Node Type . . . . . . . . . : Hybrid
NetBIOS Scope ID. . . . . . :
IP Routing Enabled. . . . . : No
WINS Proxy Enabled. . . . . : No
NetBIOS Resolution Uses DNS : Yes
Ethernet adapter NDISLoop1:
Description . . . . . . . . : MS LoopBack Driver
Physical Address. . . . . . : 20-4C-4F-4F-50-20
DHCP Enabled. . . . . . . . : No
IP Address. . . . . . . . . : 200.20.1.30
Subnet Mask . . . . . . . . : 255.255.255.0
Default Gateway . . . . . . : 200.20.1.1
Primary WINS server . . . . : 16.255.1.50
```

If you configure the TCP/IP address and other TCP/IP parameters manually, you can always verify the configuration through the Network Properties dialog box. However, if the client receives an address from a DHCP server, the only information available in the Network Properties dialog box states that the client is receiving its address from DHCP. Because the configuration information for a DHCP client is received dynamically, you must use a utility that can read the current configuration to verify the settings.

The command-line utility IPCONFIG can be used to determine how the local host is configured—whether the parameters come from manual configuration or from a DHCP server.

> **NOTE**
> A graphical version of IPCONFIG, called WINIPCFG.EXE, is included with Windows 95.

Using IPCONFIG to Resolve DHCP Address Problems

IPCONFIG can be used to resolve the problem that occurs when a DHCP client gets an IP that is not configured correctly, or if it doesn't get an IP address at all. If the client receives incorrect IP parameters, it should be apparent from the results of IPCONFIG /all. You should be able to see that some of the parameters don't match the IP address or that some parameters are completely blank. For example, you could have the wrong default gateway, or the client might not be configured to be a WINS client.

When a DHCP client fails to receive an address, the results of IPCONFIG /all are different. In this case, the client has an IP address of 0.0.0.0 (an invalid address) and the DHCP server is 255.255.255.255 (a broadcast address).

To fix this problem, you can release the incorrect address with IPCONFIG /release and then try to obtain a new IP address with IPCONFIG /renew. The IPCONFIG /renew command sends out a new request for a DHCP address. If a DHCP server is available, the server responds with the lease of an IP address.

NETWORK DRIVER INTERFACE SPECIFICATION (NDIS)

In addition to the four layers of the TCP/IP networking model, the boundary layers that connect the Internet layer to the Network Access layer and the sockets interface can also cause problems in communications.

The NDIS layer is primarily responsible for creating the logical connection between the protocols and the network adapters that are in your system. After these bindings are set, you should not have to worry about them. However, there are occasions where something (or someone) has changed these settings.

You can determine if the bindings are incorrect using the Packet Internet Groper (PING). If you can PING the loopback adapter (127.0.0.1) but cannot PING your IP address, there is a binding problem. If you discover a binding problem, you should use the Bindings tab in the Network dialog box to correct it.

> **NOTE**
>
> **DHCP Client Addresses** In many cases, the DHCP client will acquire the same address after releasing and renewing. This indicates the same DHCP server responded to the renewal request and gave out the address that had just been returned to the pool of available addresses. If you need to renew an address because the parameters of the scope are incorrect, you must fix the parameters on the DHCP server before releasing and renewing the address. Otherwise, the client could receive the same address again with the same incorrect parameters.

PING

The PING utility is one of the key utilities for diagnosing TCP/IP problems. PING sends a packet of data to a remote system (or your own system) and requests the data be echoed back to you. The command line and parameters are given here, with its options explained in the table:

```
ping [-t] [-a] [-n count] [-l size] [-f] [-i TTL] [-v TOS]
➥[-r count] [-s count]
        [[-j host-list] ¦ [-k host-list]] [-w timeout]
        ➥destination-list
```

Option	*Purpose*
-t	Tells PING to continue "pinging" until the user interrupts it. This is useful if you suspect cable problems, because you will be able to jiggle the wires without having to keep typing the command.
-a	Tells PING to resolve and display the address to a computer name.
-n *count*	The number of echo requests that the command should send. As you have seen, the default is four.
-l *length*	Increases the size of the echo packet that is sent. By default, PING sends 32 bytes of data (there is an error in the documentation about PING).
-f	Sets the "do not fragment" control bit in the IP header, allowing you to determine the maximum size of the packet that can be sent to a remote host. This information can be used to optimize TCP/IP.
-i *ttl*	Sets the time-to-live in the IP header, allowing you to control how long the packet stays on the wire. This can be used to see if your packets are occasionally being sent through alternative routes that are causing them to time out.
-v *tos*	Allows you to set the "type of service" field in the IP header. This can be used to figure out what types of services are available on remote routers and hosts.
-r *count*	Records the route that the packet took in the record route field. This can record from one to nine computers, as specified by the value given as "count."
-s *count*	Tells the system to keep the timestamp information for the number of hops given.

Option	Purpose
-j *computer-list*	The systems (routers) that you want to send the packet through. This will let you set the route that the packet will take; the maximum number you can enter is nine. The systems that are listed do not have to be joined directly to each other (there can be other hops in between).
-k *computer-list*	Similar to the -j option; however, there cannot be other hops between the computers that are listed with this switch.
-w *timeout*	Specifies the period PING will wait for the reply before deciding that the host is not responding.
destination-list	Tells PING which computers to send echo requests to.

The Bindings Tab

The Bindings tab of the Network dialog box allows you to view and set the bindings. In most cases you should not need to change the settings on this tab; however, this is a way you can optimize your system. You can do this by changing the order of the bindings—that is, which protocols are bound to which cards.

To view or change the binding order, you can follow these steps.

STEP BY STEP

15.1 Viewing or Changing the Binding Order

1. Open the Network dialog box and choose the Bindings tab (see Figure 15.1).

2. Choose the elements you want to see bindings for. The choices are all services, all protocols, or all adapters.

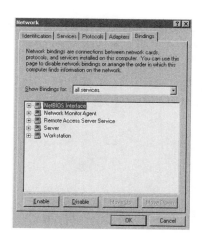

FIGURE 15.1

The Bindings tab of the Network dialog box allows you to view or change bindings.

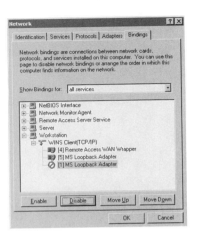

FIGURE 15.2

Here the bindings are expanded. You can see that the binding to the second network card has been disabled from the Workstation service.

3. Expand the services and check that a path to the network adapter exists from the service you are trying to use, and that all parts of the path are enabled (see Figure 15.2). If something is disabled, click on the item and then the Enable button.

4. When you are sure all the bindings are enabled, click OK; then you will need to restart your computer.

The Internet Layer

As you should recall, the Internet layer is responsible for the routing of packets. This is where you will need to carefully check the IP address, subnet mask, and default gateway. In addition to the configuration, there may be problems with the routing table or with a router somewhere between your system and the system you are attempting to communicate with.

TCP/IP Configuration Parameters

Three main parameters specify how TCP/IP is configured: the IP address, the subnet mask, and the default gateway, which is the address of the router. These parameters are configured through the Protocols tab of the Network dialog box. Although it is possible to receive an IP address from a DHCP server, for the moment this discussion focuses on parameters that are manually configured.

The three TCP/IP parameters must be configured correctly or else you cannot connect with TCP/IP. An incorrect configuration can result from typographical errors; if you type the wrong IP address, subnet mask, or default gateway, you may not connect properly or connect at all.

Whether the TCP/IP configuration parameters are wrong due to a typo or due to a mistaken number, the incorrect parameters affect communications. Different types of problems occur when the different parameters have a configuration error. Identifying and fixing the errors are covered in the following sections.

IP Address Configuration Problems

Diagnose and resolve IP addressing problems.

An incorrect TCP/IP address might not cause any problems. If you configure an IP address that is on the correct subnet and is not a duplicate, but it uses the wrong host ID, the client may be able to communicate just fine. If, however, the correct IP address has been entered in a static file or database that resolves hostnames to IP addresses, such as an LMHOSTS file or a DNS database file, there are going to be some communication problems. Typically, therefore, an incorrect IP address causes some problems.

Incorrect configuration of the TCP/IP parameters can cause different symptoms for each type of parameter. The following sections examine the effects that each TCP/IP parameter can have on IP communications.

IP Address

A TCP/IP address has two or possibly three components that uniquely identify the computer the address is assigned to. At the very least, the IP address specifies the network address and host address of the computer. Also, if you are subnetting, the third part of the address specifies the subnet address of the host.

Figure 15.3 shows the effect of an incorrect network address. In this example, the TCP/IP address assigned to a client is typed incorrectly. The address assigned to the client is 143.168.3.9, whereas the correct address was supposed to be 133.168.3.9. The network ID for the incorrect address is 143.168.x.x, whereas the network ID for the correct address should be 133.168.x.x.

With this incorrect address (143.168.3.9), the client is not able to communicate with any other TCP/IP hosts. Because the network address is incorrect, any packets this client sends will be routed to the wrong location.

If the incorrect host (143.168.3.9) sends a message to a local client (133.168.3.20), the TCP/IP configuration of the sending host indicates this is a remote address because it doesn't match the network address of the host initiating the communication. The packet won't ever reach the local client because the address 133.168.3.20 is interpreted as a remote address.

FIGURE 15.3
An example of the effect of an incorrect IP address.

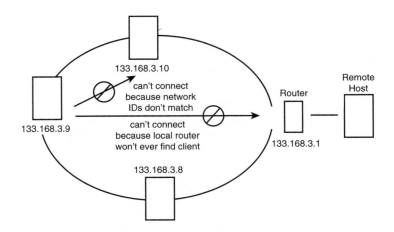

If a local client (133.168.3.6) sends a message to the incorrect host (143.168.3.9), the message never reaches its intended destination. The message is either routed (if the local client sends the message to the IP address as written) or it stays on the local subnet (if the local client sends it to what should have been the address, 133.168.3.9). If the message is routed, the incorrect client does not receive the message because it is on the same segment of the network as the local client. If the message is not routed, the message still does not reach the incorrect client because the IP address for the destination host (133.168.3.9) does not match the address as configured on the incorrect client (143.168.3.9).

Figure 15.4 gives another example of an incorrect IP address. In this case, a class A address is used (33.x.x.x). The subnet mask (255.255.0.0) indicates the second octet is also being used to create subnets. In this case, even though the client has the same network address as the other clients on the same subnet, the client has a different subnet number because the address was typed incorrectly.

This time the incorrect address specifies the wrong subnet ID. The client 33.5.8.4 is on subnet 5 while the other clients on the subnet have the address 33.4.x.x. In this case, if the client 33.5.8.4. tries to contact other clients on the same subnet, the message is routed because the subnet ID doesn't match the subnet number of the source host. If the client 33.5.8.4 tries to send a message to a remote host, the message is routed; however, the message isn't returned to the client because the router doesn't handle subnet 5—it only handles subnet 4.

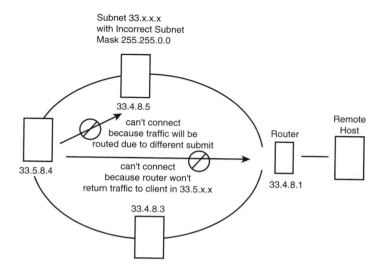

FIGURE 15.4
An example of the IP address returning an incorrect subnet ID.

If a local client tries to send a message to 33.5.8.4, the message doesn't reach the client. If the local client uses the address as configured, the message is routed, which isn't the correct solution because the intended destination host is local. If the local client sends the message to what should have been the IP address, 33.5.8.4 doesn't receive the message because the IP address isn't configured correctly.

The last component of an IP address that can cause communication problems is the host address. An incorrect host address may not always cause a problem, however. In Figure 15.5, a local client has the wrong IP address, but only the host address portion of the address is wrong. The network address and subnet match the rest of the clients on the subnet.

In this case, if a client sends a message to the client with the incorrect address, the message still reaches the client. However, if someone tries to contact the client with what should have been the address, he cannot. In fact, he could contact another host that ended up with the address that was supposed to have been given to the original host.

If the original host ends up with the same IP address as another host through the configuration error, the first client to start up works, but the second client to start up may note the address conflict and not load the TCP/IP stack at all. In this case, the second client to start up isn't able to make any TCP/IP communications.

FIGURE 15.5

An example of the effect of an incorrect IP address giving the wrong host ID.

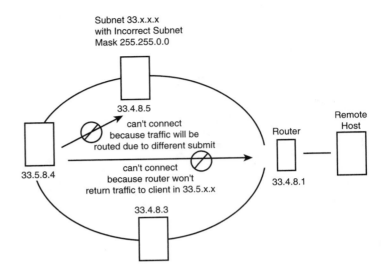

Another problem arises when the correct address is registered in static files, such as an LMHOSTS file or a DNS database. In this case, no one can communicate with this client by name because the name resolution for this host always returns the correct address, which can't be used to contact the host because the address has been typed incorrectly.

Basically, the problems you encounter with an incorrect host address are intermittent. However, if the host was configured to be a WINS client, the hostname is registered along with the incorrect address. Another WINS client trying to connect with this computer receives an accurate mapping for the hostname.

Subnet Mask

The subnet mask indicates which portions of the IP address specify the network address and the host address. Also, the subnet mask can be used to divide part of what would have been the host address into subnets. If the subnet mask is not configured correctly, your clients may not be able to communicate at all, or you may see partial communication problems.

Figure 15.6 shows a subnet on a TCP/IP network that uses a class B network address of 138.13.x.x. However, the third octet is used in this case for subnetting, so all the clients in the figure should be on subnet 4, as indicated by the common addresses 138.13.4.x.

Unfortunately, the subnet mask entered for one client is 255.255.0.0. When this client tries to communicate with other hosts on the same subnet, it should be able to contact them because the subnet mask indicates they are on the same subnet, which is correct. However, if the client tries to contact a host on another subnet, such as 138.13.3.x, the client fails.

In this case, the subnet mask still interprets the destination host to be on the same subnet, and the message is never routed. Because the destination host is on another subnet, the message never reaches the intended destination. The subnet mask is used to determine routing for outgoing communications, so the client with the incorrect subnet mask can receive incoming messages. However, when the client tries to return communications, the message isn't routed if the source host is on the same network but on a different subnet.

So, in actuality, the client really can establish communications with only one side of the conversation. Contacts with hosts outside the local network still work because they are routed.

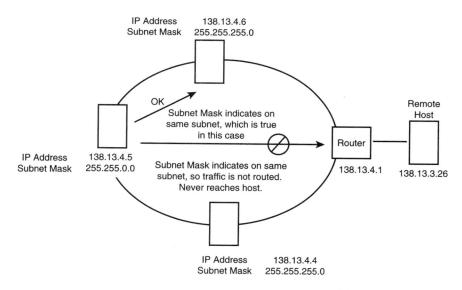

FIGURE 15.6

Even if the IP address is right, the wrong subnet ID can be used because of the subnet mask.

Figure 15.7 shows a subnet mask that masks too many bits. In this case, the subnet mask is 255.255.255.0. However, the network designers had intended the subnet mask to be 255.255.240.0, with four bits of the third octet used for the subnet and four bits as part of the host address.

If the incorrectly configured client tries to send a message to a local host and the third octet is the same, the message is not routed and, thus, reaches the local client. However, if the local client has an address that differs in the last four bits of the third octet, the message is routed and never reaches its destination. If the incorrectly configured client tries to send a message to another client on another subnet, the message is routed because the third octet is different.

Problems with the subnet mask also lead to intermittent connections: sometimes the connection works, sometimes it doesn't. The problems show up when the IP address of the destination host causes a packet to be routed when it shouldn't, or to remain local when it should be routed.

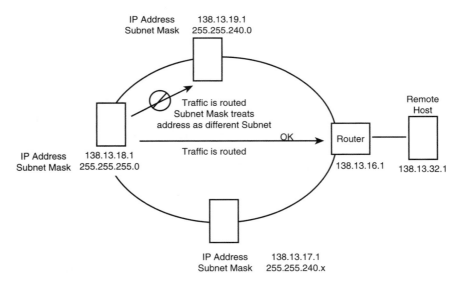

FIGURE 15.7
Communication problems will occur if the subnet mask uses too many bits.

Default Gateway

The default gateway address is the address of the router—the gateway to the world beyond the local subnet. If a client's default gateway address is wrong, it can contact local hosts but is not able to communicate at all beyond the local subnet. It is possible for the incorrect client to receive a message because the default gateway is used only to send packets to other hosts. However, as soon as the incorrect client attempts to respond to the incoming message, the default gateway address doesn't work and the message doesn't reach the host that sent the original message.

DHCP Client Configuration Problems

All the TCP/IP parameters mentioned previously can cause communication problems if they are not configured correctly. Using a DHCP server can greatly reduce these configuration problems. If the DHCP scope is set up properly, without any typos or other errors, DHCP clients shouldn't have any configuration problems. It is impossible to completely eliminate human error, but using DHCP should reduce the points of potential errors to just the DHCP servers rather than every client on the network.

Even when there are no configuration problems with DHCP addresses, DHCP clients can get a duplicate IP address from a DHCP server. If you have multiple DHCP servers in your environment, you should have scopes on each DHCP server for different subnets. Usually, you have scopes with a larger number of addresses for the local subnet where the DHCP server is located, and smaller scopes for other subnets.

Creating multiple scopes on one server provides backup for giving clients IP addresses. If the server on the local subnet is busy or down, the client can still receive an address from a remote DHCP server. When the router forwards this DCHP request to another subnet, it includes the address of the subnet it came from; this occurs so that the remote DHCP server knows from which scope of addresses to lease an address to the remote client.

Using this type of redundancy, however, can cause problems if you don't configure the scopes on all the DHCP servers correctly. The most important part of the configuration is to make sure you don't have duplicate addresses in the different scopes. On one server, for example, you could have a scope in the range 131.107.2.100 to 131.107.2.170. On the remote DHCP server, you could have a scope of 131.107.2.171 to 131.107.2.200. By setting up the scopes without overlap, you should not have any problems with clients receiving duplicate IP addresses. DHCP servers do not communicate with each other, so one server does not know anything about the addresses the other server has leased. Therefore, you must ensure that the servers never give out duplicate information; make sure the scopes for one subnet on all the different DHCP servers have unique IP addresses.

Another common problem with multiple scopes on one server can occur when the configuration parameters are entered incorrectly. For example, if you enter the default gateway as 131.107.3.1 (instead of 131.107.2.1) for the scope 131.107.2.100 to 131.107.2.170, the clients receiving these addresses will not be able to communicate beyond the local subnet because they have the wrong router address.

With one scope on a DCHP server, you are usually quite sure of what all the configuration parameters should be. With multiple scopes on one server, however, it is easy to get confused about which scope you are editing and what the parameters should be for that scope. To avoid this type of problem, check each scope's parameters very carefully to make sure the parameters match the address of the scope, and not the subnet where the DHCP server is located.

Also, if the client doesn't receive an address because the server is down or doesn't respond in a timely manner, the client is not able to contact anyone. Without an IP address, the IP stack does not initialize and the client can't communicate at all with TCP/IP.

Symptoms of TCP/IP Configuration Problems

The following sections are included to give you an overview of the common TCP/IP configuration problems and their symptoms. These are not all the possible problems; however, they are the common errors that you might see in the workplace.

Default Gateway Does Not Belong to Configured Interfaces

When you configure TCP/IP manually, you can receive the message The Default Gateway does not belong to configured interfaces. This message occurs when the address of the default gateway cannot logically belong to the same subnet as the host IP address. This can happen if the subnet mask, default gateway address, or local host address is wrong.

The TCP/IP Host Doesn't Respond

If a connection to a remote TCP/IP host is hung, you can check the status of the connection with the NETSTAT -a command. This command shows all the connections established with TCP. Successful connections should have 0 bytes in the send and receive queues. If there are bytes in the queues, there are problems with the connection. If the connection appears to be hung, but if there aren't any bytes in the queues, there is probably a delay in the connection.

The Connection Is Made to the Wrong Host

You could check everything in the IP configuration on the host and the client, yet still the client connects to the wrong host. (This can happen when you establish a session using an IP address rather than a hostname, such as when using Telnet.) This symptom can occur when duplicate IP addresses are on the network.

To fix this, you have to find the computer with the duplicate address and modify the address so it is unique. With duplicate addresses, connections are inconsistent: Clients sometimes connect to one host, sometimes to another.

Error 53 Is Returned When Trying to Establish a NetBIOS Session

Sometimes Error 53 is returned when you are trying to establish a NetBIOS session, such as mapping a drive using the NETUSE command. This happens because the computer name cannot be found on the network. In other words, TCP/IP can't find a computer name to resolve to an IP address.

You can use the normal NetBIOS host resolution troubleshooting to resolve this problem. If the hostnames are correct, it's possible you are using NetBIOS scopes. If NetBIOS scopes are configured (not blank), only hosts with the same scope ID can communicate with each other.

An FTP Server Does Not Seem to Work

FTP must be installed correctly before any clients can make connections to the server. Just as you can PING the loopback address to test a TCP/IP installation, you can also FTP the loopback address on the FTP server to test the FTP installation.

Tools to Troubleshoot the Internet Layer

There are several tools that you can use to troubleshoot problems at the Internet layer. You have already seen PING, but there are also ROUTE and TRACERT, which allow you to verify communications specific to this layer. The next few sections look at all these tools and how you can use them.

Using PING to Test Connectivity

PING is a command-line tool included with every Microsoft TCP/IP client (any DOS or Windows client with the TCP/IP protocol installed). You can use PING to send a test packet to the specified address; then, if things are working properly, the packet is returned.

As you have seen, PING is a simple tool to use: from the command prompt simply type **PING** with the IP address or hostname you want to PING. Choosing what to PING is the key to successful troubleshooting. You have already looked at using PING with the loopback address and your local address. The next sections look at using PING specifically at the Internet layer.

PINGing Local Hosts

If you are able to PING the loopback address (127.0.0.1) and your own address, you can be fairly certain that TCP/IP is set up correctly on your system. You should next try PINGing other hosts on your local network; this will ensure that your subnet mask is also correct. Make sure you PING more than one address—because it is possible the one address you choose make not be active.

If the subnet mask is wrong, you may be able to PING only some of the hosts that you normally would be able to. This will happen if too many bits are used in the subnet mask.

PINGing the Default Gateway

If you can communicate with hosts on the same subnet but not with hosts beyond the subnet, the problem may be with the router or the way its address is configured. To communicate beyond the subnet, a router must be enabled with an address that matches the subnet address for the clients on the local subnet. The router also has other ports configured with different addresses so that it can send packets out to the network at large. PINGing the default gateway address tests the address you have configured for the router and the router itself.

If the default gateway PING fails, there are several possible sources for the error:

◆ **The router has failed or is down.** In this case you cannot make connections outside the subnet until the router is brought up again. However, you should be able to communicate with hosts on the same subnet.

◆ **The IP address on the router is configured incorrectly.** The router address must match the client's default gateway address so that packets can move outside the subnet.

◆ **The client has the wrong router address.** Of course, if you PING the correct router address and it works, you also want to make sure the default gateway address configured on the client matches the address you successfully PINGed.

◆ **The wrong subnet mask is configured.** If the subnet mask is wrong, packets destined for a remote subnet may not be routed.

You should also PING each of the IP addresses used by the different ports on your router. It's possible that the local interface for your subnet is working but other interfaces on the router, which actually connect the router to the other subnets on the network, have some type of problem.

EXAM TIP

Microsoft's Recommendations for Using PING In reviewing for the exam, you should be aware of Microsoft's recommended steps for using PING:

1. Check that there is an IP address using IPCONFIG.

2. PING the loopback adapter; this ensures that the protocol is installed and functioning.

3. PING a local machine's address; this ensures that the protocol is bound correctly to the network card.

4. PING some local hosts; this checks that you have network connectivity and that your subnet mask is not too restrictive.

5. PING some remote hosts; this ensures that you are able to connect to the router and that your subnet mask is not too loose.

6. Repeat steps 2 through 5 using a hostname.

PINGing a Remote Host

As a final test, you can PING the IP address of a remote host, a computer on another subnet, or even the IP address of a Web server or FTP server on the Internet. If you can successfully PING a remote host, your problem doesn't lie with the IP configuration; you are probably having trouble resolving hostnames.

If PINGing the remote host does fail, your problems may be with the router, subnet mask, or local IP configuration. However, if you have followed the earlier steps for PINGing the loopback, local host address, other local systems, and the default gateway address, you have already eliminated many of the problems that could cause this PING to fail.

When a remote host PING fails after you have tried the other PING options, the failure may be caused by other routers beyond the default gateway used for your subnet. If you know the physical layout of your network, you can PING other router addresses along the path to the remote host to see where the trouble lies. Remember to PING the addresses on both sides of the router—both the address that receives the packet and the address that forwards the packet. You can also use the ROUTE command, as described in the following section, to find the path used to contact the remote host.

It is also possible that there is not a physical path to the remote host due to a router crash, a disruption in the physical network, or a crash on the remote host.

ROUTE

In Chapter 6, "IP Routing," you saw the ROUTE command and how it is used to view and modify the routing table. If you are having problems communicating with a selected group of remote hosts, you should check your local routing table to verify that there is not an incorrect route to the remote network.

TRACERT

If all seems to be OK with the local routing table, the problem may be with a remote router. Using the trace routing (TRACERT) utility you will be able to determine the path that your packets must take to the remote host.

To use this command, enter **TRACERT** *hostname*, where "hostname" is the computer name or IP address of the computer whose route you want to trace. TRACERT will return the different IP addresses the packet was routed through to reach the final destination. The results will also include the number of hops needed to reach the destination. Execute TRACERT without any options to see a help file that describes all the TRACERT switches.

Several options are available when you use TRACERT. The full command line is shown here, followed by descriptions of its options:

```
tracert [-d] [-h maximum_hops] [-j host-list] [-w timeout]
➥target_name
```

Switch	Description
-d	Tells TRACERT not to resolve the host names for the routers
-h *maximum_hops*	Tells TRACERT the maximum number of hops to be traced to the destination
-j *computer-list*	Tells TRACERT to use this list of computers as the route to the destination host
-w *timeout*	The timeout value for each reply that TRACERT will wait for, entered in milliseconds
target_name	The name or IP address of the system you wish to reach

The following example shows the output from TRACERT for a simple trace.

```
C:\>tracert www.mcp.com

Tracing route to www.mcp.com [204.95.236.226]
over a maximum of 30 hops:

  1    70 ms    70 ms    70 ms  tnt01.magma.ca [204.191.36.88]
  2    60 ms    70 ms    70 ms  core1-vlan5.magma.ca [206.191.0.129]
  3    70 ms    91 ms    90 ms  border2-e3.magma.ca [206.191.0.9]
  4   180 ms   131 ms   180 ms  205.150.227.1
  5   140 ms   141 ms   270 ms  a10-0-0.102.bb1.ott1.a10-0-0.102.bb1.tor2.uunet.ca [205.150.242.89]
  6   191 ms   140 ms   110 ms  224.ATM5-0-0.CR1.CLE1.Alter.Net [137.39.75.17]
  7   141 ms   180 ms   160 ms  119.Hssi6-0.CR1.CHI1.Alter.Net [137.39.31.94]
  8   161 ms   160 ms   290 ms  102.ATM3-0.XR2.CHI4.ALTER.NET [146.188.208.30]
  9   190 ms   160 ms   150 ms  194.ATM9-0-0.GW1.CHI1.ALTER.NET [146.188.208.157]
 10   200 ms   191 ms   160 ms  napnet-gw.customer.ALTER.NET [137.39.130.174]
```

```
11    110 ms    151 ms    120 ms    NChicago1-core0.nap.net [207.112.247.153]
12    110 ms    120 ms    140 ms    chi-f0.iquest.net [206.54.225.250]
13    200 ms    140 ms    121 ms    204.180.50.9
14    190 ms    190 ms    161 ms    iq-ss6-226.superlibrary.com [204.95.236.226]
```

Trace complete.

NOTE

Routers and Internet Performance
Notice the names of the routers that are shown in the example TRACERT output. If you look closely, you will see that the path goes through several different providers: magma, uunet, alternet, napnet, and finally iquest. This means the packet must flow through a router that connects each of these providers. All this traffic means the router is often congested—causing a large portion of the slowdown that can occur when using the Internet.

TRANSPORT LAYER

There is little that you need to worry about at the Transport layer. If you can PING, your transport layer should be functioning properly. The only problem that you will normally have at this layer concerns the TCPWindowSize discussed in Chapter 14, "Monitoring and Optimizing TCP/IP."

This problem will typically result in slow communications speed (similar to the 110-baud terminals used in the 1970s and '80s). However, if you have verified everything up to this point, a quick way to check TCPWindowSize is to open the Registry and see if a Window Size entry exists. If you see an entry, make a note of the setting and then delete the value. This will reset the window size to its default.

SOCKETS PROBLEMS

Assuming that you have the correct IP address and protocol, and that you are able to find a route to the remote computer, it will need to be running the service you are looking for on the correct socket. If you are providing services to the network or trying to connect to a service on the network, you need to know which port number to use.

The common port (socket) numbers are assigned by the Internet Assigned Numbers Authority (IANA); however, in some cases the service might use a different port. There is a file (described in the following section) that you will want to check to verify that the correct port is in use. After you verify this, you can use the NETSTAT command to verify that the port is ready to receive data.

The Services File

Located in the system32\drivers\etc directory is a services file, which is used by most of the services that initialize the socket numbers they use when they initialize. The following is a small portion of a services file:

```
# Copyright  1993-1995 Microsoft Corp.
#
# This file contains port numbers for well-known services as defined by
# RFC 1060 (Assigned Numbers).
#
# Format:
#
# <service name>   <port number>/<protocol>   [aliases...]    [#<comment>]
#

echo              7/tcp
echo              7/udp
discard           9/tcp     sink null
discard           9/udp     sink null
systat            11/tcp
systat            11/tcp    users
daytime           13/tcp
daytime           13/udp
netstat           15/tcp
qotd              17/tcp    quote
qotd              17/udp    quote
chargen           19/tcp    ttytst source
chargen           19/udp    ttytst source
ftp-data          20/tcp
ftp               21/tcp
telnet            23/tcp
smtp              25/tcp    mail
time              37/tcp    timserver
time              37/udp    timserver
rlp               39/udp    resource       # resource location
name              42/tcp    nameserver
name              42/udp    nameserver
whois             43/tcp    nicname        # usually to sri-nic
domain            53/tcp    nameserver     # name-domain server
domain            53/udp    nameserver
nameserver        53/tcp    domain         # name-domain server
nameserver        53/udp    domain
mtp               57/tcp                    # deprecated
bootp             67/udp                    # boot program server
tftp              69/udp
```

If you are having problems with particular services, you should check this file if they are listed to make sure the correct port is used. If a service is not listed, you may need to add it so that the system knows which port to initialize the service on. (This is a normal text file that can be viewed and edited using either Edit or Notepad.)

NETSTAT

As you saw in Chapter 14, NETSTAT can be used to view the connections to your system. Using NETSTAT -a will also include ports that are not currently active but are listening (that is, listening or server side ports). The following shows the output of NETSTAT -a:

```
Active Connections

  Proto   Local Address          Foreign Address        State
  TCP     godzilla:1026          0.0.0.0:0              LISTENING
  TCP     godzilla:135           0.0.0.0:0              LISTENING
  TCP     godzilla:135           0.0.0.0:0              LISTENING
  TCP     godzilla:1025          0.0.0.0:0              LISTENING
  TCP     godzilla:1025          LOCALHOST:1026         ESTABLISHED
  TCP     godzilla:1026          LOCALHOST:1025         ESTABLISHED
  TCP     godzilla:137           0.0.0.0:0              LISTENING
  TCP     godzilla:138           0.0.0.0:0              LISTENING
  TCP     godzilla:nbsession     0.0.0.0:0              LISTENING
  UDP     godzilla:135           *:*
  UDP     godzilla:nbname        *:*
  UDP     godzilla:nbdatagram    *:*
```

You can use this information to verify that the expected port is open and waiting for a connection, and to see the connection process. In this example, several ports are listening for connections (0.0.0.0) or broadcasts (*.*).

Testing Sockets by Establishing a Session

To test connectivity at this level, try establishing an FTP or Telnet session, or try to connect to a Web server. All of these will use the sockets interface directly and are a good test to determine if the sockets are working.

APPLICATION LAYER

Finally you come to the application layer, where you will want to verify communications. There are two main problems you may encounter at this layer: NetBIOS problems and name resolution problems. By far the most common problem will be name resolution problems, which affect both socket applications and NetBIOS applications. In the next few sections, these name resolution problems will be reviewed.

Name Resolution Problems

Diagnose and resolve name resolution problems.

If you have configured TCP/IP correctly and the protocol is installed and working, the problem with connectivity is probably due to errors in resolving hostnames. When you test connectivity with TCP/IP addresses, you are testing a lower level of connectivity than users generally use.

When users want to connect to a network resource—to map a drive to a server or connect to a Web site, for example—they usually refer to that server or Web site by its name rather than its TCP/IP address. In fact, users do not usually know the IP address of a particular server. The name used to establish a connection, however, must be resolved down to an IP address so that the networking software can make a connection.

After you've tested the IP connectivity, the next logical step is to check the resolution of a name down to its IP address. If a name cannot be resolved to its IP address, or if it is resolved to the wrong address, users will not be able to connect to the network resource with that name, even if they can connect to it using an IP address.

As you know, two types of computer names are used when communicating on the network: a NetBIOS name is assigned to a NetBIOS computer, such as a Windows NT server or a Windows 95 system; and a hostname is assigned to non-NetBIOS computers, such as a UNIX servers. In general, when using Microsoft networking to connect to a server for file sharing, print sharing, or applications, for example, you refer to that computer by its NetBIOS name. But when you execute a TCP/IP-specific command as you do when using FTP or a Web browser, you refer to that computer by its hostname.

As you saw in Chapter 8, "Name Resolution," there are several ways in which a NetBIOS name can be resolved to an IP address. You also saw that the methods used for NetBIOS-name resolution are the same as those used for hostname resolution. The following sections will review these methods and the problems that you might encounter with each.

NetBIOS Name Cache

The only name resolution method specific to NetBIOS, a name cache will contain entries for the names that you have already resolved or for items preloaded to it. To view the names in the NetBIOS name cache, use NBTSTAT -c. This will list all the names and their status.

Normally, there won't be a problem in this area unless you are preloading an entry with the wrong address. If this is the case you will need to correct the entry in the LMHOSTS file and then use NBTSTAT -R to purge and reload the name cache.

You can use the information in the name cache, however, to identify which names are being resolved to which addresses. This can tell you whether the other methods of name resolution are working correctly.

NetBIOS Name Server

In the case of Windows NT you will almost always be using a Windows Internet Name Service (WINS) to act as a NetBIOS Name Server (NBNS). An NBNS is a computer that all clients will register their names and IP addresses with so that you can simply query it for the address.

The NBNS configuration for a client is very simple: all it needs is the address of the WINS server. Check this first using IPCONFIG /all. Assuming the WINS server is listed, you should attempt to PING the address to ensure that the system can connect with it and to verify that the system is in fact running WINS.

The other problems that you will run into with a WINS server deal with the server itself. Typically, if you can see the system and the service is running, you should be able to resolve addresses.

One problem with a WINS server might be that it doesn't have an address for the requested name (check this using the WINS Manager). This can be caused by three possible problems: the database is corrupted (try stopping and starting the service); the other system did not or could not register its name with the WINS server; or the WINS server has not replicated the address for its replication partner (verify the partner is alive, and then force replication).

Local Broadcast

The major problem with a local broadcast is that it is local; this means that the server you are attempting to connect to must be on the same subnet. If it is not, the broadcast will not be able to return an IP address.

LMHOSTS and HOSTS

If a system is resorting to the LMHOSTS and HOSTS files to look up a NetBIOS name, you definitely want to check your WINS configuration. These files are not read until the primary and secondary WINS servers are tried and the local broadcast fails (a 30-second duration for each WINS server and 15 seconds for the broadcast). If you are resolving hostnames, however, the HOSTS file is one of the first places the system will look.

To troubleshoot these files, they need to be located in the system32\drivers\etc directory. First, you should verify that they are not saved as unicode. Following are several other problems that you might see:

◆ **The entry is misspelled.** Examine the HOSTS or LMHOSTS file to verify that the name is correctly spelled.

◆ **Comment characters prevent the entry from being read.** Verify that a pound sign (#) is not at the beginning of the line or anywhere on the line prior to the hostname.

NOTE

Checking the WINS Server The WINS server is intended to remove the need for a local broadcast. If your name resolution is taking a long time, you might want to use the Network Monitor to see if the system is using a local broadcast. If this is the case, the WINS server is not resolving the address.

◆ **There are duplicate entries in the file.** Because the files are read in linear fashion, only the first entry is read and all others are ignored when duplication exists. Verify that all names are unique.

◆ **A host other than the one you want is contacted.** Verify that the IP address entered in the files is valid and corresponds to the hostname.

DNS Servers

The DNS server will provide resolution of a hostname to an IP address. There is very little configuration on the client that is required. You should verify that an entry is included for the DNS server using IPCONFIG /all. If you want to use the DNS server for NetBIOS names, check the WINS Address tab in the TCP/IP configuration: NetBIOS Name Resolution uses DNS should be set to Yes.

The DNS server needs to be configured with a correct cache file (which points at the root level servers). It must also be able to connect with the Internet or be configured as an IP forwarder. When resolving local host or NetBIOS names, the DNS server needs to have the name in its zone file or an entry for a WINS server that can resolve the name.

Local Hostname

This last method, specific to hostname resolution, simply checks the local hostname to see if this is the host you are trying to connect to.

Tools for Troubleshooting Name Resolution

The following sections review the tools that you can use to troubleshoot name resolution.

PING

Probably the easiest way to test name resolution is to attempt to PING the name on the network. Even if you don't get a response from the remote system, you should see the name resolved to an IP address.

HOSTNAME.EXE

The HOSTNAME.EXE utility, located in *systemroot*\System32, returns the name of the local host. This is used only to view the name; it cannot be used to change the name. You can change the hostname from the Network dialog box.

NSLOOKUP

As you saw in Chapter 7, "Microsoft Domain Name System (DNS)," you can use the name server lookup (NSLOOKUP) command to verify the resolution that you receive from the DNS server. The basic format of the command is this:

```
nslookup name_to_look_up
```

Testing NetBIOS by Establishing a Session

The final test is to create a NetBIOS session on top of TCP/IP. This will test the NetBIOS Helper service and ensure that you will be able to use NetBIOS networking.

The quickest way to test NetBIOS is to use the Network Neighborhood. If you double-click the icon and receive a list of computers, you are able to communicate.

A common problem when making NetBIOS connections is that the wrong NetBIOS name is used. Verify that the destination host has the same name that you are using to make the connection. Another potential problem with the name configuration occurs when NetBIOS scope IDs are used. Only NetBIOS hosts with the same scope ID can communicate with each other. The scope ID is configured through the advanced TCP/IP parameters.

Incorrect share permissions can also prevent you from establishing a NetBIOS session. When you try to connect a drive to a share you have no access to, you receive an Access Denied message. This indicates that you can connect to the server, but your rights do not allow you to make a connection to this specific share. This type of failure has nothing to do with TCP/IP connectivity.

NBTSTAT

In Chapter 14 you saw the NetBIOS over TCP/IP statistics (NBTSTAT) command, which can also be used to verify NetBIOS communications. If you run NBTSTAT, you can see all the connections into and out of your system.

CASE STUDY: STANDARD TROUBLESHOOTING PROCEDURES

ESSENCE OF THE CASE

As with all networks, the example that you have been looking at is not simple. There are many different parts that must be in place to ensure that the users are able to communicate. However, there are several key areas that you will need to address as you build the procedures that will be used by the first-level support:

- The network is based on TCP/IP to allow the Internet to be used as a backbone.

- There are 61 offices that are connected.

- There is an SQL server and at least one Exchange server that all users need to be able to resolve.

- The network uses a combination of a WINS server and LMHOSTS files to perform name resolution.

- A large number of laptop users will need to be able to connect to the offices.

- Dial-in systems use PPTP as the connection protocol with TCP/IP as the encapsulated protocol.

- The entire company is one Windows NT domain with the primary domain controller (PDC) in the head office.

- DHCP is used to assign addresses to the systems in all locations.

- There is no routing internally at any of the sites, only externally through the Internet.

- DNS is used to handle resolution to the main Web server and mail servers.

As this text wraps up you will look at the problems that can occur in the TCP/IP scenario particularly in your network. This will lead to a set of standard procedures that can be used front your first-level support people.

SCENARIO

By now you should be familiar with the scenario because you have been reading about it since the beginning of this text. Essentially, you have been watching the basics of a network design take shape as you have learned about TCP/IP. The scenario of this design is basically review because all of the factors are involved.

ANALYSIS

In this case you should build up a series of steps that can be used to troubleshoot the basic problems on the network. These will be used by the first-level support to handle the majority of calls. Anything beyond this will be passed to second-level support.

There is no one solution for this; however, the flow charts in Figures 15.8–12 present a common set of steps that should be involved.

continues

continued

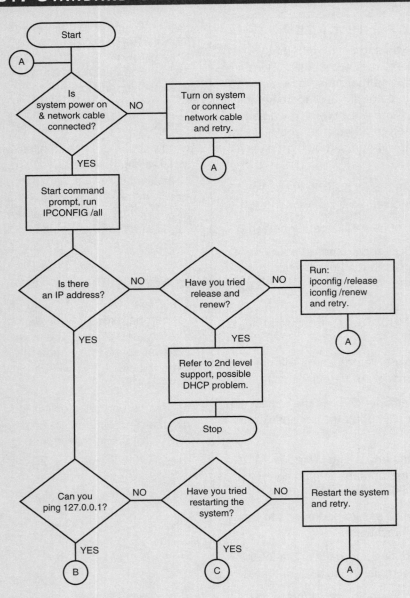

FIGURE 15.8
The first page of the troubleshooting flow chart deals the TCP/IP protocol.

CASE STUDY: STANDARD TROUBLESHOOTING PROCEDURES

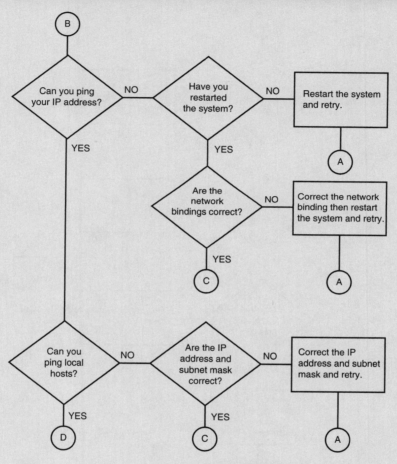

FIGURE 15.9
The second page of the troubleshooting flow chart checks the bindings and network connectivity.

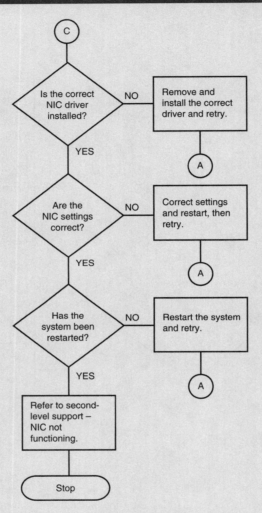

FIGURE 15.10
The third page of the troubleshooting flow chart deals with the network interface card.

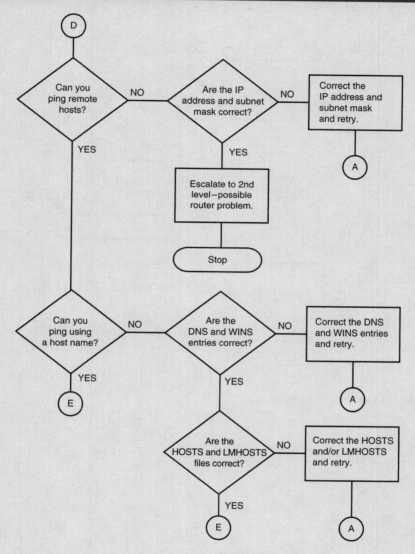

FIGURE 15.11
The fourth page of the troubleshooting flow chart checks
routing and name resolution.

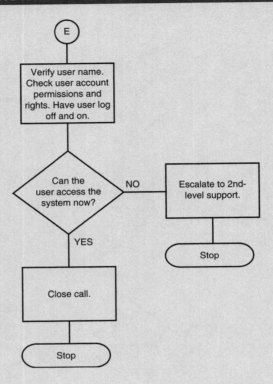

FIGURE 15.12
The last page of the troubleshooting flow chart verifies
usernames and permissions.

CHAPTER SUMMARY

There are two utilities that you should remember when you are troubleshooting the TCP/IP protocol: Performance Monitor and Network Monitor. Both of these can be used to troubleshoot the more serious problems. Generally, the quickest way to fix a problem is to isolate the component that is not working and remove and reinstall the drivers for it. This will refresh the files that are used and ensure that all links between layers are correctly rebuilt.

Some of the key points that were made in this chapter are outlined in the following list:

◆ You need to know that IPCONFIG checks that you have an address, exposes the configuration, and releases or renews DHCP leases.

◆ You should know how and in which order to use PING:

1. PING the loopback adapter; this ensures that the protocol is installed and functioning.

2. PING a local machine's address; this ensures that the protocol is bound correctly to the network card.

3. PING some local hosts; this checks that you have network connectivity and that your subnet mask is not too restrictive.

4. PING some remote hosts; this ensures that you are able to connect to the router and that your subnet mask is not too loose.

5. PING a hostname; this checks the hostname resolution.

◆ You need to know what type of resolution is in use for different connections (review Chapter 8).

◆ You need to know the parts of the TCP/IP stack and which protocols are in use for each (review Chapter 1, "Introduction to Networking with TCP/IP").

◆ You need to understand what the configuration options are and what they affect (review Chapter 2, "Installing Microsoft TCP/IP").

KEY TERMS

• address resolution protocol utility (ARP)

• bindings

• Internet Protocol Configuration (IPCONFIG)

• local hostname utility (HOSTNAME)

• name server lookup utility (NSLOOKUP)

• NetBIOS over TCP/IP statistics utility (NBTSTAT)

• Network Driver Interface Specification (NDIS)

• Packet Internet Groper (PING)

• routing table utility (ROUTE)

• SERVICES file

• trace router utility (TRACERT)

CHAPTER SUMMARY

◆ You need to know the NETSTAT and NBTSTAT utilities and what information they provide (review Chapter 14).

◆ You need to know what you can do with the Performance Monitor and the Network Monitor (review Chapter 14).

◆ You need to know about the NSLOOKUP utility (review Chapter 7).

◆ You need to understand that routing takes place at the Internet layer, and how routing can be configured and tested (review Chapter 6).

◆ You need to know how DHCP works so you can tell when it doesn't (review Chapter 4, "Dynamic Host Configuration Protocol (DHCP)").

APPLY YOUR KNOWLEDGE

This section will give you a chance to apply the knowledge that you have gained in this chapter.

Exercises

The following exercise will give you a chance to see the effect of some of the configuration errors that you have read about and the methods used to diagnose and correct them.

15.1 Correcting a Network Configuration Error

Use this exercise to see the effects that an improperly configured network card has on other networking services and protocols. Before starting, make sure you have installed Windows NT Server on a computer that has a network adapter card and TCP/IP installed.

Estimated Time: About 15 minutes.

1. Clear the System Log in Event Viewer.

2. From the desktop, right-click Network Neighborhood, and then choose Properties from the resulting menu.

3. From the Network Properties dialog box, select the Adapters tab.

4. Select your adapter card from the list and choose Properties.

5. Change the IRQ of your adapter card to an incorrect setting.

6. Close this dialog box and choose to restart your computer when prompted.

7. When your computer reboots, note the message received after the Logon prompt appears. The message should indicate A Dependency Service Failed to Start.

8. Log on and open Event Viewer.

9. Note the error message generated from the adapter card. Note the other error messages generated after the adapter card error.

10. Clear the System Log in Event Viewer.

11. From the command prompt, type **ping 127.0.0.1**. This PING fails because TCP/IP doesn't start if the adapter doesn't start.

12. From the Network Properties dialog box, change the IRQ of your adapter card back to its proper setting and restart your system.

13. Log on and check the System Log. There should be no adapter card errors or errors from networking services.

14. From the command prompt, type **ping 127.0.0.1**. This PING succeeds because TCP/IP is started now.

15.2 Using PING to Test an IP Configuration

This exercise uses PING to verify a TCP/IP installation and configuration. You should have Windows NT Server and TCP/IP installed.

Estimated Time: About 10 minutes.

1. From the desktop, right-click on Network Neighborhood, and then choose Properties from the resulting menu.

2. From the Bindings tab, expand all the networking services.

3. Select TCP/IP and choose Disable.

4. Repeat step 3 until you have disabled TCP/IP for all the listed networking services.

5. Close the dialog box and, when prompted, choose to restart your computer.

APPLY YOUR KNOWLEDGE

6. When the computer restarts, log in.

7. From a command prompt, type **ping 127.0.0.1**. This Ping works because TCP/IP is installed.

8. From a command prompt, type **ping x.x.x.x**, where x.x.x.x is your default gateway address. This PING fails because you have disabled TCP/IP for all the networking services. There isn't a way for TCP/IP packets to be sent on the network.

9. From the Bindings tab in Network Properties, enable TCP/IP for all the networking services.

10. Close the dialog box and, when prompted, choose to restart your computer.

11. When the computer restarts, log in.

12. From a command prompt, PING your default gateway. The PING works this time because a path now exists on which TCP/IP communications can reach the network.

15.3 Using ARP to Examine the ARP Cache and Add Entries

This exercise uses the ARP command to examine and modify the ARP cache.

Estimated Time: About 10 minutes.

1. From a command prompt, type **arp -g**. The contents of the ARP cache appear.

2. From a command prompt, type **arp -s 143.42.16.9 0800026c139f**. This adds a static entry to the ARP cache.

3. From a command prompt, type **arp -g** to view the revised contents of the ARP cache.

4. From a command prompt, type **arp -d 143.42.16.9**. This removes the static entry you added in step 2.

5. From a command prompt, type **arp /?** to see all the switches for the ARP command.

15.4 Using the ROUTE Command to View the Routing Table and Add Entries

This exercise is used to display the contents of the local route table and to see how this table lists the default gateway address. You should have TCP/IP installed and a default gateway address configured.

Estimated Time: About 10 minutes.

1. From a command prompt, type **route -p print**. This displays the local route table. Note the address of your client as well as the address of the default gateway in the route table.

2. Open Control Panel, Network, and then select the Protocols tab.

3. Open the TCP/IP Properties dialog box.

4. Delete the Default Gateway address.

5. Choose Apply and close the dialog box.

6. From a command prompt, type **route -p print**. Note that the default gateway address is missing from the table.

7. Follow steps 2–5 to restore the default gateway address.

8. From a command prompt, type **route /?** to see all the switches available with the ROUTE command.

APPLY YOUR KNOWLEDGE

15.5 Using NBTSTAT to View the Local NetBIOS Name Cache and Add Entries to It from an LMHOSTS File

This exercise examines the contents of the local NetBIOS name cache and loads entries into it from an LMHOSTS file. You should have TCP/IP installed, another Windows client with TCP/IP installed, and file sharing enabled.

Estimated Time: About 10 minutes.

1. Use Notepad to open the file \WINNT\ SYSTEM32\DRIVERS\ETC\ LMHOSTS.SAM.

2. Add an entry to the bottom of the file for the other Windows client, specifying the NetBIOS name and the IP address of the Windows client. Make sure there is not a comment (#) in front of this line.

3. Save the file in the same directory as LMHOSTS (without an extension).

4. From a command prompt on your Windows NT computer, type **nbtstat -c**. This displays the local cache.

5. From a command prompt, **type nbtstat -R**. This purges the cache and loads the contents of the LMHOSTS file into the local cache.

6. From a command prompt, type **nbtstat -c** to display the new contents of the local cache.

7. Using Windows NT Explorer, map a network drive to the other Windows client. The local cache was used to resolve the NetBIOS name for this connection.

8. From a command prompt, type **nbtstat /?** to see all the switches available with the NBTSTAT command.

15.6 Using NETSTAT to Examine TCP/IP Connections

You can perform this exercise to see the information returned by the NETSTAT command. You should have TCP/IP installed and access to other TCP/IP servers (for example, Internet access).

Estimated Time: About 15 minutes.

1. Connect to another TCP/IP server through a Web browser or by mapping a network drive.

2. From a command prompt, type **netstat**. This displays the statistics about your current connections.

3. From a command prompt, type **netstat -a**. Note that this command also displays any listening ports.

4. From a command prompt, type **netstat -r**. Note that this command displays the route table in addition to the connection information.

5. From a command prompt, type **netstat /?** to display all the switches available for the NETSTAT command.

15.7 Using TRACERT to Display the Path Used to Establish a TCP/IP Connection

This exercise displays the route used to establish a TCP/IP connection. You should have TCP/IP installed and access to the Internet.

Estimated Time: About five minutes.

1. Open your Web browser and connect to www.microsoft.com.

2. From a command prompt, type **tracert www.microsoft.com**. Note the route used to connect to the Microsoft Web site and the number of hops used for the connection.

3. Connect to www.microsoft.com/train_cert.

APPLY YOUR KNOWLEDGE

4. From a command prompt, type **tracert www.microsoft.com/train_cert**. See if the path is the same as that used for the prior connection.

5. Connect to home.microsoft.com.

6. From a command prompt, type **tracert**. See if the path is different than connecting to www.microsoft.com.

7. Try connecting to other Web sites and viewing the path to these sites.

8. Reconnect to some of the same sites and view the path with TRACERT. You may notice the path is not always the same; if it is, save the path as a file and then try this again after a day or so.

Review Questions

1. What addresses can you PING to test a TCP/IP configuration?

2. What is one address you can PING to prove complete TCP/IP connectivity?

3. How can you determine whether a DHCP client got an IP address? If the client didn't get an address, how can you force the client to again try to get an address?

4. You can PING a Windows NT server's IP address but you cannot connect to a share on the server. Where are possible sources of this problem?

5. What problems can occur if a client does not have the proper address configured for the default gateway?

6. What is the effect on TCP/IP if the wrong IRQ is specified for the network card? Where do you see an indication of this problem?

7. How can you test the resolution of hostnames?

Exam Questions

1. How can you see the address of the DHCP server from which a client received its IP address?

   A. Open the advanced properties of TCP/IP.

   B. Use IPCONFIG /all.

   C. Use DHCPINFO.

   D. PING DHCP.

2. Which should you do to verify that your router is configured correctly?

   A. PING a remote host.

   B. PING 127.0.0.1.

   C. Execute the ROUTE command.

   D. Execute IPCONFIG /all.

3. Your IP address is 136.193.16.1, your subnet mask is 255.255.240.0, and you are trying to PING a host with the command PING 136.193.20.23. The PING doesn't work. What could cause the PING to fail?

   A. The default gateway is not configured correctly.

   B. The subnet mask interprets the IP address as being on another subnet, and the packet is routed.

   C. The subnet mask interprets the address as being on the local subnet, and the packet is not routed.

   D. You must PING the local host first.

4. You are using Performance Monitor, but very few TCP/IP statistics are available. How can you increase the number of TCP/IP objects and counters to monitor?

   A. Install a promiscuous mode adapter card.

APPLY YOUR KNOWLEDGE

B. Configure the correct default gateway in Performance Monitor.

C. Bind TCP/IP to the Monitor service.

D. Install the SNMP service.

5. TCP/IP is not working. You recall that when Windows NT first started, the message A Dependency Service Failed to Start appeared. What is a possible cause of the problem?

  A. The SNMP service is not installed.

  B. The network card is not configured correctly.

  C. The secondary WINS server is down.

  D. The PDC of your domain is down.

6. You can PING a remote host's IP address, but you cannot connect to a share on that host. What is a possible cause of this problem?

  A. The share must be configured to enable anonymous connections.

  B. The Hostname Resolution Protocol must be installed.

  C. The LMHOSTS file does not have any entry for this server.

  D. The client has not been configured to use DHCP.

7. You made a mistake in configuring an IP address and typed the client's address as 96.82.49.208 rather than 196.82.49.208. What is the most likely result of this configuration error?

  A. The client can communicate only with hosts having the network address 96.x.x.x.

  B. The client cannot communicate with hosts beyond the local subnet.

C. The client cannot communicate with hosts on the local subnet.

D. The client cannot communicate with any hosts.

8. You are using NWLink and TCP/IP. How can you reduce the time that is needed to establish a TCP/IP session with another host?

  A. Move TCP/IP to the top of the bindings for the Workstation service.

  B. Configure the default gateway address to point to a faster router.

  C. Decrease the TTL for WINS registrations.

  D. Use SNMP to tune the TCP/IP cache size.

9. A DHCP client has failed to lease an IP address. What is the best way to have the client try again to get a lease?

  A. Issue a REQUEST command to the DHCP server.

  B. Reserve an address for the client on the DHCP server.

  C. Use IPCONFIG /release, and then IPCONFIG /renew.

  D. Restart the client.

10. What is the effect if you do not configure a router address on a TCP/IP client?

  A. You cannot communicate with any other TCP/IP hosts.

  B. You can communicate only with hosts connected to the default gateway.

  C. You can communicate only with hosts on the local subnet.

  D. TCP/IP doesn't initialize.

APPLY YOUR KNOWLEDGE

11. You have several entries for a hostname in an LMHOSTS file. Which entry is used to resolve the hostname to an IP address?

    A. The entry with the most current time stamp

    B. The first entry in the file

    C. The last entry in the file

    D. The entry with the largest IP address

12. A DHCP client has been configured to use the wrong DNS server. How can you correct the problem?

    A. Change the scope options on DHCP, and then renew the lease on the client.

    B. Use IPCONFIG /update:DNS to make the change.

    C. Enter the address of the DNS server in the advanced properties of TCP/IP.

    D. Add an entry for the DHCP client on the other DNS server.

13. A TCP/IP client had a drive mapped to a Windows NT server. You have just changed the IP address of the server and restarted. Now the client can't connect to the new server, even though the server is configured to be a WINS client. What is the most likely cause of this problem?

    A. The WINS server hasn't copied the new registration to all its clients.

    B. The client has the old IP address cached.

    C. The LMHOSTS file on the NT Server needs to be updated.

    D. The entry is still in the NetBIOS name cache.

14. On an NT computer, where does TCP/IP display its error messages?

    A. In the TCP/IP log file

    B. In the SNMP log file

    C. In the System Log

    D. In the TCP.ERR file

15. How can you test the installation of an FTP server?

    A. PING the FTP loopback address.

    B. PING another FTP server.

    C. FTP another server.

    D. FTP the loopback address.

Answers to Review Questions

1. PINGing the loopback address 127.0.0.1 verifies that TCP/IP is installed correctly. PINGing the local host address verifies that the host has a network connection and the TCP/IP stack works all the way down to the Network Interface layer. PINGing the default gateway confirms that packets can be routed to the router. PINGing a remote host verifies that the client can communicate with any client on the network. See "Network Driver Interface Specification (NDIS)."

2. PING a remote host. If the client can communicate with a remote host, it proves that the stack is installed and configured correctly, and that the router is working properly. See "Using PING to Test Connectivity."

3. Use the IPCONFIG /all command in a command prompt. If the client received an address, it is listed along with the lease life and the address

of the DHCP server that leased the address. If the client did not acquire an address, the IP address of 0.0.0.0 is specified for the client. You can use the IPCONFIG /release command to free up any IP leases and then use the IPCONFIG /renew command to force the client to try to get an IP address. See "IPCONFIG."

4. PINGing the server proves you have connectivity at the IP level. When you connect to a share on the server, you are establishing a NetBIOS session with the server. NetBIOS names can be resolved by the client requesting the connections by looking in the local NetBIOS cache, looking in an LMHOSTS file if the client is configured for LMHOSTS lookup, and querying a WINS server. You can check each of these sources of name resolution for possible conflicts or incorrect entries. See "Using PING to Test Connectivity," "Name Resolution Problems," and "Testing NetBIOS by Establishing a Session."

5. The client can communicate with any local hosts because those packets don't need to be routed. However, whenever the client tries to communicate with a remote host, the packet isn't routed because the address specified on the client for the default gateway isn't correct. See "Using PING to Test Connectivity."

6. TCP/IP won't work because it depends on other networking services that don't start if the adapter card isn't properly configured. You might see the `Dependency Service Failed to Start` message when Windows NT first starts. This indicates that networking services that depend on the adapter card are failing because the adapter card driver can't start based on its current configuration. After logging on, you might also see messages when you check the System Log of Event

Viewer. If the messages are written to the event log, you will see an error message indicating that the adapter card failed, followed by error messages from other networking services that also failed to start. You might, however, see a failure of network connections as the only visible symptom of this problem. See "The Network Interface Layer."

7. One solution is to PING the hostname rather than the IP address of the host. However, the ultimate test of name resolution is to connect to the host with FTP or Telnet, or through a Web browser. If you can connect, the name is being resolved properly and you have total connectivity with the host. See "Name Resolution Problems."

Answers to Exam Questions

1. **B.** The IPCONFIG /all command will allow you to see the address that you leased and the other parameters that were also sent from the DHCP server. See "IPCONFIG."

2. **A.** The true test as to whether your router is configured is to attempt to PING a remote host. This will verify that you can get to the router and that the router is able to forward packets. See "Using PING to Test Connectivity."

3. **C.** In this case the address will be on the same subnet as you are (136.193.16.1 to 136.193.31.254); therefore, the address is being resolved as a local address. The only answer that fits is the one that indicates this is a remote address being seen as a local address. See "The Internet Layer."

4. **D.** To enable the TCP/IP counters, you need to install the SNMP service. See Chapter 14 for more details.

APPLY YOUR KNOWLEDGE

5. **B.** Typically, if you receive the dependency service error, the network card is not working. This can be verified using the IPCONFIG /all command because the card will not show up. See "The Network Interface Layer."

6. **C.** If you can PING the IP address of a system but cannot connect to the system by name, there is most likely a name resolution problem. The only valid name resolution answer here is the LMHOSTS file. See "Name Resolution Problems."

7. **D.** The client will not be able to communicate with any of the hosts on the local subnet because they will appear to be remote. Also, to get to the remote hosts, the client will need the router, which in this case will also be remote and, therefore, not usable. See "TCP/IP Configuration Parameters."

8. **A.** Because the protocols will be tried in order of the bindings, you can use the Bindings tab to move the TCP/IP protocol to the top. See "Network Driver Interface Specification (NDIS)."

9. **C.** Although it is not essential, the IPCONFIG /release will ensure that the client does not think it has an address. The IPCONFIG /renew will then start the four-part DHCP lease acquisition; DHCPDISCOVER, DHCPOFFER, DHCPRE-QUEST, and DHCPACK. See "IPCONFIG."

10. **C.** Because the default gateway is used for packets that are destined for other networks, the effect will be that you cannot communicate outside your local subnet. See "TCP/IP Configuration Parameters."

11. **B.** The first entry that the system comes across is the entry that will be used. However, if one of the entries was preloaded to the NetBIOS name cache, that entry would be used. See "Name Resolution Problems.

12. **A.** The correct way to do this is to change the entry at the DHCP server and then renew the client's lease. This will ensure that the client con-tinues to use the correct DNS server. See "IPCONFIG."

13. **D.** The name may still be in the NetBIOS name cache. Because this is the first place the NetBIOS will always check for a resolution, you will need to remove this entry from the cache. This hap-pens automatically after 10 minutes, or you can force it by using NBTSTAT -R to purge and reload the cache. See "Name Resolution Problems."

14. **C.** As with all device drivers and services, the errors for TCP/IP are in the System Log, which you can view using the event viewer. See "The Network Interface Layer."

15. **D.** If you FTP your loopback address, FTP will connect it to your own computer, ensuring that the FTP server is functioning. See "Sockets Problems."

Suggested Readings and Resources

1. Sirockman, Jason. *MCSE Training Guide: Windows NT Server 4 Enterprise.* New Riders, 1997.

FINAL REVIEW

Fast Facts

Study and Exam Prep Tips

Practice Exam

Now that you have read through this book, worked through the exercises, and acquired as much hands-on experience using TCP/IP on Windows NT Server as you could, you're ready for the exam. This last chapter is designed as a "final cram in the parking lot" before you walk into the exam. You can't reread the whole book in an hour, but you will be able to read this chapter in that time.

This chapter is organized by objective category, giving you not just a summary, but a review of the most important points from each chapter. Remember that this is meant to be a review of concepts and a trigger for you to remember those tidbits of information you'll need when taking the exam. If you know what is in here and the concepts that stand behind it, chances are the exam will be a snap.

PLANNING

Planning is limited to a single, general objective.

Objective: Given a scenario, identify valid network configurations.

- ◆ If two physical segments are separated by a router, each segment must have a unique subnet ID.

- ◆ If two physical segments are separated by a bridge or repeater, both segments must have the same subnet ID.

Fast Facts

INSTALLATION AND CONFIGURATION

The following 10 objectives reflect installation and configuration issues.

Objective: Given a scenario, select the appropriate services to install when using Microsoft TCP/IP on a Microsoft Windows NT Server computer.

- Microsoft Windows NT 4.0 includes the following TCP/IP services:

  - Microsoft DNS Server—Provides domain name resolution services.

  - Simple TCP/IP Services—Adds client programs such as DayTime and Echo.

  - SNMP Service—Allows for monitoring and troubleshooting hosts.

  - DHCP Relay Agent—Relays DHCP broadcast messages.

  - Microsoft DHCP Server—Enables automatic TCP/IP configuration.

  - Microsoft TCP/IP Printing—Adds the LPR and LPD services for integrating printing with UNIX and network hosts.

  - Windows Internet Name Service—Provides NetBIOS name resolution services.

  - RIP for Internet Protocol—Provides dynamic routing services.

- NetBT (NetBIOS over TCP/IP) allows NetBIOS data to be transferred over the TCP/IP protocol.

- Only two parameters are required to configure TCP/IP: the IP address and subnet mask.

- The default gateway parameter is required only for remote communication.

- ARP (Address Resolution Protocol) resolves the destination IP address to the destination MAC addresses for *local* hosts by using a local hardware broadcast.

- ARP (Address Resolution Protocol) resolves the next router's IP address to that router's MAC addresses for *remote* hosts by using a local hardware broadcast.

- ARP cache entries live for ten minutes if reused, two minutes if not.

Objective: On a Windows NT Server computer, configure Microsoft TCP/IP to support multiple network adapters.

- Your network cannot be assigned a network ID of 0, 127, or a number greater than 223 in the first octet.

- A network ID must be assigned to each subnet in an environment and each router interface.

- A host ID cannot be all 1s or all 0s.

Objective: Configure subnet masks.

◆ Subnet masks distinguish the network ID from the host ID by AND'ing the IP address and subnet mask.

◆ Subnet masks are used to determine whether a destination host is on a local or remote network.

◆ The default subnet mask for a class A network is 255.0.0.0. The default subnet mask for a class B network is 255.255.0.0. The default subnet mask for a class C network is 255.255.255.0.

◆ Subnetting is the process of borrowing bits from the host ID and using them to identify a subnet ID.

◆ The more subnets you create, the fewer hosts per subnet that are available, and vice versa.

◆ To determine the number of subnets, use the calculator to figure 2^x (where x is the number of bits used in the subnet ID), and then subtract 2.

◆ To determine the number of valid hosts per subnet, use the calculator to figure 2^x (where x is the number of bits used in the host ID), and then subtract 2.

Objective: Configure scopes by using DHCP Manager.

◆ DHCP automatically assigns to clients an IP address, subnet mask, and other optional parameters.

◆ In order to forward DHCP packets, a BOOTP Relay Agent (RFC 1542) must exist on every subnet that has DHCP clients. Otherwise, you will need a DHCP server on every subnet. A BOOTP relay agent can be implemented on a router, or on a Windows NT Server by adding the DHCP Relay Agent service.

◆ Only one scope can be created for each subnet on a single DHCP server.

◆ When implementing multiple DHCP servers, Microsoft recommends that you assign 75 percent of a subnet's available addresses to the closest server and 25 percent to the next closest for redundancy and fault tolerance.

◆ DHCP servers cannot communicate with each other.

◆ If creating scopes on different DHCP servers for the same subnet, only one server can include a given address.

SUMMARY TABLE 1
FOR CALCULATING SUBNET MASK, SUBNET IDS, AND NUMBER OF SUBNETS

Position Value	64	32	16	8	4	2	1
Subnet Bits	2	3	4	5	6	7	8
Subnets Available	2^2-2 2	2^3-2 6	2^4-2 14	2^5-2 30	2^6-2 62	2^7-2 126	2^8-2 254
Subnet Mask	128+64 =192	192+32 =224	224+16 =240	240+8 =248	248+4 =252	252+2 =254	254+1 =255
Host Bits	6	5	4	3	2	1	0

- The DHCP server cannot be a DHCP client, and vice versa.

- Scopes must be activated before they distribute IP addresses.

- DHCP can also assign a router, DNS server, domain name, NetBIOS node type, WINS server, and NetBIOS scope ID to Microsoft clients.

- A WINS Server option requires a NetBIOS Scope ID option.

- User options override scope options, which override global options. All options are overridden by information manually configured on the client.

- Use Client Reservations to pre-assign an IP address to a client. The unique identifier in this configuration is the MAC address of the client.

- To create scopes on different DHCP servers for the same subnet, a client reservation must be duplicated to each DHCP server.

- IPCONFIG can be used to release and renew DHCP addresses.

Objective: Install and configure a WINS server.

- To enable a WINS client, simply configure a WINS server address in the TCP/IP properties either manually or by using a DHCP option.

- Only one WINS server is required in a TCP/IP environment.

- Microsoft recommends one primary WINS server and one secondary WINS server for every 10,000 clients. Two WINS servers provide fault tolerance.

- Install a WINS server by adding the Windows Internet Name Service in Network Properties.

- A WINS proxy agent allows non-WINS clients to retrieve information from the WINS database. A WINS proxy agent must exist on each subnet with non-WINS clients.

- A WINS proxy agent must be a WINS client and cannot be a WINS server.

Subobjective: Import LMHOSTS files to WINS.

- To import entries from an existing LMHOSTS file into the WINS database, click the Import Mappings button in the Static Mappings dialog box and specify the location of the LMHOSTS file.

Subobjective: Run WINS on a multihomed computer.

- Microsoft does not recommend running WINS on a multihomed computer in an environment with DOS clients.

Subobjective: Configure WINS replication.

- Configure replication between WINS server partners so that they can exchange database information.

- A WINS server notifies its *push partners* of changes to the database when a threshold is reached.

- A WINS server pulls information from its *pull partners* at a scheduled time.

- The Replicate Now button in the Replication Partners dialog box will replicate immediately with the partner highlighted, or with all partners if the local host is highlighted.

Subobjective: Configure static mappings in the WINS database.

◆ Static mappings allow WINS clients to locate non-WINS clients using the WINS database.

◆ To configure static mappings, add the name and IP address mapping to the WINS database using the Add Static Mapping dialog box in WINS Manager.

◆ Static mapping can be Unique (for a one-to-one mapping), Group (for broadcasting to the local subnet), Domain Name (for domain logon validation), Internet Group (for resources such as printers), and Multihomed (for computers with multiple IP addresses).

Objective: Configure a Windows NT Server computer to function as an IP router.

◆ IP is a connectionless protocol, and its packets are called *datagrams*.

◆ IP compares the source subnet ID with the destination subnet ID to determine if the destination host is on the same subnet as the source host (local) or on a different subnet than the source host (remote). If the destination host is remote, IP begins the routing process.

◆ IP on routers decrements the TTL by at least one metric, fragments packets, and is responsible for all addressing. IP routing is used only if the destination host is remote.

◆ Windows NT checks the routing table for a known route before sending a packet to the default gateway (router).

◆ The IP address of the default gateway must be the router interface that is on the same subnet as the host.

◆ *Static routing* is a function of IP. Check the Enable IP Forwarding check box to implement it.

◆ *Dynamic routing* is a function of a routing protocol, such as RIP and OSPF, that exchanges routing tables with other routers. Install the RIP for Internet Protocol service to implement it.

◆ When integrating both dynamic and static routing in an environment, static routes must be configured on both the static and dynamic routers.

◆ The following command displays the routing table: ROUTE PRINT.

◆ The following command adds a static route: ADD *destination* MASK *netmask gateway.*

◆ The following command deletes a route: ROUTE DELETE *destination.*

◆ Use the -p switch with the ROUTE command to add a permanent route.

◆ ICMP Source Quench messages from a router tell a sending host to reduce both the frequency and amount of data it is generating. Microsoft NT can react to these messages, but it does not initiate them.

◆ *Dead gateway detection* can access an alternative default gateway when the primary is unresponsive (and if a second default gateway is configured).

Subobjective: Install and configure the DHCP Relay Agent.

◆ To install the DHCP Relay Agent, first add the service, and then configure it from the TCP/IP Properties sheet.

◆ Add the DHCP Relay Agent service to allow a Windows NT computer to forward DHCP packets to other subnets.

◆ The DHCP Relay Agent service must be configured with the IP address on a DHCP server that it will relay messages to.

Objective: Install and configure the Microsoft DNS Server service on a Windows NT Server computer.

◆ A *zone* file is the local database file. If a name server has the local database file (master copy) for a zone, the server is said to be *authoritative* for that zone.

◆ *Recursive* queries require the queried name server to respond with a resolution or an error. *Resolvers*, or clients, initiate recursive queries.

◆ *Iterative* queries allow name servers to give a best answer, often referring the querying host to another name server. Servers send iterative queries to each other.

◆ Microsoft stores all service information, including the boot configuration, in the Registry.

◆ DNS files include the database, or zone, file; a reverse lookup file; the cache file; and, optionally, a boot file.

◆ Zone files are used to resolve Fully Qualified Domain Names (FQDNs) to IP addresses. Every zone file includes an SOA (Start of Authority) record, at least one NS (Name Server) record,

multiple A records, or resource records. Zone files optionally include MX (Mail Exchange) and CNAME (Canonical Name) records. An example zone filename in Windows NT is microsoft.com.dns.

◆ A sample zone file called mcp.com.dns looks like the following:

```
@           IN      SOA
➥server1.mcp.com.admin.mcp.com.      (
            2                 ; serial number
            3600              ; refresh
            600               ; retry
            86400             ; expire
            3600              ) ; minimum TTL
@           IN      NS      server1
server1     IN      A       10.10.10.50
mailsrv     IN      A       10.10.10.150
www         IN      CNAME   server1
@           IN      MX      15
➥mailsrv.mcp.com.
```

◆ A reverse lookup file is used to find an FQDN for an IP address. An example reverse lookup file name in Windows NT is 10.168.192.in-addr.arpa.

◆ All DNS servers have a cache file that contains resource records for the DNS root servers.

◆ The boot file is primarily used for migrations from BIND implementations of DNS. This file contains boot information for the DNS server. Microsoft DNS server stores in the Registry by default, but it can be configured to use the boot file.

◆ Multiple zone files can be created on a single name server. Configuring a zone under an existing zone in DNS Manager creates a subdomain.

Subobjective: Integrate DNS with other name servers.

◆ Because Microsoft DNS server is RFC-compliant, it can be integrated with any UNIX implementation of DNS.

◆ Microsoft DNS can be integrated with WINS servers to create "dynamic DNS" by using a WINS record in the zone file. The DNS server will then query the WINS server if it cannot resolve a query in a zone for which it is authoritative.

◆ Integrating a DNS server with a WINS server reduces the number of static resource records in the DNS zone file.

Subobjective: Connect a DNS server to a DNS root server.

◆ Each DNS server must be registered with a name server higher in the hierarchy. For example, both the primary and secondary name servers for mcp.com must register with the .com name server.

Subobjective: Configure DNS server roles.

◆ Each domain should have a *primary name server* that maintains the master zone files and at least one *secondary name server* that maintains a read-only copy of the zone file.

◆ When a *master name server* sends a copy of the zone file to another name server, it is called a *zone transfer*. A master name server can be either a primary or secondary name server.

◆ *Caching-only servers* do not maintain zone files. They can be used to reduce network traffic across WAN links because they do not participate in zone transfers but do maintain resolution information.

Objective: Configure HOSTS and LMHOSTS files.

◆ NetBIOS name resolution resolves a NetBIOS name, such as a computer name, to an IP address.

◆ Hostname resolution resolves a hostname, or alias, to an IP address.

◆ The four node types are b-node (broadcast), p-node (peer node, or WINS servers), m-node (mixed; or broadcast, then WINS server), and h-node (hybrid; or WINS server, then broadcast).

◆ The default node type is enhanced b-node (broadcast, then LMHOSTS file). If a WINS server is configured, the default node type is h-node.

◆ If all options are configured for NetBIOS name resolution, Windows NT will check the NetBIOS name cache, contact the WINS server, send a local broadcast, check the LMHOSTS file, check the HOSTS file, and then contact the DNS server.

◆ If all options are configured for hostname resolution, Windows NT will check the local hostname, check the HOSTS file, contact the DNS server, contact the WINS server, send a local broadcast, and then check the LMHOSTS file.

◆ The LMHOSTS file is a text file with no extension. The most common keywords are #PRE for preloading the cache and #DOM for specifying a domain name.

◆ A line in the LMHOSTS file looks like this:

```
131.107.2.200      Instructor      #PRE
➥#DOM:Classroom
```

◆ If multiple entries exist for one name in the LMHOSTS file, only the first one will be read.

◆ A HOST file is a text file with no extension. One must reside on each computer.

◆ A line from a HOSTS file looks like this:

```
131.107.2.200               instructor
➥instructor.mcp.com
```

◆ Both the LMHOSTS file and HOSTS file are stored in the *winntroot*/system32/drivers/etc directory.

◆ Comments in both the LMHOSTS and HOSTS files are indicated by a semi-colon (;) and are ignored by Windows NT.

Objective: Configure a Windows NT Server computer to support TCP/IP printing.

◆ LPD (Line Printer Daemon) is a printing service that enables any client running TCP/IP and LPR (Line Printer Remote) to send print jobs to it.

◆ LPQ (Line Printer Query) allows you to view the files in the LPD print queue, as well as its status.

◆ A UNIX client can print to Windows NT server running LPD.

◆ Windows NT can print to a UNIX print server if Windows NT has LPR.

◆ A UNIX server can print to a Windows NT printer if Windows NT has an LPD printer configured.

◆ LPD, LPR, and LPQ are installed with the Microsoft TCP/IP Printing service.

◆ To print to a UNIX printer, you must add an LPR Port in Print Manager that indicates the IP address of the server running LPD and the name of the print queue; or use the command-line utility LPR.

Objective: Configure SNMP.

◆ Simple Network Management Protocol (SNMP) is used to monitor and communicate status information between SNMP managers and SNMP agents.

◆ The Microsoft SNMP server includes four commands: get, get-next, set, and trap.

◆ Get and get-next retrieve status information from an *SNMP agent*, or client.

◆ Set allows an *SNMP manager* to configure information on an SNMP agent, but it is rarely used.

◆ The SNMP Service included with Windows NT only creates an SNMP agent. SNMP manger software must be obtained from a third party.

◆ The only command an SNMP agent can initiate is a trap, which notifies an SNMP manager of a significant event, such as an "out of disk space" error or a potential security breach.

◆ Information that an SNMP agent tracks is stored as a manageable object in a MIB (Management Information Base).

◆ Windows NT Server includes four MIBs: Internet MIB II for general TCP/IP information, LAN Manager MIB II for Microsoft–specific information, DHCP MIB for DHCP Server activity, and WINS MIB for WINS Server activity.

- *SNMP communities* provide primitive security for the SNMP service. Agents and managers will communicate only with other hosts within their designated communities. Both agents and managers can belong to multiple communities. The default community name is Public.

- The SNMP agent service can be configured to send traps to a community or specific manager.

- A trap is configured with both the community name and IP address of the SNMP management station that it sends the messages to.

- The SNMP agent service can be configured as having one or more of the following services: Physical, if the computer manages a physical device; Datalink/Subnetwork, if the computer manages a bridge; Internet, if the computer is a router; End-to-End, if the computer acts as an IP host; and Applications, if the computer runs a TCP/IP application. End-to-End and Applications should always be selected.

CONNECTIVITY

Connectivity is addressed by three objectives.

Objective: Given a scenario, identify which utility to use to connect to a TCP/IP-based UNIX host.

- Windows NT server can connect to a non-Microsoft server with NetBIOS commands if both servers use the same transport protocol and the non-Microsoft server provides Server Message Block (SMB) connectivity.

- REXEC (Remote Execute), RSH (Remote Shell), and TELNET (Telecommunications Network) allow a Windows NT computer to run applications and commands on a non-Microsoft host that does not provide SMB connectivity.

- RCOPY (Remote Copy), FTP (File Transfer Protocol), TFTP (Trivial File Transfer Protocol), and Web browsers allow a Windows NT computer to copy files to and from a non-Microsoft host that does not provide SMB connectivity.

Objective: Configure a RAS server and Dial-Up Networking for use on a TCP/IP network.

- To configure the RAS service, you must first install and configure a modem on the Windows NT Server, and then install and configure the Remote Access Service.

- For outbound communications, you need to configure Dialing Properties in Dial-Up Networking.

- From the Remote Access Service in Network Properties, select TCP/IP as the network protocol for the Server Settings in the Network Configuration dialog box.

- Select either the Use DHCP to Assign Remote TCP/IP Client Address or the Use Static Address Pool radio button in the RAS Server TCP/IP Configuration dialog box.

- Although it is not recommended, you may also select the Allow Remote Clients to Request a Predetermined IP Address in the RAS Server TCP/IP Configuration dialog box.

Objective: Configure and support browsing in a multiple-domain routed network.

◆ *Master browsers* maintain the master copy of the browse list. *Backup browsers* retrieve the read-only copy of the browse list and distribute it to clients that request it.

◆ A browse list is specific to a domain or workgroup.

◆ Browse lists (and, thus, browsing) are restricted to a single subnet unless WINS or LMHOSTS files are configured.

◆ To implement an LMHOSTS file solution for domain browsing, each master browser must have an LMHOSTS entry for the domain master browser with a #DOM tag, and vice versa.

◆ *Domain master browsers* consolidate subnet browse lists into a domain-wide browse list and offer it to other domain master browsers. Domain master browsers are always the primary domain controller (PDC) of that domain.

◆ Logon issues in a domain apply to browsing in a domain; implement either WINS servers or LMHOSTS files.

◆ To allow domain logon across subnets by using LMHOSTS files, each client requires a line in the LMHOSTS file for each backup domain controller (BDC), including the #PRE and #DOM keywords.

◆ To allow account information to be updated between domain controllers by using LMHOSTS files, each domain controller requires a line in the LMHOSTS file for each of the other domain controllers, including the #PRE and #DOM keywords.

MONITORING AND OPTIMIZATION

There is a single objective concerning monitoring and optimization.

Objective: Given a scenario, identify which tool to use to monitor TCP/IP traffic.

◆ Performance Monitor provides charting, alerting, and reporting capabilities that reflect both current activity and ongoing logging.

◆ Performance Monitor counters are enabled when the SNMP Service is installed on Windows NT Server.

◆ Network Monitor allows you to monitor, capture, and analyze network traffic, including individual packets. Capture filters can also be applied to locate specific types of packets.

◆ The SNMP Service allows a Windows NT computer to report its status to an SNMP manager.

◆ The NETSTAT command displays current protocol statistics and current TCP/IP connections.

◆ The NET command with the STATISTICS switch displays network statistics since the computer was last started.

◆ The NBTSTAT command displays current protocol statistics and current TCP/IP connections using NetBIOS over TCP/IP (NetBT).

◆ The NET command displays information since the computer was last started; both NETSTAT and NBTSTAT display current statistics, or a snapshot.

◆ The Registry setting TCPWindowSize can be used to improve TCP connections.

TROUBLESHOOTING

There are three troubleshooting objectives.

Objective: Diagnose and resolve IP addressing problems.

◆ All hosts on the same physical segment must be configured with the same subnet ID based on its subnet mask.

Objective: Use Microsoft TCP/IP utilities to diagnose IP configuration problems.

◆ IPCONFIG is the best utility to verify IP configuration.

◆ PING is the best utility to verify the availability of a host and to test network connectivity.

Subobjective: Identify which Microsoft TCP/IP utility to use to diagnose IP configuration problems.

◆ TRACERT is the best utility to verify the path to a remote host, and to troubleshoot WAN connections.

◆ Use the ROUTE PRINT command to add a view to the local routing table.

◆ NSLOOKUP is used to query and troubleshoot a DNS server.

◆ Use Event Viewer to find and troubleshoot SNMP Service errors.

◆ The SNMPUTIL utility is included with the Windows NT Resource Kit and can be used to test the SNMP Service.

Objective: Diagnose and resolve name resolution problems.

◆ Use NBTSTAT to view the NetBIOS name cache.

◆ Use IPCONFIG to view the DNS servers, WINS servers, and node type of a TCP/IP client.

◆ The NSLOOKUP command is used to query DNS servers.

Good luck on the exam!

Study and Exam Prep Tips

This chapter provides you with some general guidelines for preparing for the exam. It is organized into three sections. The first section addresses your pre-exam preparation activities, covering general study tips. This is followed by an extended look at the Microsoft Certification exams, including a number of specific tips that apply to the Microsoft exam formats. Finally, it addresses changes in Microsoft's testing policies and how they might affect you.

To better understand the nature of preparation for the test, it is important to understand learning as a process. You probably are aware of how you best learn new material. Maybe outlining works best for you, or maybe you are a visual learner who needs to "see" things. Whatever your learning style, test preparation takes time. While it is obvious that you can't start studying for these exams the night before you take them, it is very important to understand that learning is a developmental process. Understanding the process helps you focus on what you know and what you have yet to learn.

Thinking about how you learn should help you recognize that learning takes place when we are able to match new information to old. You have some previous experience with computers and networking, and now you are preparing for this certification exam. Using this book, software, and supplementary materials will not just add incrementally to what you know. As you study, you actually change the organization of your knowledge to integrate this new information into your existing knowledge base. This will lead you to a more comprehensive understanding of the tasks and concepts outlined in the objectives and related to computing in general. Again, this happens as an iterative process rather than a singular event. Keep this model of learning in mind as you prepare for the exam, and you will make better decisions on what to study and how much to study.

STUDY TIPS

There are many ways to approach studying, just as there are many different types of material to study. However, the tips that follow should work well for the type of material covered on the certification exams.

Study Strategies

Although individuals vary in the ways they learn information, some basic principles of learning apply to everyone. You should adopt some study strategies that take advantage of these principles. One of these principles is that learning can be broken into various depths. *Recognition* (of terms, for example) exemplifies a surface level of learning: You rely on a prompt of some sort to elicit recall. *Comprehension or understanding* (of the concepts behind the terms, for instance) represents a deeper level of learning. The ability to analyze a concept and apply your understanding of it in a new way or to address a unique setting represents further depth of learning.

Your learning strategy should enable you to know the material a level or two deeper than mere recognition. This will help you to do well on the exam(s). You will know the material so thoroughly that you can easily handle the recognition-level types of questions used in multiple-choice testing. You will also be able to apply your knowledge to solve novel problems.

Macro and Micro Study Strategies

One strategy that can lead to this deeper learning includes preparing an outline that covers all the objectives and subobjectives for the particular exam you are working on. You should then delve a bit further into the material and include a level or two of detail beyond the stated objectives and subobjectives for the exam. Finally, flesh out the outline by coming up with a statement of definition or a summary for each point in the outline.

This outline provides two approaches to studying. First, you can study the outline by focusing on the organization of the material. Work your way through the points and subpoints of your outline with the goal of learning how they relate to one another. For example, be sure you understand how each of the main objective areas is similar to and different from one another. Then do the same thing with the subobjectives. Also, be sure you know which subobjectives pertain to each objective area and how they relate to one another.

Next, you can work through the outline and focus on learning the details. Memorize and understand terms and their definitions, facts, rules and strategies, advantages and disadvantages, and so on. In this pass through the outline, attempt to learn detail as opposed to the big picture (the organizational information that you worked on in the first pass through the outline).

Research shows that attempting to assimilate both types of information at the same time seems to interfere with the overall learning process. Separate your studying into these two approaches, and you will perform better on the exam than if you attempt to study the material in a more conventional manner.

Active Study Strategies

In addition, the process of writing down and defining the objectives, subobjectives, terms, facts, and definitions promotes a more active learning strategy than merely reading the material does. In human information processing terms, writing forces you to engage in more active encoding of the information. Simply reading over it constitutes passive processing.

Next, determine whether you can apply the information you have learned by attempting to create examples and scenarios of your own. Think about how or where you could apply the concepts you are learning. Again, write down this information to process the facts and concepts in a more active fashion.

The hands-on nature of the Step by Step tutorials and the exercises at the end of the chapters provide further active learning opportunities that will reinforce concepts.

Common Sense Strategies

Finally, you should also follow common sense practices in studying: Study when you are alert, reduce or eliminate distractions, take breaks when you become fatigued, and so on.

Pre-Testing Yourself

Pre-testing allows you to assess how well you are learning. One of the most important aspects of learning is what has been called "meta-learning." Meta-learning has to do with realizing when you know something well or when you need to study some more. In other words, you recognize how well or how poorly you have learned the material you are studying. For most people, this can be difficult to assess objectively on their own. Therefore, practice tests are useful because they reveal more objectively what you have and have not learned. You should use this information to guide review and further studying. Developmental learning takes place as you cycle through studying, assessing how well you have learned, reviewing, and assessing again, until you feel you are ready to take the exam.

You may have noticed the practice exam included in this book. Use it as part of this process. In addition to the Practice Exam, the Top Score software on the CD-ROM also provides a variety of ways to test yourself before you take the actual exam. By using the Top Score Practice Exams, you can take an entire practice test. By using the Top Score Study Cards, you can take an entire practice exam or you can focus on a particular objective area, such as Planning, Troubleshooting, or Monitoring and Optimization. By using the Top Score Flash Cards, you can test your knowledge at a level beyond that of recognition; you must come up with the answers in your own words. The Flash Cards also enable you to test your knowledge of particular objective areas.

You should set a goal for your pre-testing. A reasonable goal would be to score consistently in the 90-percent range (or better). See Appendix D, "Using the Top Score Software," for more detailed explanation of the test engine.

Exam Prep Tips

Having mastered the subject matter, the final preparatory step is to understand how the exam will be presented. Make no mistake about it, a Microsoft Certified Professional (MCP) exam will challenge both your knowledge and your test-taking skills! This section starts with the basics of exam design, reviews a new type of exam format, and concludes with hints that are targeted to each of the exam formats.

The MCP Exam

Every MCP exam is released in one of two basic formats. What's being called *exam format* here is really little more than a combination of the overall exam structure and the presentation method for exam questions.

Each exam format utilizes the same types of questions. These types or styles of questions include multiple-rating (or scenario-based) questions, traditional multiple-choice questions, and simulation-based questions. It's important to understand the types of questions you will be asked and the actions required to properly answer them.

Understanding the exam formats is essential to good preparation because the format determines the number of questions presented, the difficulty of those questions, and the amount of time allowed to complete the exam.

Exam Format

There are two basic formats for the MCP exams: the traditional fixed-form exam and the adaptive form. As its name implies, the fixed-form exam presents a fixed set of questions during the exam session. The adaptive format, however, uses only a subset of questions drawn from a larger pool during any given exam session.

Fixed-Form

A fixed-form, computerized exam is based on a fixed set of exam questions. The individual questions are presented in random order during a test session. If you take the same exam more than once, you won't necessarily see the exact same questions. This is because two or three final forms are typically assembled for every fixed-form exam Microsoft releases. These are usually labeled Forms A, B, and C.

The final forms of a fixed-form exam are identical in terms of content coverage, number of questions, and allotted time, but the questions themselves are different. You may have noticed, however, that some of the same questions appear on, or rather are shared across, different final forms. When questions are shared across multiple final forms of an exam, the percentage of sharing is generally small. Many final forms share no questions, but some older exams may have ten to fifteen percent duplication of exam questions on the final exam forms.

Fixed-form exams also have a fixed time limit in which you must complete the exam. The Top Score software on the CD-ROM that accompanies this book provides fixed-form exams.

Finally, the score you achieve on a fixed-form exam (which is always reported for MCP exams on a scale of 0 to 1,000) is based on the number of questions you answer correctly. The exam passing score is the same for all final forms of a given fixed-form exam.

The typical format for the fixed-form exam is this:

❖ 50–60 questions

❖ 75–90 minute testing time

❖ Question review is allowed, including the opportunity to change your answers

Adaptive Form

An adaptive form exam has the same appearance as a fixed-form exam, but it differs in both how questions are selected for presentation and how many questions actually are presented. Although the statistics of adaptive testing are fairly complex, the process is concerned with determining your level of skill or ability with the exam subject matter. This ability assessment begins with the presentation of questions of varying levels of difficulty and ascertains at what difficulty level you can reliably answer them. Finally, the ability assessment determines if that ability level is above or below the level required to pass that exam.

Examinees at different levels of ability will then see quite different sets of questions. Examinees who demonstrate little expertise with the subject matter will continue to be presented with relatively easy questions. Examinees who demonstrate a high level of expertise will be presented progressively more-difficult questions. Both individuals may answer the same number of questions correctly, but because the higher-expertise examinee can correctly answer more-difficult questions, he or she will receive a higher score and is more likely to pass the exam.

The typical design for the adaptive form exam is this:

❖ 20–25 questions

❖ 90 minute testing time (although this is likely to be reduced to 45–60 minutes in the near future)

❖ Question review is not allowed, providing no opportunity to change your answers

The Adaptive Exam Process

Your first adaptive exam will be unlike any other testing experience you have had. In fact, many examinees have difficulty accepting the adaptive testing process because they feel they were not provided the opportunity to adequately demonstrate their full expertise.

You can take consolation in the fact that adaptive exams are painstakingly put together after months of data gathering and analysis and are just as valid as a fixed-form exam. The rigor introduced through the adaptive testing methodology means that there is nothing arbitrary about what you'll see! It is also a more efficient means of testing that requires less time to conduct and complete.

As you can see from Figure 1, a number of statistical measures drive the adaptive examination process. The one that's most immediately relevant to you is the ability estimate. Accompanying this test statistic are the standard error of measurement, the item characteristic curve, and the test information curve.

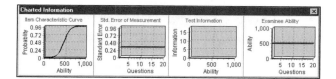

FIGURE 1
Microsoft's adaptive testing demonstration program.

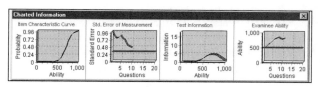

FIGURE 2
The changing statistics in an adaptive exam.

The standard error, which is the key factor in determining when an adaptive exam will terminate, reflects the degree of error in the exam ability estimate. The item characteristic curve reflects the probability of a correct response relative to examinee ability. Finally, the test information statistic provides a measure of the information contained in the set of questions the examinee has answered, again relative to the ability level of the individual examinee.

When you begin an adaptive exam, the standard error has already been assigned a target value below which it must drop for the exam to conclude. This target value reflects a particular level of statistical confidence in the process. The examinee ability is initially set to the mean possible exam score, which is 500 for MCP exams.

As the adaptive exam progresses, questions of varying difficulty are presented. Based on your pattern of responses to those questions, the ability estimate is recalculated. Simultaneously, the standard error estimate is refined from its first estimated value of one toward the target value. When the standard error reaches its target value, the exam terminates. Thus, the more consistently you answer questions of the same degree of difficulty, the more quickly the standard error estimate drops and the fewer questions you will end up seeing during the exam session. This situation is depicted in Figure 2.

As you might suspect, one good piece of advice for taking an adaptive exam is to treat every exam question as if it is the most important. The adaptive scoring algorithm is attempting to discover a pattern of responses

that reflects some level of proficiency with the subject matter. Incorrect responses almost guarantee that additional questions must be answered (unless, of course, you get every question wrong). This is because the scoring algorithm must adjust to information that is not consistent with the emerging pattern.

New Question Types

A variety of question types can appear on MCP exams. Examples of multiple-choice questions and scenario-based questions appear throughout this book and the Top Score software. Simulation-based questions are new to the MCP exam series.

Simulation Questions

Simulation-based questions reproduce the look and feel of key Microsoft product features for the purpose of testing. The simulation software used in MCP exams has been designed to look and act, as much as possible, just like the actual product. Consequently, answering simulation questions in an MCP exam entails completing one or more tasks just as if you were using the product itself.

The format of a typical Microsoft simulation question is straightforward. It presents a brief scenario or problem statement along with one or more tasks that must be completed to solve the problem. The next section provides an example of a simulation question for MCP exams.

A Typical Simulation Question

It sounds obvious, but the first step when you encounter a simulation is to carefully read the question (see Figure 3). Do not go straight to the simulation application! Assess the problem being presented and identify the conditions that make up the problem scenario. Note the tasks that must be performed or outcomes that must be achieved to answer the question, and then review any instructions on how to proceed.

The next step is to launch the simulator by using the button provided. After clicking the Show Simulation button, you will see a feature of the product, like the dialog box shown in Figure 4. The simulation application will partially cover the question text on many test center machines. Feel free to reposition the simulation or to move between the question text screen and the simulation using hot-keys and point-and-click navigation or even by clicking the simulation launch button again.

It is important to understand that your answer to the simulation question is not recorded until you move on to the next exam question. This gives you the added capability to close and reopen the simulation application (using the launch button) on the same question without losing any partial answer you may have made.

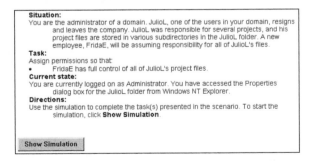

Situation:
You are the administrator of a domain. JulioL, one of the users in your domain, resigns and leaves the company. JulioL was responsible for several projects, and his project files are stored in various subdirectories in the JulioL folder. A new employee, FridaE, will be assuming responsibility for all of JulioL's files.
Task:
Assign permissions so that:
•   FridaE has full control of all of JulioL's project files.
Current state:
You are currently logged on as Administrator. You have accessed the Properties dialog box for the JulioL folder from Windows NT Explorer.
Directions:
Use the simulation to complete the task(s) presented in the scenario. To start the simulation, click **Show Simulation**.

FIGURE 3
Typical MCP exam simulation question with directions.

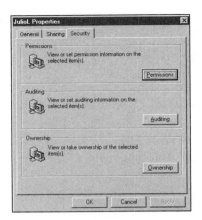

FIGURE 4
Launching the simulation application.

The third step is to use the simulator as you would the actual product to solve the problem or perform the defined tasks. Again, the simulation software is designed to function, within reason, just as the product does. But don't expect the simulation to reproduce product behavior perfectly. Most importantly, do not allow yourself to become flustered if the simulation does not look or act exactly like the product. Figure 5 shows the solution to the sample simulation problem.

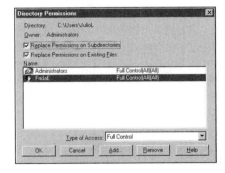

FIGURE 5
The solution to the simulation example.

There are two final points that will help you tackle simulation questions. First, respond only to what is being asked in the question. Do not solve problems that you are not asked to solve. Second, accept what is being asked of you. You may not entirely agree with conditions in the problem statement, the quality of the desired solution, or sufficiency of defined tasks to adequately solve the problem. Always remember that you are being tested on your ability to solve the problem as it has been presented.

The solution to the simulation problem shown in Figure 5 perfectly illustrates both of these points. As you'll recall from the question scenario (refer to Figure 3), you were asked to assign appropriate permissions to a new user called FridaE. You were not instructed to make any other changes in permissions. Thus, if you had modified or removed Administrator permissions, this item would have been scored wrong on an MCP exam.

Putting It All Together

Given all these different pieces of information, the task is now to assemble a set of tips that will help you successfully tackle the different types of MCP exams.

More Pre-Exam Preparation Tips

Generic exam preparation advice is always useful. Follow these general guidelines:

◆ Become familiar with the product. Hands-on experience is one of the keys to success on any MCP exam. Review the exercises and the Step by Step tutorials in the book.

◆ Review the current exam preparation guide on the Microsoft MCP Web site. The documentation Microsoft makes publicly available over the Web identifies the skills every exam is intended to test.

◆ Memorize foundational technical detail as appropriate. But remember, MCP exams are generally heavy on problem solving and application of knowledge more than they are on questions that require only rote memorization.

◆ Take any of the available practice tests. We recommend the one included in this book and those you can create using the Top Score software on the CD-ROM. While these are fixed-format exams, they provide preparation that is also valuable for taking an adaptive exam. Because of the nature of adaptive testing, it is not possible for these practice exams to be offered in the adaptive format. However, fixed-format exams provide the same types of questions as adaptive exams and are the most effective way to prepare for either type of exam. As a supplement to the material included with this book, try the free practice tests available on the Microsoft MCP Web site.

◆ Look on the Microsoft MCP Web site for samples and demonstration items. These tend to be particularly valuable for one significant reason: They allow you to become familiar with any new testing technologies before you encounter them on an MCP exam.

During the Exam Session

Similarly, the generic exam-taking advice you've heard for years applies when taking an MCP exam:

◆ Take a deep breath and try to relax when you first sit down for your exam. It is very important to control the pressure you may (naturally) feel when taking exams.

◆ You will be provided scratch paper. Take a moment to write down any factual information and technical detail that you committed to short-term memory.

◆ Carefully read all information and instruction screens. These displays have been put together to give you information relevant to the exam you are taking.

◆ Accept the Non-Disclosure Agreement and preliminary survey as part of the examination process. Complete them accurately and quickly move on.

◆ Read the exam questions carefully. Reread each question to identify all relevant detail.

◆ Tackle the questions in the order they are presented. Skipping around won't build your confidence; the clock is always counting down.

◆ Don't rush, but at the same time, don't linger on difficult questions. The questions vary in degree of difficulty. Don't let yourself be flustered by a particularly difficult or verbose question.

Fixed-Form Exams

Building from this basic preparation and test-taking advice, you also need to consider the challenges presented by the different exam designs. Because a fixed-form exam is composed of a fixed, finite set of questions, add these tips to your strategy for taking a fixed-form exam:

◆ Note the time allotted and the number of questions appearing on the exam you are taking. Make a rough calculation of how many minutes you can spend on each question, and use that number to pace yourself through the exam.

◆ Take advantage of the fact that you can return to and review skipped or previously answered questions. Mark the questions you can't answer confidently, noting the relative difficulty of each question on the scratch paper provided. When you reach the end of the exam, return to the more difficult questions.

◆ If there is session time remaining when you have completed all questions (and you aren't too fatigued!), review your answers. Pay particular attention to questions that seem to have a lot of detail or that required graphics.

◆ As for changing your answers, the rule of thumb here is *don't*! If you read the question carefully and completely and you felt like you knew the right answer, you probably did. Don't second-guess yourself. If, as you check your answers, one stands out as clearly incorrect, however, of course you should change it. But if you are at all unsure, go with your first impression.

Adaptive Exams

If you are planning to take an adaptive exam, keep these additional tips in mind:

◆ Read and answer every question with great care. When reading a question, identify every relevant detail, requirement, or task that must be performed and double-check your answer to be sure you have addressed every one of them.

◆ If you cannot answer a question, use the process of elimination to reduce the set of potential answers, and then take your best guess. Stupid mistakes invariably mean additional questions will be presented.

◆ Forget about reviewing questions and changing your answers. Once you leave a question, whether you've answered it or not, you cannot return to it. Do not skip any questions either. If you do, that question is counted as incorrect!

Simulation Questions

You may encounter simulation questions on either the fixed-form or adaptive form exam. If you do, keep these tips in mind:

◆ Avoid changing any simulation settings that don't pertain directly to the problem solution. Solve the problem you are being asked to solve and nothing more.

◆ Assume default settings when related information has not been provided. If something has not been mentioned or defined, it is a non-critical detail that does not factor in to the correct solution.

◆ Be sure your entries are syntactically correct, paying particular attention to your spelling. Enter relevant information just as the product would require it.

◆ Close all simulation application windows after you complete the simulation tasks. The testing system software is designed to trap errors that could result when using the simulation application, but trust yourself over the testing software.

◆ If simulations are part of a fixed-form exam, you can return to skipped or previously answered questions and change your answer. However, if you choose to change your answer to a simulation question, or if you even attempt to review the settings you've made in the simulation application, your previous response to that simulation question will be deleted. If simulations are part of an adaptive exam, you cannot return to previous questions.

FINAL CONSIDERATIONS

Finally, a number of changes in the MCP program will impact how frequently you can repeat an exam and what you will see when you do.

◆ Microsoft has instituted a new exam retake policy. This new rule is "two and two, then one and two." That is, you can attempt any exam twice with no restrictions on the time between attempts. But after the second attempt, you must wait two weeks before you can attempt that exam again. After that, you will be required to wait two weeks between subsequent attempts. Plan to pass the exam in two attempts; if that's not possible, increase your time horizon for receiving an MCP credential.

◆ New questions are being seeded into the MCP exams. After performance data has been gathered on new questions, they will replace older questions on all exam forms. This means that the questions appearing on exams will change regularly.

◆ Many of the current MCP exams will be republished in adaptive format in the coming months. Prepare yourself for this significant change in testing format, as it is entirely likely that this will become the new preferred MCP exam format.

These changes mean that the brute-force strategies for passing MCP exams may soon completely lose their viability. So if you don't pass an exam on the first or second attempt, it is entirely possible that the exam will change significantly in form. It could be updated from fixed-form to adaptive form, or it might have a different set of questions or question types.

The intention of Microsoft is clearly not to make the exams more difficult by introducing unwanted change. Their intent is to create and maintain valid measures of the technical skills and knowledge associated with the different MCP credentials. Preparing for an MCP exam has always involved not only studying the subject matter, but also planning for the testing experience itself. With these changes, this is now more true than ever.

Practice Exam

Exam Questions

1. You administer a network of several subnets. You have several users with laptops running a combination of Windows 95 and Windows NT Workstation. The laptop users want to be able to plug into any of the several subnets in the office. What service will allow you to accomplish this?

   A. WINS

   B. DHCP

   C. RIP

   D. MAC

   E. DNS

2. You are responsible for an environment with two locations connected with a WAN link. You want users at both locations to be able to open Network Neighborhood and see all the available resources. What service will allow you to accomplish this?

   A. WINS

   B. DHCP

   C. RIP

   D. MAC

   E. DNS

3. You are running a simple network with only 20 computers and do not want to add the additional traffic created by using a WINS server for NetBIOS name resolution, especially considering that your network is very static in its configuration. Which of the following alternatives would work in that situation?

   A. DHCP

   B. DNS

   C. HOSTS file

   D. LMHOSTS file

   E. RIP

4. You have begun designing your new TCP/IP network. How do you calculate the number of host IDs needed for your new network?

   A. Estimate one host ID per user.

   B. Estimate one host ID per computer.

   C. Estimate one host ID per network card.

   D. Estimate one host ID for each subnet.

   E. Estimate one host ID for each router interface.

5. Identify the IP addresses that are unusable in an organization for standard user addresses.

   A. 116.74.250.10

   B. 208.258.220.43

   C. 244.26.17.9

   D. 192.168.10.30

   E. 128.26.20.10

6. What is the purpose of the ARP protocol?

   A. To discover the source system's IP address

   B. To discover the destination system's hardware address

   C. To discover the destination system's IP address

   D. To discover the source system's hardware address

   E. To troubleshoot network problems

7. You have configured a server to act as a storage location for files you want to be accessible to users running on a variety of systems, such as Macintosh and UNIX boxes. Which service should you run to best facilitate that?

   A. RCP

   B. Telnet

   C. RSH

   D. FTP

   E. SMTP

8. You administer an environment with a mix of Windows, Macintosh, and UNIX systems. You want all of them to be able to easily resolve computer names for ease of communication. Which service would best accomplish this?

   A. DHCP

   B. RIP

   C. WINS

   D. FTP

   E. DNS

9. With an IP address of 155.102.15.100 and subnet mask of 255.255.255.192, what is the network portion of the address?

   A. 155.102.15.0

B. 155.102.15.64

C. 155.102.15.65

D. 155.102.15.192

E. 155.102.15.200

10. You are running a four-subnet network in which subnet 1 has a Windows NT primary domain controller and the other three are running Windows NT backup domain controllers. Each domain controller serves as the master browser of its own subnet. You don't want to use WINS. How can you make sure the BDCs always synchronize properly with the PDC?

   A. On the PDC, create an LMHOSTS file with an entry for each of the BDCs.

   B. On each BDC, change the BDC directive to 0x2f in the Registry.

   C. On each BDC, create an LMHOSTS file with an entry for the PDC.

   D. Install the relay agent service on each BDC.

   E. Configure replication on the PDC to each of the BDCs.

11. With an IP address of 155.102.15.200 and subnet mask of 255.255.255.192, how many bits of the address are used for the host portion?

   A. 2

   B. 4

   C. 6

   D. 8

   E. 10

12. What type of DNS entry would you need to enter to route all mail sent to your domain to your mail server?

   A. CNAME

B. SMTP

C. A

D. MX

E. NS

13. Which utility do you use to send text to a UNIX-based network print server?

A. LPD

B. LPR

C. LPQ

D. FTP

E. Telnet

14. Which of the following are required parameters of DHCP scopes?

A. Lease duration

B. Default gateway

C. Subnet mask

D. Continuous range of IP addresses

E. Node type

15. If you administer three subnets (S1, S2, and S3) and place a DHCP server on subnet S1, where would you place the DHCP relay agents?

A. On the routers between subnets

B. S2

C. S3

D. DHCP server

E. PDC

16. You have been assigned three class C addresses for use on your network. You want to use a subnet mask that will pool all three as one network. The network addresses are 204.110.112.0,

204.110.113.0, and 204.110.114.0. What subnet mask should you use to make the range as tight as possible?

A. 255.255.255.0

B. 255.255.192.0

C. 255.255.128.0

D. 255.255.252.0

E. 255.255.248.0

17. You want to configure your Windows NT server to act as a print server for several UNIX boxes in your environment. What do you need to do to accomplish this?

A. Assign an IP to the printer.

B. Share the printer.

C. Install the Microsoft TCP/IP printing service on the server.

D. Install LPR on the server.

E. Install LPD on the UNIX boxes.

18. Which DNS file supplies the addresses of the root DNS servers if the zone served is somecompany.com and its class C address is 209.110.27.0?

A. boot

B. somecompany.com.dns

C. 27.110.209.in-addra.arpa.dns

D. named.boot

E. cache.dns

19. If your company's assigned network address is 214.27.48.0, what should the zone name be to support reverse DNS lookups?

A. 0.48.27.214.in-addr.arpa

B. 48.27.214.in-addr.arpa

C. 214.27.48.0.in-addr.arpa

D. 214.27.48.in-addr.arpa

E. 214.27.in-addr.arpa

20. You have been assigned the network address 148.16.0.0, which you need to break down into nine subnets. You will be connecting the subnets through a router that also connects to the Internet so that you can supply Internet connectivity. What subnet mask should you use?

A. 255.255.255.0

B. 255.255.0.0

C. 255.255.192.0

D. 255.255.240.0

E. 255.255.252.0

21. The DNS server that contains your physical DNS files is referred to as the

A. primary DNS server.

B. secondary DNS server.

C. caching DNS server.

D. forwarding DNS server.

E. replication DNS server.

22. SMTP, FTP, and Telnet are examples of protocols that

A. work at the Network Access layer.

B. work at the Application layer.

C. use TCP at the Transport layer.

D. use UDP at the Transport layer.

E. use IP at the Network layer.

23. NFS, TFTP, and SNMP are example of protocols that

A. work at the Network Access layer.

B. work at the Application layer.

C. use TCP at the Transport layer.

D. use UDP at the Transport layer.

E. use IP at the Network layer.

24. You administer a network that contains several subnets. Each subnet contains its own domain, and you want all users to be able to browse each domain. What entries do you need in the LMHOSTS file for each Windows computer to be able to accomplish this?

A. One entry for the PDC in each remote domain, and one entry for each domain controller in the local domain

B. One entry for a BDC in each remote domain, and one entry for a BDC in the local domain

C. One entry for the PDC in each remote domain, and one entry for a BDC in the local domain

D. One entry for a BDC in each remote domain and one entry for each domain controller in the local domain

E. One entry for each domain controller

25. You have a number of remote salespeople who need to connect to your internal network across the Internet. Your main facility is connected directly to the Internet, but you don't want to open it up to attackers. You want the salespeople to have access, but no one else. How do you accomplish this?

A. Enable IP filtering at the server.

B. Use FTP with user-level security.

C. Configure IIS to support SSL.

D. Use RAS with SSL.

E. Implement PPTP.

26. Your computer isn't configured to use DNS, and you want to retrieve a file from a UNIX box using the computer name of the UNIX box. What do you need on your computer to accomplish this?

    A. FTP server service

    B. RIP support

    C. HOSTS file

    D. NetBIOS over TCP/IP

    E. TCP/IP supplemental services

27. You have a UNIX box on your network. You use WINS for name support on your PCs. You want the Windows users to be able to easily connect to the UNIX box by name by using FTP and other services. Given this scenario, what is the best way to configure this?

    A. Enter the NetBIOS name and IP address of the WINS server in the HOSTS file on the UNIX computer.

    B. Set up the IP address of the UNIX computer as the default gateway address of the WINS server.

    C. Add a static mapping for the hostname and IP address of the UNIX computer to the WINS database.

    D. Enter the NetBIOS name and IP address of the WINS server to the LMHOSTS file on the UNIX computer.

    E. Add the name and IP address of the UNIX box to each computer's LMHOSTS file.

28. RAS supports which connection types?

    A. PSTN

    B. X.25

    C. ATM

D. ISDN

E. HDLC

29. You need to add UNIX entries to your WINS database. Which entry type should you add?

    A. Domain name

    B. Group

    C. Internet group

    D. Multihomed

    E. Unique

30. You have just promoted the ACCT computer to PDC in the CORP domain. Its IP address is 208.140.60.20. What entry should you place in the LMHOSTS file of client PCs if you aren't using WINS?

    A. 208.140.60.20 #acct #dom:corp

    B. 208.140.60.20 corp #pre #dom

    C. 208.140.60.20 corp #pre #dom:acct

    D. 208.140.60.20 acct #pre:corp

    E. 208.140.60.20 acct #pre #dom:corp

31. Which command can be used to check your routing table?

    A. IFCONFIG

    B. NETSTAT

    C. ARP

    D. NSLOOKUP

    E. SNOOP

32. Which programs will allow you to see both IP and ethernet statistics on an NT computer?

    A. NBTSTAT

    B. NETSTAT

C. IPCONFIG

D. WINIPCFG

E. Network Monitor

33. What must you install to use Performance Monitor to view TCP/IP protocol statistics?

A. RIP for TCP/IP

B. SNMP

C. Simple TCP/IP support

D. Network Monitor Agent

E. PPTP

34. What Windows NT tool lists all current connections to your computer?

A. ARP

B. WINIPCFG

C. NETSTAT

D. ROUTE

E. IPCONFIG

35. Which tool would best be used to save TCP/IP statistics for later analysis?

A. NETSTAT

B. NBTSTAT

C. Network Monitor

D. Performance Monitor

E. ARP

36. In order to view all the NetBIOS names currently cached on a computer, which command should you use?

A. NETSTAT

B. NBTSTAT

C. Network Monitor

D. Performance Monitor

E. ARP

37. Which tool is used to capture and decode network packets?

A. NETSTAT

B. NBTSTAT

C. Network Monitor

D. Performance Monitor

E. ARP

38. Which tool allows you to use both capture and display filters?

A. NETSTAT

B. NBTSTAT

C. Network Monitor

D. Performance Monitor

E. ARP

39. If you want to examine the cache of IP addresses to outgoing MAC addresses, which tool should you use?

A. NETSTAT

B. NBTSTAT

C. Network Monitor

D. Performance Monitor

E. ARP

40. After changing some entries in your LMHOSTS file, which tool would allow you to reload the file without restarting?

A. NETSTAT

B. NBTSTAT

C. Network Monitor

D. Performance Monitor

E. ARP

41. What is the utility most commonly used when diagnosing TCP/IP connectivity errors?

A. NSLOOKUP

B. TRACERT

C. PING

D. IPCONFIG

E. ROUTE

42. An end user contacts the system administrator because her machine cannot access the Internet. After troubleshooting the user's computer using the PING utility, you are able to connect to local systems. What TCP/IP configuration is most likely the cause of the problem?

A. IP address

B. DNS server address

C. WINS server address

D. Default gateway

E. Subnet mask

43. An end user contacts the system administrator because his machine cannot access the network. After troubleshooting the user's computer using the PING utility, you are only able to get a response for the user's local IP address and a couple other local machines. What TCP/IP configuration is most likely the cause of the problem?

A. IP address

B. DNS server address

C. WINS server address

D. Default gateway

E. Subnet mask

44. An end user contacts the system administrator because her machine cannot access her favorite Web sites. After troubleshooting the user's computer using the PING utility, you are able to get a response from both local and remote IP addresses. What TCP/IP configuration is most likely the cause of the problem?

A. IP address

B. DNS server address

C. WINS server address

D. Default gateway

E. Subnet mask

45. An end user contacts the system administrator because his computer is unable to connect to other machines. You sit down to troubleshoot and discover the user's computer is able to PING the loopback address and nothing else. What TCP/IP configuration is most likely the problem?

A. IP address

B. DNS server address

C. WINS server address

D. Default gateway

E. Subnet mask

46. An end user contacts the system administrator because she can't get anything to come up in the network neighborhood window. Which TCP/IP configuration parameter is the likely cause of the problem?

A. IP address

B. DNS server address

C. WINS server address

D. Default gateway

E. Subnet mask

47. To determine the route that packets are taking when diagnosing a failed connection, which utility should you use?

    A. NSLOOKUP

    B. TRACERT

    C. PING

    D. IPCONFIG

    E. ROUTE

48. Which tool allows you to troubleshoot DNS entries?

    A. NSLOOKUP

    B. TRACERT

    C. PING

    D. IPCONFIG

    E. ROUTE

49. While troubleshooting a PC, you discover it has an old DHCP lease that contains incorrect information. You need to release and obtain a new lease. Which tool allows you to do that?

    A. NSLOOKUP

    B. TRACERT

    C. PING

    D. IPCONFIG

    E. ROUTE

50. You have a server that cannot be connected to from remote networks but can be accessed from local computers. Which parameters might be the cause of this problem on the server?

    A. IP address

    B. DNS server address

    C. WINS server address

    D. Default gateway

    E. Subnet mask

51. A Windows NT Workstation computer resides on a WINS-enabled network. In which order will that computer perform name resolution if it is configured to use an LMHOSTS file?

    A. local cache, WINS server, broadcasting, LMHOSTS file

    B. local cache, broadcasting, LMHOSTS file, WINS server

    C. local cache, LMHOSTS file, broadcasting, WINS server

    D. WINS server, local cache, broadcasting, LMHOSTS file

    E. WINS server, local cache, LMHOSTS file, broadcasting

52. When troubleshooting TCP/IP, what is the first step Microsoft recommends that you perform?

    A. PING 127.0.0.1

    B. PING your IP address

    C. PING the address of your default gateway

    D. PING IP address of a remote host

    E. PING the remote host by hostname

53. A fellow administrator comes to you with the following situation: He is responsible for administering the Los Angeles and San Francisco sites, both of which have WINS servers that he wants to replicate. The Los Angeles site is a large office with over 1,000 Windows 95 and Windows NT workstation clients and 20 Windows NT servers. The San Francisco office has about 150 clients and 4 Windows NT servers. His primary objective is to replicate the WINS database from Los Angeles to San Francisco. His secondary

objectives are to make the L.A.-to-S.F. database replication occur at least once a day and also to replicate the S.F. database to L.A. His proposed solution is to configure the L.A. WINS server as a push partner with the S.F. WINS server every 1,000 updates and configure the S.F. WINS server to pull from the L.A. WINS server once every 24 hours. Which results does the proposed solution produce?

A. The proposed solution meets the primary objective and both of the secondary objectives.

B. The proposed solution meets the primary objective and one of the secondary objectives.

C. The proposed solution meets the primary objective but neither of the secondary objectives.

D. The proposed solution meets one of the secondary objectives but not the primary objective.

E. The proposed solution meets none of the objectives.

54. Your fellow administrator comes to you with the same situation as in question 53. However, this time his proposed solution is to configure the S.F. WINS server as a pull partner with the L.A. WINS server every 24 hours and configure the L.A. WINS server to pull from the S.F. WINS server once every 24 hours. Which results does the proposed solution produce?

A. The proposed solution meets the primary objective and both of the secondary objectives.

B. The proposed solution meets the primary objective and one of the secondary objectives.

C. The proposed solution meets the primary objective but neither of the secondary objectives.

D. The proposed solution meets one of the secondary objectives but not the primary objective.

E. The proposed solution meets none of the objectives.

55. As the local system administrator, you are faced with the following situation: You have two subnets in your network and want to use two DHCP servers to assign your IP addresses. Your primary objective is to make each DHCP server act as the backup server for the other DHCP server. Your secondary objectives are to have each DHCP server provide the same IP addresses each time unless it is acting as backup, and to have DHCP assign the node type, WINS server, and DNS server addresses as well. An associate of yours suggests the following solution: Configure each DHCP server as a duplicate of the other with a scope for each subnet and the appropriate additional information; then install the DHCP relay agent on each subnet. Which results does the proposed solution produce?

A. The proposed solution meets the primary objective and both of the secondary objectives.

B. The proposed solution meets the primary objective and one of the secondary objectives.

C. The proposed solution meets the primary objective but neither of the secondary objectives.

D. The proposed solution meets one of the secondary objectives but not the primary objective.

E. The proposed solution meets none of the objectives.

56. You have the same situation you had in question 55. However, another associate of yours suggests the following solution: Configure each DHCP server with two scopes, each with the first half of available addresses for the local subnet and the latter half of the other subnet; add the appropriate additional information to each scope; set up client leases for each computer on the local subnet; and install the DHCP relay agent on each subnet. Which results does the proposed solution produce?

    A. The proposed solution meets the primary objective and both of the secondary objectives.

    B. The proposed solution meets the primary objective and one of the secondary objectives.

    C. The proposed solution meets the primary objective but neither of the secondary objectives.

    D. The proposed solution meets one of the secondary objectives but not the primary objective.

    E. The proposed solution meets none of the objectives.

57. You administer a six-subnet network that consists of Windows NT, Windows 95, and UNIX machines. Unfortunately, the Windows NT and Windows 95 computers are moved around frequently. You want to ease this problem by implementing DHCP and WINS to allow a minimum of reconfiguration and still allow for easy integration among the Windows NT, Window 95, and UNIX boxes. The company computer name policy stipulates 14-character names for all computers. Your primary objective is for all the Windows NT and Windows 95 computers to be automatically configured via DHCP. Your secondary objectives are that all Windows NT and

Windows 95 computers be able to access all UNIX boxes by hostname and all UNIX boxes be able to access all Windows NT and Windows 95 boxes by hostname. Your proposed solution is to first enable DHCP broadcast forwarding on the routers, and then set up a WINS server. The next step is to set up a DHCP server configured to supply the address of the WINS server. Finally, you will set up a reservation for the IP address of the WINS server. Which results does the proposed solution produce?

    A. The proposed solution meets the primary objective and both of the secondary objectives.

    B. The proposed solution meets the primary objective and one of the secondary objectives.

    C. The proposed solution meets the primary objective but neither of the secondary objectives.

    D. The proposed solution meets one of the secondary objectives but not the primary objective.

    E. The proposed solution meets none of the objectives.

58. You have the same situation as in question 57. But this time, your proposed solution is to first enable DHCP broadcast forwarding on the routers, and then set up a WINS and DNS server on a nonrelocating Windows NT server. Next, you will set up a DHCP server configured to supply the address of the WINS and DNS server. Finally, you will set up WINS and DNS to integrate, and set up the UNIX boxes to use the DNS server. Which results does the proposed solution produce?

    A. The proposed solution meets the primary objective and both of the secondary objectives.

B. The proposed solution meets the primary objective and one of the secondary objectives.

C. The proposed solution meets the primary objective but neither of the secondary objectives.

D. The proposed solution meets one of the secondary objectives but not the primary objective.

E. The proposed solution meets none of the objectives.

ANSWERS TO EXAM QUESTIONS

1. **B.** Dynamic Host Configuration Protocol will allow the laptops to be plugged into each different subnet and automatically request the appropriate IP address, subnet mask, and default gateway, as well as any additional information needed to properly communicate in the environment.

2. **A.** Windows Internet Name Service provides a central database in which all services can be registered. Pointing all the user stations to this service will provide them a complete list of available systems and services.

3. **D.** The LMHOSTS file provides an alternative method of mapping IP addresses to NetBIOS names. The LMHOSTS files would need to be placed on each of the 20 computers.

4. **C** and **E.** Each network card and router interface needs its own IP address. Computers cannot simply be counted because there may be computers with multiple NICs in them.

5. **B** and **C.** The second octet in B exceeds 255. The first octet in C is not a valid class A, B, or C range.

6. **B.** Address Resolution Protocol is used by TCP/IP to determine the destination network card's hardware MAC address from the supplied IP address. This destination address will be the MAC address of the default gateway if the destination is on a remote subnet or the actual destination MAC address if both systems reside on the same network.

7. **D.** File Transfer Protocol is especially suited for environments with a wide variety of platforms because it is available on nearly every system that supports the TCP/IP protocol.

8. **E.** DNS server service is the protocol responsible for hostname-to-IP address resolution on the Internet.

9. **B.** A subnet mask of 192 means there are two subnet bits in the fourth octet. This means the available network ranges are x.x.x.65 to x.x.x.126 and x.x.x.129 to x.x.x.190. Because the address indicated falls into the .65 to .126 range, the network address is 155.102.15.64.

10. **C.** Because communications between domain controllers are based on the NetBIOS computer name, the BDCs each need the ability to resolve the PDC IP address based upon its name. A simple LMHOSTS file with an entry pointing to the PDC easily resolves this.

11. **C.** 192 converted to binary is 11000000. This means that the first two bits are being used for the network address and the last six for the host address portion.

12. **D.** Mail Exchange entries are used to specify the IP addresses of SMTP mail servers for the purpose of receiving email.

13. **B.** LPR is used to spool jobs to print servers. LPD is a service that receives print jobs.

14. **A, C,** and **D.** The default gateway and node type can both be supplied by DHCP but are not required. However, a scope name is required.

15. **B** and **C.** The relay agent needs to go on the subnets without the DHCP server; this way, it can convert the broadcast into a directed datagram so it will traverse the routers to the DHCP server.

16. **D.** By converting all three to binary, the third octets are 01110000, 01110001, and 01110010. Because only the last two digits are changing, you would mask the first six. Converting 11111100 to decimal yields a subnet mask of 252.

17. **C.** To support UNIX print jobs, the print server needs to run LPD. This is installed with the Microsoft TCP/IP printing service.

18. **E.** The CACHE.DNS file is preloaded with the addresses of the nine root DNS servers.

19. **B.** To create a reverse-lookup zone, reverse the network address to the extent of the class and add in-addr.arpa to it. If you have a class C address, such as in this question, that means reversing the first three octets. If you have a class B address, reverse the first two octets, and simply use the first octet in a class A address.

20. **D.** Using a subnet mask of 240 gives you 14 possible subnets, so this is the correct answer. 192 would yield only 2 subnets and 252 would yield 62, which would be too restrictive on host addresses.

21. **A.** The primary characteristic differentiating a primary DNS server from secondary servers is that the primary contains the master files. They all respond the same, from the perspective of the users.

22. **B, C,** and **E.** Simple Mail Transfer Protocol, File Transfer Protocol, and Telnet are all TCP-based Application layer protocols.

23. **B, D,** and **E.** Network File System, Trivial File Transfer Protocol, and Simple Network Management Protocol all use UDP-based communications.

24. **A.** Supplying the PDC of the remote domains works because the PDC is always the master browser. You should supply all domain controllers of each local domain because the computer then has multiple controllers to contact for login and similar purposes.

25. **E.** Point-to-Point Tunneling Protocol is supported by RAS in Windows NT 4 and allows the creation of VPNs across the Internet.

26. **C.** All the software needed is installed by default. You just need to add an entry to the HOSTS file to map the UNIX box computer name to its IP address.

27. **C.** By adding a static mapping to the WINS database, the users can easily resolve the IP address when they need to connect. Because UNIX does not natively support NetBIOS names, the entry has to be done manually. An alternative for name resolution would be to use a DNS server.

28. **A, B,** and **D.** Public Switched Telephone Network is the standard dial-up. Integrated Services Digital Network is supported with Windows NT 4. X.25 is an older wide-area network standard that is also supported by RAS.

29. **E.** A unique entry allows you to map a single name to a single IP address, which is the appropriate selection here.

30. **E.** The format for LMHOSTS entries is IP address, computer name, optional tags. In this

case, #pre indicates to preload it into the cache and #dom:corp indicates that it is a domain controller for the corp domain.

31. **B.** NETSTAT -r will display your routing table.

32. **B** and **E.** NBTSTAT is for viewing NetBIOS information. IPCONFIG and WINIPCFG are for viewing TCP/IP parameters.

33. **B.** When you install SNMP support, it also adds the support for Performance Monitor to be able to monitor TCP/IP statistics.

34. **C.** NETSTAT shows all current connections and the respective ports.

35. **D.** Performance Monitor can log all information to a file that can later be examined within Performance Monitor or exported for use in another program.

36. **B.** NetBIOS Table Status will list all currently cached NetBIOS names on the current machine with the NBTSTAT -c command. NBTSTAT -A and NBTSTAT -a will retrieve the name caches of remote computers.

37. **C.** Network Monitor allows you to capture all traffic to and from a given machine. It will display and automatically decode those packets for you.

38. **C.** Network Monitor allows you to analyze the traffic by filtering and displaying traffic based on a wide variety of flexible options. Without filters, the sheer quantity of packets can make analysis difficult.

39. **E.** ARP -a will display the current cache of IP-to-MAC addresses.

40. **B.** NBTSTAT -R will force a purge and reload of the NetBIOS name cache.

41. **C.** Because of PING's ability to determine connectivity, it is used in four of the five Microsoft-recommended steps for diagnosing TCP/IP connectivity problems. IPCONFIG/WINIPCFG is used for the other step.

42. **D.** Connectivity to remote subnets usually occurs by way of the default gateway. Because the local connectivity works, that is the most logical thing to check next.

43. **E.** Because the local address responded, you know TCP/IP is loaded correctly. A wrong subnet mask would cause the computer to incorrectly address local computers as remote and vice versa, so this would explain the connectivity to some and not others.

44. **B.** Because you have TCP/IP connectivity, the problem is most likely a name resolution problem. Internet name resolution is accomplished by way of DNS, so a DNS-related problem is the logical cause.

45. **A.** PINGing the loopback address tells you that TCP/IP itself is loaded correctly. Failure to PING the user's own NIC indicates a failure to bind the protocol to the adapter. The most common reason for this is a duplicate IP address.

46. **C.** The contents of the Network Neighborhood are populated from the list of available services registered at the domain master browser, which will usually be set to work with the WINS server. If the WINS server address is incorrect, the master browser will not have correct information.

47. **B.** TRACERT works by sending an ICMP echo (PING) packet to the destination with an incremented TTL starting with 1. When the TTL expires, the routers along the route send back a "Packet Expired" message. The source IP of the expiration notification tells TRACERT the IP addresses of the routers in the route.

48. **A.** Name Server LOOKUP will allow you to query a DNS server directly so you can make sure the correct responses are being returned.

49. **D.** IPCONFIG/RELEASE will release the old lease, and IPCONFIG/RENEW will cause the computer to obtain a new one.

50. **D** and **E.** An incorrect default gateway would not allow the server's replies to reach the remote networks. If the subnet mask is wrong, it could be sending the remote replies as if they were local to the server instead of through the router.

51. **A.** This order is known as h-node.

52. **A.** PINGing 127.0.0.1 (loopback) will tell you if TCP/IP is loaded correctly, which is a prerequisite for everything else to work.

53. **B.** The primary objective and the replication once every 24 hours are satisfied. Both the pull and push proposed cause the data to flow from Los Angeles and San Francisco.

54. **A.** The primary and both secondary objectives are satisfied.

55. **D.** The objective of passing the DNS and other information is met; however, if either server fails, that will most likely not work properly either. By creating both of the scopes the same on each subnet, if a failure ever occurs, the servers will be sending out leases for addresses which have most likely already been leased by the other server. This will result in duplicate IP addresses.

56. **A.** The configuring of scopes using only half of the available addresses on each subnet allows each DHCP server to back up the other without risk of causing duplicate IP addresses.

57. **C.** This solution meets the primary objective, but the WINS servers as configured do nothing to allow integration with the UNIX systems. Recall that WINS only supplies NetBIOS name to IP address resolution, which UNIX does not use. UNIX requires DNS-style name resolution.

58. **A.** This solution meets all the requirements and offers complete integration of naming systems for both the UNIX- and Windows-based clients.

APPENDIXES

Glossary

A-B

address reservation   In the context of a DHCP server, an address reservation is an IP address from a scope that is reserved for a client by its MAC address.

Address Resolution Protocol (ARP)   ARP is the part of the TCP/IP protocol suite that resolves an IP address to a MAC address. A utility called ARP can be used to view the resolutions.

backup browser   Part of the Microsoft browser system, a backup browser retrieves from the master browser a list of all computers that have a server service enabled. Clients then contact the backup browser to retrieve this list.

Berkeley .rhost file   A file in the UNIX environment that lists users who are permitted to use the Berkeley remote utilities.

Berkeley Internet Name Daemon (BIND)   A service that runs on a UNIX system to provide resolution of Fully Qualified Domain Names—a DNS server.

bindings   A binding in the Windows NT networking sense is a logical connection between a redirector or server and a protocol through the transport driver interface. This could be a logical connection between a protocol and a network adapter.

BOOT file   Part of the BIND implementation of DNS, the BOOT file (or named.boot) contains the basic configuration of the BIND server.

bridge   A bridge is a physical device that works at the Physical layer of the OSI network model to connect two network segments. A bridge listens to traffic on both segments and builds a list of MAC addresses that reside on each. It forwards packets from one segment to the other if the destination system is known.

broadcast node (b-node)   One of the four node types that can be set for NetBIOS name resolution. For Microsoft networks, the order of resolution is NetBIOS name cache, broadcast on the local network, LMHOSTS file, HOSTS file, and then a DNS server.

browser elections   Part of the Microsoft browser system, browser elections are used to decide which system will be the master browser on a network segment. When an election is called, all systems respond after a set time. The system that responds first wins the election and becomes the master browser.

browser service   A service in Windows NT that handles your computer's role in the Microsoft browser system.

byte-stream communications   A type of communications in which all data being sent is treated as a series of bytes instead of a series of messages defined by boundaries. This allows data to be streamed across the network with minimum delay.

C

cache file   The cache file in a DNS implementation is the file that contains the address of servers higher in the hierarchy. The cache file that comes with Windows NT connects to the root-level servers on the Internet.

caching-only server   A DNS server that does not have authority for any zone; that is, it does not provide authoritative answers for other DNS servers.

canonical name (CNAME) record   A CNAME record in a DNS zone file acts as an alias. This allows a single server to be mapped to multiple names.

capturing   The process of grabbing data from the network and storing it so the traffic can later be analyzed.

Chart view   One of the views in the Performance Monitor. The Chart view displays a graphical representation of either real-time or logged data.

class A network   A class A network is the largest class of IP networks. There are 126 class A networks, each of which accommodates 16,777,214 hosts.

class B network   A class B network is the second-largest class of IP networks. There are 16,384 class B networks, each of which accommodates 65,534 hosts.

class C network   A class C network is the smallest class of IP networks. There are 2,097,152 class C networks, each of which accommodates 254 hosts.

convergence   In terms of OSPF (or RIP), convergence is a state in which all the routers in a network know of all available routes.

counter   Within the Performance Monitor, a counter represents the aspects of an object that can be measured.

custom subnet mask   A standard subnet mask that has been augmented to either split a large network into smaller pieces (subnetting) or combine smaller networks in a larger one (supernetting).

D-G

default gateway   The configured router on a Microsoft TCP/IP-enabled system. If a packet is bound for a remote network but there is no specified route, the packet will be sent to this address.

DHCPACK   An acknowledgment from a DHCP server to a DHCP client indicating that the request for a lease (or renewal) was successful.

DHCPDISCOVER   A message sent from a DHCP client to the network broadcast address. This is the beginning of the lease process, which causes any appropriately configured DHCP server to offer a lease.

DHCPNACK   A negative acknowledgment from a DHCP server to a DHCP client indicating that the request for a lease (or renewal) was not successful.

DHCPOFFER   A message from the DHCP server to the client that has sent a discover message indicating an address that is available.

DHCPREQUEST   A message sent from a DHCP client to the server requesting an offer or renewing an IP address lease.

Dial-Up Networking   The part of the Remote Access Service (RAS) for Windows NT used to dial remote servers to gain access to a network.

domain master browser (DMB)   The primary domain controller (PDC) in a domain environment. In addition to having the responsibilities of a master browser, the DMB coordinates the browse list among subnets. This is required because NetBIOS broadcasts do not propagate across routers.

domain name system (DNS)   The domain name system describes a method of finding computers on a large network. DNS uses a hierarchical concept called name space, which spreads the work of maintaining a list of hosts and resolving queries through many servers at different levels.

Dynamic Host Configuration Protocol (DHCP)
This protocol is an extension of the boot protocol (BOOTP). DHCP automatically leases an IP address to a client and includes configuration parameters.

dynamic routing   Dynamic routing makes the process of moving packets across networks more effi-cient by letting routers know about all the available routes. This is done using a routing protocol such as RIP or OSPF.

ethernet   A network standard that uses Carrier Sense Multi Access with Collision Detection on a bus topolo-gy. Ethernet currently runs at 10MBps and 100MBps.

extinction   On a WINS server, this is the process by which a name/IP address pair that was registered and then released is eventually removed from the database.

File Transfer Protocol (FTP) utility   A standard TPC/IP utility that uses ports 20 and 21 to transfer files. User authentication is requested, but it is sent in clear text.

forwarder   A caching-only DNS server that has been configured to send name resolution requests to another DNS server rather than attempting a full resolution itself.

global options   Options that are set at a DHCP serv-er. Global options, such as the DNS server and WINS server address, will be sent to all systems leasing an address regardless of the scope from which they lease it.

H

host ID   The last portion of an IP address. The host ID uniquely identifies the host on a network that the IP address belongs to.

host record   A record in a DNS server for a normal computer on the network. It is also known as an "A" record because that is how it is entered in the zone file.

HOSTS file   Part of all implementations of TCP/IP, this is used to resolve hostnames to IP addresses. Found in win_root\system32\drivers\etc, it is a normal text file that lists an IP address and one or more names on each line.

hybrid node (h-node)   One of four node types that can be set for NetBIOS name resolution. For Microsoft networks, the order of resolution is NetBIOS name cache, NetBIOS name server (for example, WINS), broadcast on the local network, LMHOSTS file, HOSTS file, and then a DNS server.

I

instance   After selecting a counter in the Performance Monitor, all instances (occurrences) of the object are shown so you can choose which one you wish to monitor.

Integrated Services Digital Network (ISDN)   A type of communications line that provides higher-speed access to a network. Special equipment is required on both ends of the line to acquire higher speed.

Internet Control Messaging Protocol (ICMP)   One of the core protocols of the TCP/IP suite. This protocol is used to handle error messages and to control the flow of data across a network.

Internet Explorer   A browser from Microsoft that is used to view Web pages.

Internet Group Management Protocol (IGMP)
This protocol is one of the core protocols in the TCP/IP suite. It is used with routers when you are working with multicasting.

Internet Protocol (IP)   One of the core protocols of the TCP/IP suite. IP is responsible for determining if a packet is for the local network or a remote network; if it is for a remote network, IP finds a route for it.

Internet Protocol Configuration (IPCONFIG)   A utility that can be used to view the configuration details for TCP/IP installed on a computer. IPCONFIG can also be used to release or renew an address leased from a DHCP server.

IP address   A 32-bit binary address used to identify a station's network and host ID. The network portion can contain either a network ID or a network ID and a subnet ID.

iterative query   A DNS query sent from a DNS server to one or more DNS servers in search of a system that is authoritative for the name being sought.

J-L

Joint Engine Technology (JET)   A Microsoft database engine used in such products as FoxPro and Access. It is also used for the DHCP server and the WINS server.

LAN Manager HOSTS file (LMHOSTS)   An extension of the HOSTS file that was originally used for name resolution in the network environment. The file originally appeared with LAN Manager (it is named LMHOSTS for that reason).

lease duration   Part of the configuration of a scope in the DHCP server. The lease duration is how long the client is able to use the leased address. The client will start trying to renew the address at 50 percent of the lease duration.

Line Printer Daemon (LPD)   A service run on UNIX systems to allow remote systems to print to printing devices attached to the system. Windows NT includes the equivalent Microsoft TCP/IP printing service.

Line Printer Query (LPQ) utility   A UNIX utility that allows a user to query an LPD server to see the status of the job on the print queue.

Line Printer Remote (LPR) utility   A utility that can be used to send a file to an LPD server. In Windows NT there is also an option to create an LPR Port Monitor that handles this automatically.

Local Host Name (HOSTNAME) utility   A utility that allows you to view the hostname of a system. This is not used much in Windows NT. However, in UNIX, where it is common to Telnet to many different servers, this allows you to see which system you are currently on.

Log view   A view within the Performance Monitor that allows you to capture performance data about your system.

LPR Print Monitor   A printer monitor that allows you to create a printer that can be used like all other Windows NT printers except that it prints to an LPD server.

M

Mail Exchange (MX) record   A record in the DNS zone file that indicates which system in your network will receive mail. There can be more than one MX record; however, they will be used in order of the assigned preference number.

Management Information Base (MIB)   A MIB organizes a set of manageable objects for an installed service or device. There are four MIBs included with Windows NT: LAN Manager MIB II, Internet MIB II, DHCP MIB, and WINS MIB.

master browser   The master browser on a segment gathers a list of all the servers that belong to its domain. It also assigns other computers as backup browsers, which copy this list from the master browser and provide it to clients on the segment.

master server   In the context of DNS, a master server is the server from which a secondary server obtains the zone file. This can be either a primary or secondary DNS server.

Media Access Control (MAC)   Part of the Data Link layer from the OSI model. Under the IEEE 802 model, the Data Link layer was broken down into two layers: the Logical Link Control and the Media Access Control. The address of the adapter card in the local system is stored at the MAC layer; hence, the term MAC address for the address of the network adapter.

mixed node (m-node)   One of four node types that can be set for NetBIOS name resolution. For Microsoft networks, the order of resolution is NetBIOS name cache, broadcast on the local network, LMHOSTS file, NetBIOS name server (for example, WINS), HOSTS file, and then a DNS server.

modulating/demodulating device (modem)   A modem is used to convert digital signals to analog and vice versa. This allows communications over regular phone lines.

multicasting   Multicasting is a method of sending a series of packets to a group of computers instead of a single computer or all computers on a network. Multicasting uses class D addresses (starting with 224 to 239), to which it sends the packets. Any station that wants to receive the transmission can tune to the address. The routers must support IGMP to allow multicasting to function.

N

name query/name resolution   A name request for the resolution of a NetBIOS name. Name queries can be sent to a NetBIOS name server, or they can broadcast on the local subnet.

name registration   Name registration is performed when a system starts, a service starts, or a user logs on. This checks to see if the name already exists on the network. Registrations can be sent as a broadcast on the local network or to a NetBIOS name server, where the name and IP address are added to the database.

name release   Lets other systems such as the browser know that a system is shutting down. It can be a broadcast or sent to a NetBIOS name server.

name renewal   A transmission sent to a WINS server requesting that the system be able to keep the name.

name server   A part of DNS, the name server is a computer that responds to a name query from other name servers, from a client using a local zone, or by performing an iterative query.

Name Server Lookup (NSLOOKUP) utility   Allows you to query a name server. Both a command-line mode and an interactive mode are available.

NetBIOS name   The name of the computer used for NetBIOS networking. This name can be 16 characters long: 15 provide the friendly name, and the 16th represents the service registering the name.

NetBIOS name cache   A list of systems that your computer has resolved or that you preloaded from the LMHOSTS file. The name cache is the first method of name resolution that is tried for all node types.

NetBIOS node type The node type sets the order of name resolution for NetBIOS names. There are four types: b-node, p-node, m-node, and h-node.

NetBIOS over TCP/IP (NBT or NetBT) The name given to the process of running NetBIOS network services over TCP/IP.

NetBIOS over TCP/IP Statistics (NBTSTAT) utility Allows you to verify the current connections over NBT. It also allows you to check and load the NetBIOS name cache.

Network Basic Input/Output System (NetBIOS) An Application layer networking protocol that works at the Application, Presentation, and Session layers of the OSI model. Microsoft networking uses NetBIOS as the Application layer protocol.

Network Driver Interface Specification (NDIS) The NDIS layer is used as an interface between the transport protocols and the network adapter cards. The NDIS layer facilitates the binding of multiple protocols to a single network card.

network ID The part of the IP address assigned to the station. The subnet mask is used to extract the network ID from the IP address when the IP protocol determines whether a target host is local or remote. The network ID can include a subnet ID.

Network Logon (Netlogon) service Used to validate user logon. Netlogon creates a secure channel between a client and the domain controller to pass the user's credentials. Netlogon is also responsible for replicating the user-accounts database between domain controllers.

Network Monitor A Microsoft tool that allows a user to intercept and analyze network packets. There are two versions of the Network Monitor: the limited version that comes with Windows NT (which can only read packets flowing into or out of the local systems) and the full version (which can read all packets on the network).

Network Monitor Agent The part of the Microsoft Network Monitor that actually grabs the frames from the network. By separating the tool from the agent, Microsoft allows you to monitor activity on remote subnets.

Network Statistics (NETSTAT) utility Can be used to determine which ports and protocols are in use on the local system.

nonbrowser Within the context of the Microsoft browser system, is a computer that is not configured to maintain a list of servers on the network.

O-P

object In its simplest definition, an object is a container that holds something such as a file or user account. Users will normally work with the data in the object; properties that are assigned to the object determine what a user is allowed to do with the data contained in it and with the container itself.

Open Shortest Path First (OSPF) A routing protocol that allows routers to share their routing information—making them dynamic routers. OSPF describes a method in which a network is broken down into areas; all routers in an area know of all other routers, and border routers for each area will connect to a backbone.

Packet Internet Groper Utility (PING) A utility used to troubleshoot TCP/IP problems. PING sends a packet with data asking the remote system to echo the packet.

Performance Monitor A tool included with Windows NT, this allows a user to view details about the performance of a system on many levels and to record log files containing performance data over a period of time for later analysis.

point-to-point node (p-node) One of the four node types that can be set for NetBIOS name resolution. For Microsoft networks, the order of resolution is NetBIOS name cache, NetBIOS name server (for example, WINS), HOSTS file, and then a DNS server.

Point-to-Point Protocol (PPP) A serial-line protocol that replaces the frame types found on networks when communicating over a serial line. It defines how the data is physically transmitted.

Point-to-Point Protocol—Multilink Protocol (PPP—MP) An extension of the PPP protocol that allows a user to connect to a remote RAS server using more than a single connection. For example, ISDN dial-up uses two 56Kbps channels that are bound together to make a 112Kbps connection.

Point-to-Point Tunneling Protocol (PPTP) An extension of the PPP protocol that allows a secure session to be encapsulated within a PPP session. Doing this creates a secure connection out of a normal connection. An Internet dial-in account can be made into a virtual private network (VPN).

pointer record (PTR) In DNS, a pointer record is used in a reverse-lookup file to point an IP address at a Fully Qualified Domain Name. This allows users and services to look up the name of a system that has connected to the local system.

potential browser In the Microsoft browser system, a potential browser is a system that can be configured to maintain a server list, but which is not currently acting as a master or backup browser.

primary DNS server The name server that contains the read/write (original) copy of a zone file. All changes to the zone are made at this server.

printer In Windows NT terms, a printer is a logical device that exists as a printer queue and a printer driver on a Windows NT system. The printer sends files to the physical device using a port monitor that controls the flow of information from the queue.

printing device The physical device that produces printed output.

Public Switched Telephone Network (PSTN) The normal telephone network.

Q-R

recursive query A DNS query that is sent looking for an authoritative answer or an answer indicating that there is no resolution. Normally, this is sent from the resolver to the name server. However, it can be sent from a caching-only server either configured as a forwarder or configured to use a WINS server.

Remote Access Service (RAS) The service in Windows NT that allows a station to call out or receive calls over a serial line, ISDN line, or x.25 network to another network.

Remote Copy Protocol Utility (RCP) A utility that can be used to transfer files from a TFTP server. TFTP, a connectionless transfer utility, uses the UDP transport protocol.

Remote Execution (REXEC) utility Allows you to submit a job to a UNIX workstation. It requires a username.

Remote Shell (RSH) utility Allows you to submit a job to a UNIX workstation. It requires that your name appear in the .rhosts file on the UNIX system.

repeater A physical device that takes a signal from one interface and retransmits it to another. This allows a network segment to be extended beyond the normal limits of the topology.

resolver The part of DNS that is on the client workstation. A resolver sends a name resolution query to the name server.

reverse-lookup file   Contains the reverse-lookup zone for a DNS name server. The reverse-lookup zone allows users to query an IP address and receive the Fully Qualified Domain Name of the system at that IP address.

router   A router is a system or device that has an Internet layer installed. This device receives packets sent to it, checks its routing table for the next hop, and then forwards the packets. Routing takes place at the Internet layer.

routing   The process of moving a packet from one network to another network using a router.

Routing Internet Protocol (RIP)   A protocol used by dynamic routers to share their routing tables. By sharing routing tables, routers are able to discover routes to other networks.

routing protocol   Allows routers to share their routing tables. By doing this, routers are able to discover routes to other networks.

routing table   This table, kept on a router, provides a subnet mask and network ID. The target address is ANDed with the subnet mask; if the results match the network ID, the packet is sent to the listed gateway.

Routing Table (ROUTE) utility   Allows you to view and modify the routing table.

S

scavenging   On a WINS server, the process of taking entries that have expired out of the database.

scope   When you configure a DHCP server, you create one or more ranges of IP addresses that can be leased to clients. Each of these ranges of addresses is called a scope.

scope options   After you have created a scope of IP addresses that are to be leased by a DHCP server, you can also set options that are sent to the client. These options can affect all the scopes, as with global options, or a single scope, as with scope options.

secondary DNS server   A secondary DNS name server provides name resolution for a zone. The information for the resolution comes from a zone file that is copied from a master server. The file will always be copied initially from the primary DNS server.

Serial Line Internet Protocol (SLIP)   A line protocol for serial communications that replaces the frames on a physical network. The SLIP protocol can only transfer TCP/IP packets and provides only limited security.

SERVICES file   This file, located in the win_root\system32\drivers\etc directory, lists the socket numbers for the different protocols installed on the system.

Simple Network Management Protocol (SNMP)   Used by the management station to read information from agents. It is used to manage systems and devices within a network, but it provides only limited security.

slave   A slave in DNS is a caching-only server that is configured to use a forwarder. The slave is allowed to ask only the configured forwarder for resolutions; it cannot contact any other server.

sliding window   Used in TCP to allow data to be sent and acknowledged. The transmit window on one station is set to the size of the receive window on the other. Only data within the transmit window can be sent. The window slides past data that is acknowledged to allow more data to be sent.

SNMP agent   Can reside on a device or system and responds to queries from a management station in the same community. The agent can also send a trap, which notifies the management station of significant events.

SNMP community A community in SNMP describes a group of systems that are all managed together. The management station must be a member of the same community.

SNMP manager An SNMP manager (or management station) is used to monitor SNMP agents and receive traps from the stations.

socket Describes an endpoint for communications. A socket is a combination of the IP address, the transport protocol used, and the port number. The port can be opened as either a service (listening port) or a client (active port).

standard subnet mask Describes the portion of the IP address that is used by default for the network ID. The standard subnet masks are: class A, 255.0.0.0; class B, 255.255.0.0; and class C, 255.255.255.0.

start of authority (SOA) In a DNS zone file, the SOA record tells the name servers how long the name can be cached and tells the secondary servers how long they can go before transferring the zone from the primary (or master) server. The SOA record also provides the name of the primary server and the person in charge of the domain.

static routing A routing scenario in which the routers do not share their routing tables. This means that routes to distant networks need to be added manually.

subnet Part of a larger network. You will be assigned a network ID from your Internet service provider (ISP) or InterNIC. The process of subnetting allows you to control how many hosts are on each part or subnet of your network. Using more bits in the subnet mask allows you to make different segments on your network look remote to each other.

subnet ID Part of the IP address. The network ID contains the ID that you were assigned; if you are subnetting, it will contain a subnet ID.

subnet mask The subnet mask is a 32-bit number in which the bits are turned from left to right for the number of bits you are using for your network and subnet IDs.

supernet A supernet, or CIDR (Classless Interdomain Routing), scenario involves combining several small groups of addresses (normally, class C addresses) into a larger network address.

T

Terminal Emulation (Telnet) utility This utility provides you with a terminal window to another station on the network.

token ring A form of network in which a token circulates. Systems engage the token and attach data to it. The data circulates through the ring until the system that it is intended for receives it and marks the token as such. The token then circles back to the sending system, which then releases the token.

Trace Router (TRACERT) utility The TRACERT utility allows you to view the route that packets will take on your network.

Transmission Control Protocol (TCP) One of the core protocols in the TCP/IP protocol suite. The TCP protocol is used to provide connection-oriented data transfer between clients.

Trivial File Transfer Protocol Utility (TFTP) Provides the capability to transfer files without first creating a session. The TFTP protocol is frequently used in the UNIX world to transfer start code to devices and diskless workstations.

U-Z

User Datagram Protocol (UDP)   A connectionless protocol that is part of the TCP/IP core of protocols. UDP is frequently used in broadcasts.

verify interval   The interval at which a WINS server verifies the entries it has received from another WINS server.

virtual private network (VPN)   The connection that you create when you make a PPTP connection from a system to a RAS server. The information that goes across a VPN is encrypted for security.

Windows Internet Name Service (WINS)   A service that runs on a Windows NT server and provides resolution of NetBIOS names. When you use WINS, name resolution is done using directed transmissions, resulting in a reduction in broadcast traffic and the ability to find systems on different subnets.

Windows Sockets (Winsock)   The sockets interface in Microsoft Windows NT.

WINS proxy   A WINS client on a subnet where there are non-WINS clients. The proxy agent responds to name resolution requests if it has the name in its NetBIOS name cache. If the name is not available, the proxy agent queries the WINS server and adds the name to its NetBIOS name cache.

WINS replication   The capability of a WINS server to replicate its database of names with other WINS servers.

zone   Part of the DNS name space. A server can have one or more zones for which it will be able to provide name resolution.

APPENDIX B

Overview of the Certification Process

You must pass rigorous certification exams to become a Microsoft Certified Professional. These closed-book exams provide a valid and reliable measure of your technical proficiency and expertise. Developed in consultation with computer industry professionals who have on-the-job experience with Microsoft products in the workplace, the exams are conducted by two independent organizations. Sylvan Prometric offers the exams at more than 1,400 Authorized Prometric Testing Centers around the world. Virtual University Enterprises (VUE) testing centers offer exams as well.

To schedule an exam, call Sylvan Prometric Testing Centers at 800-755-EXAM (3926) or VUE at 888-837-8616. Currently, Microsoft offers seven types of certification based on specific areas of expertise.

TYPES OF CERTIFICATION

◆ **Microsoft Certified Professional (MCP).** Qualified to provide installation, configuration, and support for users of at least one Microsoft desktop operating system, such as Windows NT Workstation. Candidates can take elective exams to develop areas of specialization. MCP is the base level of expertise.

◆ **Microsoft Certified Professional+Internet (MCP+Internet).** Qualified to plan security, install and configure server products, manage server resources, extend service to run CGI scripts or ISAPI scripts, monitor and analyze performance, and troubleshoot problems. Expertise is similar to that of an MCP, but with a focus on the Internet.

◆ **Microsoft Certified Professional+Site Building (MCP+Site Building).** Qualified to plan, build, maintain, and manage Web sites using Microsoft technologies and products. The credential is appropriate for people who manage sophisticated, interactive Web sites that include database connectivity, multimedia, and searchable content.

◆ **Microsoft Certified Systems Engineer (MCSE).** Qualified to effectively plan, implement, maintain, and support information systems with Microsoft Windows NT and other Microsoft advanced systems and workgroup products, such as Microsoft Office and Microsoft BackOffice. MCSE is a second level of expertise.

◆ **Microsoft Certified Systems Engineer+Internet (MCSE+Internet).** Qualified in the core MCSE areas, and also qualified to enhance, deploy, and manage sophisticated intranet and Internet solutions that include a browser, proxy server, host servers, database, and messaging and commerce components. An MCSE+Internet–certified professional is able to manage and analyze Web sites.

◆ **Microsoft Certified Solution Developer (MCSD).** Qualified to design and develop custom business solutions by using Microsoft development tools, technologies, and platforms, including Microsoft Office and Microsoft BackOffice. MCSD is a second level of expertise with a focus on software development.

◆ **Microsoft Certified Trainer (MCT).** Instructionally and technically qualified by Microsoft to deliver Microsoft education courses at Microsoft-authorized sites. An MCT must be employed by a Microsoft Solution Provider Authorized Technical Education Center or a Microsoft Authorized Academic Training site.

NOTE For up-to-date information about each type of certification, visit the Microsoft Training and Certification World Wide Web site at `http://www.microsoft.com/train_cert`. You also can contact Microsoft through the following sources:

- Microsoft Certified Professional Program:
  800-636-7544

- mcp@msource.com

- Microsoft Online Institute (MOLI):
  800-449-9333

CERTIFICATION REQUIREMENTS

The following sections illustrate the process of becoming a Microsoft Certified Professional.

An asterisk following an exam in any of the lists means that is it slated for retirement.

How to Become a Microsoft Certified Professional

Passing any Microsoft exam (with the exception of Networking Essentials) is all you need to do to become certified as an MCP.

How to Become a Microsoft Certified Professional+Internet

You must pass the following exams to become an MCP specializing in Internet technology (MCP+Internet):

- ◆ Internetworking Microsoft TCP/IP on Microsoft Windows NT 4.0, #70-059

- ◆ Implementing and Supporting Microsoft Windows NT Server 4.0, #70-067

- ◆ Implementing and Supporting Microsoft Internet Information Server 3.0 and Microsoft Index Server 1.1, #70-077

  OR Implementing and Supporting Microsoft Internet Information Server 4.0, #70-087

How to Become a Microsoft Certified Professional+Site Building

You need to pass two of the following exams in order to be certified as an MCP specializing in site building (MCP+Site Building):

- ◆ Designing and Implementing Web Sites with Microsoft FrontPage 98, #70-055

◆ Designing and Implementing Commerce Solutions with Microsoft Site Server 3.0, Commerce Edition, #70-057

◆ Designing and Implementing Web Solutions with Microsoft Visual InterDev 6.0, #70-152

How to Become a Microsoft Certified Systems Engineer

You must pass four operating system exams and two elective exams to become an MCSE. The MCSE certification path is divided into two tracks: the Windows NT 3.51 track and the Windows NT 4.0 track.

The following sections list the core requirements (four operating system exams) for both the Windows NT 3.51 and 4.0 tracks, and the electives (two exams) you can take for either track.

Windows NT 3.51 Track

The Windows NT 3.51 track will probably be retired with the release of Windows NT 5.0. The Windows NT 3.51 core exams are scheduled for retirement at that time.

Core Exams

The four Windows NT 3.51 track core requirements for MCSE certification are as follows (an asterisk denotes an exam that is scheduled to be retired):

◆ Implementing and Supporting Microsoft Windows NT Server 3.51, #70-043*

◆ Implementing and Supporting Microsoft Windows NT Workstation 3.51, #70-042*

◆ Microsoft Windows 3.1, #70-030*

OR Microsoft Windows for Workgroups 3.11, #70-048*

OR Implementing and Supporting Microsoft Windows 95, #70-064

OR Implementing and Supporting Microsoft Windows 98, #70-098

◆ Networking Essentials, #70-058

Windows NT 4.0 Track

The Windows NT 4.0 track is also organized around core and elective exams.

Core Exams

The four Windows NT 4.0 track core requirements for MCSE certification are as follows (an asterisk denotes an exam that is scheduled to be retired):

◆ Implementing and Supporting Microsoft Windows NT Server 4.0, #70-067

◆ Implementing and Supporting Microsoft Windows NT Server 4.0 in the Enterprise, #70-068

◆ Microsoft Windows 3.1, #70-030*

OR Microsoft Windows for Workgroups 3.11, #70-048*

OR Implementing and Supporting Microsoft Windows 95, #70-064

OR Implementing and Supporting Microsoft Windows NT Workstation 4.0, #70-073

OR Implementing and Supporting Microsoft Windows 98, #70-098

◆ Networking Essentials, #70-058

Elective Exams

For both the Windows NT 3.51 and 4.0 tracks, you must pass two of the following elective exams for MCSE certification (an asterisk denotes an exam that is scheduled to be retired):

◆ Implementing and Supporting Microsoft SNA Server 3.0, #70-013

  OR Implementing and Supporting Microsoft SNA Server 4.0, #70-085

◆ Implementing and Supporting Microsoft Systems Management Server 1.0, #70-014*

  OR Implementing and Supporting Microsoft Systems Management Server 1.2, #70-018

  OR Implementing and Supporting Microsoft Systems Management Server 2.0, #70-086

◆ Microsoft SQL Server 4.2 Database Implementation, #70-021

  OR Implementing a Database Design on Microsoft SQL Server 6.5, #70-027

  OR Implementing a Database Design on Microsoft SQL Server 7.0, #70-029

◆ Microsoft SQL Server 4.2 Database Administration for Microsoft Windows NT, #70-022

  OR System Administration for Microsoft SQL Server 6.5 (or 6.0), #70-026

  OR System Administration for Microsoft SQL Server 7.0, #70-028

◆ Microsoft Mail for PC Networks 3.2–Enterprise, #70-037

◆ Internetworking with Microsoft TCP/IP on Microsoft Windows NT (3.5–3.51), #70-053

  OR Internetworking with Microsoft TCP/IP on Microsoft Windows NT 4.0, #70-059

◆ Implementing and Supporting Microsoft Exchange Server 4.0, #70-075*

  OR Implementing and Supporting Microsoft Exchange Server 5.0, #70-076

  OR Implementing and Supporting Microsoft Exchange Server 5.5, #70-081

◆ Implementing and Supporting Microsoft Internet Information Server 3.0 and Microsoft Index Server 1.1, #70-077

  OR Implementing and Supporting Microsoft Internet Information Server 4.0, #70-087

◆ Implementing and Supporting Microsoft Proxy Server 1.0, #70-078

  OR Implementing and Supporting Microsoft Proxy Server 2.0, #70-088

◆ Implementing and Supporting Microsoft Internet Explorer 4.0 by Using the Internet Explorer Resource Kit, #70-079

How to Become a Microsoft Certified Systems Engineer+Internet

You must pass seven operating system exams and two elective exams to become an MCSE specializing in Internet technology (MCSE+Internet).

Core Exams

The seven MCSE+Internet core exams required for certification are as follows:

◆ Networking Essentials, #70-058

◆ Internetworking with Microsoft TCP/IP on Microsoft Windows NT 4.0, #70-059

◆ Implementing and Supporting Microsoft Windows 95, #70-064

OR Implementing and Supporting Microsoft Windows NT Workstation 4.0, #70-073

OR Implementing and Supporting Microsoft Windows 98, #70-098

◆ Implementing and Supporting Microsoft Windows NT Server 4.0, #70-067

◆ Implementing and Supporting Microsoft Windows NT Server 4.0 in the Enterprise, #70-068

◆ Implementing and Supporting Microsoft Internet Information Server 3.0 and Microsoft Index Server 1.1, #70-077

OR Implementing and Supporting Microsoft Internet Information Server 4.0, #70-087

◆ Implementing and Supporting Microsoft Internet Explorer 4.0 by Using the Internet Explorer Resource Kit, #70-079

Elective Exams

You must also pass two of the following elective exams for MCSE+Internet certification:

◆ System Administration for Microsoft SQL Server 6.5, #70-026

◆ Implementing a Database Design on Microsoft SQL Server 6.5, #70-027

◆ Implementing and Supporting Web Sites Using Microsoft Site Server 3.0, # 70-056

◆ Implementing and Supporting Microsoft Exchange Server 5.0, #70-076

OR Implementing and Supporting Microsoft Exchange Server 5.5, #70-081

◆ Implementing and Supporting Microsoft Proxy Server 1.0, #70-078

OR Implementing and Supporting Microsoft Proxy Server 2.0, #70-088

◆ Implementing and Supporting Microsoft SNA Server 4.0, #70-085

How to Become a Microsoft Certified Solution Developer

The MCSD certification is undergoing substantial revision. Listed in the following sections are the requirements for the new track (available fourth quarter 1998) as well as the old.

New Track

For the new track, you must pass three core exams and one elective exam. The three core exam areas are listed here along with the elective exams from which you can choose.

Desktop Applications Development (1 required)

◆ Designing and Implementing Desktop Applications with Microsoft Visual C++ 6.0, #70-016

OR Designing and Implementing Desktop Applications with Microsoft Visual Basic 6.0, #70-176

Distributed Applications Development (1 required)

◆ Designing and Implementing Distributed Applications with Microsoft Visual C++ 6.0, #70-015

OR Designing and Implementing Distributed Applications with Microsoft Visual Basic 6.0, #70-175

Solution Architecture (required)

◆ Analyzing Requirements and Defining Solution Architectures, #70-100

New Track Elective Exams

You must pass one of the following elective exams:

◆ Designing and Implementing Distributed Applications with Microsoft Visual C++ 6.0, #70-015

   OR Designing and Implementing Desktop Applications with Microsoft Visual C++ 6.0, #70-016

   OR Microsoft SQL Server 4.2 Database Implementation, #70-021*

◆ Implementing a Database Design on Microsoft SQL Server 6.5, #70-027

   OR Implementing a Database Design on Microsoft SQL Server 7.0, #70-029

◆ Developing Applications with C++ Using the Microsoft Foundation Class Library, #70-024

◆ Implementing OLE in Microsoft Foundation Class Applications, #70-025

◆ Designing and Implementing Web Sites with Microsoft FrontPage 98, #70-055

◆ Designing and Implementing Commerce Solutions with Microsoft Site Server 3.0, Commerce Edition, #70-057

◆ Programming with Microsoft Visual Basic 4.0, #70-065

   OR Developing Applications with Microsoft Visual Basic 5.0, #70-165

   OR Designing and Implementing Distributed Applications with Microsoft Visual Basic 6.0, #70-175

   OR Designing and Implementing Desktop Applications with Microsoft Visual Basic 6.0, #70-176

◆ Microsoft Access for Windows 95 and the Microsoft Access Development Toolkit, #70-069

◆ Designing and Implementing Solutions with Microsoft Office (Code-named Office 9) and Microsoft Visual Basic for Applications, #70-091

◆ Designing and Implementing Web Solutions with Microsoft Visual InterDev 6.0, #70-152

Old Track

For the old track, you must pass two core technology exams and two elective exams for MCSD certification. The following lists show the required technology exams and elective exams needed to become an MCSD (an asterisk denotes an exam that is scheduled to be retired).

Core Technology Exams

You must pass the following two core technology exams to qualify for MCSD certification under old track requirements:

◆ Microsoft Windows Architecture I, #70-160*

◆ Microsoft Windows Architecture II, #70-161*

Elective Exams

You must also pass two of the following elective exams to become an MSCD under old track requirements:

◆ Designing and Implementing Distributed Applications with Microsoft Visual C++ 6.0, #70-015

◆ Designing and Implementing Desktop Applications with Microsoft Visual C++ 6.0, #70-016

◆ Microsoft SQL Server 4.2 Database Implementation, #70-021*

   OR Implementing a Database Design on Microsoft SQL Server 6.5, #70-027

   OR Implementing a Database Design on Microsoft SQL Server 7.0, #70-029

◆ Developing Applications with C++ Using the Microsoft Foundation Class Library, #70-024

◆ Implementing OLE in Microsoft Foundation Class Applications, #70-025

◆ Programming with Microsoft Visual Basic 4.0, #70-065

   OR Developing Applications with Microsoft Visual Basic 5.0, #70-165

   OR Designing and Implementing Distributed Applications with Microsoft Visual Basic 6.0, #70-175

   OR Designing and Implementing Desktop Applications with Microsoft Visual Basic 6.0, #70-176

◆ Microsoft Access 2.0 for Windows-Application Development, #70-051

   OR Microsoft Access for Windows 95 and the Microsoft Access Development Toolkit, #70-069

◆ Developing Applications with Microsoft Excel 5.0 Using Visual Basic for Applications, #70-052

◆ Programming in Microsoft Visual FoxPro 3.0 for Windows, #70-054

◆ Designing and Implementing Web Sites with Microsoft FrontPage 98, #70-055

◆ Designing and Implementing Commerce Solutions with Microsoft Site Server 3.0, Commerce Edition, #70-057

◆ Designing and Implementing Solutions with Microsoft Office (Code-named Office 9) and Microsoft Visual Basic for Applications, #70-091

◆ Designing and Implementing Web Solutions with Microsoft Visual InterDev 6.0, #70-152

Becoming a Microsoft Certified Trainer

To understand the requirements and process for becoming an MCT, you need to obtain the Microsoft Certified Trainer Guide document from the following Web site:

```
http://www.microsoft.com/train_cert/mct/
```

At this site, you can read the document as Web pages or display and download it as a Word file. The MCT Guide explains the four-step process of becoming an MCT. The general steps for the MCT certification are as follows:

1. Complete and mail a Microsoft Certified Trainer application to Microsoft. You must include proof of your skills for presenting instructional material.

The options for doing so are described in the MCT Guide.

2. Obtain and study the Microsoft Trainer Kit for the Microsoft Official Curricula (MOC) courses for which you want to be certified. Microsoft Trainer Kits can be ordered by calling 800-688-0496 in North America. Those of you in other regions should review the MCT Guide for information on how to order a Trainer Kit.

3. Take the Microsoft certification exam for the product about which you want to be certified to teach.

4. Attend the MOC course for the path you want to be certified for. This is done so you can understand how the course is structured, how labs are completed, and how the course flows.

> **WARNING** You should consider the preceding steps a general overview of the MCT certification process. The precise steps that you need to take are described in detail on the Web site. Do not misinterpret the preceding steps as the exact process you need to undergo.

If you are interested in becoming an MCT, you can receive more information by visiting the Microsoft Certified Training Web site at http://www.microsoft.com/train_cert/mct/ or by calling 800-688-0496.

What's on the CD-ROM

This appendix offers a brief rundown of what you'll find on the CD-ROM that comes with this book. For a more detailed description of the newly developed Top Score test engine, exclusive to Macmillan Computer Publishing, see Appendix D, "Using the Top Score Software."

TOP SCORE

Top Score is a test engine developed exclusively for Macmillan Computer Publishing. It is, we believe, the best test engine available because it closely emulates the format of the standard Microsoft exams. In addition to providing a means of evaluating your knowledge of the exam material, Top Score features several innovations that help you to improve your mastery of the subject matter. For example, the practice tests allow you to check your score by exam area or category, which helps you determine which topics you need to study further. Other modes allow you to obtain immediate feedback on your response to a question, explanation of the correct answer, and even hyperlinks to the chapter in an electronic version of the book where the topic of the question is covered. Again, for a complete description of the benefits of Top Score, see Appendix C.

Before you attempt to run the Top Score software, make sure that autorun is enabled. If you prefer not to use autorun, you can run the application from the CD by double-clicking the START.EXE file from within Explorer.

EXCLUSIVE ELECTRONIC VERSION OF TEXT

As alluded to above, the CD-ROM also contains the electronic version of this book in Portable Document Format (PDF). In addition to the links to the book that are built into the Top Score engine, you can use that version of the book to help you search for terms you need to study or other book elements. The electronic version comes complete with all figures as they appear in the book.

COPYRIGHT INFORMATION AND DISCLAIMER

Macmillan Computer Publishing's Top Score test engine: Copyright 1998 New Riders Publishing. All rights reserved. Made in U.S.A.

Using the Top Score Software

GETTING STARTED

The installation procedure for the Top Score software is very simple. Put the CD into the CD-ROM drive. The auto-run function starts and after a moment, you will see the opening screen. Click Exit to quit or Continue to proceed. If you clicked Continue, then you will see a window offering you the choice of launching any of the four Top Score applications.

> **NOTE**
>
> **Getting Started Without Auto-Run** If you have disabled the auto-run function, you may start the Top Score software suite by viewing the contents of the CD-ROM in Explorer and double-clicking START.EXE.

At this point you are ready to use the Top Score software.

INSTRUCTIONS ON USING THE TOP SCORE SOFTWARE

Top Score software consists of the following four applications: Study Cards, Flash Cards, Practice Exams, and Simulator.

Study Cards serve as a study aid organized around the specific exam objectives, arranged in multiple-choice format. Flash Cards, another study aid, require responses to open-ended questions, testing knowledge of the material at a level that is deeper than simply recognition memory. Practice Exams simulate the Microsoft certification exams. Simulator emulates elements of the Windows NT interface in order to provide you with hands-on experience and practice with simulation questions like those now appearing in new and revised certification exams.

To start the Study Cards, Flash Cards, or Practice Exams applications, click the application you would like to use, then choose the Click to Run button. The initial screen of the application will appear and you will be ready to go.

To start Simulator, click the button, then follow the instructions to install it. Once Simulator is installed it will appear in your Programs menu.

Further details on using the four specific applications follow.

Using Top Score Practice Exams

The Practice Exams interface is simple and straightforward. Its design simulates the look and feel of the Microsoft certification exams. If you followed the two steps above, you should see an opening screen similar to the one shown in Figure D.1.

Click Next to see a disclaimer and copyright screen, read the information and click Top Score's Start button. A notice appears indicating that the program is randomly selecting questions for the practice exam from the exam database (see Figure D.2). Practice exams include the same number of items as the Microsoft exam.

The items are selected from a larger set of 150 to 900 questions. The random selection of questions from the database takes some time to retrieve. Don't reboot; your machine is not hung!

After the questions have been selected, the first test item appears. See Figure D.3 for an example of a test item screen.

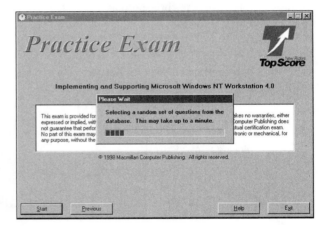

FIGURE D.2
Top Score's Please Wait notice.

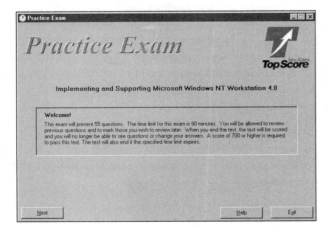

FIGURE D.1
Top Score Practice Exams opening screen.

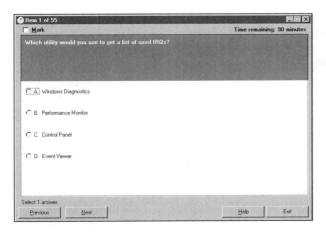

FIGURE D.3
A Top Score test item requiring a single response.

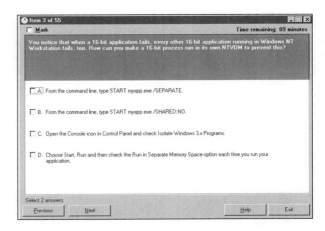

FIGURE D.4
A Top Score test item requiring multiple responses.

Notice several important features of this window. The question number, out of the total number of retrieved questions, is located at the top-left corner of the window in the control bar. Immediately below this is a check box labeled Mark, which enables you to mark any exam item as one you would like to return to later. Across the screen from the check box, you will see the total time remaining for the exam.

The test question is located in a colored section (gray in the figure). Directly below the test question, in the white area, are response choices. Be sure to note that immediately below the responses are instructions about how to respond, including the number of responses required. You will notice that questions requiring a single response, such as that shown in Figure D.3, have radio buttons next to the choices. Items requiring multiple responses have check boxes (see Figure D.4).

Some questions and responses do not appear on the screen in their entirety. In these cases a scrollbar appears to the right of the question or response. Use the scrollbar to reveal the rest of the question or response item.

The buttons at the bottom of a window enable you to return to a previous test item, proceed to the next test item, or exit Top Score Practice Exams.

Some items require you to examine additional information called *Exhibits*. These screens typically include graphs, diagrams, or other types of visual information needed to respond to the test question. Exhibits can be accessed by clicking the Exhibit button, also located at the bottom of the window.

After you complete the practice test by moving through all the test questions for your exam, you will arrive at a summary screen titled Item Review (see Figure D.5).

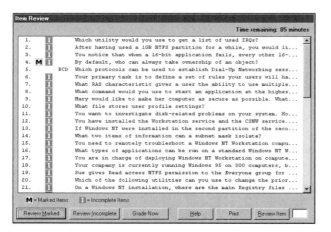

FIGURE D.5
The Top Score Item Review window.

This window enables you to see all of the question numbers, your responses to each item, any questions you have marked, and any left incomplete. The buttons at the bottom of the screen enable you to review all the marked items and incomplete items in numeric order.

If you want to review a specific marked or incomplete item, simply type the desired item number in the box at the lower-right corner of the window and click the Review Item button. After you review the item, you can respond to the question. Notice that the item window also offers the Next and Previous options. You can also select the Item Review button to return to the Item Review window.

> **NOTE**
> If you exceed the time allotted for the test, you will not have the opportunity to review any marked or incomplete items. The program will move to the next screen.

After you complete your review of the practice test questions, click the Grade Now button to find out how you did. An Examination Score Report will be generated for your practice test (see Figure D.6). This report provides you with the required score for this particular certification exam, your score on the practice test, and a grade. The report also breaks down your performance on the practice test by the specific objectives for the exam. Click the Print button to print out the results of your performance.

You also have the option of reviewing those items that you answered incorrectly. Click the Show Me What I Missed button to receive a summary of those items. Print out this information if you need further practice or review; the printouts can be used to guide your use of Study Cards and Flash Cards.

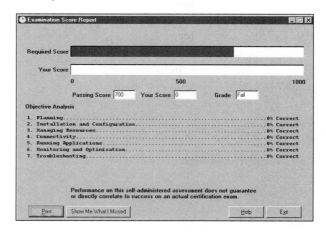

FIGURE D.6
The Top Score Examination Score Report window.

Using Top Score Study Cards

To start the software, begin from the main screen. Click on the Study Cards button, then on the smaller button displayed in the next screen. After a moment, an initial screen similar to that of the Practice Exams appears.

Click Next to see the first Study Cards screen (see Figure D.7).

The interface for Study Cards is similar to that of Practice Exams. However, you have several important options that enable you to prepare for an exam. The Study Cards material is organized using the specific objectives for each exam. You can choose to receive questions on all of the objectives or use the check boxes to select coverage of a limited set of objectives. For example, if you have already completed a Practice Exam, and your score report indicates that you need work on Planning, you can choose to cover only the Planning objectives for your Study Cards session.

You can also determine the number of questions to be presented by typing it in the option box at the right of the screen. You can also control the amount of time allowed for a review by typing the number of minutes into the Time Limit option box on the right side.

When you click the Start Test button, Study Cards randomly selects the indicated number of questions from the question database. A dialog box appears, informing you that this process could take some time. After the questions are selected, you will see a first item that looks similar to the one in Figure D.8.

Respond to the questions in the same manner as you did to Practice Exam questions. Radio buttons signal that a single answer is required, whereas check boxes indicate that multiple answers are expected.

Notice the menu options at the top of the window. File pulls down to allow you an exit from the program. Edit allows you to use the copy function and even copy questions to the Windows clipboard. The Options pull-down menu allows you to take notes on a particular question. When you pull it down, choose Open Notes. After Notepad opens, type your notes and save them. Options also allows you to start over with another exam.

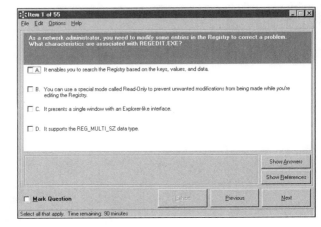

FIGURE D.8
A Study Cards item.

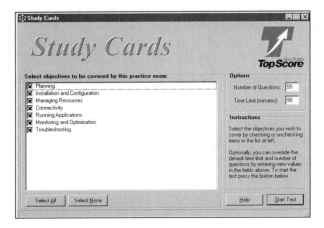

FIGURE D.7
The first Study Cards screen.

This application provides you with immediate feedback as to whether or not you answered the question correctly. Click the Show Answers button to see the correct answer(s) highlighted on the screen, as shown in Figure D.9.

Study Cards also includes Item Review, Score Report, and Show Me What I Missed features that are essentially the same as those in Practice Exams.

Using Top Score Flash Cards

Flash Cards are a third way to use the exam question database. The Flash Cards items do not offer you multiple-choice answers; instead, they require you to respond in a short answer or essay format. The idea behind Flash Cards is to help you learn the material well enough to respond with the correct answers in your own words, rather than just by recognizing the correct answer. If you have the depth of knowledge to answer questions without prompting, you will certainly be prepared to pass a multiple-choice exam.

Flash Cards are started in the same fashion as Practice Exams and Study Cards. Click the icon next to Flash Cards, then click Start the Program. Click the button for the exam you are interested in and the opening screen will appear. It will look similar to the example in Figure D.10.

Flash Cards can be chosen from the various objectives, just as in Study Cards. Select the objectives you want to cover, the number of questions you want, and the amount of time you want to restrict yourself to. Click the Start Test button to start the Flash Cards session; you will see a dialog box notifying you that questions are being selected.

The Flash Cards items appear in an interface similar to that of Practice Exams and Study Cards (see Figure D.11).

Notice, however, that although a question is presented, no answer choices appear. You must type your answer in the white space below the question (see Figure D.12).

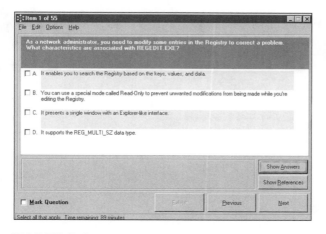

FIGURE D.9
Highlighting of the correct answer.

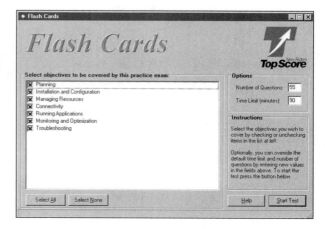

FIGURE D.10
The Flash Cards opening screen.

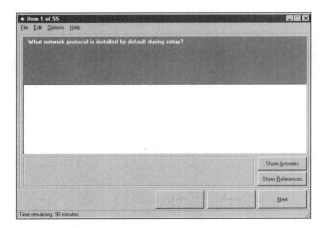

FIGURE D.11
A Flash Card item.

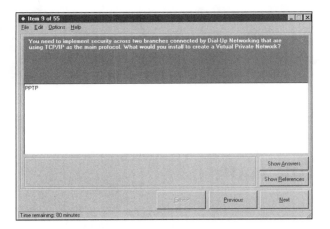

FIGURE D.12
A typed answer in Flash Cards.

Compare your answer to the correct answer by clicking the Show Answers button (see Figure D.13).

You can also use the Show References button in the same manner as described earlier in the Study Cards sections.

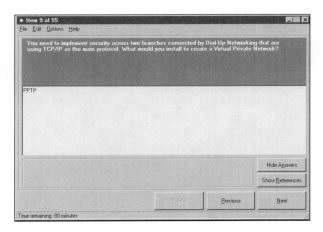

FIGURE D.13
The correct answer is shown.

The pull-down menus provide nearly the same functionality as they do in Study Cards, with the exception of Paste on the Edit menu rather than Copy Question.

Flash Cards provide simple feedback. They do not include an Item Review or Score Report. They are intended to provide you with an alternative way to assess your level of knowledge that will encourage you to learn the information more thoroughly than with other methods.

Using Top Score Simulator

Top Score Simulator is simple to use. Choose Start, Program, and click on the Simulator program name. After the application opens, go to Options, Question Set, and choose one of the three sets of questions. You will be presented with a task or question in the Task window and asked to type in an answer or choose the appropriate tool button to complete the task (see Figure D.14).

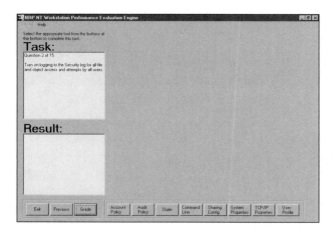

FIGURE D.14
An example of a Simulator task.

After choosing the tool, you will have to complete the task by choosing the correct tabs and settings or entering the correct information required by the task (see Figure D.15).

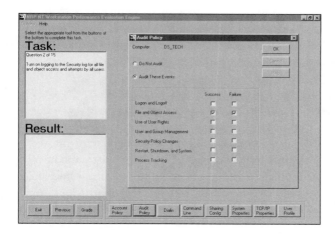

FIGURE D.15
Completing the task.

To find out if you chose correctly, click the Grade button. You will receive immediate feedback about your choice in the Result window (see Figure D.16). To move on to the next question, click Next. You can use the Previous button to go back over questions you may have missed or wish to review. The Exit button allows you to quit the program.

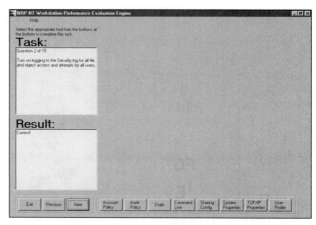

FIGURE D.16
You got it correct!

SUMMARY

The Top Score software suite of applications provides you with several approaches toward exam preparation. Use Practice Exams not only to assess your learning, but also to prepare yourself for the test-taking situation. The same can be said of the Simulator application. Use Study Cards and Flash Cards as tools for more focused assessment and review and to reinforce the knowledge you are gaining. You will find that these three applications are the perfect way to complete your exam preparation.

Performance Monitor Counters

This appendix lists the counters related to the TCP/IP protocol that are available in the Performance Monitor. There is no need to memorize these counters for the exam; they are provided here as a reference to give you an idea of what is available.

COUNTERS FOR INTERNET CONTROL MESSAGING PROTOCOL (ICMP)

The following is a list of the counters available for the ICMP Object:

- **Messages Outbound Errors.** The number of ICMP messages that your computer did not send due to internal problems with ICMP.

- **Messages Received Errors.** The number of ICMP messages received that were determined to have errors.

- **Messages Received/sec.** The number of ICMP messages received per second. (This includes any packets that were received in error.)

- **Messages Sent/sec.** The number of ICMP messages sent by the system per second.

- **Messages/sec.** The total of the Messages Received/sec and Messages Sent/sec counters.

- **Received Address Mask.** The number of ICMP Address Mask Requests received.

- **Received Address Mask Reply.** The number of ICMP Address Mask Reply messages received.

- **Received Destination Unreachable.** The number of Destination Unreachable messages received.

- **Received Echo Reply/sec.** The number of ICMP Echo Reply messages received per second.

- **Received Echo/sec.** The number of ICMP Echo messages received per second.

- **Received Parameter Problem.** The number of ICMP Parameter Problem messages received.

- **Received Redirect/sec.** The number of ICMP Redirect messages received per second.

- **Received Source Quench.** The number of ICMP Source Quench messages received.

- **Received Time Exceeded.** The number of ICMP Time Exceeded messages received.

- **Received Timestamp Reply/sec.** The number of Timestamp Reply messages received per second.

- **Received Timestamp/sec.** The number of Timestamp Requests messages received per second.

- **Sent Address Mask.** The number of Address Mask Requests sent.

◆ **Sent Address Mask Reply.** The number of Address Mask Reply messages sent.

◆ **Sent Destination Unreachable.** The number of Destination Unreachable messages sent.

◆ **Sent Echo Reply/sec.** The number of Echo Reply messages sent per second.

◆ **Sent Echo/sec.** The number of Echo messages sent per second.

◆ **Sent Parameter Problem.** The number of Parameter Problem messages your system has sent.

◆ **Sent Redirect/sec.** The total number of Redirect messages your system has sent.

◆ **Sent Source Quench.** The number of Source Quench messages sent by your system.

◆ **Sent Time Exceeded.** The number of ICMP Time Exceeded messages sent by your system.

◆ **Sent Timestamp Reply/sec.** The number of Timestamp Reply messages sent per second.

◆ **Sent Timestamp/sec.** The number of Timestamp Requests sent per second.

COUNTERS FOR INTERNET PROTOCOL

The following list describes the counters that are available for the Internet Protocol:

◆ **Datagrams Forwarded/sec.** On a multihomed system acting as a router, this is the number of IP datagrams received by your system and passed on to a final IP destination—that is, the number of packets routed. This counter includes any packets bound for a network for which you have added a route in your routing table.

◆ **Datagrams Outbound Discarded.** The number of IP datagrams that your system could not forward. This counter includes only the packets discarded for internal problems, lack of memory, and so on. Packets discarded due to errors are handled in other counters.

◆ **Datagrams Outbound No Route.** The number of IP datagrams that your system has received (or created) for which no route was found to the destination network. An ICMP message is sent to the host that originated the datagram, and the datagram is discarded.

◆ **Datagrams Received Address Errors.** If the IP datagram includes an incorrect address, an ICMP message is sent and the datagram is discarded.

◆ **Datagrams Received Delivered/sec.** A count of the IP datagrams received and delivered to the appropriate protocol per second.

◆ **Datagrams Received Discarded.** The number of IP datagrams intended for your system that were discarded due to internal IP problems, such as a lack of memory.

◆ **Datagrams Received Header Errors.** The number of IP datagrams your system received with an error of some sort in the IP header. These datagrams are discarded.

◆ **Datagrams Received Unknown Protocol.** Part of the IP header describes the protocol that the datagram should be delivered to. This counter is the number of IP datagrams for which your system does not include the protocol that is in the header. The datagram is discarded.

◆ **Datagrams Received/sec.** The number of IP datagrams received per second by your computer, including those that are forwarded.

◆ **Datagrams Sent/sec.** The number of packets sent to your IP layer from your local system and bound for transmission by the IP layer. This does not include any datagrams to be routed by your system.

◆ **Datagrams/sec.** The total number of datagrams sent to your system (not including those to be routed) and that are sent by your system.

◆ **Fragment Re-assembly Failures.** The number of IP-datagram fragments your system must reassemble but cannot.

◆ **Fragmentation Failures.** The number of IP datagrams your system attempts to fragment but cannot for some reason. This is usually due to the DF (don't fragment) flag in the IP header being turned on.

◆ **Fragmented Datagrams/sec.** The number of IP datagrams your system has to fragment per second.

◆ **Fragments Created/sec.** The number of fragments your system generates per second.

◆ **Fragments Re-assembled/sec.** The number of fragments your system reassembles per second.

◆ **Fragments Received/sec.** The number of IP datagram fragments your system receives per second.

COUNTERS FOR NETBIOS OVER TCP/IP

There are only three counters in this area:

◆ **Bytes Received/sec.** The number of bytes your system receives of the NetBIOS over TCP/IP connections that it has with other systems.

◆ **Bytes Sent/sec.** The number of bytes that your system sends over all NetBIOS over TCP/IP connections.

◆ **Total Bytes/sec.** The total number of bytes that your system sends or receives over the NetBIOS over TCP/IP ports (TCP ports 137, 138, and 139).

COUNTERS FOR TRANSMISSION CONTROL PROTOCOL

The following is a list of counters that are available for TCP connections:

◆ **Connection Failures.** The number of times TCP connections have gone directly to the CLOSED state from a state of SYN-SENT or SYN-RCVD. It also includes the number of times a TCP connection has gone to the LISTEN state from a SYN-RCVD state.

◆ **Connections Active.** The number of transitions to the SYN-SENT state from the CLOSED state.

◆ **Connections Established.** The number of connections in which the current state is ESTABLISHED or CLOSE-WAIT.

◆ **Connections Passive.** The number of transitions to the SYN-RCVD state from the LISTEN state.

◆ **Connections Reset.** The number of times connections have gone to the CLOSED state from either the ESTABLISHED state or the CLOSE-WAIT state.

◆ **Segments Received/sec.** The total number of TCP segments (packets) received per second.

◆ **Segments Retransmitted/sec.** The number of times per second that your system must retransmit a TCP segment because of a lack of acknowledgment (thus causing the retransmit timer to expire).

◆ **Segments Sent/sec.** The number of TCP segments your system transmits per second.

◆ **Segments/sec.** The total number of segments sent or received using the TCP protocol per second.

COUNTERS FOR USER DATAGRAM PROTOCOL

And, finally, here are the counters for the User Datagram Protocol:

◆ **Datagrams No Port/sec.** The number of UDP datagrams received for which there is no service listening on the Winsock port.

◆ **Datagrams Received Errors.** The number of UDP datagrams that cannot be delivered for any reason other than no service is listening on the port.

◆ **Datagrams Received/sec.** The number of UDP datagrams delivered to UDP users per second.

◆ **Datagrams Sent/sec.** The number of UDP datagrams sent from your system per second.

◆ **Datagrams/sec.** The total of all UDP datagrams both sent and received.

Index

F

G

M

TRAINING GUIDES
THE NEXT GENERATION

MCSE Training Guide: Networking Essentials, Second Edition

1-56205-919-X, $49.99, 9/98

MCSE Training Guide: TCP/IP, Second Edition

1-56205-920-3, $49.99, 10/98

MCSD Training Guide: Microsoft Visual Basic 6, Exam 70-176

0-7357-0031-1, $49.99, Q1/99

MCSE Training Guide: Windows NT Server 4, Second Edition

1-56205-916-5, $49.99, 9/98

MCSE Training Guide: SQL Server 7 Administration

0-7357-0003-6, $49.99, Q1/99

TRAINING GUIDES
FIRST EDITIONS
Your Quality Elective Solution

MCSE Training Guide: Systems Management Server 1.2, 1-56205-748-0

MCSE Training Guide: SQL Server 6.5 Administration, 1-56205-726-X

MCSE Training Guide: SQL Server 6.5 Design and Implementation, 1-56205-830-4

MCSE Training Guide: Windows 95, 70-064 Exam, 1-56205-880-0

MCSE Training Guide: Exchange Server 5, 1-56205-824-X

MCSE Training Guide: Internet Explorer 4, 1-56205-889-4

MCSE Training Guide: Microsoft Exchange Server 5.5, 1-56205-899-1

MCSE Training Guide: IIS 4, 1-56205-823-1

MCSD Training Guide: Visual Basic 5, 1-56205-850-9

MCSD Training Guide: Microsoft Access, 1-56205-771-5

MCSE Training Guide: Windows NT Server 4 Enterprise, Second Edition

1-56205-917-3, $49.99, 9/98

MCSE Training Guide: SQL Server 7 Design and Implementation

0-7357-0004-4, $49.99, Q1/99

MCSE Training Guide: Windows NT Workstation 4, Second Edition

1-56205-918-1, $49.99, 9/98

MCSD Training Guide: Solution Architectures

0-7357-0026-5, $49.99, Q1/99

MCSE Training Guide: Windows 98

1-56205-890-8, $49.99, Q4/98

MCSD Training Guide: Visual Basic 6, Exam 70-175

0-7357-0002-8, $49.99, Q1/99

FAST TRACK SERIES

The Accelerated Path to Certification Success

Fast Tracks provide an easy way to review the key elements of each certification technology without being bogged down with elementary-level information.

These guides are perfect for when you already have real-world, hands-on experience. They're the ideal enhancement to training courses, test simulators, and comprehensive training guides. *No fluff, simply what you really need to pass the exam!*

LEARN IT FAST

Part I contains only the essential information you need to pass the test. With over 200 pages of information, it is a concise review for the more experienced MCSE candidate.

REVIEW IT EVEN FASTER

Part II averages 50–75 pages, and takes you through the test and into the real-world use of the technology, with chapters on:

1) Fast Facts Review Section
2) Hotlists of Exam-Critical Concepts
3) Sample Test Questions
4) The Insider's Spin (on taking the exam)
5) Did You Know? (real-world applications for the technology covered in the exam)

 MCSE Fast Track: Networking Essentials

1-56205-939-4, $19.99, 9/98

 MCSE Fast Track: Windows 98

0-7357-0016-8, $19.99, Q4/98

 MCSE Fast Track: Windows NT Server 4

1-56205-935-1, $19.99, 9/98

 MCSE Fast Track: Windows NT Server 4 Enterprise

1-56205-940-8, $19.99, 9/98

 MCSE Fast Track: Windows NT Workstation 4

1-56205-938-6, $19.99, 9/98

 MCSE Fast Track: TCP/IP

1-56205-937-8, $19.99, 9/98

 MCSE Fast Track: Internet Information Server 4

1-56205-936-X, $19.99, 9/98

 MCSD Fast Track: Solution Architectures

0-7357-0029-X, $19.99, Q1/99

 MCSD Fast Track: Visual Basic 6, Exam 70-175

0-7357-0018-4, $19.99, Q4/98

 MCSD Fast Track: Visual Basic 6, Exam 70-176

0-7357-0019-2, $19.99, Q4/98

TESTPREP SERIES

Practice and cram with the new, revised Second Edition TestPreps

Questions. Questions. And more questions. That's what you'll find in our New Riders *TestPreps*. They're great practice books when you reach the final stage of studying for the exam. We recommend them as supplements to our *Training Guides*.

What makes these study tools unique is that the questions are the primary focus of each book. All the text in these books support and explain the answers to the questions.

- ✓ **Scenario-based questions** challenge your experience.

- ✓ **Multiple-choice questions** prep you for the exam.

- ✓ **Fact-based questions** test your product knowledge.

- ✓ **Exam strategies** assist you in test preparation.

- ✓ **Complete yet concise explanations of answers** make for better retention.

- ✓ **Two practice exams** prepare you for the real thing.

- ✓ **Fast Facts** offer you everything you need to review in the testing center parking lot.

Practice, practice, practice, pass with New Riders TestPreps!

 MCSE TestPrep: Networking Essentials, Second Edition

0-7357-0010-9, $19.99, 11/98

 MCSE TestPrep: Windows 95, Second Edition

0-7357-0011-7, $19.99, 11/98

 MCSE TestPrep: Windows NT Server 4, Second Edition

0-7357-0012-5, $19.99, 12/98

 MCSE TestPrep: Windows NT Server 4 Enterprise, Second Edition

0-7357-0009-5, $19.99, 11/98

 MCSE TestPrep: Windows NT Workstation 4, Second Edition

0-7357-0008-7, $19.99, 11/98

 MCSE TestPrep: TCP/IP, Second Edition

0-7357-0025-7, $19.99, 12/98

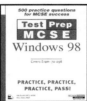 MCSE TestPrep: Windows 98

1-56205-922-X, $19.99, Q4/98

FIRST EDITIONS

MCSE TestPrep: SQL Server 6.5 Administration, 0-7897-1597-X

MCSE TestPrep: SQL Server 6.5 Design and Implementation, 1-56205-915-7

MCSE TestPrep: Windows 95 70-64 Exam, 0-7897-1609-7

MCSE TestPrep: Internet Explorer 4, 0-7897-1654-2

MCSE TestPrep: Exchange Server 5.5, 0-7897-1611-9

MCSE TestPrep: IIS 4.0, 0-7897-1610-0

HOW TO CONTACT US

IF YOU NEED THE LATEST UPDATES ON A TITLE THAT YOU'VE PURCHASED:

1) Visit our Web site at www.newriders.com.

2) Click on the DOWNLOADS link, and enter your book's ISBN number, which is located on the back cover in the bottom right-hand corner.

3) In the DOWNLOADS section, you'll find available updates that are linked to the book page.

IF YOU ARE HAVING TECHNICAL PROBLEMS WITH THE BOOK OR THE CD THAT IS INCLUDED:

1) Check the book's information page on our Web site according to the instructions listed above, or

2) Email us at support@mcp.com, or

3) Fax us at (317) 817-7488 attn: Tech Support.

IF YOU HAVE COMMENTS ABOUT ANY OF OUR CERTIFICATION PRODUCTS THAT ARE NON-SUPPORT RELATED:

1) Email us at certification@mcp.com, or

2) Write to us at New Riders, 201 W. 103rd St., Indianapolis, IN 46290-1097, or

3) Fax us at (317) 581-4663.

IF YOU ARE OUTSIDE THE UNITED STATES AND NEED TO FIND A DISTRIBUTOR IN YOUR AREA:

Please contact our international department at international@mcp.com.

IF YOU WISH TO PREVIEW ANY OF OUR CERTIFICATION BOOKS FOR CLASSROOM USE:

Email us at pr@mcp.com. Your message should include your name, title, training company or school, department, address, phone number, office days/hours, text in use, and enrollment. Send these details along with your request for desk/examination copies and/or additional information.

WE WANT TO KNOW WHAT YOU THINK

To better serve you, we would like your opinion on the content and quality of this book. Please complete this card and mail it to us or fax it to 317-581-4663.

Name _____

Address _____

City _____ State _____ Zip _____

Phone _____ Email Address _____

Occupation _____

Which certification exams have you already passed? _____

_____

_____

_____

Which certification exams do you plan to take? _____

_____

_____

_____

What influenced your purchase of this book?
❏ Recommendation   ❏ Cover Design
❏ Table of Contents   ❏ Index
❏ Magazine Review   ❏ Advertisement
❏ Reputation of New Riders ❏ Author Name

How would you rate the contents of this book?
❏ Excellent   ❏ Very Good
❏ Good   ❏ Fair
❏ Below Average   ❏ Poor

What other types of certification products will you buy/have you bought to help you prepare for the exam?
❏ Quick reference books   ❏ Testing software
❏ Study guides   ❏ Other

What do you like most about this book? Check all that apply.
❏ Content   ❏ Writing Style
❏ Accuracy   ❏ Examples
❏ Listings   ❏ Design
❏ Index   ❏ Page Count
❏ Price   ❏ Illustrations

What do you like least about this book? Check all that apply.
❏ Content   ❏ Writing Style
❏ Accuracy   ❏ Examples
❏ Listings   ❏ Design
❏ Index   ❏ Page Count
❏ Price   ❏ Illustrations

What would be a useful follow-up book to this one for you?_____

Where did you purchase this book? _____

Can you name a similar book that you like better than this one, or one that is as good? Why?_____

_____

_____

How many New Riders books do you own? _____

What are your favorite certification or general computer book titles? _____

_____

What other titles would you like to see us develop?_____

_____

Any comments for us? _____

_____

_____

_____

_____

Fold here and Scotch tape to mail

- -

New Riders
201 W. 103rd St.
Indianapolis, IN 46290

NEW RIDERS TOP SCORE TEST SIMULATION SOFTWARE SUITE

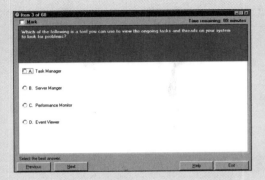

Practice Exams simulate the actual Microsoft exams. Option buttons and check boxes indicate whether there is one or more than one correct answer. All test questions are presented randomly to create a unique exam each time you practice—the ideal way to prepare.

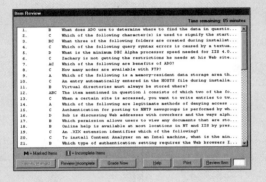

The Item Review shows you the answers you've already selected and the questions you need to revisit before grading the exam.

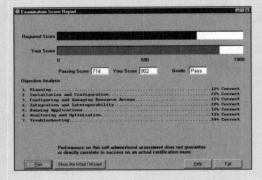

The Score Report displays your score for each objective category, helping you to define which objectives you need to study more. It also shows you what score you need to pass and your total score.

Study Cards allow you to test yourself and receive immediate feedback and an answer explanation. Link to the text for more in-depth explanations.